A. Krausse sc.

Immanuel Kant

THE LIFE OF IMMANUEL KANT

THE LIFE OF IMMANUEL KANT

By

J.H.W. STUCKENBERG, D.D.

Late Professor in Wittenberg College, Ohio

GYAN

Published by

Gyan Publishing House
5, Ansari Road
Daryaganj, New Delhi-110002
Phone: 011-47034999, 9811692060
E-mail: books@gyanbooks.com

Distribution Network
gyanbooks.com
India, USA, Canada, UK, Australia, France

ISBN : 978-81-212-6204-0 (PB)
First Published, 1882

2nd Impression 2022

Printed at: Gyan Press, Delhi.

THE LIFE OF IMMANUEL KANT
Author: J.H.W. STUCKENBERG, D.D.

THE LIFE

OF

IMMANUEL KANT

BY

J. H. W. STUCKENBERG, D.D.

Late Professor in Wittenberg College, Ohio

1882

PREFACE.

WITHIN one hundred years after the publication of the "Kritik of Pure Reason" no biography of its author has appeared in the English language. Even in Germany, where his philosophy is studied so extensively and has been the occasion of an immense number of works, but little attention has been paid to the life of Kant, and the biographies of him are far from being satisfactory. It is not difficult to discover the reasons for the neglect of the biography of this great thinker and eminent scholar. The materials for such a work are widely scattered, and require much research; and one may glean long and on many a field, and, as the result of his labours, bring home only a light sheaf, and even that nearly all straw. The difficulty is by no means over when the materials have been found. Not only are there numerous conflicting statements, owing largely to the contentions occasioned by his philosophy and the prejudices which they aroused, but there is also a lack of the variety and incident which are commonly regarded as essential to an interesting biography. Unfortunately, the friends who were his biographers were not critical, neither did they take the trouble to make researches and gather the materials within their reach. Their books are, indeed, very valuable as personal reminiscences, but they are neither scholarly nor complete. The researches made since their day, especially those by Schubert (the results of which are given in his book on "Kant's Leben"), by Dr. R. Reicke (" Kantiana "), and by the Kant Society in Königsberg, have added much valuable material; but a German biography worthy of the Critical Philosopher is still a desideratum.

The career of Kant had more variety than is generally supposed; his life was, however, that of the quiet thinker, and we must not expect the varied incidents which are found in the lives of statesmen and warriors. For the student of thought and the psychologist this fact makes it all the more interesting. The intellectual element in the career of this explorer of the reason, undisturbed by the ordinary affairs which generally absorb the attention of men, gives this life a peculiar charm and makes its study specially profitable.

The philosopher of Königsberg was too great to need unmerited praise. A colleague, in delivering his funeral oration, said, " Kant himself hated all flattery, and abhorred all untruth. Should not then the truth, the pure, unadulterated truth serve us as our only guiding star ?" Our age is free from the prejudice and bitterness excited by the advent of the Critical Philosophy; and one hundred years after the appearance of the " Kritik " we can calmly contemplate its author, and weigh impartially the testimony for and against him. However profound the reverence which is inspired by a great name and exalted virtues, it is the duty of the biographer to use honestly the materials found after conscientious research. If there are paradoxes, inconsistencies, and weaknesses, they should no more be hid than the excellencies should be obscured; but there ought to be careful discrimination between the exceptional failings, which are found in the best lives, and the exalted principles and motives, which are the rule. The distinction between biography and fiction is easily obliterated when the greatness of the subject has elements of the sublime, and when the temptation to add to the interest of the description by means of exaggerations is strong. One of Kant's biographers says, "His mind had embraced the whole domain of human knowledge, and everywhere had entered into the most minute details. There is no object within the sphere of the serious sciences, as well as of common life, which he did not subject to exact investigation, and of which he did not know all that was worth knowing." This, and much more that was written about the profound thinker who needed no eulogies, is not biography, but hero-worship. Instead of desiring such hyperbole, the true admirer of the author of the Critical system will agree with the philosopher Herbart, who said of Kant, "We can show no honour to the sincere inquirer after truth, at the expense of truth;" and with Bouterwek, also referring to him, "Merit shines brightest in its own light where no desire to deify envelops it in clouds of incense."

Kant is known chiefly as the author of the "Kritik of Pure Reason." In giving an account of his life, however, a much more comprehensive view of him must be taken; he must be considered in the various relations he sustained. As his works culminated in ethics and theology, and were intended to establish these on a firm basis, his moral and religious views deserve more attention than they generally receive from English writers on his philosophy, especially since they are so intimately connected with his life. A critical discussion of his abstruse philosophy would be out of place in a biography. The English reader has access to excellent works on the Kantian system, and others, as well as translations of Kant's books, are in process of preparation. This biography aims to concentrate all the light on the man himself and his life. The great interest now taken in Kant's philosophy in England and America justifies the hope that the life of the Father of German metaphysics will be welcomed by English readers. If his works throw light on his life, it will also be found that his life aids materially in understanding his works.

While the student of the Critical system is naturally expected to take a special interest in its author, this biography is also intended for students and scholars in general, and for all who take an interest in intellectual conflicts and triumphs. As this broad aim has determined the character of the book, some things may be found in it which the student of the Critical Philosophy might be willing to dispense with, but which the more general reader will find indispensable. As

Kant should be studied in the light of his times, much contemporary history has been considered in the preparation of this book. The thoughtful reader will prefer to consider the philosopher in his relation to his age, rather than to view him in an isolation which would place him in a false light.

I am indebted chiefly to the Royal Library of Berlin for the materials used in preparing this biography. The principal authorities are referred to in the Appendix, especially in the first note.

All the translations from Kant's works are made directly from the original. I have generally used "Kritik" to designate the "Kritik of Pure Reason." Unless otherwise stated, "mile" always designates the English mile.

The picture of Kant represents the philosopher at the age of sixty-seven, the original having been painted by Döbler in 1791.

This biography was intended to appear during the Centennial year of the "Kritik of Pure Reason;" but the work was so much more laborious, and required so much more time, than was anticipated, that this was found to be impossible.

BERLIN, HEGEL PLATZ 2.
Jan. 16, 1882.

CONTENTS.

CHAPTER IV.

PHYSICAL BASIS.

CHAPTER V.

MENTAL CHARACTERISTICS.

CHAPTER VI.

HOME AND SOCIAL LIFE.

CHAPTER VII.

KANT AND HIS FRIENDS.

CHAPTER VIII.

KANT'S AUTHORSHIP.

CHAPTER IX.

AUTHORSHIP CONTINUED.

CHAPTER X.

MORAL AND RELIGIOUS VIEWS AND CHARACTER.

THE LIFE OF IMMANUEL KANT.

THE LIFE OF IMMANUEL KANT.

CHAPTER I.

KANT'S BOYHOOD AND EARLY SURROUNDINGS.

1724–1740.

Königsberg—Relatives—Home influence—The Pastor—Pietism—The Gymnasium—Its Rector, religious influence, and intellectual advantages—His speciality—Special friends—Sensitiveness—General character of his early life.

IMMANUEL KANT is so identified with Königsberg that a sketch of this city is essential to a correct knowledge of the life of her most famous son. Here he was born and educated, here he taught and died; and this city, with its immediate vicinity, was the scene of all his labours, hardships, and triumphs. Its social, religious, and intellectual condition exerted a potent influence on his character and views; but he, on the other hand, gave the city a fame such as it had never before enjoyed, and has for ever associated its name with one of the most important epochs in philosophy, so that for his sake it was called "The Capital of Philosophy," and also "The City of Pure Reason."

Königsberg is a frontier city of Germany, being situated in the north-eastern corner of Prussia, near the Russian border. Formerly it was the capital of the province of Prussia; but when that province was divided a few years ago, it became the capital of East Prussia. The city is built on undulating ground, in an attractive region, and its position is favourable for commerce. It is situated at the mouth of the Pregel, a river which forms an important means of communication with the interior of the province and also with Poland, though for its mercantile importance it is mainly indebted to its location on a bay of the Baltic. Last century its extensive commerce brought the city into communication with numerous sea-ports of Europe, Asia, Africa, and America, as well as with the whole province of Prussia and the adjoining countries.([2])

In the beginning of the eighteenth century Königsberg was prosperous and wealthy; but during the Seven Years' War its prosperity was checked and much of its wealth was lost. In 1800 the city, consisting of the towns of Altstadt, Löbenicht, and Kneiphof, was about nine miles in circumference, and contained 4000 houses. Its inhabitants during last century numbered from 40,000 to 50,000, exclusive of the military.

As might be expected in a maritime port, there was considerable variety in the character of the population. The city had been wrested from the Slavs by the Germans, during the Middle Ages, and traces of Slavic elements were still found among the inhabitants. Representatives of different nations were brought to the city by commercial interests; such as Polish, Russian, Scandinavian, Dutch, and English merchants and seamen. The religious differences were also considerable. The Catholics were greatly in the minority, having only one church; the Protestants were principally Lutherans, who were, however, divided into the Orthodox and Pietistic; parties there were also adherents of the Reformed faith. In 1729 the city had fourteen Lutheran and three Reformed churches. Owing to the nearness of Russia, members of the Greek Church frequently came to the city. The active trade also attracted many Jews, who had their own social and religious institutions.

Besides its commercial advantages, Königsberg was the religious, political, judicial, military, and literary centre of the province. It was the home of numerous civil and military officers, as well as of scholars and prominent ecclesiastics. Besides its elementary schools, it contained five gymnasia and a university. In the higher classes of society there was considerable culture and literary inspiration; even outside of the university there existed a good degree of intellectual activity, and among the merchants were found a number of men who cultivated a taste for letters. Hamann, Hippel, and others, acquired a reputation by means of their books, and many of the officers took an interest in scholarship. Isolated as the city was from other literary centres, it had in itself many of those elements which are calculated to develop a taste for learning. Even among the poorer classes there was an ambition to give their sons a learned education, an ambition which the schools helped to realize as well as to inspire; and many sons of mechanics took a university course.

His surroundings, as we shall see, had an important influence on Kant. This busy, stirring city afforded variety and inspiration enough to make it a favourable abode for a scholar; and yet it was free from those distracting influences which are apt to interfere seriously with study. Its advantages and disadvantages must, of course, be judged by last century, not by our age. The merchants from different lands, and the seamen with large, varied, and interesting experience, gave the scholar special opportunities to study men and to gain a knowledge of the world. That Kant highly appreciated the advantages offered by the city, is evident from a note to the Preface of his "Anthropology:" "A large city, the centre of a government, in which the officers of the Government are found; which contains a university for the culture of the sciences, and is also so situated as to have commerce by sea; which is favoured with communication, by means of rivers, with the interior of the country, as well as with more distant adjoining lands of various tongues and customs; such a city, for instance, as Königsberg on the Pregel, may be regarded as a suitable place for enlarging one's knowledge of men and of the world, a place where this knowledge may be gained even without travel."(3)

Immanuel Kant was born in this city, on the 22nd of April, 1724, in a house in Saddler Street. This house, which has been torn down, stood near the Green Bridge, which was the centre of a lively trade during the summer, where especially the Germans, Dutch, English, Poles, and Jews, carried on an extensive traffic. The boy was thus early brought into contact with representatives of these nationalities, and he had an opportunity for observing the peculiar manners and customs of different nations; afterwards the study of national characteristics and of different countries became his chief literary recreation and delight.

In the almanac for Eastern Prussia, the 22nd of April is designated "Emanuel:" this circumstance determined his Christian name at his baptism, which took place the day after his birth. The very meaning of the word commended it to his pious parents; and Kant also became attached to the name.

In his relatives, so far as they are known to us, we find no evidence of extraordinary intellectual endowments. His parents were plain people, belonging to the class of mechanics, and there was little to distinguish them from others of the same grade in society, except perhaps their eminent morality and piety. But while there is no trace of family genius, we have in Kant a union of the blood of the two nations which are most distinguished for their metaphysical speculations, namely the Scotch and the German.

His father, John George Cant (4), born near Memel, in Prussia, was the son of Scotch parents who had emigrated thither from Scotland. Kant himself states that for some unknown reason quite a number of Scotch families emigrated to Sweden and Germany, at the close of the seventeenth and the beginning of the eighteenth century, and that his paternal grandparents were among these emigrants. Of these ancestors, and of Kant's other paternal relations, nothing is known. Even of John George Cant scarcely anything is recorded; his celebrated son, with his characteristic reticence respecting his early life, rarely referred to him. Kant's father was a saddler in humble circumstances, whose strict morality seems to have been the most striking trait of his character. He was industrious and conscientious, and was specially intent on training his children to habits of industry and to the formation of an upright character; and as he regarded truthfulness as the most essential of the virtues, he took particular pains to inculcate a love for the truth. Immanuel esteemed his character highly, and on the occasion of his death, in 1746, he wrote in the family Bible: "On the 24th of March, my dear father was taken away by a happy death. May God, who did not grant him many joys in this life, permit him to share the eternal joys."

The character of Immanuel's mother was more positive than that of the father; and though she died when her son was only fourteen years old, and eight years earlier than his father, she made on him the deepest and most lasting impression. Her parents were German, and her maiden name was Regina Dorothea Reuter. She was an affectionate mother and a devoted Christian, and together with her husband belonged to the Pietistic party in the Lutheran Church. In her character the religious element was predominant, while her husband laid the emphasis on morality. On the day of her marriage, November 13th, 1715, she wrote the following in the family Bible: "May the Lord our God be pleased to keep us in constant love and unity, and give to us the dew of heaven and the sweetness of the earth, till He brings us to the marriage of the Lamb; for the sake of Jesus Christ His Son. Amen." She was greatly influenced by her pastor, Dr. F. A. Schulz, who in the pulpit and in his pastoral visitations exhorted his people to have stated times for prayer and other religious exercises, to strive earnestly for a change of heart, and to learn definitely the time of this change. She was faithful in following these directions, and strict in attending to religious devotions at home and in church. In the training of her children she was most anxious about their spiritual welfare, and it was largely to her influence that Immanuel was indebted for his high ideal of holiness and the development of his character.

In harmony with the prevalent low views of woman's intellectual capacities and calling, the facilities for female education were very meagre. When broad intellectual culture was regarded as unnecessary or even inappropriate for women who belonged to the higher classes of society, it is not surprising that a few rudiments of knowledge were thought sufficient for the daughters of mechanics and labourers. We must, therefore, not expect to find Kant's mother a woman of superior education; but she had more than the ordinary intelligence of the women of her own rank. Kant, who said that he was the picture of his mother, regarded her as a woman of good natural powers, of noble heart, and of devout piety. In his old age he still spoke of her with reverence and even with tenderness, saying, "My mother was a lovely, affectionate, pious, and upright woman, and a tender mother, who led her children to the fear of God by means of pious instruction and a virtuous example. Often she took me outside of the city, directed my attention to the works of God, spoke with pious rapture of His omnipotence, wisdom, and goodness, and impressed on my heart a deep reverence for the Creator of all things. Never shall I forget my mother, for she planted and nourished in me the first good seed, and opened my heart to the impressions of nature; she aroused and enlarged my thoughts; and her instruction has had an abiding and blessed influence on my life." She died December 18th, 1737, her death being an offering on the altar of affection. A friend, whom she tenderly loved, had been engaged to a man who forsook her and married another. This faithlessness so deeply affected the friend, that she was attacked by a fatal fever, during which she refused all remedies. Kant's mother, who attended her during her illness, urged her to take some medicine; but she declined it, under the pretext that the taste was too disagreeable. In order to convince her that this was not the case, his mother tasted it, using for that purpose a spoon which had already been in the mouth of the patient. A feeling of disgust came over her immediately, she became greatly excited, and the effect on her imagination was increased when she discovered spots on the body of her friend which indicated that tho disease was spotted fever. She became sick on the same day, and soon died.

The peace, morality, and piety of his home exerted a marked and lasting influence on Kant, and to his early training he himself ascribed his moral strictness and his power to resist evil inclinations. The circumstances in which he was placed were calculated to develop strength of character and self-reliance. Without being in absolute need, he was obliged to practise self-denial; and without insuperable obstacles in the way of an education, he early encountered and mastered difficulties. The very hardships of his youth served to unfold his powers, and led him to prize the more highly the learning which cost him so much effort. His home was admirably adapted to the development of those qualities which Kant learned to appreciate above all others, and which are really the best; and he appreciated its excellence and recognized its beneficial effect on his character. Though he inherited from his parents no money, he received from them treasures inestimably more valuable. His father died poor, but without debts. Only a few years before his own death, Kant described his parents as models of moral propriety. "They gave me," he said, "a training which, in a moral point of view, could not have been better, and for which, at every remembrance of them, I am moved with the most grateful emotions." In comparing his humble home with others of wealth and of rank, he spoke of its superior excellence. "Kant said that when he contemplated his work as a tutor in the house of a count not far from Königsberg . . . he had often thought, with deep emotion, of the incomparably more excellent training which he had received in his home, where, as he gratefully boasted, he had never seen or heard anything that was immoral."(5)

While in many instances Pietism had degenerated, we have reason to believe that this was not the case with the religion of Kant's parents. From all we can learn of them, we are justified in concluding that they were free from bigotry, hypocrisy, and fanaticism. That their religion was sincere and earnest, and that it moulded their characters and lives, is evident from the testimony of their son. Speaking of his parents, he said, "Even if the religious views of that day, and the notions of what was called virtue and piety, were not clear and satisfactory, nevertheless the thing itself was found. Let men say what they will of Pietism, those who sincerely adopted it were honourably distinguished. They had the highest which a man can possess—that rest, that cheerfulness, and that inner peace, which no passion could disturb. No need and no persecution disheartened them; no contention could excite them to anger and enmity. In a word, even the mere observer was involuntarily inspired with respect. I still remember how a quarrel about their rights broke out between the guilds of the harness-makers and of the saddlers, from which my father suffered considerably; but in spite of this, even in the conversation in the family this quarrel was mentioned with such forbearance and love toward the opponents, and with such firm confidence in Providence, that the thought of it, though I was only a boy then, will never leave me." ([6]) This testimony is the more significant, because Kant had no sympathy with Pietism when it was given. The influence of this home must indeed have been exceptional, since Kant, the strict and even severe moralist, frequently said, "Never, not even a single time was I permitted to hear anything improper from my parents; never did I see in them anything that was wrong."

There were ten children besides Immanuel, three sons and seven daughters; six of these, two sons older than Immanuel, and four daughters, died quite young. He was the fourth child. His only brother who attained years of maturity, John Henry, was eleven years younger, and chose the ministry as his profession, studying theology in the University of Königsberg. After spending some time as family tutor in Courland, he became the rector of a school in Mittau; and from 1780 until his death in 1800 he was the pastor of a church in Rahden, Courland. He had an original mind and was well informed; his attainments in history, of which he made a speciality, were superior, and he also had a good knowledge of mathematics, was a critical student of the classics, read extensively, and was an admirer of practical philosophy, but not of metaphysics. It is said that in his youth he received instruction from his brother, which probably means that he attended some of his lectures while at the university. He read his writings until his book on "Religion within the Limits of Reason" appeared, then refused to read any more of them, because, he said, his old head could not adapt itself to a new terminology. The early home-training left a moral impression on him similar to that made on his celebrated brother, and he was upright and candid, and had the strictest regard for the truth. He published nothing, his sphere being practical life rather than speculation or literature; but till the close of his life he was a student of learned works. While conscientious and energetic in the discharge of his duties, he also had admirable qualities of heart. His studies, his religious views, his pursuits, and, in fact, his whole life, were so different from those of his brother that there was little congeniality between them. They rarely corresponded with each other, and for many years not at all. Immanuel seems to have cherished no fraternal affection for his only brother, who was also the only relative who could lay any claim to scholarship; though after his brother's death he generously aided the family, which had been left in poverty.

Of the three sisters who survived the age of childhood, one was older than Immanuel and died unmarried; the other two were married to humble citizens of Königsberg. They had enjoyed only the extremely meagre educational advantages of girls in their circumstances, had no opportunities for refinement and culture, and never rose above their lowly station in life. Only one of them, Mrs. Theuer, survived her brother.

The early intellectual advantages of Kant were by no means equal to the superior moral ones. It is not easy to transfer ourselves from the enlightened Germany of to-day, with its masterly educational system, to the Germany of the first decades of the eighteenth century. The letters and biographies of that period must be read, in order to form a conception of the people who were still painfully struggling to rise above the ruins of the Thirty Years' War; a people that had just passed through the saddest century of their history, a century of wretchedness and despair; a people depressed, depreciating themselves in comparison with other nations, with neither political unity nor independence, with no national literature, and without the consciousness of intellectual strength. While various departments of learning flourished in England, France, and the Netherlands, Germany had little or no intellectual influence among the nations, a fact which will become more evident when we follow Kant to the gymnasium and the university, but which also must be taken into account in connexion with his entire education. The day when Pestalozzi and others radically reformed the educational system of Germany had not yet come. In the primary schools, both in the city and in the country, the instruction was very defective. Girls were taught to read, and perhaps to cipher, and they also received religious instruction, but rarely anything more. There were no schools for the higher education of girls; hence, unless parents could afford a private tutor, their education was confined to these elements; and the boys, unless they were to be prepared for the gymnasium, generally fared little better. The teachers were frequently incompetent, many of them being mechanics who taught in connexion with their trade, in order to eke out a living.

Kant at first attended what was called the Hospital School. The pastor of the family, Dr. Schulz, who was the first to notice the abilities of the boy, called the attention of his parents to his talents, and urged them to promote their development. His connexion with one of the gymnasia as rector, and with the university as professor, made the way for the higher education of Kant more easy; and the fact that both the gymnasium and the university were in Königsberg made it possible to give him the advantages of these institutions with comparatively little expense. If it had not been for this faithful pastor, there seems to have been little probability that his parents would have thought of sending him to the gymnasium. Jachmann, one of the biographers of the Königsberg philosopher, says of this pastor, "Kant is indebted to him for what he became, and the learned world is under obligation to him for what it gained through Kant's culture." But in spite of the limited expense, his parents could not afford to give him a liberal education; their pastor, however, gave substantial help by sending them fire-wood free of charge. Whether the powerful influence of Schulz secured stipends, or other pecuniary aid, is not known. Being a devout Pietist, the minister was desirous that Kant should study theology, and this met the wishes of his parents, especially of his mother. When eight years old, he was accordingly sent to the Collegium Fridericianum, the gymnasium of which the pastor was rector.

Kant gratefully recognized the services rendered him by this excellent man, and Borowski, his friend and biographer, says, "In Kant's estimation, Dr. F. A. Schulz was one of the first and most excellent of men. During lucid intervals in his old age, and often in former years, he expressed a desire to erect a monument to the memory of Schulz, and also thought that others ought to erect one." Late in life Kant regretted that in his writings he had not reared a memorial to the memory of his friend and benefactor. He was also indebted to a maternal uncle, named Richter, a shoemaker of some means, who assisted him while a student and afterwards.

Neither of the parents lived to witness the beginning of their son's fame; the mother, however, lived to see him in the gymnasium, preparing for the university, and the father saw him complete his course in the university, but died a year before his first book was published.

If we examine Kant's youth with the hope of finding some prophecy of his future greatness, we shall be disappointed. This may be due partly to the fact that we know so little about that period of his life; but there seems to have been nothing extraordinary in it, as otherwise it would probably have been recorded. During the first years at school he manifested no preference for the subject in which he achieved his great fame; and even during his studies at the university he did not make it a speciality. Impelled by a thirst for knowledge, he was a diligent student, and in some branches his attainments were more than ordinary; he, however, gave no evidences of striking brilliancy of intellect, and even his most intimate friends discovered in him no indications of the profound metaphysician or of any extraordinary philosophical genius. While but little is known about him personally during this period, we, fortunately, have the data for a knowledge of the two most important factors in his early life, namely, the religious and intellectual influences to which he was subject.

The gymnasium which Kant attended was, like his home, subject to Pietistic influence; and to a large extent this is also true of the university. At home, therefore, in church, in the gymnasium, and in the university, he was in this religious atmosphere; and for the sake of understanding his youth, and also his character and life, it is important to examine this powerful religious tendency. When we consider what his pastor and the Pietistic schools did for Kant, it is not too much to say that the world is indebted to Pietism for saving from obscurity the greatest of modern metaphysicians.

The great religious movement begun by Spener in the second half of the seventeenth century, called Pietism by its opponents, was a powerful revival of religion, to which in many respects the later Methodist movement in England was similar. Its influence was by no means confined to the Lutheran Church, in which it originated, but extended to all the churches. Unlike Methodism, it did not organize a new denomination, but aimed at the spiritualization of the Lutheran Church. Spener has been called a second Luther; and the great work begun by him was in many respects a real reformation. Instead of the cold and formal orthodoxy generally prevalent, he wanted to introduce more spiritual life into the churches and a more practical Christianity. While not aiming to set aside the orthodox doctrines, he did not want mere intellectual assent to them to be regarded as constituting a Christian; but he aimed to quicken the doctrines, and to apply them to the heart as well as the head, so that they might form a character which should attest itself in daily life, as well as in profession and in acts distinctively religious. But in giving so much emphasis to the character of the heart and the life, the self-sufficiency of a sterile intellectualism in religion and of a dead orthodoxy was attacked, and the doctrines themselves received a relatively different position and value. By means of such views, and through his efforts to spread them, Spener exerted an almost unparalleled spiritual influence throughout Germany. Among the few signs of life after the Thirty Years' War, Pietism was the most important. Although its direct aim was only religious, it affected all departments of life, stimulated education and government, aroused the latent energies of the masses, and gave the people inspiration, hope, and enthusiasm. In many places, spring with its warm breath, and teeming with life, followed a cold, dead winter. Becoming an absorbing passion, it concentrated all the energies in religious aims. While the nobility and the heads of Government were affected by it, Pietism was essentially a popular movement, and the neglected classes, the masses, were the recipients of its greatest benefits. Catechization, which had been neglected, was generally introduced, and was made a spiritual as well as an intellectual exercise; meetings for prayer and biblical study were held during the week; pastoral visitation, with religious counsel and exhortation, became common; the preaching, which had been coldly intellectual, was quickened; theological instruction, which had become scholastic, dry, and polemical, was made more spiritual and more ethical; and the whole aspect of the spiritual life was changed. The movement aroused the missionary activity of the Church, established benevolent institutions, and culminated in founding the University of Halle, and Francke's Orphan Asylum in the same city. In Prussia, Pietism became a great power, and this university was especially favoured by the Government; and Francke's Asylum, and the various institutions connected with it, became the model for other Pietistic establishments.

It is evident that a movement so vigorous, and so radical in the changes it effected, could not escape opposition. The Orthodox party denounced it and persecuted its leaders. A bitter controversy arose between the two parties, in which impure motives, personal attacks, and abusive epithets, bore a prominent part, produced distraction and religious indifference, and promoted scepticism. Even the most ardent advocate of Pietism cannot deny that in the course of time it laid itself open to serious charges. It lost much of its original freshness, simplicity, and power, and became formal and artificial; and before the first half of the eighteenth century had closed, the period of its degeneracy had come. Its piety became constrained and affected, and was a matter of rules rather than of spontaneous spiritual life. It developed a painfully anxious spirit, and encouraged an introspection which frequently led to gloomy brooding over the state of the heart; those who were obliged to submit to its regulations, and to listen to its frequent exhortations, were apt to find much in them that was irksome and insipid; and it is not strange that in many instances the heart, instead of being won by its appeals, turned from them with aversion. The constant playing on the emotions, and the persistent efforts to bring about conversion, sometimes produced effects which were very different from those intended. Add to this the fact that many Pietists, in their extreme opposition to amusements, gave to life a gloomy and unnatural aspect; that learning was frequently spoken of disparagingly, all the emphasis being laid on the heart and its experiences; that a supposed superiority to others often engendered a spiritual pride; and that hypocrisy was apt to assume the garb which seemed to be most devout—and it will readily be understood that the degenerated Pietism, for only that is meant, had a deleterious influence, especially on the minds of the young and the scholarly. It became too narrow, too little human, and too unhealthy, to satisfy deep and scientific natures. From a persecuted party it grew in many places to be the dominant one, and it also became a persecutor. When through its instigations the philosopher Wolf was obliged to leave Halle, and when it sought to force others to refrain from teaching what it regarded as irreligious, Pietism created the suspicion that it was hostile to freedom in scientific investigation, a suspicion which is specially potent in its influence on students. There were indeed many Pietists during the period of its degeneracy who were free from the faults mentioned; but their example did not counteract the evil influences of an unhealthy Pietism.

The religious influences to which the sensitive, impressible mind of Kant was subject at home and in the gymnasium were such as were exerted by the better class of the Pietists of that day; but that these influences were not wholly beneficial is evident from the testimony of numerous reliable witnesses. Excesses occurred which bore evil fruit, and there were methods which, in spite of the purity of the motives which prompted them, frustrated their intended aim.

The Fridericianum was founded by a dealer in wood, named Gehr, who was a Pietist, and was desirous of having his children educated in his own faith. For this purpose he procured from the celebrated Orphan Asylum in Halle, in 1698, Dr. Lysius, a superior instructor, who modelled the institution he founded in Königsberg after the one in Halle, both religiously and intellectually. At first the school was only a private one, intended for the children of the founder, and the teacher was a family tutor; but his extraordinary success led other parents to ask permission to send their children to him. Besides granting this request, Gehr also gave free instruction to some poor children. The popularity of the institution soon aroused the opposition of the educational authorities in Königsberg; and in order to quiet the unfavourable rumours respecting the school, Gehr requested a full examination of its instruction and methods. The committee appointed for this purpose gave an exceedingly favourable report, declaring that they were surprised and gratified at the attainments of the pupils in Latin, Greek, history, geography, and other branches, as well as in the catechism and in the Scriptures.

The school continued to be a private institution

till 1703, when it received the royal privilege of a gymnasium with the name, "Collegium Fridericianum." In granting this privilege, the king declared that it was his aim "to extend God's glory and to bring souls to heaven." Besides the gymnasium, the institution had a German school for the elementary instruction of boys and girls. It was the only institution in Prussia which had a boarding department, a feature which attracted many foreigners, especially Russians, Lieflanders, and Courlanders. In 1732 schools for the poor were also added.

Kant spent eight and a half years in this gymnasium, entering it in the spring of 1732. Rejoiced as the poor lad no doubt was that, in spite of his humble condition, his desire for knowledge was to be gratified, the impression of the institution cannot have been very cheerful. A description of the building a hundred years later shows that its effect must have been gloomy; for the small rooms, with low ceilings, were "suffocating in summer and cold in winter;" some of them were so dark as to make study difficult, and "in this semi-twilight, reading and writing injure the eyes and put the mind into a despondent mood." The kitchens of the professors' apartments were contiguous, and sent their fragrance into the cheerless recitation rooms.(7)

The rector of the gymnasium, Dr. F. A. Schulz, is of special interest to us on account of the important service he rendered Kant. Like his predecessor, Lysius, he had been educated at Halle, where he was known as an ardent Pietist and a zealous disciple of the Wolfian philosophy. Having spent some time in pastoral work in other places, he was called to Königsberg in 1731, to become the pastor of one of the churches and also a member of the consistory. Other influential positions were soon added, for which he was indebted to the royal favour; thus, he was appointed Professor of Theology, and he became a member of the academic senate; he was made rector of the Fridericianum, and served on important ecclesiastical and educational committees. Schulz was a fine scholar; and at Halle, through the influence of the philosopher Wolf, he obtained permission to deliver mathematical and philosophical lectures in the university before he had taken a degree. He possessed great mental vigour, superior organizing talent, and indomitable zeal. As pastor, rector, teacher, and administrator, he was eminently successful. As general inspector of schools his service to the cause of education in Königsberg and throughout the kingdom was of inestimable value; and it was chiefly through his activity that 1600 new schools were established. After his death, one of his pupils said, "What a great mind Schulz must have had, is evident from the fact that for the greater part of his life he patiently, actively, cheerfully, with great intelligence, and with blessed results, held more than six distinct offices, with all their labours and burdens." ([8])

This is the man to whose memory Kant was desirous of erecting a monument. He became the pastor of the family when Kant was but seven years old; and next to the parents he was most influential in forming the character of the boy. His Pietism was the basis and the impulse of all his activities. He was a faithful pastor, was an excellent and a powerful preacher. The pupil already quoted says, "What an impression was made by his edifying, simple, moving eloquence! He reached the soul, the bones, and the marrow. As little as one with open eye can avoid seeing the lightning, so little could one escape his power to move."

Not only at home and in church, but also in the gymnasium, Kant was brought under the influence of Schulz. The rector was too much occupied with other matters to attend to the business affairs of the gymnasium; these were left to his assistant, Schiffert, who was also a zealous Pietist and a good scholar. But Schulz was the ruling spirit in the Fridericianum, and his power was especially felt in its religious management. The spiritual element was the most prominent in the institution, and everything had a Pietistic hue. (9) From the character of Schulz, as well as from the testimony of the best pupils of the school, including that of Kant, we infer that the Pietism was sincere and zealous, and was in general free from fanaticism. (10) At the same time there is no doubt that there was an excess of effort to arouse religious emotions. One is surprised at the amount of time devoted to devotional exercises in Pietistic schools, which were chiefly emotional and aimed at a conviction of sin and to effect conversion. While in the other schools of the city two hours a week were given to religious instruction, in the Fridericianum the first hour of each day was devoted to it, and every recitation was begun and closed with prayer. Besides the Bible, the catechisms of Luther, Spener, and Dietrich were used in the school. On Sunday there were two sermons and two catechizations in the church connected with the institution. All the instruction had a religious aim, and exhortations were frequently connected with the recitations. The original New Testament was the principal book used in the study of Greek, and the interpretation of that book was the aim in the study of that language. The historical instruction was mostly confined to the history of the Old and New Testaments. And Scheffner, who was a pupil a little later than Kant, states that on every Sunday two boys from the upper classes had to stand before the pulpit, while Dr. Schulz, with a sharp voice and in a severe tone, catechized them on his sermon.

The discipline of the institution was stern, and the pupils regarded its severity as an element of the religion. ([11]) Whatever benefits might flow from them, Pietism and its discipline in the gymnasium could not fail to excite aversion and opposition, particularly on the part of those who were predominantly intellectual and had a passion for knowledge. These influences were by no means such as were calculated to attract Kant, in whose nature emotional religion never struck a sympathetic chord. Borowski says of him that he "had no taste at all for the forms of piety or religiousness which many of the pupils adopted, sometimes from very impure motives."

Whatever excellences there may have been in the religion of his home and the gymnasium, Kant's opinion of Pietism in general was by no means favourable. Sometimes he spoke of it with bitterness; and taking his own words as a commentary on its character, we are not surprised that he turned from it with aversion. He says, "But it is not contempt for piety which has made Pietism a name to designate a sect, with which a certain degree of contempt is always associated; but it is the fantastic and, with all appearance of humility, proud assumption that they are distinguished as the supernaturally favoured children of heaven, though their conduct, as far as can be seen, has not the least advantage over those who are called by them the children of the world." ([12])

Pietism thus had its favourable and its unfavourable elements, and Kant was subject to both kinds of influence. Its excesses, its emotional character, and its controversies, had a bad effect on many minds. Though powerful in the province, it left no enduring literary monuments, because its sermons and books lacked depth and breadth; its glory consisted in its ethical features, in promoting education among the masses, and in establishing eleemosynary institutions. In the schools its aims were often frustrated; and it is probable that both Kant and his friend Ruhnken refused to enter the ministry, though they were sent to the gymnasium by their parents to prepare for that profession, because they were unfavourably affected by Pietism. But while its religious features repelled Kant, its moral elements exerted the deepest influence on him. In his ethical system, especially in his stern morality and in his views of the radical evil in human nature and the need of conversion, we see the effect of his early religious training. Pietism did not win his heart, but it moulded his conscience. "The weakness of Pietism was its drill system, into which it fell in its exaggerations. When the religious instruction of children became a strait-jacket, it lost its attractions for the youthful mind; nevertheless, in its onesidedness, Pietism forged that brass logical chain whose last link is the Categorical Imperative." ([13])

In intellectual character and educational advantages the Fridericianum compared favourably with the other schools of that day. Not only was it the best of the five gymnasia in Königsberg, but it was the best and most celebrated in the province. It introduced improvements which were also adopted by other institutions, and it sent into the churches, schools, civil offices, and various other spheres, more eminent and successful men than any other school in eastern Prussia. Kant was a pupil in its most flourishing period, namely, during the first years of the rectorate of Dr. Schulz. His predecessor, Lysius, who has been pronounced, next to Francke, the best teacher of his day, devoted thirty years to the development of the school; and Dr. Schulz continued to conduct and develop it in his spirit.

But notwithstanding its superiority for that day, it was very inferior when compared with the excellent Germau gymnasia of the present. Owing to the preponderance of the Latin language in the gymnasia, they were commonly called Latin schools; but both the Latin and the Greek were taught mechanically, as a system of rules and as a discipline for the memory, while the spirit of the classics was neglected. "As late as 1779, Frederick the Great found it necessary to enjoin upon the Prussian gymnasia, by means of a cabinet order, a more diligent and better study of the Greek and Latin authors, in order that the pupils might get the substance as well as the words, and ideas as well as a good diction." ([14]) The German language was not thoroughly taught; and the instruction in general was scholastic and formal, rather than real and living.

The Fridericianum was not free from the defects then common in the Latin schools, and it also suffered from the fact that, on account of its limited means, it was obliged to depend largely on students of the university, and candidates for the ministry, for its instructors. The employment of so many new and inexperienced instructors made much machinery necessary. "The frequent change of teachers obliged the directors to follow a certain plan of instruction, which prescribed the lessons for every course, every month, every week, and even for every hour. The teacher was a wound-up watch, which, in the opinion of the Pietists, was set correctly and went right." ([15])

It is evident from these facts, that the general character of the gymnasia and the peculiar condition of the Fridericianum give no assurance that Kant enjoyed the advantages of a deep and broad culture while preparing for the university. The Fridericianum had the merit of being the first Latin school in the city which introduced history, geography, and mathematics, as regular branches of study; but the instruction in them was by no means thorough. The course of study included Latin, Greek, Hebrew, French, history, logic, mathematics, and geography; and the German language was taught in connexion with rhetoric and poetry, but the time for its appreciation as a branch of study had not yet come. There was no instruction in natural history or physics. It is not strange that in his mature years Kant's opinion of the intellectual character of the gymnasium was not very favourable. The very thought of the instruction in logic and mathematics made him laugh; and in speaking of his teachers in these branches, he said, "These gentlemen could probably not have kindled into a fire any spark of philosophy or mathematics which might have been in us." Cunde, his fellow-pupil, to whom he made this remark, answered, "They could blow it out or quench it." Scheffner relates that his teacher used the Greek New Testament as a text-book, and had the translation written between the lines. One teacher, by the name of Heydenreich, was, however, an exception to the general rule. He was connected with the school from 1737—1740, and taught the first Latin class, which had from sixteen to eighteen lessons a week. Besides teaching the language, he explained the text, caught and communicated the spirit of the classics, and interested and inspired his students. Kant rarely referred to his teachers in the gymnasium; but Borowski says that he spoke with great esteem of Heydenreich more than a hundred times. To this "elegant Latin scholar," as Kant called him, he was indebted for that inspiration which he failed to find in the other branches, and he devoted himself to the study of the Latin classics with great zeal. Not only was this his favourite study in the gymnasium, it was the only one for which he manifested a preference, and in which he made any special progress. Kant, Ruhnken, and Cunde, frequently met to read Latin authors who were not included in the course; and Ruhnken, who had more money at his command than his comrades, took pains to furnish the best editions of the classics. They were all gifted young men, with intellectual tastes and aspirations; they were diligent and successful students; and in the pursuit of their favourite study they not only learned the Latin language, and cultivated a good Latin style, but they also developed a taste for the spirit and the beauties of the classics. His association and study with these friends made oases in Kant's youth, and he remembered with great pleasure the happy hours spent with Ruhnken and Cunde over his favourites among the ancients.

The diligent study of the classics was of great and permanent value to Kant. Not only did it enable him to use the Latin language easily and gracefully, which is evident from his dissertations in that language, but it also laid the basis for that broad humanistic culture which was so noticeable in his conversations and lectures. In his first book, written when the impression of the classics was still fresh, Horace, Virgil, and Lucretius, are quoted. In his conversations he frequently referred to the Latin authors; and even in old age, when his memory for recent impressions had become very weak, he was still able to quote easily and correctly numerous passages from Latin writers, especially from the work of his favourite author, Lucretius, "De Natura Rerum." In 1801 a friend of Kant, speaking of his association with Ruhnken at the gymnasium, wrote, "Kant never forgot the charming entertainment furnished him by the ancients; and even now, at his great age, his memory does not merely retain the most beautiful verses and sentences of the Latin poets, orators, and historians, but the remembrance of them frequently inspires him." ([16])

When we consider the character of the gymnasium, we are not surprised that Kant manifested no preference for the subjects which afterwards engrossed his attention. It is explained by the fact that natural science had no place in the curriculum, and that mathematics and logic were not taught in such a way as to inspire any love for them; and the boy had not yet developed sufficient taste for these branches to make them subjects of independent study. He was still dependent on his teachers and surroundings for his inspiration and preferences, and there was no evidence of a decided natural inclination or gift in any particular direction. Not until he was brought under the influence of other instructors, in the university, was there any indication that his speciality would not be philology. Ruhnken said that at the gymnasium he himself had a preference for philosophy, Kant for philology; yet the former made his reputation in philology, the latter in philosophy, and Ruhnken's last work was "Scholia in Platonem," while Kant's last intellectual labour was devoted to the completion of his philosophy. Kypke, another fellow-pupil of Kant, said that at that time they did not, and could not, have the least idea that Kant would ever devote himself to philosophy. And Ruhnken afterwards regretted that Kant had abandoned the green fields of the humanities, to wander on the barren steppes of metaphysics.

Already at the gymnasium Kant was ambitious for authorship. As scholars sometimes Latinized their names, he proposed to write his "Kantius," on the title-pages of his books, while Ruhnken expected to become known as "Ruhnkenius," and Cunde as "Cundeus." Ruhnken was the only one who carried out this intention, and as Ruhnkenius he attained fame as an authority in classical literature.

Kant and Ruhnken never met each other after they left the gymnasium. The latter went to Wittenberg, to study the classics, philosophy, and law; then to Leyden, to pursue Greek under the eminent Hemsterhuys. Having lost faith in speculative philosophy, he devoted his life to philology, was appointed professor in Leyden, and stood in the front rank of the classical scholars of last century. Ruhnken was one year older than Kant, and died in 1797.

Cunde, Kant's other intimate friend at the gymnasium, was also his fellow-student in the university. After finishing his studies at Königsberg, he taught for awhile in the Fridericianum, and then became rector of a Latin school in Rastenburg. He was an excellent man and a superior teacher. It is said that he had stupendous learning, "which would have been an honour to any university, an incomparable method in teaching, and a deep insight into human nature." He was a man of strict integrity and sterling worth; and the three friends were congenial morally as well as intellectually. Overworked while a teacher in the Fridericianum, Cunde's health was already undermined when he went to Rastenburg. The school-building at this place was so bad that its miserable condition was the occasion of his premature death in 1759. This trio, Kant, Ruhnken, and Cunde, seem to have displayed the most intellectual vigour among the students at that time in the gymnasium, and this, together with their moral character and their aspirations, formed the basis of their intimacy.

Kant was eight years old when he entered the gymnasium, and sixteen when he left it to enter the university. While he saw the defects of the school, he also saw its excellences, and he was grateful for the advantages which he there enjoyed. He spoke with appreciation of the paternal spirit of the institution, and of the earnest efforts to form the characters and develop the minds of its pupils. The school at least prepared him for the university, and thus opened the way for him to a learned career. That he was diligent and successful in his studies is evident both from his associations and his attainments.

Little else is known of Kant's youth. We have reason to regret this fact, for it is always interesting to watch the first unfolding of the aspirations and powers of one who has moved the world out of its usual course, and we are anxious to learn whether the great man is really found in the boy. Even the biographies of him by intimate friends give very unsatisfactory accounts of his early years. Nearly all who had known him in his youth had died before him; and the sister who survived him probably remembered nothing that was striking or characteristic. Kant himself did not like to speak of his youth, its memory evidently having little that was attractive. Being the child of a poor mechanic, small, timid, weak and even delicate, it is not singular that the busy world paid no attention to this boy, who gave no promise of his future greatness. It was a sad period of life, with but few of the pleasures and scarcely any of the poetry of youth. He was extremely sensitive; this is confirmed by the story that he was so annoyed because a boy said that his name "Cant" should be pronounced as if written with a "Z," that he afterwards wrote it Kant. He was predisposed to melancholy; and his poverty, his self-denial, and the difficulties which beset him, were calculated to deepen his gloom. His family was not so situated as to give him any social standing, nor had he powerful friends to encourage and help him. Thrown almost wholly on his own intellectual resources, his only hope was in achievements resulting from severe personal efforts. Most persons of mature years find a melancholy pleasure in reflecting on the joys, the hopes, the inspirations, and the enthusiasm of the spring of life; but when Kant had grown to manhood, and had learned to estimate everything from an intellectual standpoint, he looked on youth as the period of weakness. Hippel, Kant's acquaintance for many years, in speaking of the Egyptian bondage in which many children were kept, states that Kant had experienced the miseries of the slavery of youth in full measure, and that he declared that fear and horror seized him when he reflected on the bondage of his youth. This is an exaggeration, but it is, no doubt, based on remarks of Kant. Rink says, "It was not on account of the slavery of his youth that Kant depreciated the years of childhood, but his reasons were deeper, namely, the defective knowledge and judgment of childhood; for this reason he declared him to be a child who had the vain wish to return from the age of manhood to that of childhood." But the misery of which Hippel speaks probably helped to form Kant's view of youth.

Two stories are related of Kant's boyhood: the one an evidence of occasional absent-mindedness; the other, of unusual presence of mind when aroused. Forgetfulness of ordinary affairs was characteristic of him; and he said that during his whole life absent-mindedness had been one of his failings. When he first went to school he was frequently punished for forgetfulness. Once, when on his way to school, he laid down his books to play with other boys, and after the play he went to school, never thinking of the books till the teacher asked for them. But on another occasion his presence of mind probably saved his life. When about eight years old, he attempted to walk over a log lying across a ditch filled with water. He had taken only a few steps when the log commenced to roll and he began to get dizzy. As he could neither retreat nor stand still, he fixed his eyes on a point, on the other side of the ditch, in a line with the log, ran towards it without looking down, and thus escaped.

CHAPTER II.

STUDENT IN THE UNIVERSITY. BEGINNING OF AUTHORSHIP. FAMILY TUTOR.

1740—1755.

Change in the Government—University of Könisberg—Matriculated as Student of Theology—Studies—Favourite teacher—Reasons for not entering the ministry—Struggles with poverty—Recreation—First book—Family tutor—Work on Cosmogony.

JUST before Kant entered the University of Königsberg a change occurred in the Government of Prussia, which seriously affected the religion, the literature, and the life of the kingdom. When Frederick William I. died, on the last day of May, 1740, his son, Frederick II., commonly called the Great, ascended the throne. The predilection of Frederick William for military affairs is characteristic of the Hohenzollern family; his passion for giants as soldiers was but a whim of that propensity. His military exactness and routine had left their impress on the people, and the age itself was mechanical. For present notions his government was too paternal and too personal. Strictly orthodox himself, he expected his people to have the same faith, and he even used constraint to make them devout in his sense; and in governing his people, as in training his son, he seems to have had no idea of tolerance. The spirit of his administration was most powerfully felt in cities like Königsberg, where the civil officers, who were his instruments rather than his agents, were numerous. In every department of life there was a cramped feeling, a lack of room for development, and a want of spontaneity. But on the accession of Frederick II. to the throne, who himself had keenly felt the galling tyranny of his father, the change, as is usual in reactions, was very marked; in some cases there was a bound from one extreme to the other. Not that his reign was less personal than that of his father, but its spirit was different. For a long time sceptical tendencies had run parallel with Orthodoxy and Pietism; the Government had, however, used its power to suppress them. Under the new king there was no longer to be any religious restraint; for, as he said at the beginning of his reign, every man was to have the liberty to be saved in his own fashion. The era of tolerance which he introduced did not merely affect religion; he emphasized the freedom of thought, always excepting cases where it conflicted with his political supremacy. Persons who had been exiled during his father's reign were recalled; and it was one of his first acts to invite the philosopher Wolf to return to Halle. His French teachers, as well as the literary tendency of the age, had created in him a preference for the French language and literature; his libraries in Potsdam, consisting almost wholly of French books, still testify to this preference. He corresponded with eminent Frenchmen, invited them to his court, and was greatly under their influence, being especially intimate with Voltaire. The royal favour promoted French frivolity and scepticism, as well as the popularity of French literature.

The new king inaugurated a new era for Prussia, and during his long reign the revival of letters began in Germany. The literary activity of Lessing, Herder, Jacobi, Hamann, Schiller, Goethe, Winckelmann, and many other eminent men, belongs wholly or in part to this reign, during which the modern literature of Germany had its birth. His great achievements for the enlargement and the glory of Prussia, and his consequent popularity, made his views all the more influential; and under him who was called the Great, *the* King, the Royal Philosopher, the Only One (der Einzige), a great change was wrought in the thought and life of his kingdom during the forty-six years of his vigorous reign.

The first sixteen years of Kant's life belonged to the reign of Frederick William. During the twenty-seven years of his sovereignty the people became addicted to his mechanical ways; and Kant imbibed this spirit of the times during the formative period of his character, and his life was characterized by a regularity which became mechanical and monotonous. His earliest religious impressions were such as this king himself had fostered. The whole tenor of the Government was changed when Kant entered the university; and it is probable that by the change his religious views were also affected. We find that he passed from the Pietism by which his youth was influenced, to the free-thinking of the age of Frederick the Great; just such a reaction is found in his case as that which took place in the Government when the new monarch ascended the throne. Kant, however, retained the stern morality which characterized the preceding king, and this saved him from the frivolity which was encouraged by royal example under Frederick the Great.

The University of Königsberg, which Kant entered in the autumn of 1740, and with which he was connected during the greater part of his life, was founded in 1544, by Duke Albert. Melanchthon, whom he consulted respecting the teachers, sent his son-in-law, Sabinus, who was made rector for life. For the first two centuries the history of this institution was not brilliant; and at the close of its second century, when Kant became a student, it occupied an obscure position among the German universities. Neither its intellectual life nor its educational advantages were such as to give it prominence.([17]) Its strength was in its theological faculty, to which at times nearly one half of the students belonged, while there were comparatively few in the philosophical faculty. The students were mainly from the Province of Prussia, Courland, Pomerania, Silesia, and the Protestant portion of Polish Prussia. Thus its students, as well as its location, belonged rather to the border of Germany than to its heart.

If we take a map of Germany and glance at the surroundings of Königsberg, we are at once struck with its intellectual isolation; before the introduction of railways, and in the eighteenth century, this was much more complete than at present. It was a frontier city which had little communication with the heart of Germany, being remote from other universities, as well as from Berlin, Weimar, and other intellectual and literary centres. The literature and science from other quarters reached it slowly, if at all; consequently there was a lack of that inspiration which is communicated by contact and rivalry with intellectual characters and centres. In 1736 Professor Bock, of the University of Königsberg, wrote, "As is well known, I live where books and periodicals from other places are seen only after long years." As a rule, only books specially ordered by purchasers were brought to Königsberg by the booksellers, so that it was difficult to keep up with the literature of the day. As late as 1781, another writer, Baczko, said, with reference to the Province of Prussia, of which Königsberg is the capital: "Prussia is decried in Germany as almost a learned Siberia; and owing to our great distance from Leipzig, the centre of the German book trade, it is natural that we should suffer, since all literary novelties come late to us, and authorship is not favoured by facilities for selling books." Another writer speaks of Kant as working out his system "on the Pregel, in one of the most completely forgotten corners of Europe." This isolation particularly affected the life of the university, and it partly accounts for the fact that the first books of Kant were almost wholly unnoticed.

Other facts must also be taken into account in considering Kant's studies at the university, and his whole intellectual career. In the universities of Germany, as well as in the gymnasia and the other schools, the instruction, both as respects matter and method, was far from being satisfactory. The lectures were generally prosy and lifeless, dealing rather with the forms of thought than with thought itself, making nice but useless scholastic distinctions, rich in tedious subtleties concerning matters of little importance, and burdened with a method which made a show of learning without real, living scholarship. A stiff and stilted pedantic mannerism still prevailed. The teachers were often incompetent, and many of the lectures were delivered in Latin which was anything but classic. Instead of promoting genuine and thorough scholarship, it seemed rather to be the principal aim of the instruction to furnish the student with the means of successfully passing the examination required by the state.

The German language was greatly neglected, and it was depreciated by Germans themselves, when compared with the Latin, French, and English; indeed, it was still a matter of dispute, which of the various dialects should be used for a national literature. The right to use the German language for scholarly works was just beginning to assert itself. When C. F. Wolf published the first philosophical work in German, it created surprise; and in an appendix he explained German words by means of the Latin. A vigorous, independent literature hardly seemed to be a desideratum in the estimation of writers, so persistently were foreign models chosen for imitation. Gottsched, who left Königsberg for Leipzig in the same year that Kant was born, contended for French models, while Bodmer and the Swiss preferred the English; and it required men of genius like Lessing, Schiller, and Goethe, to reveal the power of the German language and to prove the possibility of an independent German literature. The founder of æsthetics as the science of the beautiful, Baumgarten, was indeed living, but his system was not published till the middle of the century, and then it gave elements rather than a science. The literary disputes of the day prove that the whole subject of taste and criticism was involved in confusion and uncertainty. Lessing, Winckelmann, Kant, and Schiller, introduced light and order. In the natural sciences, the mechanical views of nature absorbed the attention of philosophers, the chief authorities being Newton and his school, together with Descartes and Leibnitz, and their followers. In metaphysics, the dogmatism of the Wolfian school held almost undisputed sway.

The revival of letters was imminent when Kant entered the university, but he did not have the benefit of it during his studies. Klopstock was born in the same year as Kant, but he began his university course five years later; Winckelmann entered the university of Halle two years before Kant entered that of Königsberg; Lessing was five years younger than Kant, and was still a school-boy when the latter was already a student; Kant had ended his university course several years before Goethe's birth, and had been a teacher four years when Schiller was born; Herder, Wieland, Jacobi, and, in fact, the whole galaxy of Germany's brightest literary period, belong to a later time than Kant's student life. These names, however, indicate the character of the period which was about to be inaugurated, a period in which Kant's name was one of the most eminent. With all the disadvantages of the day, it was a time of fermentation and of grand opportunities. As an epoch was approaching, it was an age when great problems demanded solution, when doubts developed the intellect, when sharp conflicts aroused thought, and when the confusion itself created opportunities for a master-mind. The man who could master the different tendencies, and could harmonize their conflicting elements, would find the crisis itself the occasion for the greatest intellectual results. Only when we consider the difficulties, on the one hand, and the rare opportunities, on the other, can we comprehend the career of Kant.

The University of Königsberg suffered more than many others from the evils enumerated. At the opening of the century the Aristotelian philosophy was still taught; in the second decade a Privat-Docent introduced the Wolfian system. In 1729 Professor Bock wrote, "The university is in so miserable a condition that it does not seem unlike a trivial school; philosophy is afflicted with a hectic fever, and the other sciences are also badly enough cultivated." The affliction of philosophy was probably connected with the fact that Wolf was expelled from Halle and Prussia in 1723, and it was dangerous to teach his system in the universities of the kingdom. A few years later, however, an alliance was formed between Pietism and the Wolfian philosophy in Königsberg, mainly through the influence of Dr. Schulz, after which this philosophy prevailed in the university.

For the study of mathematics no superior advantages were afforded. Professor Kraus, who taught mathematics in the university many years later, declared that Königsberg had always had men who understood mathematics, and still has; but that as long as the sun had shone on the city, it had not been able to boast of a good mathematician. Nor did chemistry, natural history, technology, or political science, fare any better. The division of labour was far less complete than at present, and the exclusive devotion of a teacher to a speciality, and the consequent great proficiency in it, were exceptions. Even theology and mathematics were taught by the same man, Langhausen being professor extraordinary of theology and professor in ordinary of mathematics.([18]) J. G. Bock was at the same time professor of speculative philosophy and of poetry, an evidence that speculative philosophy was not made very prominent. It was, however, characteristic of the age to apply philosophy to everything, and two professors were appointed to teach practical or applied philosophy. Most of the professors in the philosophical faculty were unknown in science and letters, and not one of them was celebrated. There were among them men of respectable scholarship; but in general the teaching had become lifeless, and was little calculated to arouse and inspire the intellect.([19])

Kant's preference for the Latin language and literature might have continued at the university if he had there found a good instructor in Latin. The revival of interest in the classics, which had begun in Leipzig and Göttingen, did not yet affect the University of Königsberg. Probably Ruhnken went to Wittenberg, after graduating at the Fridericianum, because Königsberg offered few attractions in his favourite departments, especially in philology. Kant, who was greatly influenced in his intellectual preferences by the ability of his instructors, now made specialities of other subjects, in none of which the gymnasium had offered any advantages.

He was matriculated as a student of theology, though it is doubtful whether even then he had any inclination for that study. His mind and his preferences were too little developed, and he knew his own powers too little, to determine finally his intellectual course. At that time parents generally decided the calling of their children, even without consulting them. He had been sent to the gymnasium to prepare for the ministry; and it is probable that the memory of his mother, and the influence of his father and of Dr. Schulz, determined his matriculation in the university as a theological student. This did not interfere with the hearing of lectures in other departments, nor did it oblige him to make a speciality of theology; and whenever he desired it, he could be transferred to another faculty. Indeed, theological students were expected to take a course in philosophy first, in order that they might be the better prepared for theology.

Professor Teske, who was a good scholar, had the department of physics. Kant attended his lectures, and was more indebted to him than to any other professor in ordinary. But Martin Knutzen, professor extraordinary, more than any one else, moulded his intellect and determined his preferences and his future career. Born in 1713, he was appointed professor extraordinary at the age of twenty-one, was twenty-seven years old when Kant entered the university, and was never promoted to a professorship in ordinary. ([20]) His lectures extended over many subjects of philosophy and physics, including logic, metaphysics, rational psychology, natural philosophy, morals, natural law, rhetoric, mnemonics, and mathematics. Kant not only attended his lectures, but also took part in the meetings which he held for disputations and for the examination of students on the subjects of his lectures. Knutzen was a disciple of the Leibnitz-Wolfian philosophy, and in religion was a Pietist; his attainments were unusual, his reading was varied and extensive; and as his gifts as a teacher were extraordinary, he was deservedly popular with the students. Besides being a laborious student, he lectured four or even five times a day, and overwork is supposed to have been the cause of his death, in 1751, when only thirty-seven years old. His activity was not confined to the university, but he extended his reputation by means of writings on philosophical, theological, physical, and mathematical topics. ([21])

Professor Knutzen's lectures embraced the subjects which Kant pursued with most pleasure while a student in the university; and after he finished his course, mathematics, physics, metaphysics, and morals were his specialities. Kant, however, did not at this time make the study of metaphysics prominent. Now and for years afterwards he devoted himself chiefly to mathematics and physics. The influence of his mathematical studies is apparent in his great works, being evident from his frequent references to mathematics, and from his demand for exact definitions and for demonstrations which have mathematical certainty; and his entire philosophy reveals the mathematical mind.

The personal intercourse of a professor may be more influential than his learned lectures, in giving the student intellectual inspiration, and in developing his mental tastes and his moral character. The young teacher who can enter with warmth into sympathy with an eager student, may have a decided advantage over the aged professor. Kant entered into closer personal relations with Knutzen than with his other teachers. Besides hearing his lectures and taking part in his reviews and discussions, he also consulted him about his studies, and conversed with him on learned subjects. The teacher, pleased with his abilities and thirst for knowledge, placed his library at Kant's disposal, and gave him directions in his reading; and it was in this way that the eager student became acquainted with the works of eminent scholars, including those of Newton. But this favourite teacher did more than influence his students to become learned; he aimed to make them originators of thought, not mere imitators; and thinkers, instead of mere learners.

There was a striking resemblance between this teacher and his aspiring and susceptible pupil; and much that has been said of Knutzen might also be said of Kant. Their intellectual specialities were the same till the end of life; but in religion they differed, since Kant did not adopt his teacher's Pietistic views. They were both laborious students; both were learned and were polymathists; both were thinkers, and both aimed to make their students thinkers. While Kant, at the age when Knutzen died, had probably displayed more originality than his teacher, it is doubtful whether on the whole he had revealed more mental breadth or greater intellectual vigour. The pupil, however, attained a lasting and world-wide fame, while the teacher was forgotten.

In the university, Professors Knutzen and Teske took the place of Heydenreich in the gymnasium; and mathematics and physics took the place of the classics. A writer, speaking of Kant, says, "His teachers in mathematics and physics, Professors Knutzen and Teske, were among the clearest and most learned men in Königsberg. Kant not only heard all their lectures most attentively, but he also took pains to obtain explanations of difficult points by means of private conversations with both, and to procure books from them for the independent study of these branches. During his academic course he still kept philosophy proper in the background; and Kant's university friend, Kypke, afterwards his colleague as Professor of Oriental Literature, remarked that at that time he showed little inclination for metaphysical studies." (22)

Kant no doubt attended many lectures of which no mention is made; but we know that he heard those of Professor Schulz on dogmatics, though he did not take a full course in theology. It was his aim to include all the sciences in his investigations, and he regarded some knowledge of theology necessary for a complete education, even if the ministry was not chosen as a profession. Heilsberg, who was his fellow-student at the university, states that this breadth of culture was Kant's object. "For this purpose, Wlömer, Kant, and I, decided to attend the public lectures of Dr. Schulz during the next half year. We did not miss an hour, diligently wrote the dictations, reviewed the lectures at home, and in the examinations which the worthy man frequently held with his numerous hearers, our answers were so satisfactory that at the close of the course he requested us to remain. He asked for our names, inquired about our knowledge of languages, and desired to know what professors we were hearing, and what was the aim of our studies. Kant answered that he intended to devote himself to medicine;

Wlömer, that he had chosen the law; I was undecided." The professor then asked why they heard theological lectures? Kant replied, because they had a desire to learn. Dr. Schulz informed them that if they concluded to enter the ministry, they should come to him with confidence, and they should have the choice of places in the country and cities, adding, "This I promise you; and if I live, I will keep my word. Here is my hand; go in peace." ([23])

From this it is evident that Kant had not yet found the sphere of his future activities. He may have had serious intentions of studying medicine. Later in life he manifested a preference for medical works, and his first book was dedicated to Bohlius, a medical professor. In the undecided state of his mind he may sometimes have inclined to one profession and then to another.

But why did Kant fail to comply with the desire of his parents to enter the ministry? His lack of sympathy with the prevalent religion was no doubt one of his strongest reasons. His inquiring mind could hardly escape agitation through religious doubts, which Schulz's lectures, highly as Kant appreciated them, were not calculated to remove. They contained a strange mixture of Pietism and mathematical demonstrations of Christian dogmas, such as might have been expected from the man of whom Wolf said that if any one understood him, it was Schulz of Königsberg. Hippel, who was one of Dr. Schulz's students, gives a hint of his method in teaching theology:—"This remarkable man taught me to look at theology from a new point of view; for he introduced so much philosophy into it that one would have thought that Christ and His apostles had all received instruction from Wolf in Halle."

It was an age of theological agitation, of religious inquiry and doubt; and the unsettling of faith had a strong influence on the young men in the universities. It is a significant fact that Winckelmann, Lessing, Ruhnken, and Kant, were all sent by their parents to the university to study for the ministry, and that not one of them entered that profession. There was much in the university during Kant's student-life which was calculated to alienate him from religion. The quarrels of the religious factions produced distractions, and made an unfavourable impression on the students. The theological faculty was the most powerful, and exercised an authority which some of the other professors regarded as oppressive. Dr. Schulz, who became the most influential man in Königsberg soon after his arrival in the city, was the leading spirit in the theological department, and had warm adherents in the other faculties; but he also met with decided opposition, and his supremacy was disputed by those who rejected his religious views. When Frederick II. began his reign, the royal favour bestowed on Dr. Schulz by his predecessor was withdrawn, and the king, displeased with his Pietistic zeal, deprived him of some of his offices, and greatly curtailed his power; and he was also energetically opposed by a strong party in the churches of Königsberg. This change in his influence occurred about the time when Kant entered the university. The hot disputes in the churches embittered the feelings of the different parties, and also affected both the professors and the students. Professor Fisher had been banished from

Königsberg in 1725, because he ventured to advocate Wolf's philosophy, and to defend some of the very tenets for which, on pain of death, that philosopher had been banished from Halle. He had also spoken in uncomplimentary terms of the Pietism in Königsberg. A royal decree banished him from the city within twenty-four hours, and from the province within forty-eight. As the new king had restored Wolf to Halle, so he permitted Fisher to return to Königsberg. In 1743 he published a book on "Nature," in which he advocated deistic and pantheistic views. The Pietists, including Dr. Schulz, secured the prohibition of the book; the author was severely attacked, and was not permitted to partake of the communion. The sensation thus produced could not fail to affect the students, so easily aroused to indignation even by the semblance of intolerance. It is not difficult to imagine its influence on Kant, absorbed in the study of mathematics and physics; and these early experiences no doubt had much to do with his later hatred of all forms of oppression, and particularly of religious intolerance. If aversion to Pietism already began in the gymnasium, it could only be increased by the contentions which occurred during his studies in the university. Taking into account these facts, together with his intellectual preferences, we need look no farther to discover his reasons for not entering the ministry. ([24])

Kant's quiet, uneventful life was marked by a regular and steady development of his powers, without abrupt inner or outer changes. Hungry for knowledge, and absorbed in its acquisition, he pursued the even tenor of his way, apparently little affected by distracting or disturbing influences. The conflicts of his life were mostly inner and hidden from the world. Even the processes of his mind in producing his great metaphysical speculations are very imperfectly known; with the exception of his works, we have hints about them only in his letters. We know nothing of his mental conflicts and religious struggles in youth; but he could not pass through the Pietistic influences without mental agitation, and it no doubt required much earnest thought to determine his vocation. It was not in his nature to break easily with the religious associations of his early life, and it must have cost him a severe struggle to resolve not to comply with the ardent desires of his parents and helpful pastor.

Kant was obliged to contend with poverty while at the university, and he found the road to learning beset with difficulties. He, however, mastered the lectures, especially those of Knutzen and Teske, so successfully that he could aid other students in reviewing them. Sometimes he rendered this assistance as a matter of friendship; but his necessities also compelled him to give instruction for which he received compensation, the students paying him what they pleased. He occupied a room, for some time, with Wlömer, an intimate friend, probably receiving his lodging gratis. Heilsberg says, "Kallenberg, now councillor of war, gave him free lodging and considerable support when Wlömer went to Berlin. From the deceased Dr. Trummer, whom he also instructed, he received much help, but more from his relative, the manufacturer Richter, who paid the expenses of his promotion to the degree of magister." Kant lived very economically, an art which he was obliged to learn early and to practise long. Although he did not absolutely suffer from want, Heilsberg informs us that when an article of Kant's clothing was sent away to be mended and he was obliged to leave the house, "one of the students would remain at home while Kant sallied forth with the coat, pantaloons, or boots borrowed from him. If a garment was entirely worn out, the party" (those to whom Kant gave lessons, and perhaps other friends) "made contributions, of which no account was kept, and which were never refunded."

There may be more than a compensation for poverty in the very discipline it gives a man while mastering the difficulties he encounters; and it may prove a blessing to many a mind by leaving open but one way to eminence—that of intellectual supremacy,—though that may lie through deserts, or over mountains almost impassable. There are victories whose greatest blessing is in the battle. Kant's necessities proved to be blessings in disguise. In pursuing his purpose resolutely, he learned self-denial, mastered circumstances, and developed remarkable will-power; and his poverty obliged him early to cultivate the gift of communicating instruction. He was only a student when he became a teacher.

He shared but few of the common joys of life. However much a hostile fortune was to blame for this, his tastes seem to have been too predominantly intellectual to seek the ordinary pleasures of youth. His friend Heilsberg says, "Kant was fond of no pleasures, and still less was he inclined towards any species of fanaticism; and he imperceptibly accustomed those who heard him to similar views. His only recreation consisted in playing billiards, a game in which Wlömer and I were his constant companions. We had developed our skill almost to the utmost, and rarely returned home without some gain. I paid my French teacher altogether from this income. As a consequence, persons refused to play with us, and we abandoned this way of making money, and chose l'hombre, which Kant played well." Study was the main source of his enjoyments, and when afterwards he advised young men to cultivate a love for work, and to deny themselves pleasures so that they might the longer retain the power of enjoyment, he gave them a rule which he himself had adopted.

Kant probably ended his university course in 1744, at the age of twenty. In this year he began the preparation of his first book. In harmony with his preferences and principal studies at the university, the book is mathematical, treating of the kinetic forces. ([25]) The title-page bears the date 1746; but the dedication was written on his birthday, April 22, 1747, and in the book itself there is a reference to a work which appeared in the spring of 1747, so that the publication may have been delayed till the autumn of that year or still later. As he was too poor to pay for the printing, he was aided by his uncle Richter. The book has only historic interest, which consists in the fact that it gives us a knowledge of the mind and views of young Kant; but in this respect it is invaluable. It is characteristic that at the age of twenty he chose a subject so abstract and necessarily involving much dry discussion. The book throws light on his university course, showing what studies chiefly occupied his attention, and it also reveals the tendency to abstract reasoning which is so marked in his metaphysical works.

The standpoint of the book is essentially that of his teacher, Knutzen. (26) In the Wolfian philosophy, of which the teacher was a disciple, a pure mechanism prevailed, and a dogmatism that was defended by mathematical demonstrations, which it applied to every subject. Both in the natural sciences and in metaphysics this method promoted a lifeless formalism. Kant is not wholly satisfied with this method, and he subjects it to criticism; but he does not transcend it, and has no other to put in its place. The author is bold and self-confident, and yet modest; he is critical, and at the same time positive; and he reveals a fearless, energetic mind and a resolute will. "If I venture to reject the thoughts of Leibnitz, Wolf, Herrmann, Bernoulli, Buelfinger, and others, and to give my own the preference, I would not like to have worse judges than these men; for I know that if their judgment rejected my opinions, it would not condemn my aim." There is much in the book which in a youth just out of his teens may savour of impertinence, and of this Kant is aware. "My freedom in contradicting eminent men will produce unfavourable results for me. The world is much inclined to believe that he who is better informed on some points than a great scholar, imagines himself superior to him. I venture to say that this is a mistake." Connected with this freedom, which characterizes the independent thinker, there is also respect for great men and their opinions; but it is not a reverence which makes their authority final. We have here a mind striving to emancipate itself from the bondage of authority while respecting those who imposed it; hence there is a mingling of the defiant tone with modesty, and the wrestling of a critical spirit with the system in which it is entangled. He is convinced that the time is past when the opinions of great men can be regarded as settling disputed questions. "One can now boldly hold as nothing the authority of the Newtons and Leibnitzes if it conflicts with the discovery of the truth, and can fearlessly resolve to yield to no persuasion but that of the understanding." And in a characteristic passage he says, "In the pursuit of this discussion I shall not hesitate to reject freely the proposition of any man, however celebrated he may be, if to my understanding it appears to be false." As he is well aware that a pigmy in learning may in some department surpass a scholar who excels him in every other, he of course does not claim to be superior to the eminent men whom he criticizes. He admits that there is presumption in the declaration, "The truth for which the greatest masters of human knowledge have striven in vain, first of all presented itself to my mind;" but he significantly adds, "I do not venture to justify this thought; but, on the other hand, I would not like to disclaim it." He thinks it important that a man should have a noble confidence in his powers, since it inspires the mind and gives it a degree of exaltation which is advantageous in the investigation of the truth.

The author is convinced that by means of this book he has done science considerable service, and thinks that his views will help to settle one of the greatest controversies at that time dividing the geometers of Europe; and he ventures to predict that the controversy will either be settled soon, or that it will never end. But aside from its spirit there is nothing especially striking in the book, and there are no new theories which claim attention. It received little notice when it appeared, created no reputation for its author, and is not now prized by mathematicians. Greatly as he was indebted to his teachers Knutzen and Teske, the work must have cost him much research and earnest thought, and it proves that at the university he laid a solid foundation for his eminent career. We look in vain for the profundity and the peculiar views of the "Kritik," which appeared thirty-four years later; but the independent and critical spirit of his first book is the germ from which the "Kritik" could grow.

There can scarcely be a doubt that at this time Kant had already chosen the sphere of his activity, and that he was intent on fitting himself for it. With a resoluteness peculiar to him, he says in this book, "I have marked out for myself the course which I have determined to take. I shall begin my career, and nothing shall keep me from continuing it." He chose the learned career of a teacher in the university, though years of toil were still necessary before he could enter that sphere.

His father died in 1746, and in the same year he became a family tutor. It may be that his father's death threw him more completely on his own resources, and made it necessary for him to support himself. In order to become a teacher in the university, he was obliged to take a degree and to habilitate, and this required money; he may also have found it advisable to prepare himself more thoroughly for the degree and for the delivery of lectures. It was common for young men after completing their course, whether they were candidates for the ministry, or aimed at the position of a teacher in the university, to become family tutors; frequently this was the only available means of support. The position was far from being an enviable one. The pay of such a tutor was small, and frequently he was regarded as scarcely more than a servant, received but little respect from the children, and was expected to attend to other matters besides teaching.([27]) Kant, however, seems to have been unusually favoured while family tutor; still, the nine years which he spent in this position could not have been otherwise than irksome. He had no taste for teaching the mere rudiments of knowledge, and his own confession indicates that the occupation was not congenial. Speaking humorously of the matter, he declared that there probably never was a worse tutor, and said that he had never been able to acquire the art of adapting himself to the capacities and views of children.

Kant was at first tutor in the family of a Reformed preacher near Königsberg; then in the family of Von Hüllesen, at Arnsdorf, about sixty miles south-west of Königsberg. This was the limit of his travels. He visited Pillau, about thirty miles distant, and other places in the vicinity; but Arnsdorf is the greatest distance he ever journeyed from his native city. His friendly relations with the family of Von Hüllesen were continued after he ceased to be tutor, and his work there cannot have been a failure. The letters of his pupils proved their warm regard for their teacher, and after he left the house he was invited to participate in the most interesting festivities of the family. One of the young men was afterwards placed in his charge at Königsberg while pursuing his studies at the university. His pupils in this family were among the first in Prussia to free their peasants from the subjection in which they were at that time held; and for this act the king conferred on them the title of count.

The third and last family in which he lived as tutor was that of Count Kayserling, whose residence was near Königsberg, and who lived much of the time in the city. This position was of great advantage to him, and had much influence on his social relations. The count, who had studied at Leipzig, Halle, and in other universities, was a man of admirable qualities of mind and heart, and had gained a reputation in diplomatic service in various countries. The countess was a woman of unusual talent, with superior culture and attractive manners. She aided her husband in literary work, and also translated a Compend of Philosophy into French. Her rare talent in painting procured for her the distinction of an election to honorary membership in the Berlin Academy of the Arts and Mechanical Sciences. In one of his books Kant calls her "the ornament of her sex." It was in this family that he became acquainted with the rules of refined society. Here he met many persons of rank and distinction; and owing to his superior mental powers and his scholarship, he soon became a favourite guest in the most cultivated families of Königsberg. At table, French, Italian, and English literature, as well as political affairs, were discussed; this stimulated him to master these subjects thoroughly, and gave him an opportunity to use his excellent conversational powers. His experience in this family was of great value; here he gained an ease, culture, and polish, which could hardly have been expected in a man with his early associations and his studious habits.

If we judge Kant's tutorship, not by his estimate, but by the esteem in which he was held by the two noble families in which he lived, we must conclude that it was eminently successful. It cost him an effort to adapt himself to those under his charge; but this had its value in preparing him for his future career. "This long residence in strange families, the various social relations he entered, and to which he soon adapted himself admirably; the necessary victory over his bashfulness; the fact that he was thrown on his own intellectual resources; the many demands made on him by his duties as tutor, and the conscientiousness with which he strove to perform them; all this was calculated to exert an extraordinary influence on his life, especially in developing the marvellous versatility of his mind." (28) The union of scholarship and refinement in Kant is noticed by the same writer: "We now recognize in him the thorough scholar and the cultivated man of the world, without any interference of the qualities of the one with those of the other."

These niue years of tutorship also afforded him opportunities for the pursuit of his favourite subjects. His first book, which appeared soon after he became family tutor, was probably finished while occupying this position. The time which was his own he devoted chiefly to mathematics and physics, astronomy perhaps receiving most attention. In 1754 he published a brief discussion of the question, "Has the Earth been subject to any Change in its Revolution on its Axis?" In the same year he briefly considered the question, "Is the Earth growing Old?" But the work to which he devoted most of his energies, and which is the most important of all his earlier publications, is the astronomo-geological book which appeared in 1755, with the title, "General Natural History and Theory of the Heavens; or an Essay on the Constitution and Mechanical Origin of the Whole Universe, discussed according to Newtonian Principles." (29)

The great astronomers had given the laws of the motions of the heavenly bodies; Kant goes farther back and attempts to account for the very origin of these bodies, and his book is really a cosmogony of the universe. Supposing matter to have been originally in a state of chaos, he proceeds to give a purely mechanical explanation of the formation of the celestial bodies according to Newton's laws of attraction and repulsion. He regards matter, created by God, as originally hovering in a nebulous state. First the sun is formed by the attraction of particles of matter; then the chaotic matter which still hovers around the sun is formed into the planets and their moons. Kant was the first to propose this theory of the origin of the universe, but a few years later, Lambert, without knowing anything of Kant's book, advocated the same theory in his "Cosmological Letters;" and later still, Laplace, in his "Exposition du Système du Monde," proposed and more firmly established the same theory, without knowing anything of the books of his predecessors. In Germany it is still called the Kant-Laplace theory.

While Kant adopts the great laws discovered by Newton, and applies them in explaining the construction of the universe, he criticizes and transcends some of the principles of the great English philosopher. Newton accounts for the order in the world by the direct interposition of God; but Kant thinks that it can be accounted for by the laws of matter. These laws were placed there by God, but they work without the necessity of divine interposition. God is still regarded as the author of all things; His activity is, however, put farther back. Law, not chance, rules the universe, and this makes it so harmonious in its organization and movement; and God has so constituted this law that it works without His interposition.

This hypothesis of the origin of the world is not the only significant feature of the book. Near the beginning he expresses the conviction that there may be planets beyond Saturn, and also a planet between Mars and Jupiter. When, twenty-six years later, Herschel discovered Uranus, Kant rejoiced at the confirmation of his prophetic view. It is, however, strange that Kant's suspicion that there are planets beyond Saturn, which is often praised as revealing a deep insight into the planetary system, rests on an hypothesis which was proved false by the discovery of those planets. It is Kant's theory that the eccentricity of the orbits of the planets increases with their distance from the sun, the exception to this rule in the case of Mercury and Mars being regarded by him as due to disturbing influences; consequently, the further a planet is removed from the centre of the system, the more will its orbit resemble that of a comet. He therefore regards it probable that there are planets beyond Saturn whose orbits are still more eccentric than that of Saturn, and, consequently, still more closely related to those of comets, so that, by a regular gradation, the planets at last become comets. When, however, Uranus and Neptune were discovered, it was found that their orbits were less eccentric than that of Saturn.

While the book discusses the mechanical forces, Kant does not regard them as capable of explaining organisms; they are, however, much better understood than the organic powers. He thinks that, in a certain sense, it may be said without presumption, "Give me matter, and I will construct a world! That is, give me matter, and I will show you how a world may originate therefrom; for if the matter exists, it is not difficult to discover the causes which have co-operated in the formation of the world." But insuperable difficulties appear when we begin to deal with organisms. "Can we boast of the same ability with respect to the least plant or insect? Can we say, Give me matter, and I will show you how a caterpillar can be produced?"

Among other things, the book also discusses the density of the different planets, the origin of the comets, the revolutions of the planets on their axes, the origin of Saturn's rings, the zodiacal light, and the history of the sun. Kant thinks it very probable that most of the planets are inhabited; and he holds that in proportion as a planet is distant from the sun, its inhabitants, animals, and plants, will be formed of lighter material, and their form and structure will be more perfect. He ascribes vice, error, and the inertness of thought to the coarseness of the material from which the body is formed; man must therefore be more perfect if the material of his physical nature is finer. He consequently reasons that in proportion as human beings are removed from the sun, their bodies will be fine, and the power of thought, the quickness of the intellect, the clearness and vividness of their impressions from external objects, their skill in executing their purposes, and the whole range of their endowments, will be perfect. This seems to him so probable that he regards it as almost certain. The highest intelligences would therefore be found on Jupiter and Saturn, and the lowest on Venus and Mercury; on the former, a Newton would be regarded as an ape, and on the latter, a Greenlander or a Hottentot would be esteemed a Newton. In speaking of the blessings of the most fortunate inhabitants, he gives a loose rein to his speculations, and this part of the work abounds in what may be called illustrations of a speculative imagination.

The style of the book is easy, and between the arguments beautiful passages are interspersed. Those who are familiar only with his dry speculations are not prepared for the perspicuity and beauty of style in his earlier works. He calls worlds and systems "mere sun-dust," as compared with the whole of creation; and among others this poetic passage occurs, "A view of the starry heavens on a brilliant night inspires noble souls with ecstatic delight. Amid the universal stillness of nature and the peace of the spirit, the mysterious activity of the soul utters an indescribable language, which thrills, but which human tongue cannot express."

Kant had consecrated his life to thought, and the time spent by so many in idleness or dissipation was devoted by him to severe mental toil. The following words were evidently written from the fulness of his heart: "The discernment of the understanding, when it possesses the proper degree of completeness and clearness, has far more lively charms than sensuous allurements have, and is able to conquer these completely and trample them under foot."

In judging of the merits of the book, it should be remembered that its author was only thirty-one when it was published, and that he had never been connected with a university except as a student. It was chiefly the product of his diligent study as family tutor. The work was dedicated to Frederick II., who, however, probably never saw a copy of it. The publisher failed while the book was in the press, his entire stock was seized by the court for the creditors, and in this way the circulation of the book was hindered. When Lambert published his "Cosmological Letters" they excited much attention, while Kant's book was scarcely known.

CHAPTER III.

TEACHER IN THE UNIVERSITY.

Habilitation—Privat-Docent—Subjects and character of his lectures —Aim in teaching—Popularity—Testimony of Herder—Distraction—First salary—Contest for a prize—Promotion to a professorship—Efforts to induce him to leave Königsberg—Condition of the University—Dean and Rector.

MOST of the instructors in German universities are included under the classification of tutors, professors extraordinary, and professors in ordinary. (30) A tutor may become a professor in ordinary without passing through the intermediate grade of professor extraordinary; but it is unusual to appoint any one a professor who has not been a tutor. Kant desired to become a tutor in the philosophical faculty, and for this purpose it was necessary for him to present to the dean of that faculty two Latin dissertations. These he was obliged to defend before the dean and professors against any one who might see fit to attack them. Persons were also appointed to dispute with the author, the whole proceeding being conducted in Latin. Kant's first dissertation was presented for the purpose of taking the degree of magister. It was a treatise on "Fire," (31) and was defended before the faculty on the 12th of July, 1755. Teske, his former teacher, was much pleased with it, and declared that it had been instructive to him. To secure the privilege of lecturing in the university, he presented and defended another dissertation, on the 27th of September, entitled, "A new Explanation of the First Principles of Metaphysical Knowledge;" (32) which was the first metaphysical discussion from his pen. According to a royal decree of 1749, no person was to be proposed for the position of professor extraordinary who had not presented and defended three Latin dissertations. To prepare the way for a professorship, Kant accordingly prepared a third treatise, "On the Advantages to Natural Philosophy of a Metaphysic connected with Geometry," (33) which he defended in April, 1756.

It is worthy of note that in these dissertations there is a discussion of mathematical, physical, and metaphysical principles, and that they belong to the departments of which he made a speciality while a student and also afterwards. But it is evident that at this time his strength still lay in mathematics and physics. His books and treatises show that he was thoroughly prepared for his new sphere. He had mastered the results of the researches of Newton, Leibnitz, Hales, Boerhave, and others; and the comprehensiveness of his knowledge is as surprising as his penetration, his bold speculation, and his ability to systematize the results of his investigations. He, however, never made experiments in physics.

Any one who has a good character and the requisite scholarship, can become a tutor in a German university by complying with the conditions of habilitation; but after the laborious preparation necessary, and after passing through this severe ordeal, he has nothing but the privilege of delivering lectures. He is thrown entirely on his own resources, and on the assistance of friends; from the university he receives no remuneration. Only a professor in ordinary is eligible to the position of rector, dean, or member of the academic senate; in the management of the university the tutor is not consulted. For his income he depends on the fees of the students who hear his private lectures, the public ones always being free; and necessity may compel him to give private lessons, or to resort to other means for a livelihood. No student is obliged to hear his lectures; and while the exalted position of a professor is likely to attract students, that of a tutor is too humble to be attractive. He is, in fact, simply a private teacher, with the privilege of lecturing if he can get an audience. Until the year when Kant became professor, neither his name nor that of any other tutor appeared in the catalogue, so that even the subjects on which he lectured were not published by the authority of the institution. But the first year of Kant's professorship was also the first in which the catalogue contained the names of the tutors, and the subjects of their lectures, thus giving them public and official recognition. ([34])

Among the uncertainties of a tutorship is the promotion to a professorship. It may be a long time before a vacancy occurs; in case of a vacancy, other tutors may be preferred to him, or may have stronger claims because they have waited longer; and thus years and life itself may be spent, without attaining the coveted goal. The history of German universities furnishes examples of fine scholars who have worn out their lives in toil, with but dim hopes of promotion. But the difficulties connected with the position are a spur to effort and they arouse the mind to the utmost exertion; and it is not surprising that among those who overcome these obstacles, so many stand in the front rauk of deep and broad scholarship. It would be difficult to create a sphere more desirable or more advantageous for the intellectual man than the position of a teacher in a German university; and well is his course called pre-eminently "the learned career."

The vocation which Kant chose was the one to which he was best adapted by his tastes, his habits, and his scholarship; but on account of his poverty his position was peculiarly trying. Considerable expense was connected with his promotion, such as the payment of fees, and the printing of the dissertations; in meeting this he was aided by his uncle Richter. The ordinary difficulties of the position were increased soon after he became tutor, by the Seven Years' War, by means of which Königsberg, being near the Russian border, suffered greatly.

Kant's books were no doubt known at the university. He had aroused expectation, and when his treatises were presented, he was honoured by unusually large audiences. In the autumn of 1755 he began his first course of lectures, delivering them in a large hall in the house where he lodged. Borowski, who was present at the first lecture, says that this hall, "together with the vestibule and steps, was filled with an unusual number of students. This seemed to embarrass Kant exceedingly. Being unaccustomed to the affair, he almost lost his composure, spoke less audibly than usual, and frequently repeated himself. But this only served to increase our admiration for the man who, in our opinion, had the most extensive knowledge, and who impressed us as not fearful, but only very modest. In the next hour everything was different. Then and afterwards his lectures were not only thorough, but also easy and agreeable." The same writer informs us that there was so exalted an opinion of his attainments, that he was thought capable of teaching anything belonging to the philosophical faculty. For his first courses of lectures he, however, chose subjects to which he had thus far specially devoted himself. During that winter he lectured on mathematics and physics. At that time compends were generally used as the basis of the lectures; and he chose a compend by Wolf for his lectures on mathematics, and one by Eberhard for those on physics.

To the two courses of the first winter he soon added lectures on logic and metaphysics, using for the former a compend of Meyer, for the latter that of Baumeister and afterwards that of Baumgarten. Soon he lectured regularly three or four times a day. He was not content with giving theoretical knowledge, but wanted also to give it a practical application; accordingly, he prepared lectures on fortification, applying to this subject his knowledge of mathematics. From the very beginning of his connexion with the university he aimed to connect the practical with the theoretical, a tendency which characterized his whole life afterwards, but which is largely ignored, because his eminence in speculation has obscured his practical efforts. The lectures on fortification were intended for military men, and by means of them he extended his influence beyond the limits of the university. The numerous military officers in the city made such a course important, and it is probable that he discussed the subject in compliance with their request.

While we should hardly expect from Kant anything pertaining to war, still less should we look to him for a discussion of subjects referring chiefly to amusement. We regard fireworks as playthings, whose discussion hardly lies within the sphere of a philosopher's serious investigations. Yet Kant delivered lectures on pyrotechnics. His interests were, in fact, far more general than is usually supposed, and in his earlier years, especially, he was greatly influenced by his surroundings, and popular subjects frequently engaged his attention. The age itself helps us to understand these lectures. "It must be remembered that during the first half of the eighteenth century pyrotechnics were valued very highly, that unusual sums of money were spent for them, and that authors and artists did not think it beneath them to prepare folios, with expensive plates, for the explanation and exaltation of things which cannot possibly be described. Kant aimed to infuse life into the dead, mechanical knowledge, and to connect it with science; he, however, abandoned such pursuits when the more earnest spirit of the century consigned the idle sport to its proper place." (35)

Belonging to the philosophical faculty, to which are assigned all departments of learning not peculiar to theology, law, and medicine, he had a wide range of topics from which to choose. As tutor he was not obliged to lecture on any particular subject, but was entirely free in his choice. His previous preparation and preferences were by no means the only considerations in the choice of subjects, and at times they may have been overbalanced by others, for he was dependent on his lectures for his living, and his income from them depended upon their popularity; he also had a reputation to make as well as to sustain. These were important factors in his case; and it was natural that in the selection of his subjects, he should carefully consider his condition and his surroundings.

We know the various subjects on which Kant lectured during his long connexion with the university, but not the exact order in which he took them up. It would be interesting to follow him from theme to theme, so as to trace the development of his mind as indicated by his lectures; but as the catalogues did not give his name until he became a professor, this neglect prevents us from following the earlier progress of the work of the greatest man ever produced by the university. From the scattered accounts of pupils and others we learn that he soon increased considerably the subjects of his lectures. As the time of the laborious student permitted and as his mind developed he took up new topics.

In 1757 he began to lecture on physical geography. He made this course popular rather than strictly systematic or profoundly scientific. As he had never travelled, he was chiefly dependent on the accounts of others, and he made these lectures the repository of his thoughts and reading on the earth and its phenomena. In the programme announcing the subject for the first time, he proposes to discuss the sea, continents, islands, fountains and wells, rivers and brooks, the atmosphere and winds, the seasons in different countries, the changes to which the earth has been subject, and the animal, vegetable, and mineral kingdoms; surely he gives himself ample room for using his accumulated stores of geographical and physical knowledge. These lectures, which were published in 1802, contained many interesting facts and generalizations, as well as vivid descriptions, practical hints, and anecdotes; there was also a vein of humour, and free play was given to the imagination. They attracted officers, professional men, and merchants, as well as students; and they are frequently mentioned as exceedingly interesting and inspiring. For more than thirty years he delivered them every summer, and they were very popular. In 1778 the Cabinet Minister, Von Zedlitz, wrote to Kant that he was reading a manuscript on physical geography, written in the lecture-room by one of the students; and he was so delighted with what he learned from that imperfect manuscript that he beseeches him to send a more perfect copy. The aim to adapt the lectures to a mixed audience made their popular character surpass their scientific value; and while they contain much interesting material, they are now of little importance to the student of physical geography, and have not materially promoted the progress of the science.

From January, 1758, till 1762 the Russians had possession of Königsberg. They had the management of the university during this period, but permitted it to take its usual course. Some of them encouraged literature, and the number of Russian students increased. Having been repeatedly invited by Russian officers to lecture to them on physics and physical geography, Kant complied with their request.

In 1759 he published a short article on "Optimism," having previously lectured on the subject; and in 1763, a brochure on "The only possible Proof of the Existence of God," having previously delivered a course of lectures on "Criticism on the Proofs of the Divine Existence." It is also probable that he lectured on "The Emotion of the Beautiful and the Sublime," on which subject a small volume by him appeared in 1764.

This gives a wide range of topics for the period of his tutorship, and there may have been others. The students requested him to deliver lectures on German style, but the subject was too remote from his studies, and he therefore declined; the request is, however, significant. After he became a professor he also lectured on the encyclopedia of the philosophical sciences, natural law, ethics, or moral philosophy, as he afterwards called it, anthropology, natural theology, and pedagogics.([36]) His lectures on physical geography, anthropology, and moral philosophy were the most popular among the students as well as in other circles, and were the means of giving him an extensive, social, moral, and intellectual influence in the city and province.

The compends used as the basis of most of his lectures were merely general guides, for not only in the details, but frequently also in the plan and the general arrangement he went his own way. His copies of the compends were interleaved with blank pages, and he used them as long as he lectured; and while professors in other universities were already lecturing on the Kantian philosophy, he still used Meier on logic, and Baumgarten on metaphysics. An account of him in 1795, two years before he ceased to lecture, says of his use of Meier's Compend, "He always brings the book along. It looks so old and soiled, I believe that he has brought it with him daily for forty years. All the blank leaves are covered with writing in a small hand, and besides, many of the printed pages have leaves pasted over them, and in other cases lines are frequently crossed out, so that, as is evident, scarcely anything of Meier's Logic is left. Not one of his hearers brings the book, and they are intent on writing only his own words. He does not, however, seem to notice this, and faithfully follows his author from chapter to chapter, and corrects everything, or rather says everything in a different way, but with the most innocent air, so that it is evident that he makes no pretensions on account of his discoveries."(37)

Besides the notes on the blank leaves of the compends and on the margins of the printed pages, he was in the habit of making memoranda for his lectures on slips of paper, on envelopes addressed to him, and on the blank parts of letters. He rarely wrote out his lectures in full; as a rule, he did this only when they were to be published. But after carefully elaborating them mentally, he spoke freely, using notes and compends only as skeletons; and the frequent repetition of his lectures made even these almost unnecessary in the course of time.

While his lectures were learned and often profound, being the result of his extensive researches, penetrated and moulded by his master-mind, they differed materially from his profound metaphysical works. His "Kritik of Pure Reason" was never delivered in the form of lectures. When he spoke to the students, his style was generally clear, and he used numerous illustrations. But in metaphysics, the subject itself being full of inherent difficulties, it frequently required close attention to follow his discussions.([38]) He would conduct various processes of thinking before the students, developing one thought from another, and indicating errors here and there in the processes, thus guiding his hearers in the construction and development of thought. For able minds this was very interesting and instructive; but there were many who would lose the thread of his discourse; he did not, however, read for dull minds, and is reported to have said repeatedly, at the beginning of his lectures, "I do not read for geniuses, their endowments being such that they will make a way for themselves; nor for the stupid, for they are not worth the trouble; but I read for the sake of those who stand between these two classes, and want to be prepared for their future work."

While in his profounder lectures he gave the students the results of his own investigations, it was his principal aim to teach them to think, and he so frequently emphasized this that his hearers could not make the mistake of imagining that he expected to do the thinking for them. According to his Logic, a philosopher is one who philosophizes. One man cannot make another a philosopher, however much learning he may impart, though he may help him to become one; for it is only by the exercise of his own reason, by thinking for himself, that one becomes a philosopher. "Every philosophical thinker builds, so to speak, his work on the ruins of another." The systems of philosophy are constantly changing; this is owing to the fact that none exists which is satisfactory. "As none exists, philosophy of course cannot be learned; and even if it existed, no one who learned it could claim to be a philosopher, for his knowledge would only be historical." Whoever wants to become a philosopher must view all systems of philosophy as merely a history of the use of reason and as material on which to exercise his philosophic talent. "The true philosopher must therefore, as a thinker, make an independent, not a slavish, imitative use of his reason." Kant's aim in his metaphysical lectures was to arouse the mind to activity, and to make thinkers and philosophers, rather than to teach a system of philosophy. As he repeatedly said, he wanted his hearers to learn to stand on their own feet; hence he would say to them, "You will not learn philosophy from me, but to philosophize; not merely thoughts for repetition, but to think." In his Logic he gives three important rules for thought: First, to think yourself; second, to put yourself in the place of others; third, always to think consistently. The first is the enlightened, the second is the enlarged, and the third is the consequent method of thinking. It was the aim of his lectures to promote these methods; and while he could not think for his students, he could help them both to think and to think consistently; and he could also help them to put themselves in the place of others. While his lectures were repositories of rich scholarship, it is self-evident that he was no mere collector of facts; everywhere and always he was the thinker, appropriating, elaborating, and generalizing what he had gathered.

After 1773 his lectures on anthropology were the popular course for the winter, as those on physical geography were for the summer. They, too, were attended by others than students. As those on physical geography contemplated nature as a traveller who makes thoughtful journeys, so those on anthropology thoughtfully but pleasantly explore the mind's connexion with the body, giving the results of his observations on himself and others, and also of his extensive reading, drawing, it is said, especially from English novels. He states that he aims to reveal to his hearers the principles of morals, of skill, of the intercourse of persons with one another, and of the methods of developing and governing men; that is, the principles of all that is practical. He discusses phenomena and their laws rather than the possibility of modifying human nature, and avoids, as useless, all subtle investigations of the manner in which the organs of the body are connected with the mind. Kant states that it is his purpose to give the results of his observations in such a way that his hearers will never find any part dry, but everything attractive; and that he hoped by means of these lectures to train young men in skill, in prudence, and in wisdom.

With his keen sense of the paradoxical, his high appreciation of the humorous, and his skill in relating anecdotes, it is not surprising that he made the subject entertaining as well as instructive. The lectures were published in his Anthropology. The learning of this work, its perspicuity, its clear discriminations, its sententious passages, its deep insight into human nature, its anecdotes and illustrations, its revelations of the freaks, contrasts, and paradoxes of men, its humour and its wit, made it deservedly popular, and enable us to understand why its author so often aroused and inspired his hearers.([39])

Kant disliked exceedingly every kind of affectation, and his manner was free from it in the lecture-room. With little more than his head visible, he sat behind a small desk, on which lay his compend, and sometimes slips of paper with notes. A description of him at the age of seventy-one states that his delivery was not attractive, but altogether in the conversational tone; occasionally he would draw his hand from his buttoned coat and make a slight gesture; his voice was no longer clear; the writer, however, says that the excellence of the matter amply compensated for any defects in the delivery, and adds, "When one has become accustomed to his voice so as to be able to understand his words, it is not difficult to follow his thoughts. Recently he spoke of space and time, and it seemed as if I had never comprehended any one so fully; and now he has come to that part of logic where he must speak of cognition. This gives him an opportunity to discuss its perfection, and also logical, æsthetic, and other kinds of cognition. The principal thoughts of his 'Critique of the Judgment' are given as easily, clearly, and entertainingly as can be imagined. It must be extremely interesting to hear his whole course, since in this way one readily becomes acquainted with all his thoughts."([40])

These facts enable us to understand why Kant at once became popular as a teacher. There was a marked contrast between his fresh and sprightly lectures and the dull pedantry which prevailed in learned circles; he laid the sciences, poetry, general literature, and, in fact, all the departments of thought under contribution, in order to make them rich in interest as well as in instruction. Minds which were active as well as receptive found his philosophical lectures mines of thought; such were strongly attracted by him, and over many of them his influence was astonishing. The majority of his hearers could not appreciate his profundity, and at best they became mere echoes of his opinions; but numerous young men received from him impulses which determined their whole future career. His moral lectures especially made a deep impression; they frequently inspired his students and filled them with enthusiasm. There were some who almost worshipped him, and occasions were gladly seized by his auditors for manifesting their appreciation. While he was still a tutor he attracted persons from a distance to Königsberg, and one gentleman came from his possessions in Poland, for several winters, solely for the purpose of enjoying the benefit of his superior instruction.

Of the enthusiasm aroused by Kant while a tutor, we have a striking illustration in the case of Herder, who spent from 1762 to 1764 at the university. Although he was a student of theology, Kant, who permitted the indigent young man to hear his lectures gratis, made the deepest impression on him, and wonderfully stimulated his mind. Herder heard him on logic, metaphysics, morals, mathematics, and physical geography. Thirty years after leaving the university, he wrote, "I had the good fortune to know a philosopher, who was my teacher. He was in his best years, and possessed the cheerful vivacity of youth, which, I believe, he preserves even in his old age. His open brow, formed for thought, was the seat of undisturbed serenity and joy; language freighted with thought flowed from his lips; wit and humour were at his command; and his instructive lecture was a rich entertainment. In the same spirit with which he investigated Leibnitz, Wolf, Baumgarten, Crusius, and Hume, and traced the laws of Newton, Keppler, and the scientists generally, he examined the writings of Rousseau then appearing, namely, his 'Emile' and his 'Heloise.' He placed the true estimate on every physical discovery which came to his notice, and always returned from other studies to an impartial scrutiny of nature and the moral worth of man. He drew the inspiration for his lectures from the history of men, of nations, and of nature, as well as from natural science, mathematics, and his own observations. He was not indifferent to anything worth knowing. No cabal, no sect, no advantage to himself, no ambition, had the least influence over him compared with the development and illustration of the truth. He encouraged, and obliged his hearers, to think for themselves; despotism was foreign to his mind. This man, whom I mention with the highest esteem and gratitude, is Immanuel Kant." ([41])

Herder, receptive and yet original, ambitious for learning and for fame, with a warm heart and a vivid imagination, was marvellously influenced by his favourite teacher, and at times his fervour bordered on rapture. A fellow-student says of him, "Eagerly he seized every thought, every word of the great philosopher, and afterwards at home he arranged the thoughts and language. Often he communicated to me what he had written, and we would talk it over in a retired arbour of an unfrequented public garden by the old Rossgart Church. Once, in the early morning hour, Kant, the man of exuberant spirits, spoke with unusual mental exaltation, and, when the matter admitted, with poetic inspiration, quoting his favourite poets, Pope and Haller. With bold conjectures he discoursed on time and eternity. It was evident that

Herder was powerfully affected; and when he came home he put the ideas of his teacher in verses which would have done honour to Haller. Before the lecture on the next morning he handed them to Kant, who, struck with the masterly poetic representation of his thoughts, read them with warmth and with praise to his auditors." (42)

Herder did not, however, hear all the lectures of the philosopher with enthusiasm. He preferred those on mathematics, physical geography, and physics; but for his metaphysical lectures he had no taste, desiring more life and less abstraction, more that pertained to reality and less logic. After many a metaphysical lecture he would take a poet, Rousseau, or a similar author, and hasten into the fresh air to get rid of the unpleasant impression.

As it was his principal aim to teach his students to think, Kant was not a friend of dictation; and he believed that the students who were best able to grasp his thoughts were those who during the delivery of the lecture wrote only the main points for meditation, while those who wrote most were the ones who were least able to distinguish the more from the less important thoughts, and consequently mixed a lot of misunderstood stuff with the clearly apprehended views. When he noted that the less important things were carefully written, while the more weighty ones were omitted, it would disturb him.

Judging from the power of abstraction revealed in his books, one would hardly suspect that the great metaphysician could have been disconcerted by trifles; yet a little noise in the lecture-room, or something unusual in the appearance of the students, easily embarrassed him. Sometimes even the sound made by the pens of his hearers disturbed him, and once he said, "Gentlemen, do not scratch so; I am no oracle." He was in the habit of fixing his eye on some student who sat near him, and from his countenance he would infer whether he was being understood. Frequently the expression or dress of the student whom he watched became the occasion of confusion. Jachmann gives a striking instance: "One hour his distraction specially arrested my attention, and at noon Kant complained to me that his thoughts had been interrupted continually because a button was wanting on the coat of one of his hearers. Involuntarily his eyes had been attracted to this defect, and it was this which had so distracted him. At the same time he remarked that this is more or less the experience of every one; thus, when a person has lost a front tooth one naturally looks constantly at the place where the tooth is wanting. He also makes this remark several times in his Anthropology." Peculiarities in the appearance of students were apt to disturb him, such as a bare neck, an exposed breast, or long hair hanging carelessly over the neck and brow, which were regarded by some youths as evidences of genius. It is said that when he became especially serious, and thought deeply furrowed his brow, he would fix his eyes on a certain student who always sat immediately before him, was extremely uncouth and dull, and found the lectures, which went far beyond his horizon, very tedious. He manifested his weariness by long yawning, which at one time so disturbed Kant that he said with some excitement, "If one cannot avoid yawning, good manners require that the hand should be held before the mouth." The narrator adds, "I believe that afterwards the amanuensis effected a change of place between him and another student." (43)

After Kant became a professor and received a fixed salary, it was his rule to lecture only twice a day, from seven to nine in the morning, thus leaving more time for his literary labours. (44) His course on natural religion he delivered only twice, discontinuing it in 1794, because the Government had called him to account for his theological views. In 1795 he brought all his private lectures to a close, on account of his age and feebleness. From that time until the end of the summer semester of 1797, when he closed all his lectures, he delivered only public ones, namely, four a week on logic in summer, and the same number in winter on metaphysics. Long before this his delivery had lost much of its vivacity, owing to his weakness and the frequent repetition of the same lectures. In 1791 Fichte found them uninteresting and drowsy. When Kant was seventy, a hearer reported that his metaphysical thoughts were digressive and lacked perspicuity. "A young man of fifteen or sixteen could comprehend but little connectedly in these lectures; the benefit which I received was from occasional bright thoughts which flashed into my soul. I believe that at that time older students fared no better." Rink says, "It cannot be denied that already in the eighth decade of last century his lectures lost so much of their life that it seemed as if he must be on the point of falling asleep, an opinion which was confirmed when, with a vigorous movement of the body, he was seen to arouse himself suddenly. But in spite of this he continued to the last to be a very conscientious teacher, and I cannot remember that he missed a single hour."

With all his popularity, his circumstances while a tutor, especially in the beginning of his connexion with the university, were not easy. Once a student, who was himself poor, brought him the pay for his lectures; Kant took only so much of the money as he still needed for the payment of his rent, and returned the rest. In order to be free from debt, which he resolved to avoid at all hazards, he was obliged to live very plainly. The income from his lectures being meagre, he occasionally took charge of some young men whose education he superintended. With the statement to this effect, approved by Kant himself in Borowski's sketch, Jachmann agrees, but he is more explicit. "During the first years of his tutorship in the university, the receipts from his lectures were small, and he was often obliged to live very economically, so as to avoid pecuniary embarrassment. He had laid aside twenty Louis-d'or which he never touched, so that in case of sickness he might be secure from absolute need. In order not to use this fund, he found it necessary to sell his library of choice books, since he could not meet his expenses with his income.

His first appointment to a position with a salary was in 1766, when he became second librarian in the Royal Library. The Government in Berlin, in the letter appointing him, designated him as "the able Kant, made famous by his books." His salary was sixty-two thalers a year. There were many excellent books in the library, especially among the accounts of travel; and constant access to these was of advantage to the voracious reader. About the same time he was also appointed superintendent of a private cabinet of natural and ethnographical objects, being chosen for this place on account of his knowledge of natural history. The cabinet, being one of the sights of Königsberg, was visited by many strangers, to whom he was obliged to exhibit the curiosities. This was disagreeable to Kant, because it interfered with his studies, and since those who visited the cabinet were generally more impelled by curiosity than a desire to learn. He soon resigned this position, and in 1772 the one in the Royal Library, which he also disliked. Kant had neither tact nor inclination for business of any kind; and whatever took time from his studies or made him the agent in gratifying idle curiosity was irksome.

It seems incredible that a man with his gifts, with his scholarship and his extensive reputation, should have been obliged to toil for fifteen years as a mere tutor; but such was the case. In 1756, one year after he became a tutor, he applied for the extraordinary professorship of mathematics, logic, and metaphysics, which had been vacant since 1751, when Knutzen died; but as the country was much disturbed, the Seven Years' War being imminent, the Government decided not to fill that position. In 1758 the professorship in ordinary of logic and metaphysics became vacant by the death of Professor Kypke, and Kant applied for the appointment. Professor Schulz, the friend of his youth, favoured his application, though it is evident that he was suspicious of Kant's religious views. Besides abandoning theology, the philosopher had probably given him other reasons for suspecting the soundness of his faith. He requested Kant to call on him. When he entered the room, Schulz asked him solemnly, "Do you in your heart fear God?" The academic senate, to which the application was made, however decided in favour of Dr. Buck, who had been a tutor longer than Kant. The city was then in the possession of the Russians, whose commanding general confirmed the choice of the senate.

But his merits were too conspicuous and his reputation too extensive for the general government to lose sight of Kant. In 1763 he was a contestant for a prize offered by the Berlin Academy of Sciences. His dissertation was entitled, "Investigations respecting the Clearness of the Principles of Natural Theology and Morals." (46) The first prize was given to Moses Mendelssohn, the most eminent representative of the Popular philosophy; the second was awarded to Kant. This distinction introduced his name to the Government, as well as to scholars in Berlin. From various official documents it is evident that in Government circles he was highly esteemed on account of his scholarship, and that the authorities intended to appoint him to the first vacant professorship in the philosophical faculty. Accordingly, in 1764, when the professorship of rhetoric and poetry became vacant, the minister of education wrote to the authorities at Königsberg to inquire into Kant's fitness for the appointment, and his willingness to accept it if tendered. The letter says, "A certain magister, Immanuel Kant, has become known to us through his works, which give evidence of thorough scholarship." Kant was not yet the abstract metaphysician, and he had given sufficient evidence that he could write beautifully; and it was perhaps thought that his varied attainments fitted him for any position. But to imagine the mathematical and metaphysical Kant as spending the remainder of his days on rhetoric and in versification, and in trying to teach aspiring geniuses the art of torturing words into metre and rhyme, and of giving to airy nothing a local habitation and a name! The incumbent was obliged to prepare the official poems for the special occasions and numerous celebrations connected with the university; and it is self-evident that neither nature nor his education had adapted him to this professorship. The minister, being informed that he did not desire the appointment, wrote to the Königsberg authorities that the Government had decided to offer him some other position in the university, saying, "The very able magister Kant, who teaches with such general approval, shall be promoted at the first opportunity, and you are to announce this to him; and when such an opportunity occurs you are to propose him immediately."

Nevertheless he was obliged to wait six years longer before a suitable vacancy occurred. Meanwhile his reputation attracted the attention of other universities to his superior abilities. In 1769 an effort was made to secure him as professor of logic and metaphysics in Erlangen, and a correspondence with him took place on the subject. Seeing no hope of a speedy promotion to a professorship in Königsberg, he thought seriously of accepting; and the report that he was coming excited much joy among the students in Erlangen. At the same time he was urged to accept the professorship of philosophy in Jena. If the professorship of mathematics in Königsberg had not become vacant at that time, Kant would probably have been lost to this city. This position was, however, placed at his disposal. In view of his early preference for mathematics, he might have accepted it, and then the world would probably never have known him as the great metaphysician; but Professor Buck desired the chair of mathematics, and offered Kant his professorship of logic and metaphysics. Kant accepted this offer, and in 1770, after fifteen years of toil as a humble tutor, and when forty-six years of age, he became professor in ordinary of logic and metaphysics, never having occupied the intermediate position of professor extraordinary.

In order that he might become a professor, it was necessary for him again to present a Latin dissertation. In its subject and treatment the one prepared for this occasion was worthy of the man who was called to teach metaphysics, and it is historically significant from the fact that in it Kant for the first time publicly gave some of the most important principles afterwards developed in the "Kritik." It was a discussion of the difference between sensation and understanding, with the title, "The Form and Principles of the World of Sense and of the Intellect." ([47])

After he became a professor, he could lecture on subjects not immediately connected with his professorship, for in this, as in so many other respects, there is great freedom in German universities. But a professor must lecture on the subjects for which he is appointed, is expected to make a speciality of them, and is supposed to have for them a preference and special adaptation. Kant's position now in a measure defined the sphere of his intellectual activity; and from his correspondence we learn that for years he had given particular prominence to the study of metaphysics. Henceforth he is less a mathematician and physicist than formerly, and in his thoughts and lectures and books he restricts himself mainly to speculative and moral philosophy.

Kant began his career as professor under the most favourable auspices. He was in his best years, had the favour of the Government, had learning which was as extensive as it was solid, and had acquired an enviable reputation for scholarship. The popularity which he enjoyed while a tutor was increased after he became a professor, and culminated when the "Kritik" gave him celebrity. In May, 1786, Hamann wrote that he went with his son at six in the morning to Kant's lecture-room, an hour before he read, the attendance being so large in the first months of a semester as to make this necessary in order to secure a place. A few years before this, Hamann stated that Kant was reading on philosophical theology, and that the rush to hear him was astonishing. At the time when his fame was at its height, many persons not connected with the university attended his lectures, and numbers came from a distance to hear him.

His position as professor not merely gave him greater influence and authority, but also an opportunity to concentrate his efforts, since he was no longer obliged to lecture so frequently for the sake of a livelihood; still, when he began his professorship he was very busy, partly in preparing new lectures. A letter written at this time states that a literary project was necessarily delayed on account of his "laborious academic work." His salary was four hundred thalers; besides this, he had an income from those who attended his private lectures. This was more than enough for a man with so few wants, and whose whole life had been disciplined by an enforced economy. The king, in

1789, increased the sum by the addition of 220 thalers, making his stated income 620 thalers, or about 90*l.*, the highest salary ever received by Kant. As the attendance at his lectures was large, this must have been a source of considerable revenue; and in his later years he also received an income from his books.

It is not surprising that Kant's extraordinary popularity aroused some opposition to him in the faculty; his religious views may also have given occasion for attacks. Some of his older colleagues, finding themselves overshadowed by Kant, made insinuations against him in their lectures; but by his younger colleagues, most of whom had been his pupils, he was respected and kindly treated, one only excepted. This one was a tutor and an enthusiastic follower of the philosopher Crusius. Having made rude attacks on Kant in his lecture-room, just as he had on Wolf and others, he was silenced for awhile; when he proposed to read again, the students, who had come for that purpose, interrupted and so disconcerted him that he was obliged to desist, and he abandoned his lectures altogether.

About a year after Kant was appointed a professor, Von Zedlitz became minister of public instruction. He took great pains to improve the condition of the universities. A letter from him to the civil authorities in Königsberg gives an idea of the condition of the university in that city, and also of the esteem in which Kant was held by the Government. The minister finds fault with the institution because modern literature seems to be ignored in the lectures; because the professors, with the exception of Kant and Reuss, read on compends which are antiquated; because on some important subjects no lectures are announced—such as Public and German Law, Botany, and Prussian and Brandenburg History; and because the philosophy of Crusius is still taught by some, though generally it has been found to be unsatisfactory. The teachers who are disciples of Crusius are ordered to abandon their lectures on philosophy, unless they can free themselves from his system, and are to chose some other topics. Another professor is admonished to avoid verbosity "as much as possible, since the discourse which has been most thoroughly elaborated is always the most condensed." The teachers are also exhorted to accumulate new stores of knowledge by diligent study. Sad indeed must have been the intellectual character of the university to make such a letter necessary or even possible; but the general stagnation made Kant's broad learning, and fresh, vigorous, and profound thoughts all the more powerful, and his position the more conspicuous.

Von Zedlitz, who was a warm admirer of Kant, in 1778 offered him the professorship of metaphysics in Halle, where the number of his students would have been much larger than in Königsberg, and his influence much greater; he, however, declined the position. The minister, who was very anxious that he should accept, renewed the offer, and presented for his consideration the advantages of Halle, hoping in this way to induce him to accept the place. A salary of 800 thalers was offered, just double the amount which he was then receiving; Von Zedlitz also states that the climate of Halle is much healthier than that of Königsberg, and that the number of students is from 1000 to 1200, or more than twice as many as in the latter city; and as another inducement, he mentions the fact that he is desirous of restoring Halle to its former pre-eminence, and of making it the centre of learning in Germany, by attracting thither the most eminent men. Nevertheless Kant refused to leave his native city. A letter written by him in the same year enables us to understand his reasons for rejecting this tempting offer. He states that he is not ambitious for gain, nor for fame in a conspicuous position, but prefers a quiet place where he can devote himself to study, speculation, and society, and where his easily affected mind, and still more easily affected though never really sick body, can be properly preserved, and adds, "All change makes me fearful, even if it gives the greatest promise of an improvement in my condition; and I believe that I must heed this instinct of my nature if I want to extend to its full length the thread which the Fates have spun very thin and weak." As the "Kritik" was approaching completion, he may also have feared that a change might involve him in new labours which would interfere with the progress of that work.

Kant became a member of the academic senate in 1780, and held this position until his feebleness led him to resign it in 1801. He was the dean of the philosophical faculty six times, and twice the rector of the university; but celebrated as he was for scholarship, he did not distinguish himself in either position. Even for the business affairs of the university, except so far as they pertained to learning and morals, he had no taste, and he gladly left their management to others. When his official position of dean or rector required him to act alone, he generally followed the precedents, not venturing on innovations; and when he transacted business in concert with the other members of the senate, he generally voted with the majority. In his old age, he preferred to be excused from serving as dean or rector; and when he was elected dean in 1794 and again in 1798, he was excused; and he was also released from the duties of the rectorate when in 1796 it was his turn to fill that office.

It was charged that as dean, Kant was too lenient in his examination of the students. He cared more about their judgments than their memories, and less about the amount they knew than how they knew. Professor Kraus remarks, with reference to the charge that Kant did not examine sharply, and that as rector he was not strict, "If he did not examine rigorously, it was because the whole affair was exceedingly disagreeable to him, and to such a mind, and with his pursuits, it could not be otherwise. He disliked the rectorate on account of the many cases of dishonesty with which he became acquainted. All evidences of dishonesty and immorality were odious to him."

When Prussia was elevated to the rank of a kingdom in 1701, Frederick I. came to Königsberg, his native city, and placed the crown on his head; since that time it has been the coronation city of the Prussian kings. It was during Kant's rectorate that Frederick William II. ascended the throne and went to Königsberg to be crowned. The philosopher, who took no prominent part on festival occasions, nor delivered any public addresses, except when required to do so by his official position as rector, was at this time introduced to that monarch. Shortly after this, Kant's salary was increased by the king, and he was also elected a member of the Berlin Academy of Sciences.

CHAPTER IV.

PHYSICAL BASIS.

Appearance—Head—Peculiar experience with his eyes—State of Health—Study of his physical condition—View of medicine—Dietetics—Mastery of mind over body—Art of prolonging life.

KANT'S physique was not proportionate to his massive intellect. He was below the medium size; and when somewhat bowed by old age, he was described as scarcely five feet high. "His body seemed to have received from nature the impress of feebleness as its characteristic." His bones were small and weak, but proportionately his muscles were still weaker. One who had been his acquaintance for fifty years, said, "Ever since I knew him, his body was extremely emaciated, and at last it was dried like a potsherd." On Rauch's celebrated monument of Frederick II., in Berlin, Kant is represented with other eminent men of that monarch's reign. The artist had much difficulty in modelling a figure worthy of his great fame and yet true to nature. He is represented as raising his right hand to make a gesture while talking with Lessing, who is at his side, and in his left he holds a cane and his three-cornered hat. He wears a wig, tied to which is a bag which hangs on his shoulders. His forehead is broad and square; his cheek-bones are high and the cheeks are sunken; his lips protrude and the chin recedes; the chest is depressed and the abdomen is prominent. The compressed chest was an inheritance from his mother. His right shoulder was turned backward and was considerably higher than the other: in old age this deformity became more apparent, and gave him the appearance of being very much bent. With the exception of his crooked nose, the rest of his body was symmetrical. Most of the pictures of Kant in old age, judged by descriptions of him by his acquaintances, flatter him.

After his death, his head was carefully examined, but there was no dissection. While there were a number of prominences on the forehead, there were scarcely any on the back part of the head. The measurement through the head, from the root of the nose, was seven and three-quarter inches (German), its width from ear to ear, six and a half. The forehead, which receded gradually, was narrow at its base and broad at the top. From the base of the nose to the top of the head the measurement was five inches.

When in 1880 the remains of Kant were transferred to the chapel erected in honour of his memory, his skull was subjected to the most minute examination. As the result of this investigation, his head was declared to be large in proportion to the rest of the body. The capacity of the skull was unusual, being much larger than the average of Prussian and Lithuanian skulls; its height and length were only medium, but its width in some parts was remarkable. The breadth at the temples, of the forehead, and of the entire front part of the head, was found to be only ordinary, while in the middle and the back part it was extraordinary; and the right side of the skull was larger than the left. (48)

The appearance of Kant indicated the student; his narrow chin and thin cheeks gave his head special prominence, and impressed the beholder with the preponderance of the intellect. His eyes, which were not large, were lively, tender, and penetrating; their colour was blue, a fact on which, for an unknown reason, Kant laid some stress. When he became animated in his lectures or conversations, there was an irresistible fascination in his look. Jachmann describes his face as pleasing, and thinks that in youth it must have been handsome. With the enthusiasm characteristic of him when speaking of his beloved teacher, he says, "Where shall I find words to describe his eyes! Kant's eye looked as if it had been formed of heavenly ether. . . . It is impossible to describe his enchanting look and my emotions when he sat opposite and suddenly raised his eyes to look at me." Borowski writes, "It did one good to behold his eyes. In viewing his fine forehead one immediately perceived the deep thinker, and a glance at his eyes revealed the good-natured man." "His hair was blond; there was a fresh colour in his face, and even in old age his cheeks retained a healthy redness." All his senses were strong and keen, his hearing being especially distinguished for sharpness and delicacy. If he heard a peculiar voice, or if any one spoke in an unusual key, it at once attracted his attention; and he disliked exceedingly an affected or unnatural tone. As might be expected from the structure of his chest, his voice was weak, and at a little distance it required close attention to understand him. He sometimes pitched it very high, and until he was seventy it could stand a severe strain.

His organization was so delicate that he was extremely sensitive to impressions from external objects, and Jachmann relates that a newspaper fresh from the press and still damp could give him a cold. This extreme sensitiveness partly accounts for the fact that, in spite of his singular power of abstraction, he was so easily disturbed in the lecture-room.

In old age the appearance of Kant was not calculated to impress a stranger favourably at first sight; his elevated shoulder and bent form made his diminutive stature still less imposing than in the vigour of youth. Professor Kraus describes him in later years as "almost always keeping his head bowed down and hanging on one side, the bag of his wig mostly disordered and lying on one shoulder." With a sudden motion of his head he would throw the bag back, and the servant, passing behind his chair, frequently restored it to its proper place; but it would soon fall to the left again. Strangers who knew nothing of his appearance were disappointed when they saw him. An English letter says, "It is generally supposed that the greatness of a celebrated man must be evident from his appearance. If you come to Kant with this notion, you will be astonished to find before you a small, emaciated man, always bowed down while walking, whose eyes, as well as the rest of the features, are a reproach to physiognomy." This is no doubt too strong; those who knew him best, say nothing of repulsiveness in his appearance. A better acquaintance, a closer study of his features, and repeated conversation with him, revealed hidden attractions and removed any unfavourable impressions made at first sight.

He had peculiar experience with his eyes. This was the case for the first time when he was already past forty; afterwards the same phenomenon occurred occasionally, and in one year several times. Sometimes while reading, the letters would suddenly become indistinct, mixed, and unreadable; this never lasted longer than six minutes. He said that for a preacher who was in the habit of reading his sermons, such an experience might be very serious, but for himself in the lecture-room, since he was not confined to his notes, it had no other effect than to cause the apprehension that it might be the forerunner of blindness; but after having several such attacks, and finding that his sight was not affected thereby, his fears were allayed. Once, whilst subject to this strange experience, he closed his eyes, and put his hand over them in order the more effectually to exclude the light. He then saw a figure resembling the last quarter of the moon as represented in the almanac, as if drawn, in the dark, on paper with phosphorus, but with an indented border on the convex side. The figure gradually lost its brightness, and disappeared altogether within six minutes.

Once, in returning from a walk, he for a long time saw the steeple of a church double. But still more singular is the fact that his left eye became totally blind without his own knowledge or that of his friends. One day, while taking his usual walk, he seated himself on a bench and tried to determine with which eye he could see best. Taking a paper from his pocket, he closed his right eye, and to his astonishment discovered that he could see nothing with the other. He did not know when the eye had become blind, but supposed that it must have happened three or four years before he made the discovery. The fact was ascertained by him a good many years before his death, and it is thought that for the last twenty years of his life his left eye was sightless.

In spite of his compressed chest and the delicacy of his system, Kant's life was remarkably free from sickness. He said that he remembered no illness in earlier life except an attack of ague, and of that he had cured himself by a vigorous walk. Frequently, however, he was indisposed, and to a lady inquiring about his health, he said that, properly speaking, he was never well and never sick; not the former, because he was never free from pain, there being a constant pressure below the chest, on the pylorus; not the latter, because he had never been sick a day, nor had he ever needed medical aid, excepting a few pills which he had taken by the advice of a friend, to relieve constipation. His digestive organs seem to have been early deranged; to this he ascribed his frequent ailments, and to the last it caused him perpetual trouble.

In the year 1770, in which he was appointed professor, he speaks of long indisposition during the summer, and says that the excessive burden of his lectures prevented the needed recreation and interfered with his correspondence; he hopes in the future to be less pressed by his lectures and to recover the small measure of health which he formerly enjoyed. His excessive labours were, no doubt, partly the cause of his disorders. Instead of entirely recovering his health, we find that from this time his letters frequently mention his indisposition. During the preparation of the "Kritik" and the works which followed it, he was in delicate health. He wrote in 1778 that for many years he had been accustomed to regard himself well with a degree of health so small that many would have complained. This condition, he says, admonished him to take care of himself and attend to recreation. He also says, "I find myself in my usual, that is, weak way, healthy; I never enjoyed a much greater degree of health." A year earlier he complained that he was suffering considerably, and that he was daily indisposed.

This physical debility interfered greatly with his intellectual labours; his works were delayed thereby, and some plans may have been entirely frustrated. He regarded it as a great obstacle in the execution of his projects, and in 1789 he wrote to a friend in Berlin, "Think of it, most worthy friend! Sixty-six years old, constantly disturbed by indisposition in plans only half completed, and diverted from my course by all kinds of written and even printed appeals; how difficult it is for me to perform, without some neglect here or there, what I regard as my duty!" In the same year he wrote to Professor Reinhold about the disadvantages of growing old, since it obliged him to work mechanically, and added, "For several years I have found it necessary to refrain from devoting myself to uninterrupted study, whether in reading a book or in reflection." He could still work in the forenoon: but in the evening he was obliged to change the subjects of study frequently, as otherwise he could not sleep. "In the sixty-sixth year, subtle investigations always become more difficult, and one would gladly avoid them if only others could be found to undertake and complete them." In order to secure time for study and authorship, he was obliged to take his well moments from the culture of friendship and from his correspondence, and to concentrate them on his intellectual pursuits; and his feeble health is frequently mentioned in his correspondence as his apology for delay in answering the letters of friends.

Kant was fully aware of his frail condition, and made his physical state a subject of special study and of scrupulous care; he studiously investigated the means of preserving health and diligently practised the art of prolonging life. Hygiene was one of his favourite topics of conversation in all kinds of company; and he so often discussed the same subjects and repeated the same thoughts, that they became monotonous. He watched the moods of his body critically, and inquired into the physical condition of his acquaintances; he was eager to learn the experience of his friends respecting the effects of food and climate, and the remedies used when ill; he studied meteorology in its relation to health, and carefully examined the statistics of mortality, which, at his request, were sent to him weekly by the director of the police. It was his ardent desire to reach a ripe old age; and he frequently mentioned persons who had attained a great age, and estimated his own probable chances of life.

For awhile he made a frequent use of quinine, but afterwards abandoned it. Until extreme old age, he took very little medicine; he spoke disparagingly of its use, declaring that it was synonymous with poison (pharmacon). He regarded it as peculiarly injurious to himself, and wrote to a friend, "On account of my sensitive nerves, medicine, without exception, is poison to me." When old, he said, "I shall die, but I do not want to die by means of medicine. When I am sick and weak, they may do with me what they please, I shall submit to anything; but I shall take no preservative." He humorously related the story of a man who had drugged himself to death. Although in good health, he constantly took medicine to ward off sickness, and by this means destroyed his life. This was his epitaph: "N. N. was well, but because he wanted to be better than well, he is here." But while he had little faith in medicine, Kant took a deep interest in medical books, partly on account of his interest in science in general, but chiefly for the sake of his health. In the last decade of the century, when the system of the Scotch physician, John Brown, became popular among medical men in Germany, Kant became its advocate, and recommended it to his friends; but he had little faith in the power of doctors to cure the ills of the flesh. There were, indeed, a number of physicians among his personal friends, but he did not esteem them because they belonged to the medical profession. He even thought that doctors might be dispensed with altogether, unless they occupied their time with the study of chemistry, galvanism, and new discoveries in science.

Kant regarded dietetics as the most important element in hygiene. Regularity in eating, drinking, and sleeping, with proper recreation after work, he esteemed of far more importance than medicine, because they prevent sickness. In 1778 he writes that his constitution is so feeble that he can preserve his health only by means of great uniformity in his method of life, and in his mental state; and five years later he says that a hygienic rule which he found long ago in an

English author had been adopted by him, namely, that every person should have his own peculiar way of being healthy, which he cannot alter without risk. In following this rule, he finds that though he is always obliged to contend with indisposition, he is never sick. And he has come to the conclusion that those live longest who are least anxious to prolong life, yet are careful not to shorten it by interfering with the beneficent natural powers of the body.

Kant made frequent experiments with his body, and in the course of time gained such control over it as to make it the obedient instrument of his mind. In a letter to Dr. Hufeland, he discusses the art of being the master of one's sickly feelings by mere force of will. His own power in this respect was extraordinary, of which the following is an illustration. "On account of my flat and narrow chest, which affords but little room for the movement of my heart and lungs, I have a natural predisposition to hypochondria, which in earlier years bordered on weariness of life. The reflection, however, that the cause of this oppressive feeling was probably only mechanical, and could not be removed, soon brought it to pass that I paid no attention to it; and while I felt oppressed in my chest, my head was clear, and I possessed a cheerfulness which I could voluntarily communicate in society; and I was not, as hypochondriacs usually are, subject to variable moods. Since we enjoy life more on account of what we do than what we receive, intellectual labours can resist those interferences which proceed solely from the body, by promoting a different kind of feeling. The oppression in my chest remained, for its cause lies in the structure of my body;

but I have become master of its influence on my thoughts and actions, by turning my attention away from this feeling altogether, just as if it did not at all concern me."

Kant, as a close and thoughtful observer of his physical condition, sought to discover the causes of his frequent indisposition and to learn the remedy. Some of the experiments which he made with himself were entirely successful. Finding that he was subject to colds which disturbed his sleep, he resolved to draw his breath, with closed lips, only through his nostrils. This succeeded admirably in overcoming the difficulty; it prevented coughing, and enabled him to fall asleep immediately. In this way he so effectually formed the habit of breathing through his nostrils only, that he did it even in his sleep.

Sometimes he suffered from thirst immediately after retiring. In order to get water he would have been obliged to go into another room in the dark; to avoid this he made the experiment of drawing several deep draughts of breath, at the same time expanding his chest, and drinking, as it were, the air through his nostrils, by which means the thirst was quenched in a few seconds. He regarded the thirst as an irritation which was relieved by a counter-irritant.

His power of abstraction was of great service to him in mastering his sickly feelings. Even in old age he could overcome sleeplessness by withdrawing his thoughts from the object on which they were fixed, and concentrating them on another. At that time a pain in his head similar to a cramp interfered with his sleep; but by withdrawing his attention from it he overcame the difficulty. He was able to concentrate his mind so perfectly on a chosen subject that the pain was treated as if it did not exist, and the consciousness of it was lost. Being subject to what he called rheumatic attacks, he overcame the sleeplessness caused thereby in the same way, by sheer force of will. "That these were, however, not imaginary pains was proved by the glowing redness which was seen early the next morning on the toes of my left foot." ([49]) His own experience made him confident that many rheumatic attacks, and also cases of epilepsy and podagra, can be resisted by a firm resolution of the will, and that in the course of time they may be completely cured.

Life was prized by Kant on account of its opportunities for intellectual development and moral culture, and the body was valued as the means to this end. He was accustomed to say that one should know how to adapt himself to his body; and by carefully studying his physical system, and by strenuous efforts of his resolute will, he conquered unfavourable conditions to which others would have succumbed. There is no doubt that he was often supposed to be in excellent health, when it was only by force of will that he kept his mind from brooding over his indisposition. Thinking it ignoble to be continually complaining, he was disposed to say but little about his ailings, until in his old age his infirmities increased and his will lost its resoluteness.

Kant was never confined to his bed by illness except in the last year of his life, and then only a few days, though for a number of years he was very weak and subject to considerable suffering. In his old age he at one time declared that he was only vegetating, being still able to eat, drink, walk, and sleep, but no longer of any benefit to society. Physically he regarded himself well; but so far as social life was concerned he was ill; and he spoke of himself despondently as "this candidate for death." This condition he viewed as the result of his previous efforts to prolong life, the wisdom of which he now questioned. "It is to this that the art of prolonging life leads, namely, that one is merely tolerated among the living, a state which is not the most enjoyable." He fears that he may be in the way of a younger generation; "but it is my fault," he says, thinking that if he had not been so intent on prolonging life, he might have ended his earthly career when he ceased to live intellectually and socially.

CHAPTER V.

MENTAL CHARACTERISTICS.

Intellectuality—Memory—Judgment—Opposition to Dogmatism, Prejudice, and Fanaticism—Power of analysis and synthesis —Sense of the ludicrous—Wit—Abstraction—Originality—Union of Excellencies—Strange psychological fact—Study and appreciation of other systems—Political views—Imagination—Emotional nature—Transformation—Dogmatic spirit—Æsthetic culture—Views of music, oratory, poetry, and genius—Reading—Library—Depreciation of history—Polymathist.

In his small, lean body and capacious mind we have a symbol of Kant's physical and intellectual interests and relations. This gives the point of view from which the man himself and his whole life must be considered. His intellectuality almost amounted to a passion; and history furnishes few examples of men whose minds were so completely on the throne, and were so absolute in their sway as to subject the whole being to their supremacy. If the sovereignty of the intellectual was ever disputed, it was only by his moral interests and tendencies. That these were potent factors is as evident from his profoundest metaphysical as from his ethical works; and both the purpose and the result of the "Kritik" are practical. In contrasting the theoretical with the practical, he does not hesitate to give the latter a decided preference;

he places the practical reason above the speculative, and morality is the culmination of his whole philosophy. Owing to his undisputed supremacy in metaphysical abstractions, the relation of his thoughts, his works, and his life, to realities is generally overlooked. While this is a serious mistake in forming an estimate of his philosophy, it is still more serious in considering the man himself. But while recognizing the union of the abstract and the concrete, of the theoretical and the practical, we nevertheless find that his exaltation of the practical and the moral is chiefly intellectual. He, indeed, applied his moral rules to himself, both for the formation of his character and for the government of his life, and his success was remarkable; yet, taking his life as a whole, we find that the intellect was his domain, that the study was his home, and that thought was to him the essence of life. As far as morality is concerned, he was chiefly intent on finding for it a firm basis and on giving an intellectual system of the theory of practice. When the theory was found, its practical application was for Kant a matter of course. His speculations have been made the basis of morals, as well as of philosophical systems, and his works are rich in theories which admit of important practical applications; and his disciples have applied them to various departments of life, making applications, even, of which Kant never thought. While, however, there is so much in Kant which belongs to the practical and to morals, the intellect must be viewed as the focus of his being. Now it takes a purely speculative turn, then it deals with physics or with mathematics; now it contemplates theology, then morality; but whatever the subject may be, he lifts it into the region of the intellect, and there disposes of it. In the ordinary sense, he was certainly not a practical man; but it may be said that he was speculatively practical, or if it did not seem too paradoxical, that he was theoretically practical. An expression of Kant himself indicates the deepest tendency of his being: "I am an investigator from inclination. I feel a burning thirst for knowledge and eager unrest to make progress in it, but also gratification with every advance."

In examining his mental faculties, we find that his memory was prodigious. Professor Kraus says that it was "incredibly strong;" and another acquaintance states, "His memory is astonishing. Even now, in his old age, when free from physical pain, he remembers perfectly all he has read on a subject." This exaggeration shows how remarkably retentive his memory must have been, as otherwise it could not have made such an impression. Late in life, when he readily forgot recent impressions, he still remembered earlier ones, and could correctly and easily repeat long passages from favourite authors. Professor Knutzen delivered lectures on mnemonics, which may have aided him in the development of this faculty; and in his Pedagogics, Kant specially commends a system of mnemonics. He admonishes teachers to be particularly careful to cultivate the memory of their pupils, an evidence of the importance he attached to this faculty. To secure this end, he thinks the memory should be occupied only with important objects, such as are worthy of being remembered. Consequently, he pronounces the reading of novels injurious to children; it weakens the memory, since the novel is intended only for amusement, not for retention in the memory or for repetition.

It would be ridiculous to desire to remember novels and relate them to others. Therefore all novels ought to be taken from children." It should be remembered that both in character and in literary importance the novel of the eighteenth century differed greatly from the better class of more recent works of fiction. Being himself a master of method, he advised his students so to classify their knowledge as to be able at once to place what they learned into its own department, because this would not merely aid them to systematize, but also to retain their knowledge.

His forgetfulness of ordinary affairs, which has been mentioned, arose largely from the fact that they did not much interest him or attract his attention. It was altogether different with the subjects which he studied. He was interested not merely in principles but also in details; and as he had an excellent memory for words and events, as well as for thoughts, his knowledge was exact as well as comprehensive. Jachmann, who suggests that his study of mathematics probably developed this exactness, gives some illustrations of his memory for details. Once he described Westminster Bridge in the presence of a resident of London, giving its form, its dimensions, and the arrangement of its parts, so accurately and minutely, that the Englishman inquired how many years he had lived in London, and whether he had devoted himself especially to architecture? With surprise he learned that Kant had never been outside of the province. On another occasion he spoke so familiarly about Italy with an Italian, that he was asked how long he had resided there? When already sixty years old, he devoted himself with great zeal to the study of chemistry, and so completely did he master the nomenclature and the details of experiments made by others, that he gave an exact account of some of these experiments in a conversation with an eminent chemist. Surprised at the accuracy of the details, the chemist exclaimed that he did not see how it was possible for any one to understand experimental chemistry so perfectly without having made or seen any experiments.

While Kant certainly cannot be classed with those who depreciate memory in order to exalt speculative thought more highly, he did not place a high estimate on learning unless connected with reflection and sound judgment. Memory was to him but the storehouse in which are deposited the materials for reflection. He himself combined vast learning with profound philosophical acumen; and with his metaphysical mind he could not value highly erudition without philosophic insight. His "Anthropology" says, "There is gigantic learning which is frequently found to be cyclopean—it lacks one eye." And in his "Pedagogics," he calls those who have a good memory, but little judgment, "the asses of Parnassus," which are useful in carrying material for others, even if they themselves construct nothing valuable.

The character of Kant's judgment may be inferred from the fact that mathematics was a favourite study, that he criticized systems of metaphysics and generally accepted methods of logic, and that he subjected the reason itself to the most searching critique in the history of philosophy. Where others were satisfied with probability, he demanded certainty; he undermined arguments which had withstood the attacks of centuries; and where others fell back on intuition and on propositions held as self-evident, he demanded mathematical demonstration. No one knew better than he that the problems of mathematics are entirely different from those of philosophy, and that consequently the method of the one should not be adopted by the other, and for this reason he opposed the method of the Wolfian philosophy; but at the same time he aimed to secure for philosophy all the possible definiteness and certainty of mathematics. A philosophical writer says, "Kant's purely logical contemplations were easily connected with the mathematical, to which they were intimately related;" and of his system he says that it is permeated by a logical, mathematical spirit.(50) In his criticisms, Kant aimed to make his judgment pure; that is, free from the influence of authority, prejudice, and emotion. He regarded it as the first requisite of a philosopher that he be consequent; and we find that he resolutely and remorselessly follows the dictates of his reason, equally regardless of the authority he destroys, and of the practical consequences. Without looking backward, forward, or aside, his critical spirit moves on as coldly and resistlessly as fate; and he was, what Mendelssohn called him, "the all-destroying one" (der Alles Zermalmende).

But Kant's judgment was slow in its decisions. He admired the readiness with which an acquaintance, who was a judge, decided complicated questions, stating that he could not do it so readily. We can understand this slowness, when we consider with what thoroughness he investigated problems. A judgment may be quick because superficial or ignorant; Kant's was slow because so deep and learned and scrupulously careful. He was accustomed to view an argument from all points and in every possible light, to see whether it could stand the severest tests. This required time; and haste in the solution of problems such as he investigated, might have proved fatal to his whole philosophy. His dread of error, and the earnest desire to make his position impregnable, made him slow and cautious. Convinced that this is the only safe course, he says, "To move with rapid steps in undertakings which lead to a great and remote goal, has at all times been disadvantageous to a thorough insight." Much of his life was spent in plodding, and in digging at the roots of thought to find their last and deepest fibres. This work required great care and clear discrimination, and it was necessarily slow; but it was thorough, and has produced lasting results.

Closely connected with the critical spirit which controlled his judgment, was his bitter opposition to dogmatism, whether found in philosophy or in religion; it almost seems as if he personified it and then pursued it with a personal hatred. His own earlier entanglement in its meshes may have contributed to inspire his later animosity. He defines as dogmatism all positive assertions without preceding criticism; or "a general confidence in principles without a previous criticism of the power of the reason itself." Scepticism, the opposite of dogmatism, is a general mistrust of reason without such criticism. It was his hope that he might destroy dogmatism by his "Kritik," and he says, "This is certain: whoever has tasted critique is for ever disgusted with all the dogmatic products with which he was formerly obliged to content himself because his reason needed something and discovered nothing better for its entertainment." An arrogant tone was intolerable to him, and he rebuked it severely.

Kant himself, however, was considerable of a dogmatist, but in a sense different from his definition of the word; that is, after making such a criticism as he demands, he makes assertions of the most dogmatic character. He wants all to think for themselves; and yet his tone is at times such as to leave the impression that he thinks he has so absolutely settled certain points that henceforth they cannot be questioned. Perhaps this is necessary in a system; then it proves that a certain dogmatic spirit is unavoidable. Even this expression escapes him in his "Prolegomena," "I am security for the correctness of all these proofs;" just as if one can be such an authority for another as to make the investigation of the processes which lead to certain conclusions unnecessary. His dogmatism was, of course, that of a mind conscious of its strength, very conscientious in its processes, and perfectly convinced of the correctness of its conclusions. Compared with many of his professed disciples and also with some of the later philosophers, Kant is very moderate in the use of that intolerable spirit in metaphysics which regards its own system as the absolute philosophy, and which has done so much to bring metaphysical investigations into disrepute. He himself published a brochure against the aristocratic tone which was beginning to be heard in philosophy.(51)

Prejudice he treated with a bitterness similar to that directed against dogmatism. In his first book he speaks of the great number over whom prejudice and the authority of eminent persons have a "horrible dominion." At the age of forty-two he wrote, "I have purified my soul from all prejudices; I have destroyed every blind devotion which ever crept into my mind for the purpose of creating in me much imaginary knowledge. Now I esteem nothing as of consequence or worthy of respect except what honestly takes its place in a mind which is calm and accessible to all evidences, whether confirmative or destructive of my former opinions. Wherever I find anything that instructs me, I accept it. The verdict of the man who refutes my arguments is my verdict after I have weighed it against self-love and my reasons, and then have found its evidence the stronger. Formerly I viewed the common human understanding only from the standpoint of my own; now I put myself in the place of a reason foreign to me and outside of me, and view my opinions, together with their most secret occasions, from the standpoint of others."

But with all his efforts, he could not wholly free his mind from bias, and this he himself admits. "I do not find that any dependence whatever on my part, or that any inclination before the investigation, deprives my mind of that receptivity which tries all the reasons *pro* and *con*, one only excepted. The scales of the understanding are not entirely impartial, and one arm bearing the inscription, *The hope of the future*, has a mechanical advantage, as a consequence of which even light reasons which fall on the scale on that side raise speculations of much greater weight placed on the other scale. This is the only inaccuracy which I cannot well remove, and which, in fact, I shall never want to remove." ([52])

His dislike of every species of fanaticism must be

put in the same category with his opposition to dogmatism and prejudice; and the book just quoted gives striking instances of this aversion. It is directed mainly against Swedenborg, and is a compound of logic and ridicule aimed at superstition. He says, "I do not blame the reader if instead of regarding the ghost-seers as semi-citizens of another world, he treats them summarily as candidates for an asylum, and thus relieves himself of all further need of investigation." Whilst he thus advises others to deal with superstition or fanaticism in a summary manner, he carried his own rule into practice. A man who was generally reliable once told him a ghost story, namely, that he had heard something walk with a tread as heavy as if made by iron. Kant coolly asked him whether he was willing to attest the story with an oath? This led the man to reflection, and he admitted that it was possible that he himself had not heard the steps, but that the story had been related to him by others. At another time J. H. Schoenherr, who had a peculiar theosophy, went to Kant to call his attention to the defects of the Critical Philosophy, and to reveal to him his own theosophic views. He told the philosopher that man was made and preserved by two primitive beings, namely the primitive Light and the primitive Water. Kant replied, "If that is the case, man ought to be able to live on light and water." The theosophist answered that this is possible. The philosopher advised him to try it, and if he succeeded, to let his success be the proof of his theory. It is said that Schoenherr did try it for some days, and was convinced by the experiment that his theory was false.

In spite of his desire to be impartial, he was too

much influenced by his surroundings to be entirely successful; and even Kant was in many respects the creature of his age and a partaker of its prejudices. It is natural that this should have been the case particularly with matters which he had not made subjects of special investigation. Hamann, after the "Kritik" had given its author celebrity, wrote, "Kant is a man of great talents, as well as of good and noble disposition, who permits himself to be greatly influenced by prejudices, but who is not ashamed to recall and renounce them; it is only necessary to give him time to reflect. He rather talks than listens. On account of his system and the fame gained thereby, he is at present the more ticklish and the more opinionated, which you yourself can easily understand. This is not wholly his fault, but chiefly that of the dear public; therefore he cannot be blamed for it altogether."

With all his liberalism in religion, he did not rise above the prevalent prejudice against the Jews, which is the more surprising because Moses Mendelssohn was at the summit of his fame, and Marcus Herz, a Jewish physician in Berlin, was one of Kant's favourite pupils and most intimate friends. In Königsberg the prejudice against this people was so general that the Englishman Motherby, a warm friend of Kant, is said to have been the only one who was superior to it. "Motherby esteemed in the Jew the man, and despised the Jew in the Christian." When Lessing's "Nathan the Wise" appeared, Hamann wrote, "Last week I read the first ten sheets of Nathan, and enjoyed them exceedingly. Kant, who received them from Berlin, pronounced them only the second part of 'The Jews,' and will admit no hero among this people. So fearfully severe is our philosophy in its prejudices, with all its tolerance and impartiality!" Although he could not free himself from the influence of his immediate surroundings respecting ordinary affairs and questions of the day, it was different with philosophical questions; in their investigation he was remarkably successful in freeing himself from the influence of authority and of his own preferences. As a philosopher, he was impelled by the love of truth, and everywhere it was the only object of his search.

In power of analysis Aristotle and Kant have a pre-eminence which is almost solitary; and it is this power which contributed so largely to the influence of the one in Greek and the other in German philosophy. It would be interesting to draw a parallel between Kant and Aristotle, on the one hand, and between the German metaphysician and Plato, on the other, for Kant united prominent characteristics of both; though it would be unjust to the Greek philosophers not to admit that in some respects he was surpassed by Plato and in others by Aristotle. While there is much in Kant which suggests the idealistic philosopher of the Greeks, there is also much which suggests the marvellous analytical power of the great Peripatetic philosopher. Kant of course applies this power chiefly to the operations of the mind. He makes discriminations where the ordinary understanding sees no distinctions, and where even speculative minds find it difficult to follow him in his dissecting and distinguishing processes. Hamann calls his acumen (Scharfsinn) his "evil demon." He readily analyzed his own thoughts and those of others; and in his critical works this power becomes very evident in testing arguments and in exposing fallacies. (53) The extreme difficulty in following him in his distinctions has been the occasion of many conflicting views respecting his meaning. It is said that the power which forsook him last was that of analyzing thoughts and tracing them to their sources.

His power of synthesis is closely connected with the analytic. In following thought from its genesis to its ultimate consequences, he observed close analogies as well as nice distinctions; but the synthetic power is less apparent in his works than the analytic. The former might have been more manifest if he had retained his mental vigour long enough to complete the last work on which he laboured, which was intended to embody and complete, in a final system, the result of all his speculations. As that was not finished, he gave the world preparations for metaphysics, not the system itself. But according to the "Kritik," a complete scientific synthesis is impossible; for while we may use the ideas of God, of the Spirit, and of the Cosmos, practically, we dare not use them speculatively or scientifically. We have phenomena in nature, and we can discover their laws, and these are objects of science; but the idea of a cosmos, the synthesis of all natural laws and phenomena, is speculatively impossible. His conclusion respecting man is the same. Thought and its laws are subjects for philosophical inquiry; but the idea of the spirit, in which these inhere, while practically very useful, cannot be used speculatively. The same is true of the idea of God, the final and absolute synthesis. For practical purposes this idea is necessary; but speculatively it, as well as that of the cosmos and that of the spirit, is involved in inextricable difficulties and in contradictions. The very conclusions of the Critical Philosophy thus deny the possibility of a complete synthesis; it is therefore not surprising that its strength is seen chiefly in its analytic processes. Not only is this power of analysis seen in the separation of heterogeneous elements, but also in distinguishing those which are analogous but not alike. It is this which enabled Kant to detect error so readily, and which made him the great critic. However much ardent Kantians may resist the conclusion, the final verdict will probably be, that the Critical Philosopher was greater in what he destroyed than in what he scientifically constructed.

With his quick perception of analogies and contrasts, it is natural that he should have had a keen perception of the ludicrous. He quickly observed the incongruous and the paradoxical, and they furnished him sport and relaxation. In his books and conversations we find him frequently leaving his serious contemplations, to ridicule foibles and follies, and to promote cheerfulness with his pleasantry. His book against Swedenborg is the most striking illustration of his union of profound and serious contemplation with humour and ridicule: and the union is so complete that there is danger of taking the one for the other. Bouterwek suggests that it might be worth while to show how many thoughts used sportively by Kant were regarded by his disciples as scientific judgments which they seriously commented and illustrated. He was particularly fond of humorous works, and in the last years of his life he read in Lichtenberg's books and marked the passages which specially pleased him. His praise of satire was extravagant, and in speaking of its influence he declared "that no metaphysician could do as much good in the world as Erasmus of Rotterdam and the celebrated Montaigne of France had accomplished. He also recommended the 'Essays' of the latter for constant reading; he himself could repeat many passages from them." In the department of belles-lettres he read satirical books with a marked preference, such as Swift's works, Butler's "Hudibras," and "Don Quixote." But he rarely laughed, and admitted that this was a defect in his nature. He thought laughing a blessing for children, as it tends to make their disposition more cheerful. Whenever persons indulged in a laugh, he wanted it to be harmless and good-natured, not at the expense of one who was wounded thereby, though he admitted that one may be the occasion of a laugh without being laughed at. Concerning empty and silly laughter, he said, "A mechanical laugh is superficial and makes society insipid;" but he also added, "He who does not laugh at all is morose or pedantic."

Kant had a keen appreciation of wit and was himself witty. "His wit was easy, merry, ingenious. There were lightning flashes of wit, which played in the serene heavens and illuminated his lectures as well as his conversations." In his "Anthropology" he defines wit as the power that couples and assimilates heterogeneous ideas which, according to the law of association, are remote from each other; it is the peculiar ability to liken things which are diverse. He says, "It is agreeable, pleasing, and cheering, to discover similarities among things dissimilar, and thus to give, as wit does, the understanding material to make its ideas general." Wit is play, judgment is work. "Wit is rather a flower of youth; judgment more the ripe fruit of age." Being a special talent, it cannot be learned in the schools. In puns, wit is superficial.

In speaking of his physical condition, his power of abstraction, which enabled him to conquer pain, was mentioned. In his critical works it is seen in a marvellous degree; and in abstract metaphysical speculations, where others are lost in inextricable confusion, he is perfectly at home. But at the same time we have seen that he was frequently subject to distractions, especially in his lectures. Sometimes in the development of a subject he lost sight of the main thought; then he would suddenly end the digression, and again resume the consideration of that thought. This wandering in his lectures made it difficult to follow him; and there are similar digressions in his works which increase their obscurity. In his letter to Hufeland he states that his thoughts were subject to distractions which were very painful to him; and that while speaking he would sometimes ask himself quietly or his hearers, "Where was I? From what point did I start?" He thinks that this tendency to distraction may be somewhat diminished, but that with all possible efforts it cannot be wholly avoided.

If greatness is measured by originality and by the contribution of new thoughts to the stock of human knowledge, Kant must be placed very high. "Everywhere he wanted to go his own way." This originality is seen in his methods as well as in his thoughts; and even when he reproduces the views of others, Kant is seen in them. Never satisfied with looking at the surface of things, but ever striving to penetrate objects and to get behind them, we find that every subject which he considers, receives the peculiar impress of his spirit. By giving the leaven of his own mind to a subject, thus making his discussion of it thoroughly Kantian, he made his books so suggestive and his philosophy such a revolutionary power. His originality is especially seen in his cosmogony, his moral philosophy, and in his æsthetical views in the "Critique of the Judgment;" and the "Kritik" teems with original thoughts, such as the distinction between sensation and understanding, the views of time and space, and the categories, while the method of the book, as well as the subject, is altogether his own. Whether we consider the destructive elements in the speculative portions of the book, or the constructive elements in its more practical parts and in his ethical works, this originality is striking. It is not surprising that with his creative mind he produced so grand an epoch in philosophy.

The superiority of Kant's mind is universally admitted. While some of its powers were more marked than others, and are worthy of special mention, there was, nevertheless, rather a union of excellencies than the solitary prominence of a single faculty. The philosopher Herbart says of Kant's mental characteristics: "With this depth, so much learning; with this extreme delicacy of moral feeling, so much clear, sound understanding; with this ability to grasp whatever is greatest and remotest, such great calmness of mind, such accuracy in details, such moderation, such critical self-control!" W. von Humboldt, who was induced by Schiller to study the Critical Philosophy, was astonished at the greatness of intellect revealed in it, and says of its author, "Kant undertook and accomplished the greatest work for which the philosophical reason will probably ever be indebted to one man. He tested and sifted the entire philosophical process in such a way as obliged him to meet the philosophers of all times and nations; he measured, limited, and smoothed the basis of this process; he destroyed the false structures built on this basis. And after completing this work, he established principles whose philosophical analysis often agreed with common sense, which had frequently been led astray or ignored in the former systems. In the truest sense, he led philosophy back into the depth of the human heart. In the fullest sense, he possessed everything which characterizes the great thinker, and united in himself gifts which ordinarily seem to be opposed to each other; namely, profundity and acumen, a dialectic power which was probably never surpassed, while at the same time he did not depreciate that truth which the dialectic process could not discover; and he also had that philosophic genius which spins out and holds together, by means of the unity of the idea, the threads of an extensive web of conceptions running in all directions, a genius without which there can be no philosophical system." Jean Paul says, "Kant is no planet, but an entire solar system radiating light."

While the intellectual character and development of Kant are full of interest to the student of the mind, there are some psychological facts which are worthy of special study. It is a strange fact that in the course of time his mind became so wholly absorbed by his own philosophy that, as a seeming penalty, he became unable to appreciate the speculations of others. The supreme concentration of his mind on the "Kritik" and the works which followed, made him lose himself in his own reflections, so that he could not find his way out, and at last it became impossible for him to place himself on the standpoint of other thinkers. This fact was too striking and too surprising to escape the notice of his friends, and Jachmann wrote, "Every person will admit that Kant's intellectual powers were original in the highest degree, and if ever a philosopher went a new and untrodden way, it was Kant. I must, however, make a few remarks about the originality of his intellect. The richness of his own mind in thought, and the habitual ease with which he drew all philosophical ideas from the inexhaustible fountain of his own reason, brought it to pass that at last Kant scarcely comprehended any one except himself. Understand me correctly; I speak of abstract philosophical conceptions. He who was an original thinker in the most peculiar sense of the word, found everything in himself, and thus lost the ability to find anything in others. At the very time when his mental powers had attained their highest development, namely, when he worked out his Critical Philosophy, nothing was more difficult for him than to appreciate the system of another. Even the writings of his opponents he could understand only with the greatest difficulty, since he found it impossible to leave, for any length of time, his own system of thought. He was aware of this difficulty, and therefore generally requested his friends to read other systems and communicate to him the relation of their principal contents to his own views. The consciousness of his inability to comprehend views foreign to his own may account for the fact that he left it to his disciples and friends to defend his philosophy against the attacks of his opponents."

Kant makes repeated reference to this strange effect of his long introspection and of the intense concentration of his mind on his own philosophy. When he was sixty-six years old, he wrote to his friend Herz that in his advanced age he cannot well succeed in understanding purely speculative thought, foreign to himself, but is obliged to let himself go his own way in the track he has followed for many years. Four years later, he says that he can think well yet, but that he finds it difficult to appreciate another person's train of thought, and attributes this inability partly to his physical condition. He asserts that he does not understand what Maimon means with his proposed improvement of the Critical Philosophy, and that he must leave it to others to refute his views. When Kant was only sixty-one, four years after the "Kritik" appeared, Hamann wrote to Herder, "Kant is too full of his own system to judge yours impartially." For many years he was so absorbed in evolving his own philosophy, that he had neither time nor inclination to study other systems; and the result was an unusual intellectual exclusiveness and isolation. After he had elaborated the critical system, that community of thought which generally exists among scholars, ceased in his case; he could still give to others, but he could take their peculiar views only by doing violence to himself. Rink states that after his great works were published, Kant knew what other thinkers had produced only through fragments, and that consequently he did not properly estimate their views, not even in those cases where he held notions which, if developed, would have led to the same conclusions. Kuno Fischer says, "In general, the accuracy of Kant's apprehension of systems foreign to his own is questionable. He was so occupied with his own thoughts that he found it difficult to appreciate the spirit of another philosophy; in old age he found it altogether impossible."

Authors are generally desirous of learning what is thought of their works, and they frequently find the criticism of scholars suggestive of improvements; but after the "Kritik" appeared, Kant, as a rule, did not even read what was written for or against his views. That this was not the result of indifference to the influence of his philosophy, or to the relation sustained to it by philosophical thinkers, is proved by his letters and his sensitiveness with reference to adverse criticism. Sometimes he made arrangements to have his friends reply to the attacks on his system, and he was anxious that the answers should not be too mild. But his own speculations absorbed his attention too much, to consider seriously the confirmation or refutation of his works by reviewers: and after the "Kritik" became celebrated, it was the occasion of so many works, both favourable and unfavourable, that it would have consumed entirely too much time if he had read all of them. Even if Kant had taken a deeper interest in the discussions occasioned by his philosophy, it would not have been surprising if he had become tired of the extensive Kantian literature produced between 1786 and the close of the century. His confidence in the principles of his philosophy and in their final success may have made him less concerned about the opinions of cotemporaries. And it should also be considered that he was incessantly labouring to complete the works he had planned, and that attention to other matters might have interfered with this aim. Hamann took a deeper interest in the relation of scholars to the Kantian philosophy than its author. At one time Kant sent him three publications against his philosophy, which he had not thought it worth while to read himself; so, as he said, he turned them over to "the inquisitive old man." Kant was vexed that they had come to him without a letter, and because he had been obliged to pay the postage.

The fact that Kant wove a web around himself, which he could not break, and thus imprisoned himself in his own system, enables us to understand expressions which otherwise seem inexplicable. Hippel makes this statement, "Kant repeatedly said, I do not understand the catechism, but I understood it formerly."(54) And he adds, "Kant also said that he could not understand Montesquieu;" which is the more remarkable because he had been a favourite author. But not only did he, later in life, fail to appreciate the authors he read; he never made the study of the philosophical works of his predecessors such a speciality as his preference for metaphysics would lead one to expect. In his works he repeatedly speaks of other systems of philosophy in such a way as to make the impression on some of his cotemporaries that he depreciated them for the purpose of exalting his own, a charge which is no doubt unjust. He admitted that he understood neither Spinoza nor Jacobi's explanation of his system; (55) and he also acknowledged that he had never studied Spinoza carefully. (56) As he habitually went to his own mind for his principles, and evolved his system from them, it is not strange that he sometimes imagined a thought to be original, when the thought itself, or at least its germ, had already been given by another. Kuno Fischer, who has carefully studied Kant's relation to his predecessors, and cannot be charged with a want of admiration for him, says, "He knew Leibnitz only after the manner of the Wolfians, and Spinoza, as it were, not at all. The scholastics were outside of the range of his studies. He constantly apprehended and judged the Greek systems according to their most general characteristics; and even in these he frequently misses the mark, Plato and Aristotle not excepted. When he cites the doctrines of the ancients, he groups them more to suit his convenience than according to their peculiar order." While this neglect of other philosophies may have prevented him from doing them justice, it did not seriously interfere with the development of his own system. The writer just quoted adds, "We mention this defect once for all, in order not to revert to it again. As far as the merit and the philosophy of Kant are concerned, it is of little importance, and really of no influence. In a certain sense it is even an advantage to his cause. The task which Kant pursued had to be accomplished through his own efforts, and the most thorough knowledge of the preceding philosophies could not have aided him in its performance." In his works Kant gives a summary of the history of philosophy, which he used in his lectures; it is extremely meagre, occupyiug only about eight pages.

Kant was too deeply interested in individuals and nations to neglect politics, and in his old age he was engaged in planning a book on the subject. ([57]) From his views of the freedom and dignity of man, it is evident that he would oppose all forms of despotism. But he did not think a mere revolution capable of freeing a people from tyranny; for while it may remove personal despotism and many other evils, it cannot change the mode of thinking. Unless the masses are enlightened, there can be no real freedom; new prejudices will be added to the old ones, and the people will be under their dominion. The freedom of the press will, however, promote the needed enlightenment. He sympathized with the American colonies in their war with England, and took a deep interest in the French Revolution, from which he expected great benefits, and which he defended zealously, even when it was very unpopular in Königsberg. Although his advocacy of that cause gave offence, he was too much accustomed to have his own way to let the opinions of others interfere seriously with the free expression of his own in company. For a long time even the atrocities perpetrated in France did not alter his opinion, and he still advocated the cause of the Revolution when Burke, and many other of its early friends, saw and denounced the pernicious tendencies of the movement.

Kant based his political views largely on Montesquieu, and advocated the strict separation of the legislative, the judicial, and the executive functions. He denounced Pitt's course, because he believed that this statesman was promoting the encroachment of the legislative on the executive power, and he did not hesitate to declare that his policy tended to barbarism.

In his opinion, the people ought to have a voice in

the legislative body, and for this reason he favoured the American colonists in their dispute with England. At the beginning of the French Revolution he hoped to see the realization of the desired separation of the three functions of government; when his confidence was, however, at last shaken, he opposed the new despotism as anarchy allied with atrocious passion and bloody barbarity. After this his tone was changed, and he defended more vigorously the prerogatives of rulers, and spoke less emphatically in favour of the rights of subjects. Formerly he had spoken of subjects as if they had rights which they might defend against rulers; now his language implied that all opposition to the existing authorities is wrong; formerly he had defended the Revolution with a degree of passion; now he spoke of revolutionists as if they were criminals and even traitors; and if there had been protests against his former views on the part of royalists, now he met with opposition from the advocates of freedom.

In his brochure on Eternal Peace, published in 1795, Kant wants to introduce his exalted moral principles into politics, both in national and international affairs. In legislation as well as in the execution of the laws, the controlling principle ought to be right, instead of expediency. Freedom and equality should prevail because they are right, and selfishness or happiness should not be the motive of their advocacy. Kant holds that the Categorical Imperative is the supreme law in politics as well as in private morality; and he gives this maxim to the politicians who seek to promote eternal peace: "Seek ye first the kingdom of the Practical Reason and its *righteousness*, and the end you seek (the blessing of eternal peace) shall be added unto you." In order that war may be avoided, he advocates the formation of a federation of states (*fœdus pacificum*) for the settlement of the disputes which may arise between them. While at first only a few states may join this federation or league, its aim should be to extend its influence until it embraces all states, and thus puts an end to war. He attaches less importance to the form of government than to the supremacy of law, the real sovereign to which the ruler and the ruled are alike subject. This pamphlet was very popular, and was translated into several foreign languages.

Kant was not a poet, though he composed a few blank verses on the occasion of the death of colleagues in the university. Their poetic value is small; they contain no flights of imagination, and reveal neither enthusiasm nor inspiration. They are didactic compositions which present good moral thoughts in the form of blank verse. (58) It would, however, be a mistake to suppose that imagination and enthusiasm were foreign to his nature, an impression which is favoured by his cold metaphysical works. In old age, after he had encased himself in his philosophy, this was largely the case, though even then some subjects, especially moral ones, kindled his enthusiasm. In his early manhood there were many evidences of an enthusiastic nature, though his admirable self-control and his effort to subject everything to reason might interfere with its free exercise. His fondness for the Latin poets leads us to suspect a strong imagination and its special culture until he entered the university. While he was afraid to give a loose rein to the imagination when advanced in years, in his earlier productions, especially in his cosmogony, this faculty sometimes gets the mastery over dry theories and mathematical calculations. Aside from the Latin classics, however, his studies were mostly such as were calculated to curb the imagination; and neither the Wolfian philosophy, in which he was trained, nor the one which he himself developed, was calculated to promote its cultivation. Bouterwek writes, "It is certain that this speculative mind, with its strivings after pure knowledge, was afraid of the imagination and its inventions, just as if he had been a Wolfian." In his efforts to attain mathematical certainty he demonstrated the imagination away; but the dry, logical, unimaginative Kant of later years was not a product of nature, but of discipline.

What has been said of his imagination is essentially true also of his emotional nature. Kant feared that feeling might interfere with the working of the intellect, and prevent the attainment of that pure knowledge which he sought. Even in morals and religion he treats the emotions, those of a nobler kind not excepted, as a hindrance rather than a help. The emotional religious influences of his youth and the general sentimentality of the times no doubt promoted this depreciation of feeling. He saw the injurious influences of extravagance and fanaticism, and liked to present the antidotes to the evils of the day as strikingly as possible; it is no wonder, then, if one extreme led him to another. It was an age fond of extravagant expressions of love and friendship, an age of kisses and sighs and tears; and he was a mortal enemy of all affectation and sentimentality. His fear of the influence of the emotions was also promoted by the fact that he regarded the prevalent errors in philosophy as largely the product of prejudice and feeling, and their removal as possible only through pure reason.

His writings impressed some of his contemporaries with the belief that Kant was heartless; and one of them calls attention to the fact that in his letter to Hufeland he stated that he had succeeded in so completely separating his head from his chest that the oppression of the latter does not affect the former. This was a revelation to him respecting the head products of Kant, and in a letter he says, "Let us rejoice, my dear friend, that in our case head and heart still go together." This separation of the head from the heart is striking even in works where it might be expected that prominence would be given to the feelings. Soon after Kant's death an author wrote, "The cold understanding was the ruling power in Kant's unwearied mind; he did not even trust enthusiasm in those cases where a noble emotion, instead of depressing, arouses the power of thought. Respecting the dignity of man, Kant felt a powerful inspiration only when some moral interest was connected with the pure contemplations. . . . All violent emotions, in the possession of which many think themselves great, had something petty in Kant's eyes." And he adds, "Not a little did this intellectual coldness contribute to the imposing authority which the Kantian philosophy gained among the cold Germans." (59)

In considering this subject, however, we must discriminate between the utterances of the youthful and the aged Kant, both as found in his lectures and in his books. Knowing his own later aversion to enthusiasm, it seems hardly possible that he could have been the author of the following: "Whoever is more powerfully inspired by a moral emotion as a principle than others, on account of their cold and often ignoble heart, are able to appreciate, is, in their estimation, an enthusiast;" and this is followed by the declaration that without enthusiasm nothing great has ever been accomplished.(60) This was written when he was forty, a period in which many of his utterances indicate emotion as well as enthusiasm. Therefore, while the marked predominance of his intellectual faculties at last largely suppressed the emotional element, there is abundant proof that by nature Kant was not lacking in feeling. As is usual in natures which are emotional and yet intellectually profound, we find in him a conflict between the head and the heart, between the longings of the one and the demonstrations of the other; and this gives us the key to his distinction between the speculative and the practical reason. Though so wary of impulses, he found in his own nature those which he could not suppress, in spite of all the negative conclusions of his philosophy. When his dogmatism was shaken, he found it impossible to rest in scepticism; and the demand for a scientific basis for hope and aspiration was the mighty impulse which produced the Critical Philosophy. In his cold Critiques of Pure Reason and of Judgment, Kant is only partially seen; in other works he deals with flesh and blood as well as with skeletons. How can we account for the marvellous enthusiasm with which he inspired his best students? The spark which kindled a flame in others was communicated from his own being; such heat could never have emanated from an iceberg.

Jachmann states that in his lectures on morality Kant was not merely a speculative philosopher, but also a spirited orator who moved the heart while he satisfied the mind. "It produced a heavenly rapture to hear this pure and sublime morality coming from the lips of its author with such powerful philosophic eloquence. O how often he moved us to tears! How often he powerfully agitated our hearts, and lifted our spirits and our emotions out of the trammels of a selfish love of pleasure to a high realization of pure freedom, to unconditional subjection to the law of reason, and to the sublime emotion of disinterested duty! At such times the immortal philosopher seemed to be inspired by a divine power, and he also inspired us who listened to him full of admiration. Surely his hearers never left one of his lectures on morality without being made better." The same enthusiastic admirer mentions Kant's animation during conversation when specially interested in his subject. "How often did Kant speak with rapture of God's wisdom, goodness, and power, when conversing with his friends on the structure of the world! How often he spoke touchingly of the blessedness of a future life! And here the heart both of the philosopher and the man spoke, giving indubitable testimony of his emotions and honest convictions. One such conversation on astronomy, during which Kant was constantly inspired by his theme, was not merely enough to convince every one who heard him that he believed in God and providence, but it would also have changed an atheist into a believer." Even if at other times he spoke coldly and critically on these subjects, and though Jachmann may transfer some of his own enthusiasm to Kant, still there is evidence enough to show that there were times when he was unusually inspired and inspiring.

Some persons laud Kant's speculative philosophy to the skies and speak contemptuously of his moral system, while others praise his moral philosophy and reject his speculations; and there are others, still, who form their opinions of Kant and his life mainly either from his speculations or from his moral principles; consequently, he is seen and judged very imperfectly. To hold before men his speculative philosophy and say, "This is Kant," is as misleading as to hold up his sublime moral principles and say, "So Kant lived." Sometimes life is greater than a theory, sometimes immeasurably less; and a true biography carefully discriminates between the theory and the life. In order to form a correct estimate of the author of the Critical Philosophy, we must not merely distinguish between his speculation and principles on the one hand, and his life on the other, but also between that which nature had made him, and what he became through the stern discipline to which he subjected himself. That the impulsive and extremely sensitive Kant became so complete a master of himself as to subject his emotions almost wholly to reason and calculation, is remarkable but not inexplicable. There were evidences of sensitiveness and of impulses to the last; but with the advance of years they became more subordinate. Few lives furnish so striking an illustration of the transformation possible by means of circumstances and discipline. The ardour of youth may yield to cold calculation; the sensitive may become callous, and the gentle harsh; the enthusiast and the devotee may change to the critic and the sceptic; indifference may take the place of ardent affection; the sociable man may become a hermit; a passion or interest, however strong, may be weakened or even expelled by the cultivation of another; and thus the transformation between youth and age may be so complete that at last the antipodes of the early characteristics appear. This will enable us to explain apparent contradictions in the life of Kant. The severe struggles of many years gave him a training which qualified him for the mastery over himself. According to his own testimony, his inclination to yield to impulses, whose results he had occasion to regret, induced him to form maxims for his conduct with a view of making reason, and not impulse, the arbiter in all things. Being early disciplined in self-reliance, he developed a degree of self-sufficiency which enabled him to dispense largely with the assistance and affection of friends. Besides, he possessed an intense desire for knowledge; a worship of pure truth, and a religious zeal to promote its spread; a critical spirit which controlled him in his researches and was characteristic of the tendencies of the age; an intellect conscious of its great strength, and ambitious for the full development and manifestation of its powers; and a will which could master the body with its ailings, could control the emotions, and, as the pure practical reason, could set up its throne in his moral system, just as the speculative reason set up its throne in the "Kritik." When all these things are considered, as well as the years of absorbing and abstract intellectual toil in preparing the great "Kritik," we can in some measure understand the remarkable transformation to which he was subject, which, however, was not so great as to enable his reason, his maxims, and his will to prevent the original elements of his nature from asserting themselves strongly at times.

Long after he had passed the period of youth, Kant gave unmistakable evidence that he was not always the cold, calm philosopher. Being very fond of dried fruits, he occasionally requested his friend Motherby to import some for him. At one time he was eagerly expecting a vessel with French fruits which he had ordered, and he had already invited some friends to a dinner at which they were to be served. The vessel was, however, delayed a number of days by a storm. When it arrived, Kant was informed that the provisions had become short on account of the delay, and that the crew had eaten his fruit. Kant was so angry that he declared they ought rather to have starved than to have touched it. Surprised at this irritation, Motherby said, "Professor, you cannot be in earnest!" Kant answered, "I am really in earnest," and went away. Sometime afterwards Motherby met him and again referred to the matter, when the philosopher immediately declared that he was sorry for his hasty remark.([61])

It is now generally admitted that by suppressing his emotional nature he became one-sided. Formerly it was the fashion, in certain circles, to extol him as a prodigy in every department of learning, and as a complete, full-orbed, harmoniously developed man; to dissent from these views, or to question his authority, was regarded as sufficient cause for violent attacks. But with the strongest admiration for Kant on the part of those who profess to be his disciples, such hero-worship can never return again. It is plainly seen now that he was not only thoroughly human, subject to ordinary human infirmities, but that in some respects he was much more one-sided than many who, compared with him intellectually, were only pigmies. It was the very fact that he devoted himself so wholly to his critical speculations which gave him his real greatness and the sublime elevation on which he stands alone. "The quietness and firmness with which Kant confined himself to the domain of thought, the boldness and resoluteness with which he pressed unceasingly forward in this realm as far as it seemed possible, constitute one of the great characteristics in Kant's scientific personality."(62) It would have been impossible for him to have attained his speculative pre-eminence if he had developed all his powers harmoniously.

Having but little appreciation of the systems or even thoughts of others after he developed his own philosophy, Kant became very much set in his opinions. His stern discipline, his intellectual isolation, and his riveting the attention so exclusively on subjects elaborated by his own mind, at last gave his thoughts an unusual rigidity, and made him so impervious to the arguments of others that, after reasoning out a matter to his own satisfaction, he was apt to be immovable,—a spirit which of course increased with old age. His assertions respecting the French Revolution, for instance, were often peremptory, and sometimes he even ignored facts. A contemporary says, "It was difficult and almost impossible to convince him that his views were wrong; even when facts were presented against these views, he was not convinced, at least not immediately and not always."(63) This person, as well as Wasianski, gives an instance of Kant's habit of demonstrating things *à priori*, even if there was proof to the contrary. He had come to the conclusion, in 1798, that Napoleon could not have the intention of landing in Egypt, but that while he pretended to be fitting out an expedition against that country, he was really preparing to enter Portugal. It was his opinion that England would feel most keenly the capture of Portugal by the French, owing to the important commercial relations between those two countries. So satisfactorily had he demonstrated to himself this supposed stratagem of Napoleon, that even after the French had landed in Egypt, and the Government had announced the fact to all Europe, he still asserted that the expedition was against Portugal, and that the announcement to the contrary was only a pretext to mislead the English.

His dogmatic spirit seems at last to have become his second nature, and the dictatorial tone of the authoritative professor could not escape the notice of his friends. These, indeed, plead age and great learning as an apology ; but even those who charitably considered these facts could not wholly escape the unfavourable impression made by this spirit. Count Purgstall, whose enthusiastic admiration for the great philosopher cannot be questioned, after spending some time at Königsberg and in Kant's society, says, "The result of my observation respecting Kant is this : he is certainly honest, his soul is pure, he is childlike, and does not consider himself a great man. This is admitted by all who know him well. . . . His knowledge of men is extensive, he has studied the world, and knows how to speak admirably of many things which do not belong to his speciality. He alone is a great speculative philosopher. . . . Only once in a thousand years is a *Kant* born; and nature has very wisely arranged this, for only once in a thousand years is a speculative philosopher necessary.

"Now, as surely as I believe that Kant's *morality* and *humanity* have not suffered through the dangerous position of a professor, so sure is it that he has not escaped all the faults and imperfections of his office. Thus, he cannot bear to hear others talk much, becomes impatient, at least for the moment, if any one professes to know anything better than he does, monopolizes the conversation, and professes to know everything about all countries, places, divisions of the earth, and the like. For instance, he professed to know better than I do what kind of fowls we have, how our country looks, what degree of culture our Catholic priests have attained, and similar things. In all these matters he contradicted me."[64] And this was done in spite of the fact that he had never been in the region under consideration.

We do not expect much æsthetic culture from one who devotes himself as exclusively as Kant did to the rigid sciences. It is true that he made art, and beauty in general, a subject for analysis and speculation in his "Critique of the Judgment," and he wrote a small volume on "The Emotion of the Beautiful and the Sublime." But aside from his scrupulous care in his dress, especially in his early manhood, he gave no marked evidence of taste. In furnishing his house he proved that he was not actuated by a love of the beautiful; and no man of taste could have written as he did in his "Anthropology," "In complete solitude, no one would adorn or polish his house; nor will he do it for the sake of his wife and children, but only for the sake of friends, in order to show himself to them to advantage." In his "Critique of the Judgment" he, however, gives some profound thoughts on the nature of the beautiful. Respecting Kant's appreciation of art, Borowski says, "He never seemed to pay much attention to paintings and engravings, even when of a superior kind. In galleries and rooms containing much admired and highly praised collections, I never noticed that he specially directed his attention to the pictures, or in any way gave evidence of his appreciation of the skill of the artist."

Of music he spoke disparagingly, and one of his friends declared that he preferred noise to harmony. Kant charges music with a lack of politeness, in that it forces itself on the attention when not wanted, and in this way disturbs society. It differs in this respect from the arts which address the eye, since one can turn away from them if he does not desire to see them. Music is like an odour, which spreads in every direction and must be breathed even when not wanted. "He who draws a perfumed handkerchief from his pocket, treats all who are about him to an odour against their will, for if they breathe at all, they are obliged to inhale it; for this reason it has gone out of fashion. Those who recommend the singing of spiritual songs as a part of family devotions, do not consider that they inflict a great annoyance on the public by means of such a noisy (and for that very reason usually Pharisaic) devotion, since thereby the neighbourhood is obliged either to join in the singing, or else to suspend the effort to think." He advised some young friends not to study music, because it would take too much time from their scientific pursuits; and he also thought its tendency was to make effeminate. He rarely attended concerts at any time, and never during the latter part of his life. Military music he liked best; funeral dirges he disliked exceedingly. When the Jews in Königsberg commemorated the death of Moses Mendelssohn, Kant was present. In giving an account of the affair, he spoke of the music as an "eternal, disagreeable moaning," and he could not think of it without extreme aversion. It is said that he never attended a concert after this experience, in order not to be subjected again to similar torture.

There being a prison near his house, he was greatly annoyed by the singing of the prisoners during their religious exercises. In 1784 he wrote a characteristic letter to his friend Hippel, who was police-director and prison-inspector, asking to be relieved "of the stentorian devotion of the hypocrites in prison." In this appeal he says, "If their voices were so moderated during singing that they can hear themselves with closed windows, I do not think that they will have reason to complain that their soul's salvation will be endangered unless they bawl at the top of their voices. Even without making so much noise, they might procure a certificate from the prison-keeper (which is probably their principal aim), testifying that they are very devout persons; for he will be able to hear them at any rate, and I only want their voices to be toned down to that pitch which the pious citizens of our good city find loud enough for their edification."

Kant had a low opinion of oratory, regarding it as the art of deceiving people, and opposed teachers of eloquence, comparing them with lawyers. He wanted cold logic, without any art of persuasion, as the means of conviction; and said that the reading of a beautiful poem always gave him pleasure, while in the perusal of the best speeches of Roman, parliamentary, or pulpit orators, he experienced a feeling of disapproval, because he perceived in them the deceitful art which persuades people to form, in weighty affairs, conclusions which lose all significance on calm reflection.

The first place in the beautiful arts is assigned by him to poetry, which he regarded as almost wholly the product of genius and as the art which is least governed by rules or models. He was fond of the poets and frequently quoted them. Besides his favourite Latin authors, Lucretius, Horace, Juvenal, and Virgil, he had a preference for Pope among the English and Haller among the German poets. The time for the study and appreciation of Shakspeare in Germany had not yet come; the deep insight into human nature revealed by this wonderful seer would no doubt have made him most attractive to Kant. He read Milton, Wieland, Buerger, and others; but Young's "Night Thoughts," which were very popular in Germany, were too monotonously serious for him. Though Herder had been his pupil and once a great favourite, Kant did not read his poems, being prejudiced against him on account of one of his earlier prose works. For Lessing's dramas he manifested no fondness, and he was not acquainted with the poetical works of Schiller and Goethe. He read Schiller's "Æsthetic Letters," which were in his own immediate line of thought, he himself having written on the same subject. His knowledge of German poetry did not extend to a later period than that of Klopstock; and for his poems he had no taste. When the

Augustan era of German literature began, he was either too old to appreciate it, or was too much occupied with his own works to give it any attention.

It is only in art that Kant acknowledges genius. He defines it as a gift, in distinction from an acquisition; as a law unto itself and the creator of its own laws, in distinction from the ability to work according to rules prescribed by another. Wherever law rules instead of spontaneity, as in science, philosophy, and morals, he recognizes no genius. The appellation of a philosophical or speculative genius he would have declined as a misnomer.

Kant began his studies in the gymnasium when about eight years old; and his intellectual career may be regarded as ending with the last book which he wrote, namely, in 1798. This gives a period of sixty-six years of severe and uninterrupted mental application. Study was not only his life-work, it was also his delight. With contempt he speaks of "the apes of genius," as he calls those who despise study and without it expect their genius to grasp and evolve everything. What is to be done in view of these so-called geniuses? "What else except to laugh at them and patiently pursue one's course with diligence, order, and definiteness, without regarding such jugglers." He had a genius for work, and never expected to accomplish anything except by hard and persistent labour.

Aside from his special studies, his reading was extensive and varied. When he had already attained his seventieth year, it was said, "He reads all that is new, especially history and geography, and has a fortunate memory which retains even the most difficult names." Christian theology excepted, there was scarcely a department of learning which did not interest him and become an object of his investigations. So far was he from being a narrow specialist, that he was in the true sense a polymathist.

A glance at the subjects which engaged his attention gives some conception of the breadth of his mind and the extent of his interest in learning. His partiality for the classics, mathematics, physics, astronomy, and for metaphysics, has already been mentioned, as well as his interest in medical works. Law was included in his reading, which is evident from his discussion of "The Metaphysical Principles of Law;" books on morals and natural religion also, since he lectured and published works on these subjects. Besides his deep interest in those laws of the mind which lie even beyond the ken of most philosophers, he was interested in the manners, customs, politics, trades, religious opinions, the institutions, and the life of nations, and embodied the results of his investigations in his "Anthropology." And while he applied Newton's discoveries and developed metaphysical principles in physics, he also studied the surface of the earth, its mountains, valleys, forests, rivers, lakes, seas, and atmosphere, together with their inhabitants, and made his "Physical Geography" the depository of his researches on these subjects. He did not need the metaphysical speculations of others to impel him to philosophize, for he could evolve abstractions enough from his own mind without this impulse; and when his mind was weary with speculation, it naturally turned to those subjects which were calculated to give it freshness and recreation. Accounts of travel were his favourite reading for relaxation, and he read all important books of this kind which were accessible.(65) Eagerly he sought for original writers, and took delight even in their paradoxes. Professor Kraus says, "Thinking was a necessity for his active mind, which always sought that which was new and transcended the usual conceptions. Hence his love for paradoxical writings."

English and French writers were among his favourite authors. In his study of physics he was most indebted to Newton. Frequently he refers to Locke, and repeatedly to Berkeley; but owing to the critical spirit of Hume and the impulse which he had received from him, Kant placed him higher than any other Scotch or English metaphysician. While he spoke highly of Shaftesbury, he particularly esteemed Hutcheson as a moral philosopher, and recommended him to those engaged in the study of ethics, just as he did Hume in metaphysics. Among French authors, he had read Montaigne while still a student, and knew many passages of his "Essays" by heart. Montesquieu's political views and his knowledge of various nations made him a great favourite. While the German metaphysician was averse to Voltaire's flippancy, he shared his antagonism to real or supposed fanaticism. But of all French writers he preferred Rousseau, whose views of human nature, of education, and of the freedom and rights of man, deeply interested Kant and made a lasting impression on his mind. The only picture which adorned his house was one of Rousseau. His "Emile" so engrossed the philosopher's attention that for several days it kept him from his usual walk. This author and Montesquieu had most influence in moulding his social and political views. Speaking of his own thirst for learning, and of the fact that he had made knowledge the criterion of human excellence, he says, "There was a time when I thought that this could determine the worth of man, and I despised the masses who know nothing. Rousseau, however, set me right. This apparent advantage disappears; I am learning to honour men, and I should regard myself as much more worthless than the common labourer, if I did not believe that the pursuits I am following can promote the worth of others, by aiding in restoring the rights of man."

As he had never travelled, he depended chiefly on books for his knowledge of countries and nations; but his contact with persons from different lands also aided him. Kant took pleasure in meeting persons of diverse opinions, occupations, and degrees of culture, in order that he might study man in various circumstances and relations. With men who had made specialities of them, he liked to discuss chemistry, galvanism, and even craniology. Though Königsberg had no large libraries, it possessed many books of interest and value; and besides the public ones, there were circulating libraries which contained works of scientific and literary importance. The book-stores were the common resorts of literary men and scholars, where they wrote letters, examined new books, had access to periodicals, and discussed the literary news of the day. Among the booksellers who visited the book-market in Leipzig, and came in contact and corresponded with men of letters, were persons of literary taste and promoters of literature. They cheerfully placed their books and journals at Kant's disposal without pecuniary consideration. While Königsberg suffered intellectually from its literary isolation, its advantages, though inferior to those of Berlin, Leipzig, Weimar, and other intellectual centres, were still considerable, and Kant had much opportunity for the gratification of his varied scholarly tastes. Professor Kraus says of him, "As soon as he received the semi-annual catalogue of books, he marked nearly all accounts of travel, as well as the chemical, physical, and other works from whose authors he had reason to expect something instructive. These books he read successively, and was generally through with the list long before the new catalogue appeared, which he treated in the same way. While writing, he always had a new unbound book lying beside him, which he would read when mentally wearied, in order to prepare himself again for meditation and composition."

Owing to the generosity of the booksellers who permitted him to read books and then return them, it was not necessary for him to purchase many works. At the time of his death his library consisted of about five hundred volumes, including many pamphlets. Professor Gensichen, who inherited this library, says of it, "Among the older books I find more on mathematics and physics than on philosophy. The newer volumes are, of course, mostly philosophical, and those occasioned by Kant's philosophy are considerable in number; it is probable that he did not buy a single one of them, but that the most of them, if not all, were sent to him by their authors. I am, therefore, inclined to believe that Kant furnished his library chiefly with books on mathematics and physics (chemistry included)." He also makes this statement: "In the library left by Kant I miss all his works preceding the "Kritik of Pure Reason," and also his

"Critique of the Judgment." Probably Kant gave away some of his books, especially in his last years, and loaned others which were never returned; this seems likely from the fact that of works containing a number of volumes, only a few of the set are on hand." (66)

In speaking of the learned peculiarities of different nations, Kant says that among the Germans genius develops into roots; among the Italians, into foliage; among the French, into flowers; and among the English, into fruit. According to this generalization, he himself was thoroughly German, though we also find flowers and fruit in his scholarship. The breadth in his scientific studies is worthy of special note. He did not want the sciences to be isolated, and it is a significant fact that he attached so much importance to the study of mathematics and physics in connexion with speculative philosophy. In his "Logic" he states that the improvement in metaphysics in modern times is due, partly to the more diligent study of nature, partly to the union of mathematics with natural science. The connexion of mathematics, physics, and metaphysics, is a characteristic of his studies as well as of his works. The book just quoted gives a hint of his aim in his studies: "Mere polymathy is cyclopic learning, which lacks an eye, namely the eye of philosophy; and a cyclop in mathematics, history, natural history, or philology, is a scholar who is great in all these, but regards a philosophy respecting them as unessential."

Although Kant read historical works, he did not sufficiently appreciate history to give it the place it deserves. His depreciation of this department of learning will be the more easily explained if we remember that his education belonged to a period when there was but little taste in Germany for general history and when there were no attractive historical books. The impulse given to this study by Moser, Frederick II., Schiller, and John von Müller, belongs to a later age. Kant's habit of demonstrating propositions *à priori* led him to ignore historical facts. He wanted to carry his mathematical spirit into history, and it is said, "A report which did not give time and place, however reliable it might otherwise be, he never trusted and did not think worthy of notice." In his "Logic" he shows that he was eager to discover and to teach those principles and methods which would enable their possessors to find what they wanted without burdening the memory; and he thought that the man who would sum up history under permanent ideas would be a praiseworthy genius, rendering special service to the human mind. He also says, "Teachers of reason are generally ignorant of history." In his religious views his effort to substitute reason for history is very apparent.

His contemporaries were not blind to his depreciation of history in the interest of *à priori* knowledge. Herder wrote to Hamann, "It is strange that metaphysicians, like your Kant, even in history want no history, and as much as boldly banish it from the world. I will carry together fire and wood, in order to make the historical flame large, even if again, as in the case of my 'Urkunde,' it should be the funeral pyre of my philosophy. Let them speculate in their cold ice-heaven!" One who studies Kant's writings carefully, cannot avoid the conclusion of a recent writer who says,

"At the same time, it is to be said that the historical element in its widest sense never received its full due at the hands of Kant, whose deficiency in the historical interest was remarkable." ([67])

However, in spite of these defects which only blind admiration can be disposed to deny, those who know him merely as the eminent speculative philosopher have no conception of his many-sided and extensive attainments. His most intimate friends were astonished at the breadth of scholarship and the philosophic depth revealed in his conversations, as well as in his lectures and books. In fact, he was treated as if a living library, and was consulted personally and by letter on the most varied subjects. His fame, however, rests mainly on his metaphysical works, and among these chiefly on his "Kritik." His influence on morals has been great, and his postulates have permanent value, but he did not succeed in establishing moral philosophy on a firm basis. In mathematics, physics, and astronomy, he is rarely mentioned now, except in connexion either with his metaphysical views or his cosmogony. He gave a new impulse to æsthetic studies at a period when the revival in literature made this impulse specially potent. His "Anthropology" and "Physical Geography," being popular rather than profound, exerted only a temporary influence, this being especially the case with the latter. But in metaphysics he attained an eminence unparalleled in modern philosophy, and the "Kritik" has deservedly made his name one of the most celebrated in literature.

CHAPTER VI.

HOME AND SOCIAL LIFE.

The philosopher's home—Regularity—Carefulness in trifles—Lampe —Dress—Recreation—Table-talk—Social power—Self-respect —Relatives—Views of woman and marriage—Love-affairs.

THE world has learned to know Kant as a toilsome student and a great metaphysician; what wonder, then, if it has regarded him as an ideal German professor who buries himself in his study, and disregards the world and its affairs, society and its attractions? Such a picture of the Königsberg philosopher is purely imaginary. Instead of being a hermit whose study was his cell, and whose sole companions were his books and his thoughts, we find that his interests, like his reading, were extensive and varied, that he was very sociable, was frequently in company, and exerted a powerful social influence.

For a number of years after he became a teacher in the university, he lodged in private dwellings, and Borowski speaks of five different houses in which he had his abode. His studious habits led him to seek localities and houses which were quiet, this being the more essential to him because he was so easily disturbed: but for a long time his limited means neither permitted him to purchase a house nor to choose just such locations as were best suited to his purpose. With respect to his rooms and surroundings he was particular and even peculiar. While lodging in one house he was disturbed in his meditations by the crowing of a cock in a neighbouring yard. Although he offered a considerable sum for the noisy fowl, the obstinate owner refused to sell him, as he could not conceive how a cock could annoy a philosopher. As the disturber of his meditations could not be silenced, Kant removed to another locality.

While occupying lodgings he dined at some public-house, the choice of which depended mainly on the probability of meeting agreeable company. One house he left because a guest was in the habit of speaking very deliberately, and with a degree of pathos, even when he talked of unimportant affairs. Kant found the presence of this man intolerable, and so he took his dinner elsewhere. He ceased to patronize another restaurant because some of the guests expected him to play the professor at dinner and converse on learned subjects, whereas he desired rest and recreation. At these public houses he liked to read the papers and discuss the news of the day, and in earlier years he also played billiards and cards.

In 1783 he purchased the house which was his home during the remainder of his life. It was centrally located on Princess Street, but not in a noisy part of the city, and had a small garden. There were eight rooms; his lecture-room, the kitchen, and the chamber for his aged cook, on the ground floor; his own rooms, five in number, were on the first floor, consisting of the study, library, the dining, bed, and reception rooms; the attic was occupied by his male servant.

His furniture was exceedingly plain, and it was evident at a glance that it was selected for service, not for ornament. In general a table or two, a few chairs, and a sofa, constituted the furniture of a room. His study contained a few tables, covered with papers and books, and also a chest of drawers. The bare walls of his rooms were relieved by no picture, save the solitary portrait of Rousseau, which was the gift of a friend. His table-ware and kitchen-utensils were also very plain, being merely such as were necessary to entertain a few friends at dinner. The entire inner arrangement of his house revealed a philosopher who was extremely simple in his tastes and mode of life.

While the home is not the man, its air is generally an expression of his spirit, especially if neither wife nor child disputes his supremacy. Our philosopher at home is so interesting to us because we there come into more intimate contact with him than in other relations, and also because we get views of him which are not so familiar as those of the eminent professor and the distinguished author. We, indeed, see him in his home only during the last twenty years of his life; but these are the years of his greatest celebrity. Kant was sole lord in his house, and his will was the supreme law. We must not be astonished if he is not found to have been the neatest of housekeepers, and if sometimes things were permitted to go their own way; there is a compensation in the fact that in most of the affairs he was sure to make his supremacy felt and to have his way. A bachelor has a right to poor furniture and black walls; but Kant was a philosopher as well as a bachelor, and elegance or annual house-cleaning might have interfered with his speculations.

About his personal habits, however, he was careful, and with respect to his appearance he was very particular.

It was fortunate for his purse that his happiness required no beauties of art. He blamed those who spent money for furniture which was not needed, and in himself he would never have excused extravagance in this respect. The whole house had a sombre appearance, the effect of which was increased by the deathlike stillness which prevailed during study hours. According to the testimony of Professor Kraus, "Kant's rooms were not only badly furnished, but were so astonishingly black from the smoke of the fire and the lamp, that it was possible for a person to write his name on the walls." Cobwebs are not mentioned, but they were no doubt there. What wonder if the scholar becomes attached to such things for their associations, and for the thoughts and symbols which he puts into them! His surroundings may become a part of himself, and the desire not to be disturbed may be applied by him to things as well as to his person. That revolutionary spirit which is eternally restless, and ruthlessly demands domestic change and renovation, was foreign to Kant; and it is a relief to find that the philosopher who regarded the old metaphysics as consisting mainly of rubbish that must be removed, was so extremely conservative respecting his mode of life and his home. Scheffner, another friend of the metaphysician, says, "The walls of his sitting-room were grey, being covered with dust, and with smoke from his morning pipe; and as at one time while listening to a conversation between him and Hippel, I made some marks on the wall with my finger so that the white ground became visible, Kant said, 'Friend, why will you disturb the ancient rust? Is not such a hanging, which arose of its own accord, better than one that is purchased?'" It is quite natural that Kant should regard as vandalism that spirit which takes pleasure in destroying the precious relics of antiquity.

During the first few years after he had his own home, he continued to dine at some public house; since 1786, however, he took his meals at home. In the evening he would give the orders for the dinner of the following day, which the servant, well aware how particular Kant was in exacting implicit obedience, was careful to execute to the letter.

One of the friends and guests of Kant gives a description of his home, and a picture of the philosopher waiting for the arrival of the persons invited to dine with him. His imagination saw even in the exterior of the building evidences that it was a thinker's home, which he describes as rather antique and situated on a street which was but little travelled, while back of it was an old castle, with its moat and gardens, its towers and prisons. "Both in summer and in winter the region was quite romantic, but this he did not appreciate." It is, however, the interior and the occupant which are of the greatest interest. "When one entered the house, it was found that a peaceful quiet reigned within; and if the savoury odour of the kitchen, a barking dog, or a mewing cat, favourites of the cook, had not convinced him of the contrary, he would have thought that it was uninhabited. When he ascended the steps the servant was seen to the right, preparing the table; the guests, however, passed to the left through a very plain, cheerless, smoked vestibule, to a room which represented the parlour, which was also devoid of ornament. A sofa, several chairs covered with linen, a cupboard with a glass-door through which some porcelain was visible, a bureau which contained his silver and his money, a thermometer and a console (whether under a mirror or under a bust I do not remember), constituted the furniture which concealed a part of the white walls." Passing through this apartment, "which represented the parlour," the visitor came to a plain door which led to what the writer calls the "Sans Souci," namely, the study. With a cheerful "Come in," the philosopher answered the rap on this door. The study had "an air of simplicity, and was a quiet retreat from the noise of the world. There were two common tables, a plain sofa, several chairs, and a chest of drawers under a medium-sized mirror; sufficient room was left for a passage to the barometer and thermometer, which he frequently consulted. The windows had small panes of glass; and the little green silk curtains which hung before them were perhaps the most costly articles in the room. Here, as on a tripod, the thinker sat in his semicircular chair, which was wholly of wood, either still engaged in study or else, because he was hungry, with his eyes turned to the door, longingly expecting his guests. Till the close of life he approached his guest from this place, opened the door and welcomed him. Wherever and however one might meet him, though the exalted expectations of the stranger who saw him for the first time might not be quite realized, his countenance was spirited, his look friendly; and when he spoke he delivered oracles and charmed his hearers. At the arrival of the guests, he would order his servant to bring the dinner, while he himself brought the silver spoons (called *the silver*) from the bureau, and hastened to the table. His guests preceded him to the dining-room, which was just as unadorned as the rest of the house." (68)

After the death of Kant, the house which had been his home for twenty years was sold and turned into a tavern, with a bowling-alley and billiard-room attached; and thus the quiet abode of the philosopher, which was so rich in the most interesting associations, became the scene of noise, confusion, and carousals. A marble tablet was placed in the front wall, bearing this inscription :—"Immanuel Kant wohnte und lehrte hier von 1783 bis zum 12 Feb. 1804." The name of the street on which it stood was changed from Princess to Kant Street. In the spring of 1881 the house passed over to a new owner, who intended to demolish it, to make room for another building.

Kant's manner of life was as simple as his surroundings, its most striking feature being its extreme regularity. The military order in his life was partly the result of his youthful training, and partly the result of the requirements of his health. In order that his body might be the fit instrument of his mind, he found that great physical and mental regularity was essential. He feared even slight changes, lest they should affect his health or interfere with his studies; hence he was rigorous with himself, and made his life singularly methodical. There was a painful anxiety in his strict conformity to rules, which at last got the mastery over him and excluded spontaneity.

He regarded seven hours of sleep as sufficient, and

accordingly limited himself to that number, until in old age when he found that more was necessary. Promptly at ten he retired, and his servant had strict orders never to let him sleep longer than five, however strongly he might plead for more rest. Five minutes before five o'clock, the servant entered his room every morning, with the stern, military call, "It is time!" And even in the rare case of loss of sleep during the night, Kant never hesitated a moment to obey the summons. With a degree of pride he would sometimes ask the servant, in the presence of his guests, whether in thirty years he had ever been obliged to wake him twice? His answer was, "No, very noble Professor!" He rarely slept during the day. "Half jokingly, half seriously, he would say, that as Mohammed believed that a definite portion of food was designed for each person, and if that was consumed rapidly death would come the sooner; so still more does this apply to sleep, which should accordingly be enjoyed sparingly, in order that one may sleep long, that is, may live long."

When the clock struck five, Kant already sat at the table in his dressing-gown and night-cap, over which he wore a small three-cornered hat. His breakfast consisted of weak tea and a pipe of tobacco. He took, he said, one cup of tea; but being absorbed in thought, and in order to keep the tea warm, he filled the cup repeatedly, and frequently drank two or more cups. He was very fond of coffee; but he regarded its oil as injurious, and avoided it altogether.

According to Jachmann, he spent till seven in the morning in thinking over his lectures; then he dressed, and lectured for two hours; at nine he immediately donned his gown, his night-cap, his hat, and his slippers, and studied from that time till a quarter to one, when he arose and called to his cook, "It is a quarter to one!" As he never appeared at dinner in his dressing-gown, regarding it as a slovenly habit, he would then dress and return to his study, to await the arrival of his invited guests. Even the least delay beyond one o'clock, the hour for dinner, whether on the part of his cook or his guests, made him impatient. During the meal itself he disliked haste, and generally spent three hours at the table, sometimes, when the company was large, still longer. This habit of sitting long at table was not confined to his own home. Hippel said, "Professor Kant liked to dine at my house, and more than once we sat from one till eight; this, however, was not for the purpose of regaling the body, but the mind." On rising from the table he usually took a walk of an hour. Between dinner and the walk he was careful to avoid sitting, otherwise he could not resist sleep, which he was determined to prevent. Neither bad weather nor any other circumstance was apt to interfere with his customary exercise. In summer he walked very slowly, so as not to perspire; if he noticed that he was about to do so, he at once stopped, because he thought that his constitution required that he should by all means avoid perspiration. And it is stated as a remarkable fact that even in the hottest weather he never perspired.(69) In his younger years he frequently had company while taking his exercise; in his old age he preferred to walk alone, because the conversation wearied him and made him breathe through his mouth, which he regarded as injurious. After returning home he spent the rest of the day in reading and meditation, or in preparing his lectures for the next day. This was his usual routine after he had his own table, one day passing like another. While he ate at public houses, and when as tutor he still had lectures in the afternoon, his life must, of course, have varied considerably from this outline.

The clock-like regularity of Kant's life surprised his friends, and became the subject of frequent remark. The poet Heine describes it rather poetically than with historical accuracy, as follows:—"It is difficult to write the history of the life of Immanuel Kant, for he had neither life nor history. He lived the mechanically ordered and almost abstract life of a bachelor, in a quiet, retired little street of Königsberg, an old city on the north-eastern border of Germany. I do not believe that the large clock of the cathedral did its daily work with less passion and with greater regularity than its countryman, Immanuel Kant. To rise, drink coffee,* write, deliver lectures, eat, take walks, everything had its appointed time; and the neighbours knew that it was exactly half-past three when Kant, in his grey coat and with the Spanish reed in his hand, stepped out of his door and walked towards the small Linden Avenue, which is still called after him, 'The Philosopher's Walk.' Eight times he walked up and down there, at all seasons of the year; and when the weather was unfavourable or the grey clouds portended rain, his old servant, Lampe, might be seen wandering anxiously behind him, with a long umbrella under his arm, like a picture of Providence.

"Strange contrast between the outer life of this

* Should be tea, for he drank no coffee.

man and his destructive, world-crushing thoughts! . . . The good people (citizens of Königsberg) saw in him nothing but a professor of philosophy, and when he passed, they greeted him kindly and perhaps set their watches by him."(70)

That he daily passed eight times up and down "The Philosopher's Walk," is probably a product of Heine's imagination; yet it can hardly be said that the poet exaggerates the undeviating regularity of Kant's life. It is extremely difficult to find a parallel to his methodical order and promptness. There is, therefore, a degree of satisfaction and a kind of poetic justice in the fact that in punctuality he found his match in an Englishman named Green, a native of Hull, but a resident of Königsberg, where he had an extensive commission business. Green was probably the most intimate friend of the philosopher, and was more a scholar than a merchant. In his extensive reading, the discoveries and inventions of the English particularly interested him, and he no doubt exerted an important influence in cultivating Kant's taste for accounts of travel and enlarging his knowledge of English literature. Like the philosopher, he was a bachelor, and his house also had three inmates, himself, a business companion, and a servant. Kant and Green, who were very fond of each other's company, agreed one evening to take a drive at eight the next morning. Green was a genius of punctuality, and it is said that on the occasion of such an appointment he would begin to walk about his room a quarter before eight, with watch in hand; would put on his hat ten minutes before eight, would take his cane five minutes later, and at the stroke of the clock would enter the carriage.

Unfortunately Kant was not on hand when the clock struck, and Green, who never waited a moment for any one, drove away. He had proceeded but a short distance when he met his belated friend walking rapidly. Kant greeted him and beckoned him to stop; Green returned the salutation, but at the same time bade him adieu and drove on.(71)

Even in trifles the great thinker sometimes manifested an anxiety which revealed his characteristic painstaking care. One day at dinner the servant broke a wine-glass, and Kant ordered all the fragments to be gathered on a plate and placed before him. Scarcely was dinner over, when he requested his guests to go with him for the purpose of burying the pieces, a duty which he could not entrust to his servant. A spade was brought, and the whole party entered the garden, to find a suitable place for interment. Every proposition to bury it here or there was met by Kant with the objection that it might one day injure some person. At last a secluded spot was found beside an old wall, a deep hole was dug, and in the presence of the party the glass was carefully buried.

No picture of Kant's house is complete, unless his old servant, Martin Lampe, is made a prominent figure in the background. In his way he was quite a character, and he was a very essential person in the odd household. As the cook ruled over the kitchen on the ground floor, with the cat and dog as her sole companions, so Lampe was perched on the attic, a symbol of his elevation to the position of general overseer, being the presiding genius of all the business of the house; Kant, the lone philosopher, was placed between these two guardian angels. In rigid routine,

Lampe was the counterpart of his master, an element which must have contributed much to the esteem in which the philosopher held him. He had been a soldier, and in the army had acquired that mechanical regularity which characterized his service of Kant for more than thirty years. Being careful to execute orders promptly and literally, and knowing how to adapt himself to the peculiarities of Kant, he had made himself very essential to his comfort. Unfortunately he was given to drink. His master was liberal towards him at first, but this encouraged him in his intemperate habits, and he was sometimes drunk in the presence of Kant, abused his trust, demanded additions to his salary, came home at unseasonable hours, and, in spite of promises to do better, became worse, and at last was regarded as incorrigible. Kant became very suspicious of Lampe, and regarding severity as the only successful method of dealing with him, he treated him quite harshly. Finally, just when his services seemed most necessary, he had to be dismissed. It was suspected that he had made an assault on Kant, who would never tell what he had done, but said, "Lampe has so acted towards me that I am ashamed to state what he did." He was discharged with a pension of forty thalers a year for life, with the condition that if he or an emissary ever importuned for more money, the pension should be withdrawn.

Lampe was exceedingly ignorant; but his long service with Kant made him conceited, evidently thinking that contact with the famous philosopher had enabled him to absorb considerable wisdom. It is said that Kant and he frequently disputed about the names of things, the titles of books, and the pronunciation of words: For over thirty years Lampe had been sent twice a week to fetch the Hartung newspaper; and to avoid the confounding of this with the Hamburg paper, Kant was always obliged to repeat its name to the servant; still he could not remember it, and constantly called it the Hartmann paper. Kant would order him to say Hartung; but the implication that he must learn its name from his master vexed him, and in a rough tone he would say, "Hartung's paper;" but the very next time it was brought, the name was sure to be wrong again. There was, however, one thing which Kant did succeed in teaching him, namely, who was king of England. Jokingly he would ask him in the presence of his guests, "Who is the King of England?" He was taught to reply, "Mr. Pitt." And it is stated that at last the notion that Pitt was king took such complete possession of Kant's own mind, that he wanted to know of no other King of England.

Not till his old age was Kant's bedroom heated in winter, but his study was kept very warm. Lampe had the most explicit orders about the temperature; but as he consulted the thermometer only when he made the fire, the study was generally too hot, a condition of things to which Kant became accustomed, and which he at last actually required, so that he wanted seventy-five degrees Fahrenheit, and sometimes even had a fire in July or August.

While Kant was all theory and thoroughly unskilful in mechanical affairs, Lampe was as innocent of skill as he was of theory, but possessed much rude force. As a consequence, both were apt to be perplexed over trifles, especially when things were out of repair. Kant would plan how to mend a broken article, whereupon Lampe would proceed to put the theory into practice; but by the application of excessive and unskilled force he often succeeded in reducing the article to a condition which put all future repair out of the question.

Kant was exacting, and demanded implicit and literal obedience. Lampe was not only required to manage the affairs of the house just as he had received directions, but also to appear before the guests dressed as his master desired. In waiting on the table he wore a white coat with a red collar; on one occasion, however, he ventured to appear in a yellow coat, instead of the regulation uniform. Kant was indignant, and ordered him to sell the coat at once, promising to make good the loss sustained in the transaction. Then he learned to his astonishment that Lampe was a widower, that he expected to be married again on the next day, and that he had purchased the coat as his wedding garment. This was a revelation to Kant, who had all along been under the impression that his servant stood with himself on the exalted plane of bachelorhood; and Lampe fell greatly in his estimation. It was not merely the yellow coat, instead of the white one with a red collar—but to think that the servant should have been married, and Kant not know it, and that he contemplated marriage again on the morrow without consulting his master! We are, therefore, not surprised to learn from Rink, "It is true that Kant was very indignant on account of Lampe's marriage, and it was the first cause of his dissatisfaction with his old servant." And in a note-book the philosopher wrote, "Lampe is a poor servant; first, because he cannot write, and second, because he is married, not only without my consent, but even against my will."

Kant paid an attention to dress which is scarcely to be expected from the hard student and learned professor, and least of all from the speculative philosopher. French fashions, as well as French manners, language, and literature, were popular in Germany. The courts aped Paris and set the fashions for the people; but after the French monarchy had been overthrown, these courts were less inclined to follow slavishly the modes of Paris, and the Revolution also introduced more simplicity of dress in that city than was characteristic of the old styles. Before that time, the French fashions had made bright colours common in gentlemen's apparel, and Kant's costume formed no exception to the general rule.

We should naturally expect our philosopher to appear in society dressed in black; but his friend Borowski states that he never wore black except when there was national mourning. Kant declared that it was better to be a fool in fashion than to be out of fashion, and this was his rule in the choice of his garments. Instead of regarding minute attention to such affairs as unworthy, he thought it showed a proper esteem for our fellowmen. Nature, he said, particularly the flowers, teaches the most important lessons in the choice of colours for garments; thus the auricula shows us that a yellow vest belongs to a brown coat. Jachmann says, "He wore a little three-cornered hat, and a small, blonde, powdered wig with a bag attached; a black necktie, and a shirt with ruffles around the throat and wrists; a coat, pantaloons, and vest of fine cloth, generally a mixture of black, brown and yellow; grey silk stockings, and shoes with silver buckles; he also wore a sword while it was still fashionable, but afterwards carried an ordinary reed cane. According to the prevailing fashion, the coat, vest, and pantaloons were bordered with gold cord, and the buttons were covered with gold or silver threads. This was his usual dress, even in the lecture-room, where the worn garments did their last service." To this strict compliance with the requirements of fashion his hat formed an exception. For over twenty years he continued to wear the same three-cornered one; at last he used it while reading, the brim being turned down so as to shield his eyes.

To another acquaintance of the philosopher we are indebted for a description of his dress in old age. "He was always neatly dressed; and his deeply serious face, his head drooping somewhat to one side, his regular though not too slow step, attracted reverential looks towards him. The bright sandy colour of his dress, which afterwards yielded to a deeper brown, must not surprise us; all kinds of bright colours were at that time preferred, and black was reserved for funerals and mourning. On warm days he went, according to the prevailing custom, with his head uncovered, his hat held on the gold head of his reed cane, a finely powered wig adorning his head. Silk stockings and silk shoes also belonged to the usual dress of a well-clad man."

We can even catch a glimpse of Kant's attire in his study. Count Purgstall, who called on him early one morning in 1795, states that he found the little philosopher at work in his study, in a yellow dressing-gown, a red, silk, Polish necktie, and with a night-cap on his head! (72) Over this night-cap he usually wore his three-cornered hat.

He was as particular about the portraits of himself as he was in the matter of dress. A Jew had made an engraving of him which so displeased Kant that he threatened to sue the artist if he sold any of the pictures. His anger was no doubt justifiable, for Hamann says that the picture made him look like a monster, at the sight of which women and children should cross themselves. When the sculptor Schadow sent an artist to Königsberg, to make a model of the aged philosopher, for a marble bust, the man asked Kant whether he should model him altogether faithfully? His answer was, "So old and ugly as I am now you must not make me."

Kant understood the rare art of making his relaxation the means of recreation as well as of culture. Between study and recreation he drew a sharp line, regarding the one as work and the other as play,—but he knew how to make the play profitable, using it to rest the mind and yet as a stimulus and the means of mental development. He who reduced the operations of the intellect to their laws was not disposed to leave anything to chance, but reduced conduct to maxims, and even gave rules for table-talk. As he desired the mind to have room for spontaneous activity at table and during walks, he wished to avoid the consideration of abstract and profound themes on such occasions, and to give free play to the imagination. Reading or meditation he regarded as injurious then, and he also says, "Music at the feast of great lords is the most insipid nonsense which gluttony ever invented." His delight at table was in lively and cheerful conversation, of which he gives the natural order as follows :—First, the news of the day, namely, home news, then foreign, whether received by letter or from papers; second, discussion of subjects; third, wit and humour, so that the repast may end with laughter, which is calculated to promote digestion. For a banquet, he gives the following :—A subject should be chosen which will interest all and give to each one an opportunity of saying something; there must be no dead silence, but only momentary pauses; the subjects should not be varied often, for at the end the mind takes pleasure in reviewing the course of the conversation; an entertaining subject should be nearly exhausted before it is dropped, though if the conversation begins to drag, one must understand how to iutroduce an allied subject; there should be no dogmatic spirit, and as the aim of the conversation is play rather than work, the tendency to be dogmatic should be checked by a skilfully applied joke; in serious disputes, which cannot be avoided, care must be taken that they are carried on properly, so that the disputants may not lose respect for each other, which depends more on the tone of the voice than on the subject under discussion.

Our philosopher knew how to practise as well as to formulate these rules. In order to make the occasion cheerful and to avoid being left to his meditations, he generally had two guests for dinner; on special occasions there were five, his household arrangements not being adapted to entertain more than six persons.(73) It was only on his birthday that this number was exceeded. He regarded Chesterfield's rule as excellent; namely, that the company at table, the host included, should not be less than the Graces nor more than the Muses; and he thought that for the most enjoyable company the number of the Graces should not be greatly exceeded. It was his wish that the guests should come for the special purpose of enjoying each other's company, not for the sake of the eating, which they could do at home.

For many years he ate only one meal a day, but that with a keen appetite. The dinner usually consisted of three courses, namely, soup, dried pulse with fish, and a roast, together with a dessert of cheese, to which fruit was added in summer. When he entertained a large company, an extra course was provided and also cake. Every guest had a pint bottle of wine beside his plate, red or white, whichever he preferred. Kant had the reputation of being a very hearty eater, but it should be remembered that for many years, aside from the tea in the morning, he took no other refreshment between his dinners. He always drank wine and water at dinner, never beer, against which he had a strong prejudice. If he heard of any one who died in the prime of life, Kant would say, "He probably drank beer;" and if the indisposition of a person was mentioned, he was apt to ask, "Does he drink beer at night?" He regarded that beverage as slow poison.

As a host, Kant made special efforts to please his guests, and noted their favourite dishes, in order that he might provide them when they appeared at the table the next time. In the invitation of his guests he manifested unusual delicacy, never inviting them on the preceding day, lest the acceptance of his invitation at that time might interfere with accepting any other invitation which they might receive; but he always invited them on the day their company was desired. For awhile Professor Kraus dined with him daily, Sundays excepted; yet Kant had him invited every morning, thinking that this was required by politeness; and though Kant was a regular Sunday guest at the house of au English friend, named Motherby (Green's partner), this friend, in deference to his views, was careful to send him an invitation every Sunday morning.

His usual guests, knowing his rigid punctuality, were careful to arrive in time; and promptly at one o'clock Lampe would open the door and say, "The soup is on the table." In passing from the study to the dining-room the weather was the usual subject of conversation, the theme being continued after they were seated. This was one of his favourite topics. He made his observations of its state with curious care, frequently consulting the barometer and thermometer, which were hung conveniently near for that purpose; he discussed the influence of the weather on health and mortality, and liked to have his guests speak on the same topic. Instead of regarding it as a hackneyed theme which should be excluded from society, he thought it the most natural topic to introduce a conversation. Other subjects might seem abrupt, but the weather naturally suggests itself when one has just come into the house, and especially is it an excellent and easy theme for young persons and those easily embarrassed.(74)

When seated at table, Kant would say, "Now, gentlemen!" which was the signal for beginning the dinner. He wanted his guests to feel as much at home as if in their own house; ceremony was banished, and each guest, contrary to the rules prevalent in society, was expected to help himself. Kant set the example of freedom from restraint, to promote which he sometimes used provincialisms, and encouraged his guests to do the same. As no ladies were present, the conventional forms of mixed society were the more easily laid aside.

Careful as Kant was to provide for the appetite of his guests, he was still more solicitous to promote their social enjoyment. In his estimation, hearty cheerfulness was the best spice for the entertainment, and towards furnishing this he did his part. Not only was he fond of talking, but he also had remarkable conversational powers; and even if his guests had little to say, he was satisfied if they were good listeners. Philosophy was usually excluded, since it required too much reflection, and he rarely made mention of his own books. It usually displeased him to hear unfavourable comments on others; nor did he like allusions to crimes or great evils of society, since they suggest unpleasant reflections. But he liked to consider the news of the day, especially if political in its character; medicine and sanitary affairs; accounts of travel, together with the peculiarities of countries, people, and individuals; general literature; and also ordinary topics, such as the preparation of food. His fondness for tracing etymologies, as well as for humour and the ludicrous, was displayed to advantage at the table. His satire was keen, but amusing rather than stinging. He understood the art of combining the serious and the ludicrous, without detriment to either. A rich fund of anecdotes was at his command; he told them admirably, relating with most pleasure such as took a humorous turn. His favourite Latin and German poets were also made tributary to the enlivening of the entertainment. Sometimes he became deeply interested in a subject, spoke with much animation, and for the time forgot his dinner. In fact, Kant was the most entertaining of hosts, as well as the most critical of philosophers, and his guests describe his table-talk with an enthusiasm such as could only have been inspired by a man of rare conversational powers. He surely must have had remarkable social qualities who daily interested, instructed, and charmed his guests by the hour. The philosopher was lost in the agreeable companion, and the isolated student in the man of society and the brilliant conversationalist. But what to him was a mere play of the faculties would to many others have been work; for in the close distinctions, the careful analysis, the broad generalizations, the sententious and wise suggestions, the philosopher would appear in spite of himself, so that even in his play he could not get out of the atmosphere of his study altogether. His ready memory brought to his command rich stores of learning gathered from various departments of literature and science, and the whole was illuminated and permeated by his genial spirit. Here, as well as in his books, the marvellous fertility of his mind was revealed. "Even on his guests he lavished an incalculable wealth of ideas; he often gave utterance to numerous sagacious thoughts, of which he himself was scarcely conscious afterwards, or which he did not think it worth while to expand farther or to prove."

While this daily meeting with a few select friends

occurred only during the last seventeen years of his life, he occupied a prominent social position for over fifty years. Before he had his own table he accepted invitations frequently; subsequently he found more pleasure in the company of his own guests than in general society, which he, consequently, entered only occasionally after he was sixty-three years of age. Company was a necessity to him, in order that he might give expression to his views and exercise his social nature. Rink, one of his guests, says, "For the last twenty-five years of his life Kant belonged to the world only during dinner; and then, too, he was, in a certain sense, in his study. The rest of his time was devoted to speculation, even when he was engaged in considering subjects of general interest. On this account his views were generally very attractive, those of the most ordinary affairs not excepted, and his conversation was as entertaining as it was instructive. But he gave himself to company rather because it was a necessity to him than for the sake of learning anything from society." Formerly he went into company in the evening; but these social entertainments generally lasted so long as not merely to interfere seriously with his studies, but also with his sleep, and therefore he generally avoided them in later years.

The circle in which he moved was not confined to scholars, but included persons of various occupations and degrees of attainment. Class distinctions were much more marked in Germany, during last century, than at present, and the nobility were more aristocratic and exclusive; but in spite of his humble origin, Kant's intellectual and social superiority made him a frequent and welcome guest in noble families, who felt complimented by the presence of so eminent and entertaining a scholar. In meeting merchants, seamen, military and civil officers, literary and scientific men, in society, he not only received new impulses, but also had an opportunity to use his varied attainments and to exercise and develop the popular elements of his nature. With all classes he became a favourite, and with some of the highest he became quite intimate, including generals, governors of the province, and the first of the nobility. Those who occupied the most prominent positions and held the highest rank were not ashamed to sit at his feet as learners and to do honour to his ripe scholarship. It is natural that his fame and his learning should have especially attracted men of intellectual tastes and aspirations, and he frequently associated with professors, students, ministers, physicians, authors, and booksellers, was free and lively with all, appreciated intellect wherever he found it, and his superior knowledge of men and his versatility enabled him to adapt himself to the most varied tastes and degrees of mental attainments. The world of children he scarcely knew except from his observation of them during his walks; nevertheless when he met the little ones in the homes whose hospitality he accepted, he made an effort to adapt himself to them, and was so successful in winning their confidence that they anticipated his coming with glee, and gladly talked to him about their studies.

While the speculative works of Kant give no idea of the popular elements in him, he wrote other books which reveal these qualities almost as clearly as they were seen in his social intercourse. That this dry metaphysician could also be sprightly and popular is evident from his book on "The Emotion of the Beautiful and the Sublime." Rosenkranz portrays the author as he imagines him to have appeared when this book was published, in 1764, at the age of forty. ([75]) "Kant, at the time he wrote this book and so diligently enlarged it, seems to have studied man in his empirical reality with much pleasure. The very contrast with his former abstract studies probably made his naturally naive and penetrating observation the more keen. Imagine the 'beautiful magister,' as they called him in the city, in elegant attire, when, his morning lectures being finished, he visited a restaurant before dinner, took a cup of tea or coffee, and played a game of billiards; picture him to yourself after this at table, entertaining his companions with his humour; and then, after he has worked again and taken his walk, see him in the evening, as Herder describes him, shining in all classes of society! Would one not believe that I am not speaking of last century, least of all of Kant, but of a philosopher of our own times in Paris?" The company which he entered, as well as his books, was a study to him, and it was the means of enlarging his views of human nature. The same author says, "It is astonishing how, without ever having travelled, he studied the whole world, and became acquainted with every people, with every class, and with every important city."

The time just described, namely, when he was forty years of age, was probably his most brilliant social period. Aspiring, spirited, and versatile, he was hearty in his social relations as he was profound in his studies. It was at this time that Hamann wrote, "Kant loves the truth as much as he does the tone of good society." Herder was his student during this period, and his enthusiastic account of the philosopher introduces him to us as a popular lecturer and brilliant companion, as well as a metaphysician. Much of his sprightliness and vigour were lost in old age; but his fondness for company and his social influence continued as long as he was able to enter society. We have a sketch of him in the social circle at the age of seventy, which represents him as still lively and entertaining. In 1794 one who belonged to the number of his guests invited him to his wedding. "Seated at table, opposite the bridal couple, he not only entertained them with continual conversation, but the entire company, which was pretty large, listened eagerly to his remarks made in a low tone; when he lost himself too deeply in thought, he would skilfully and gracefully change the current by means of a joke, which gave occasion for a laugh." ([76])

Another account of the philosopher about the same time, or perhaps a few years later, reveals him as he appeared in his own house. "He receives you kindly, converses on the most sublime or the most ordinary affairs, as you please, and does not become impatient at your long stay. How significant this patience is in the case of a man like Kant, you can imagine when you remember that his name is known from the rising to the setting of the sun, and his fame has spread everywhere; that nearly every traveller desires to see him, and that he rarely refuses any one this privilege; and that among these curious ones are, no doubt, many who know little or nothing of him except his name, and who think of the great Kant only as a giant. . . . If you come with a letter of recommendation, or if he takes a fancy to you, he will probably invite you to his small dinner-party; for he rarely eats alone, but has one or two friends, though never a large company. These small gatherings have this pleasant feature that, independent of what a dainty palate may find there, they have great attractions for the mind, since Kant makes a constant effort to entertain his friends. And when I tell you that this man unites a comprehensive genius with a great mass of choice knowledge gathered from all branches of science and literature; that his conversation is most agreeable, and that he speaks much and with pleasure: then you will readily believe me that a person cannot hear him enough, and that, without longing for them, one is reminded of the symposia of the wise men of Greece. He is particularly fond of physical geography and politics; especially are political affairs his favourite themes, or rather his recreation. A large part of his spare hours, especially Sunday forenoons, he spends in reading newspapers and other periodical literature. It is exceedingly interesting and instructive to hear his opinions of the subjects discussed, for he throws light on many points, and through his keen insight much which seems insignificant becomes highly important; he espies unsuspected causes of effects which seem to be altogether heterogeneous; and finally he draws conclusions from the present respecting the future, some of which have proved to be only too true. Especially must his remarks, descriptions, and anecdotes, respecting geography, particularly physical geography, rivet the attention of every one." The writer says that Kant is acquainted with the "situation, climate, government, and remarkable and peculiar features of all lands," and adds, "You can well imagine that every intelligent person desires and seeks the company and conversation of such a man. The first merchants of Königsberg seek to draw him into their circle, and he by no means lives like an anchoret in the lonely Princess Street. Gladly and frequently he enters society . . . and is, as it were, the soul of these social circles; for he likes to talk alone and to monopolize the conversation, which in others is generally regarded as a fault, but is gladly seen in his case." We are not surprised that the author of this sketch says that one would hardly believe this merry companion to be the author of the "Kritik of Pure Reason." (77) Indeed, this bachelor philosopher was declared by friends to be the most agreeable man they had ever met in society.

While a dogmatic tone in company offended him, direct and persistent contradiction angered him. His great attainments, his social position, his fame and influence, gave him confidence in himself and a supremacy which could not easily be disputed. If contradicted, he was sometimes free in showing his displeasure, and in giving unmistakable proof that his emotional nature was not wholly suppressed. Kant knew full well what was due to him, and he demanded from others that respect which he was himself ready to manifest towards them. In his advanced years he required that the strangers who desired to meet him at the houses of friends should first call on him, a rule to which persons high in authority were no exception. Nicolavius, Kant's publisher in Königsberg, invited him to his house to meet Count F. L. von Stolberg, who was on his way to St. Petersburg; but as the count had not called on him, he refused to go. When, however, on the count's return to Königsberg, he visited the philosopher, Kant accepted the invitation of his publisher to meet the distinguished nobleman.

A spirit of servility and expressions of excessive devotion and humiliation were common even among scholars. In proportion as genuine worth decreased, the love of its counterfeit, empty titles, seemed to increase, together with the tendency to use hyperbolical expressions of regard. Kant, especially in his later years, despised this spirit, whether it appeared in society or literature, and desired a politeness which was deeper than the surface, and a refinement in which there was truth and honesty, heartiness and independence.

But little can be said of the relation of Kant to his kindred. Between him and his brother there was no intimacy while the latter was a student. Borowski, who lived in Königsberg, says, "Here their relation and intercourse amounted to nothing more than that the younger heard the lectures of his brother Immanuel, and after the lectures they perhaps exchanged a few words with each other." For many years his relatives in Königsberg received no attention or recognition from him, and he rarely spoke of them to his acquaintances. Though he lived in the same city with his sisters, it is said that he did not speak to them for twenty-five years. ([78]) They had been servant-girls, and had married according to their rank; but however illiterate they were, and however humble their station, this conduct is surprising, and the most charitable construction that can be put on the matter suggests a weakness in this man who was so truly great in many respects. Jachmann attempts to explain this treatment of his sisters, by the statement that his studies and position had taken him altogether out of the sphere of his family; that he was at that time in such moderate circumstances that he could not give them the help which they probably expected; and that he feared lest he might prove a burden to them; but such reasons have little or no weight where there is any family affection. In his old age he held more communication with them, and also gave them pecuniary aid. He presented to each niece a wedding-gift, and bestowed a pension on his younger sister, as well as on the widow of his brother, giving annually two hundred dollars or more to his relatives, who also inherited the greater part of his property.

His younger sister was brought to his house some six months before his death, in order to assist in nursing him. She was six years his junior, and resembled him strikingly; in early life they had been much attached to each other. When brought to his house it seemed to require a special effort on his part to realize that she was his sister; when he recognized her as such he apologized for her lack of culture. ([79])

When we consider the breadth and depth of Kant's knowledge, his profound views of human nature, and his observations in society, we are surprised that in his views of woman he did not rise above the ordinary prejudices of the day. Her intellectual and social position was lower then than at present, though there are still many in Germany who have a mortal dread that the higher education of woman may transcend the limits fixed by nature for her intellectual development. Those who expect from Kant broad views respecting woman, must not forget to study his opinions in the light of that day; even then they will likely conclude that the philosophic bachelor, limited in his observations of humanity to Königsberg, early losing his mother, and avoiding all intercourse with his sisters, was not the man to do justice to woman. Touching many womanly qualities he speaks beautifully and justly, saying much that is apt and striking; but, taken as a whole, his views of her are unworthy of his great name.

In his book on "The Emotion of the Beautiful and the Sublime," he characterizes the female as the beautiful, and the male as, essentially, the noble and the sublime sex; and his effort to be consistent with this classification makes him unjust, so that he fails to discover the noble and sublime qualities so often found in woman. He regards the difference of sex as the peculiar charm of woman, and places a low estimate on her mental attractiveness. She may study profoundly, but it will be at the expense of her real charms. "A woman who has her head full of Greek, or who can dispute learnedly on mechanics, might also have a beard, for this would probably help to give more fully that look of profundity which she seeks to obtain." ([80]) "The beautiful understanding chooses, as objects of study, whatever is related to the finer feelings, and leaves abstract speculation or knowledge, which is useful but dry, to the diligent, thorough, and deep understanding; therefore woman will not study geometry."

His notion of woman's education corresponds with his opinion of her intellectual capacities and mission.

The view of a map of the world is to be made pleasant to her, and a general and superficial knowledge of the earth is all that women need. "Neither is it necessary for them to know anything more of the universe than is required to make a view of the heavens, on a beautiful evening, affecting, after they have in some measure apprehended the fact that there are other worlds than ours, and that in them beautiful creatures are found." Her science is not reasoning, but the emotions; and he says with respect to her education, "There should never be cold and speculative instruction, but always emotions, and these should be such as lie as near as possible to her sexual relations."

He does not regard woman capable of great moral strength, and thinks that she will not avoid evil because it is wrong, but because it is ugly. For women there must be "nothing of shall, nothing of must, nothing of duty. . . . They do a thing only because it pleases them, and the art consists in making them love only what is good. I scarcely believe that the beautiful sex has capacity for principles; and I hope that in making this statement I do not offend, for these are very rare even among men. Instead of these, Providence has put into their bosom kind and beneficent emotions, a fine sense of propriety, and an obliging soul. By no means let sacrifices and grand self-restraint be required. A man must never tell his wife if he risks a part of his wealth for the sake of a friend. Why should he fetter her cheerful talkativeness by burdening her mind with weighty secrets which belong only to him? Even many of her faults are, so to speak, beautiful faults."

When woman remained in what he regarded as her proper sphere, he spoke of her kindly and respectfully. Heilsberg, his friend from his youth, said, "He was no great admirer of the female sex, and declared that they deserved esteem nowhere except at home, and for their domestic virtues." Regarding their social influence as refining, he advised his young friends to associate with ladies of culture. He said, "A man has taste for his own sake; a woman makes herself an object of taste for every one." But while admitting this refining influence of ladies' society, he did not want them to converse with him on learned topics, and disliked to hear them speak about his "Kritik;" and though he spoke frequently and even passionately on the French Revolution, he did not want a woman to talk to him on the subject. Once a lady persisted in speaking with him on learned affairs, which he as persistently tried to avoid; observing this, she remarked that women might be learned as well as men, and that there had been scholarly women. Kant answered, "Yes, indeed, such as they were!" At another time, having discussed at length the preparation of food, one of his favourite topics, a lady highly esteemed by him said, "It really seems, dear professor, as if you regarded all of us as mere cooks." He then spoke of cooking and its supervision as an honour to any woman, and presented such cogent reasons as to win the favour of all the ladies present.

In society he frequently showed much attention to ladies, and gave evidence of fondness for their company. Nor was the critical philosopher blind to the fascinations of artless and beautiful young ladies; on the contrary, he took pleasure in conversing with them. He prized the presence of women chiefly as a means of recreation; and he says that the society of women is not intended for conversation which leads to reflection, but for the recreation of men. The ladies whom he appreciated most were those who were endowed with taste and with the power to charm, but who nevertheless cultivated the domestic virtues. Holding that womankind has a passion for dominion, he said, "Woman, because she always wants to rule, does not hesitate to marry a fool." Instead of seeking to rule, he wants her to be humble, retiring, and satisfied with her domestic sphere.

Sometimes woman was the subject of his playful humour. He compared her with a town clock, saying that she ought to be like one, so as to do everything punctually, to the very minute; and yet not like one in proclaiming all secrets publicly. Again, he compared her with a snail, declaring that she should be domestic and attached to her home; and yet she should not be like a snail so as to carry all she has on her back. Once he proved to some ladies that they could not get to heaven; for, he said, in Revelation it is stated that there was silence in heaven for half an hour, a condition of things which cannot be imagined where there are women.

Kant's views of woman were too common in Germany, during the eighteenth century, to occasion much surprise; ([81]) and they did not affect his position in society, nor did he forfeit the admiration of the ladies of Königsberg. His learning and fame, his cultivated manners and remarkable conversational powers, won their admiration. Countess Kayserling was only one of the many ladies who admired his superb talents and sought his company. After his death a noble lady wrote, "I have enjoyed beautiful and spirited conversations with this interesting and celebrated man. In the house of my cousin I daily conversed with this lovely companion. . . . Kant was a friend of this family for thirty years. . . . Often I saw him there when he was so entertaining that one would never have suspected in him the deep thinker who brought about so great a revolution in philosophy. In conversation he sometimes clothed even abstract ideas in a lovely garb, and he lucidly explained every statement he made. Charming wit was at his command, and occasionally his conversation was seasoned with light satire, expressed naturally and in the driest tone."([82]) In spite of his dread of learned women, some ladies studied his philosophy and became his professed disciples.

With such views of woman and with his depreciation of the emotions, we cannot expect exalted views of marriage from the bachelor philosopher; he, in fact, regarded it rather as a yoke for both husband and wife.([83]) The "Anthropology" says, "He who loves, may still be able to see; he who falls in love is unavoidably blind towards the beloved object; but in a week after marriage he usually regains his sight." He gave friends the advice to marry from rational considerations rather than for the sake of the affections; and he enforced his advice by relating the experience of a man who had married twice, his first wife chiefly for her wealth, the second because he loved her, and in the end he found that he had been as happy with the one as with the other. Kant thought that money would outlast beauty and all other charms, and would confer enduring benefits.

While he was not really averse to marriage, and sometimes even desired to aid a friend in the choice of a companion, he nevertheless extolled the advantages of single blessedness. His most favourite poem was an epithalamium, which praised celibacy, mentioning as illustrious examples the Pope, Democritus, Thales, Descartes, and Leibnitz. With special pleasure and marked emphasis he always gave the thought, "Permit me to say that I have no wife."(84) The poem closed with a special reference to the couple for whose wedding it was written, making them an exception to the general rule that single life is preferable to marriage. This close particularly pleased the philosopher, and he frequently quoted it when any exception to a rule was discussed :—

> "The rule remains, One should not marry ;
> But we except this worthy pair."(85)

Kant, the confirmed bachelor, might extol single blessedness ; but in his younger years he had doubts whether he himself ought not to form an exception to the rule that one should not marry. Even the critical metaphysician was not wholly a stranger to the emotion of love. One of his books, written at the age of forty, contains this passage, where he speaks of the charms of woman: "I do not like to enter into detailed analyses of this kind, for in such cases the author always seems to describe his own affections. Where the poet writes a sonnet to become master of his heart, the philosopher writes a treatise." It has been suspected that this was written when he was moved by the attractions of some lady. There are evidences of at least three love affairs, and there is no doubt that he had serious intentions of marriage. Once his heart was touched by a gentle and attractive widow, who was visiting relatives in Königsberg. Kant came to the conclusion that she would make him a suitable companion, and he would have liked to marry her; but he who was so prompt in other affairs, weighed this serious matter so philosophically, and to determine whether he could afford to marry, he estimated his income and expenses so mathematically, that while he was still trying to solve the knotty problems involved, the charming widow left the city and married another man. The second time he was captivated by a pretty Westphalian maiden, who came to Königsberg as the travelling-companion of a noble lady. She was clever and had received a careful domestic training, and Kant repeatedly gave evidence that he took pleasure in her society. It is probable that in theory it was already settled that she should be Mrs. Kant, but his matrimonial did not surpass his mechanical skill; he again delayed his proposal, and she was already on the border of Westphalia before he knew of her departure. At another time he was disposed to marry a lady who lived in Königsberg; but on a nearer acquaintance she lost her attractions, and he regarded her as unfit for his companion.([86])

While his heart may have held secret treasures of affection, those mentioned are the only cases known to have led our philosopher to the verge of matrimony. If he had been less deliberate, he might have had occasion to praise married life as he did the single state. After these three experiences in love affairs, he seems to have abandoned all thought of marriage, and sometimes he would leave a company in displeasure where, even in sport, he was exhorted to marry.

Some of his friends were solicitous that he should enter the matrimonial state; and one day, when Kant was already seventy, a friend entered his room and asked him whether he was not going to marry, at the same time presenting the advantages of the married state. The philosopher, however, treated the affair humorously. The friend then gave him a small pamphlet on marriage, declaring that he had published it chiefly in the hope of inducing him to marry. Kant took the pamphlet politely, paid the expense of its publication, and treated the whole matter as a good joke.

CHAPTER VII.

KANT AND HIS FRIENDS.

Views of friendship—Excellence of heart—Countess Kayserling—General Meyer—Green—Motherby—Hamann—Von Hippel—Scheffner—Borowski—Jachmann—Kraus.

KANT was too cold, critical, and calculating, to be ardent as a lover or a friend; and even if his emotional nature had been more developed, he lived too much in his speculations, and yielded too little to the impulses of the heart, to cultivate enthusiastic friendship. "He was never diffuse in compliments or in empty phrases, and least of all was he lavish in the effusions of his heart. His friendship always remained good, substantial prose." This statement of Borowski is confirmed by Wasianski: "Kant had adopted the delusive paradox of Aristotle, 'My friends! there are no friends.' He seemed not to give the expression *friend* the usual meaning, but rather to regard it somewhat as *servant* is used at the close of a letter." In speaking of him as an old man, he adds, "Till now he had been sufficient unto himself; and as he knew suffering only by name, he had needed no friend." But in his helplessness, Kant admitted that Aristotle's paradox is false, and that friendship is something real.

There were only two or three friends whom he

addressed with the familiar "Du" (Thou), which among the Germans implies special intimacy; and these had all been fellow-students. Even in their case this mode of address at last became distasteful to him, but he declared that it was then unavoidable. To his most intimate guests his relation was that of a kind, spirited, and familiar acquaintance rather than of affectionate friendship. In one of his books he says that a friend in need is much to be desired; "but it is also a great burden to be tied to the fate of others and to be loaded with their needs." Whilst it may be consonant with love to accept a benefit from another, he thinks it lowers esteem for self, and that, consequently, one prefers to bear his burdens alone and to conceal them from others, though he will flatter himself that in time of need he can depend on the assistance of his friend. Expressions like these, made when he was seventy-three, give an insight into his emotional nature, and create the suspicion that he had no conception of a love which sacrifices cheerfully, expects no recompense, implies no subjection on the part of the recipient, has its source in the very nature of the heart, and finds a rich reward in obeying its own impulses. Instead of an affectionate, he wants a moral friendship, which he defines as the full confidence of two persons in each other in the mutual communication of their private views and feelings so far as they harmonize with the esteem of each for the other. He in fact makes this esteem, and not affection, the essence, and affirms that this moral friendship which he advocates is different from the affectional. His friendship is rather a matter of maxims than the communion of soul with soul.

But while he was far from being demonstrative or impulsive as a friend, he was very kind, and at times obliging to an unusual degree. Childlikeness was one of his most marked characteristics; this made him frank and cordial, though the rules to which he rigidly bound himself restrained the expressions of his heart. His truthfulness, integrity, and sincerity, were crowned by a generous nature; but he had so disciplined this nature that its generosity ran in the grooves of maxims, instead of being a freely flowing spring bubbling spontaneously from the heart. While later in life the halo of glory thrown around him by his great fame no doubt helped to inspire that enthusiasm with which numerous admirers speak of him, the devoted and lasting attachment of so many can only be accounted for by admitting the existence of the excellencies of heart and mind which they ascribe to him. Wasianski says, "He was very humane, was free from all desire to domineer, was no one's enemy, treated his colleagues with confidence and friendship, aided young scholars with counsel and otherwise, and introduced young authors to the public by writing prefaces for their books." Jachmann's brother was desirous of studying in Edinburgh and travelling afterwards. Kant became interested in the project, and set aside five hundred thalers on which the young man was at liberty to draw at any time; and when he found no occasion to use the money the philosopher was disappointed. Having recommended a young man to a chaplaincy, he discussed the trial sermon with him several days before it was preached, so as to make sure that it would prove acceptable; and when it was delivered he sent a friend to the church to hear it, and immediately report the impression it made. For the same person he afterwards secured a position as teacher, and used his personal influence to secure pupils for the school. Many who were in perplexity or need were recipients of his kindness, and some of the letters from his students are filled with expressions of gratitude for the many benefits received from him.

Although he did not like to visit sick friends, he kept himself informed respecting their condition. When his friend Motherby was dangerously ill, Jachmann was required to report his condition, and the opinions of his physicians, twice a day. After the decease of acquaintances, he preferred not to converse about them; but when they were mentioned, he would say, "Let the dead rest with the dead," or, "It is all over."

During the life of the countess, Kant's intimacy with the Kayserling family continued. Hamann says of this family, "This house is the crown of our nobility, and is distinguished above all others by its hospitality, benevolence, and taste." Professor Kraus, who had also occupied the position of family tutor in this house, says of the table-talk of the countess, "She speaks incessantly to me alone; and of what, do you think? Of the theories of light by Euler and Newton; of the Edda; of superstition and unbelief, which of the two is worse; of new discoveries and new books. . . . . She takes all the French journals and does nothing but read." This countess, who of all women, his mother alone excepted, seems to have exerted the greatest influence on Kant, gathered around her the scholars, literary men, and nobility of Königsberg. Kant, Hamann, Kraus, Hippel, and other men of letters, besides the highest civil and military officers, were frequent guests in the Kayserling palace. In this illustrious company she took special delight in honouring Kant, whose talents and scholarship had received so much of their polish under her refining influence. In refinement and social culture he was adapted to the most elegant society, while in intellect and in conversational powers he surpassed all others who frequented this house. Here the popular and brilliant Kant shone to the best advantage. Unless strangers were present, he always occupied the seat of honour next to the countess. His position in this circle gives an idea of his social standing in the city, he being the most popular as well as the most entertaining and the most inspiring member of the most cultivated society.

His more popular lectures arrested the attention of the officers of the city soon after he became a teacher, and the governors and military commanders admired his scholarship and sought his company. In 1764 Hamann speaks of Kant's relation to General Meyer, who was commander of a regiment of dragoons and also governor of the province. "He is now lecturing on mathematics and physical geography, to General Meyer and his officers, which brings him much honour and is of great advantage. He dines with the General almost daily, and is brought to his lectures in a carriage. Swept along by a whirlpool of social distractions, he has a number of projects in his head, such as a system of morality, an essay on a new metaphysic, an extract from his geography, and a number of minor schemes, from which I also expect to reap some benefit. Whether the least of these will be accomplished, I still doubt." Hamann probably thought that society would interfere with his authorship. This union of social distractions and literary projects is characteristic of a large part of his life.

General Meyer was a man of unusual culture, and, like Kant, was a bachelor. He was fond of giving dinner parties, to which officers and the leading scholars of the city were invited. His partiality for Kant was very marked. The General laid special emphasis on dignity of deportment; and if anything unbecoming or unskilful was done by the officers at his table, he was not backward in expressing his disapproval. "Accordingly, one day they could not suppress their fear when Kant, who sat opposite the General, spilt some red wine on the expensive tablecloth. The General, in order to relieve the embarrassment, intentionally upset his own glass; and as they were conversing about the Dardanelles, he traced the course of the strait in the wine with his fingers. One aim was to show the officers that the scholar stood much higher in his estimation than they did."(87)

His most intimate friend was won in a peculiar way, and their first encounter promised anything else rather than friendship. Walking in a garden one day, Kant came upon a company in which he found an acquaintance with whom he entered into a conversation, in the course of which he spoke rather bitterly of the policy pursued by England. Suddenly one of the company sprang up angrily, and placing himself before Kant, he avowed that he was an Englishman, and declared that he as well as his whole nation had been insulted by the remarks made; and in his anger he demanded satisfaction by means of a duel. Kant, not in the least disconcerted, continued the discussion of the subject which had given the offence, and with such eloquence gave the principles according to which events like that should be judged, that the Englishman, quite astonished, gave him his hand, cordially acknowledged the justice of Kant's exalted ideas, asked pardon for his anger, accompanied him to his house, and invited him to pay him a visit. This was the philosopher's introduction to Green, whose pedantic punctuality has already been mentioned. (88)

Green had a good mind, was well informed, and read much; he was peculiar and even whimsical, but at the same time upright and noble. The esteem in which Kant held this merchant's intellectual capacities is shown by the fact that, as he informed Jachmann, he did not write a sentence in the "Kritik" which he had not first submitted to Green. For years the philosopher and the merchant were daily companions, regularly spending several hours together. Jachmann gives an amusing scene in connexion with their daily meeting, in which we find an exception to Kant's rule not to sleep in the day-time, though it may be that it occurred before he had adopted that rule. He went every afternoon to the house of his friend, who at that time could not go out because he suffered from podagra, and would usually find him asleep in his arm-chair. Seating himself at Green's side, he would give himself to meditation and also fall asleep. Generally another friend, a bank-director named Ruffmann, also came and took a nap. At an appointed time, Motherby, Green's partner, entered the room and awoke the trio, when they engaged in conversation till seven. So punctually did they separate at this hour, that the writer says,

"I have often heard the inhabitants of the street say, 'It cannot be seven yet, for Kant has not gone by.'" On Saturday evenings these friends, joined by a few others, generally remained together and took tea.

Green died in 1787, and his death is said to have seriously affected Kant's mode of life. After this he rarely went into company in the evening, which has been attributed to the loss of his friend; he, however, began about this time to have his own table and guests, and this fact more than any other probably led him to decline invitations.

Robert Motherby was another intimate friend of the metaphysician, who esteemed him highly and frequently accepted his hospitality. He had come from Hull to manage the business of Green, who preferred to devote his time to reading, and in the course of time he was made a partner in the firm. The sons of this merchant also became warm friends of the philosopher. In one of his letters, Kant speaks of Dr. Wm. Motherby as his special friend, just as his father had been, and adds, "Uprightness is his native character as well as that of his father." It was this son who, after Kant's death, proposed that his friends should meet annually on his birthday, to keep fresh the memory of the great philosopher. In associating with these Englishmen and with their countrymen, namely, the merchants and seamen whom he met at their houses, Kant had an opportunity to cultivate his knowledge of English literature and politics; and we know that he was not slow in improving such opportunities.

Among the literary men in Königsberg with whom Kant associated, John George Hamann was by far the most eminent. Our interest in him is the greater because we are indebted to him for many important hints respecting the philosopher and his labours. The rank assigned to him in literature is indicated by an article which appeared in 1853, in a journal published in Königsberg, where both he and Kant were born and where they lived and died. (89) It speaks of Hamann's fame as promising to surpass that of the Critical Philosopher, although during their lives Kant was famous and the "Magician of the North," as Hamann was called, was obscure and neglected. "Verily, while Kant's activity almost lies closed behind us, the present judges otherwise respecting the Magician of the North, who is now honoured as one of the greatest and deepest thinkers of last century." But since this was written, the revival of interest in Kant has again exalted him, and has opened a new and important activity for his philosophy, and promises for it great things in the future; and there can be no question that in intellectual greatness, especially in speculation, he was far superior to his literary friend. Hamann is, however, now receiving some of the merited recognition which his own age refused him, and his words have a prophetic ring: "One easily overcomes the double grief of being misunderstood and therefore abused by his own age, by cherishing confidence in the abilities of a better coming generation."

Hamann was six years Kant's junior, and died sixteen years earlier than the philosopher. Having completed his studies in his native city, he became a family tutor, and afterwards went to London on business for a firm in Riga, but was wholly unsuccessful. Becoming dissipated, he spent money entrusted to him by the firm, and became indebted to them to the amount of

300*l.* sterling. When on the verge of despair, he read the Bible and professed to have been converted "by means of a descent to the hell of a knowledge of self." He wrote an autobiographic sketch of his experience in London, giving a minute account of his career in that city, and presented it to one of his employers in Riga, at the same time asking for the hand of his sister in marriage. The man was shocked by the perusal of this confession, and as its author still continued the course of idleness into which he had fallen, his request was refused. The sketch created such aversion to him that the firm felt inclined to have him imprisoned for having wasted their money.

After visiting Riga, Hamann went to Königsberg, and Mr. Berens, a member of the firm, also went to that city. This gentleman became intimate with Kant, and the two tried to rescue Hamann from the gloom which had settled upon him, and to induce him to work and form regular habits of industry. Not only was he melancholy and shiftless, idle and restless, but he also insisted on continuing in his idleness and on letting his mind brood or revel as it pleased. Their efforts to induce him to change his mode of life incensed him, and to lead them to desist he wrote his "Socratic Memorabilia," in which Kant and Berens are represented as sustaining to him the relation of Alcibiades to Socrates. In this little book he claims that he must go his own way, guided by "the word in his heart," which is the light of the Gospel. Hamann warmly defends himself, and it is evident that, on account of his religion, he regards himself as superior to Kant, whom he does not think devout enough. When this book appeared, Kant was thirty-five years old, and had been a tutor in the university for four years.

Lindner, a mutual friend in Riga, interposed to restore harmony. The firm forgave the debt; and in spite of Hamann's passionate words in his book, he and Kant remained on friendly terms. In some respects they were antipodes. The metaphysician was cold, logical, systematic, and severely regular; Hamann was passionate and imaginative, a creature of moods and impulses. Kant made reason the rule of his life and the source of his philosophy; Hamann found the source of both in his heart. While Kant dreaded enthusiasm in religion, and suspected in it superstition and fanaticism, Hamann revelled in enthusiasm; and he believed in revelation, miracles, and worship, differing also in these points from the philosopher. In some respects they complemented each other; but the repelling elements were too strong to make them fully sympathetic. The difference in their stand-points, however, makes Hamann's views of Kant all the more interesting.

In the course of time Hamann secured employment as a secretary in a government office; but business was irksome to him, and literature largely absorbed his attention. Following the bent of his own mind while at the university, he had spent his time there chiefly in studying the humanities, instead of preparing for the ministry, as his father desired, or of studying law, though inscribed as a juridical student. After settling down in Königsberg, he devoted himself to theology, philosophy, ancient literature, oriental languages, and desultory reading. He was a voracious reader, the ancient classics and English authors being among his favourites. His mind was receptive and creative, and was easily aroused; his imagination was vivid, his heart passionate. While not the man to treat a subject exhaustively or systematically, he was original and had genius. Gifted with a keen prophetic insight and remarkable intuition, his writings are peculiar, rich in apothegms, dark sayings, and riddles. His style is his own; and the sententiousness, the real profundity, and the peculiar use of figures and symbols, make his books obscure, and there are passages which he himself did not understand some time after they were written; (90) but from the dark clouds lightning flashes give, as it were, revelations of nature, the heart, and divine things. Uniting in himself so much that is poetical, romantic, wild, and weird, he well deserved the regard of Kant, the high esteem in which Goethe and other literary men held him, and the name by which he is known in German literature, "The Magician of the North."

Hamann, who frequently met Kant, had a profound admiration for his intellect, and appreciated the excellence of his heart; but he was not blind to his faults, and never became an advocate of his philosophy. Kant aided him in various ways, and permitted his son to hear his lectures without compensation; Hamann recognized his indebtedness, and was so anxious not to offend his benefactor that he hesitated to criticize his books as severely as he thought they deserved. He wrote to Herder, "Through kindness to my son, Kant has put me under obligation to him, so that I desire, as much as you, to avoid all unpleasantness. Aside from the old Adam in his books, he is really obliging, unselfish, and at heart a good and noble-minded man of talent and of merit." They frequently discussed literary subjects. Both were more eager to talk than to listen, and as their differences were very marked, their disputes at times became quite warm; both, however, loved the truth and were sincere in their inquiries, and each respected the views of the other.

Soon after the troubles with the firm in Riga, Kant and Hamann, who had both been family tutors, planned to write a book for children, on "Physics." Hamann was, no doubt, better fitted for such a task than Kant, being better able to enter into sympathy with children. For some reason the philosopher dropped the matter, and Hamann, with considerable passion, and in an imperious tone, wrote to him, to reprove him for abandoning the project. Ho admits his learning, and recognizes him as a philosopher, but charges him with vanity and a lack of candour. Probably hinting that if Kant aided in writing such a book as that contemplated, he would accomplish something more useful than he had yet done, he says, "It is as easy to preach to scholars as it is to cheat honest people; nor is it a dangerous or a responsible work, because most of them are already so perverted that a venturesome author cannot any more confuse their mode of thinking. Even the blind heathen had regard for children; and a baptized philosopher ought to know that, in order to write for children, more is required than the wit of Fontenelle and a coquettish style. One would injure children by that which petrifies beautiful spirits and inspires beautiful marble." Evidently regarding the philosopher as too far removed from the simple nature of children to adapt himself to their needs, he warns him that he who would write for them must have a knowledge of children, such as neither the gallant nor the academic world can give. This was said when Kant was as brilliant in society as in the lecture-room. Hamann's severity is seen in the following: "The spirit of our book must be moral; but if we ourselves are not moral, how can we impart a moral spirit to our books, and communicate it to our readers? We should obtrude ourselves as blind leaders of the blind; obtrude ourselves, I say, without a calling and without necessity." This is probably merely a hint that Kant was not frank towards Hamann in this matter. Kant did not reply to these insinuations and appeals, and the project of writing the book, of which the philosopher seemed to think little, while Hamann regarded it as very important, was dropped.

Their temperaments and stand-points made such conflicts unavoidable. The impulsive, unreserved Magician could not put himself in the place of the self-possessed Critical Philosopher. If Hamann was one-sided, was Kant less so? Were not the qualities which had been excessively developed by the one, the very things which the other had neglected? In later years Hamann dealt less passionately with his eminent friend, and frequently speaks of him with great praise. He, indeed, thought that the remarkable fame of the thinker had made him somewhat vain, but for this he blamed him less than the public. Once he exclaimed, "How long was this great man obliged to be a tutor in the university! How miserable was his condition as a student! But with what modesty he afterwards enjoyed his great triumphs!" His conflicting views of Kant must be ascribed largely to the changes in his own variable moods.

Another of the more noted of Kant's acquaintances in Königsberg was T. G. von Hippel, an author of some repute, who by means of his indomitable energy had worked his way from obscurity and poverty to position and wealth. Like other associates of the philosopher, he was capricious; a strange man, in whose character apparently contradictory elements were constantly cropping out. Being unsettled in his plans after finishing his studies at Königsberg, his love for a young lady of rank led him to study law with great zeal and sacrifice, in the hope that he might gain a position which would enable him to make her his wife; but after completing this study he abandoned all thought of marriage, in order to devote himself completely to intellectual and practical pursuits. He wrote a book on "Marriage," and a play on "The Man regulated by the Watch;" but "the greatest eulogist of marriage remained unmarried, and the author of 'The Man regulated by the Watch' never possessed a watch. He loved money, but rarely had any; he collected the emblems of death, and placed them about him, and often spoke and wrote about dying, yet he was afraid of death; he found that life insipid which he was loth to leave." (91)

Kant, who was attracted by that which was peculiar and paradoxical, took pleasure in Hippel's company, at whose house he was accustomed to meet men like Hamann, Borowski, Scheffner, Jensch, a lawyer, Lawson, a poet, and Fischer, who was a preacher. Jensch was also a bachelor, as well as Hippel and Kant. Hippel's house was, in fact, a favourite rendezvous for the literary men of the city. He himself was greatly influenced by English authors, Fielding and Sterne being his literary models.

Hippel published a book on "Marriage," in 1774, and one on "The Course of Life," in 1778, both of which appeared anonymously. They contained so many thoughts which were afterwards found in Kant's metaphysical works, that it was suspected that he was either their author, or had aided in their preparation. After Hippel's death in 1796, Kant, being requested to indicate his relation to these books, stated that he took no part in preparing them; and of the thoughts which were so similar to his own he gives this explanation: "They gradually passed, fragmentarily, into the manuscripts of my hearers; but I could not bring these thoughts into a system until the period between the years 1770 and 1780. The notes of my pupils on my lectures on logic, morality, natural law, &c., but especially those on anthropology, were (as is usually the case when the teacher does not read) very imperfect. These notes fell into the hands of the deceased, and were sought by him because, besides the dry scientific elements, they also contained much that is popular, and which the enlightened man could use in his writings." There is, however, still another way of accounting for at least some of Kant's thoughts in these books. Hippel is said to have caught much of his inspiration, and to have taken many of his thoughts, from the conversation of the literary men who were frequently his guests, and is reported to have made arrangements to be called away from the table at stated times, in order that in a neighbouring room he might jot down the most important thoughts he had heard.

Of the literary men who frequented Hippel's house, J. G. Scheffner, councillor of war, was another strange character. He was twelve years younger than Kant, and was one of the last survivors of his friends, dying August 20, 1820. Scheffner associated with all the literary characters of Königsberg, composed military poems, made translations from foreign languages, and was the author of books, essays, and reviews; and through these various labours, and by means of his counsel, deeds, and social power, he exerted a great influence, and has been called "The Franklin on the shore of the Baltic." That like other friends of the great philosopher, he, too, was eccentric, is seen in his arrangements for his funeral. Some time before his death he had a plain coffin made for himself, chose the place where his remains were to be deposited, and arranged all the details of his burial. He even composed the hymns to be sung on that occasion, and named certain persons who were to be invited to his house a few days after his funeral, where they were to partake of a dinner and be of good cheer. They came, but felt their loss too keenly to enjoy the occasion.

Although Scheffner was not one of Kant's more intimate guests, he frequently entertained the philosopher, and he also visited him when too feeble to leave the house. In his Autobiography he relates an incident which illustrates the desire of the philosopher always to help himself and to be independent of others. "During a visit, made about a year before his death, he could not find the word he wished to use in the conversation. When I wanted to help him, he seized my hands, saying, 'No, no, friend! do not help me; my head must itself find it.' He then went over different expressions until he found the right one, which he accompanied with a well-satisfied "Do you see, friend?" His attachment to the philosopher was proved some time after Kant's death by his efforts to make the surroundings of his grave worthy of the memory of his eminent friend.

L. E. Borowski was not only a friend of Kant, but also his biographer. Having entered the University of Königsberg in 1755, the year in which Kant became a teacher, he heard the first lectures of the philosopher. He spent his whole life in Königsberg, became Archbishop of the Evangelical Church, the only functionary of that rank in Prussia, and died in 1831. His acquaintance with Kant for fifty years, and his residence in the same city, gave him unusual facilities for obtaining a knowledge of the life and character of his teacher. When requested to deliver an address before the German Society of Königsberg in 1792, he chose "Kant" as his subject, and sent the manuscript of his speech to the philosopher, stating his purpose, and requesting him to make erasures, remarks, or additions, as he thought best. Kant complied with his request, but at the same time expressed his desire that the address should not be delivered, much less published, during his life, though he willingly consented to let the manuscript become the basis of a biography to be published after his death. Borowski respected this desire, and after Kant's death he published the manuscript, with the philosopher's emendations, and added other biographical material so as to bring the history of the great man down to the close of his life. Of the various biographies of Kant, by friends and cotemporaries, that of Borowski is the most valuable, and peculiar significance is, of course, to be attached to that part which received Kant's review and sanction.

R. B. Jachmann entered the University of Königsberg, his native city, in 1784, became Kant's amanuensis, and remained in intimate relation with him for ten years. The philosopher, four years before his death, requested him to write his biography, and promised to lend his aid. Jachmann prepared a sketch of his life and, according to agreement, sent it to him for review; but the aged savant was already too weak to revise it. In 1804 he published an account of Kant's life and character, in eighteen letters; and although a critical spirit is lacking in them, they contain much valuable material. The author's enthusiasm for his teacher led him to idealize his subject, and repeatedly one finds extravagance and hero-worship instead of reliable biography.

Among the numerous pupils of Kant during his active connexion of more than forty years with the university, four or five are mentioned for whom he had a special regard. One of these was C. J. Kraus, with whom he became more intimately associated than with the rest. He entered the university at the age of seventeen, in 1770, the year in which Kant became a professor. Kraus heard all his lectures eagerly, and, like so many other bright and talented youths, became an enthusiastic admirer of his favourite teacher. Kant's instruction powerfully stimulated his mind, and excited doubts and inquiries about which he was anxious to consult his instructor; but the distance between professor and student was at that time greater than at present, friendly communications between them were more unusual, and Kraus was so modest that he did not venture to visit him for consultation. He, however, became a member of a society formed by Kant for the discussion of subjects connected with his lectures, and in one of the meetings he presented such deep thoughts that the philosopher, surprised at his unusual intellect, addressed him at the close in order to make his acquaintance. ([92]) Kant after this took a deep interest in the young man, and aided him also in other respects than in his intellectual development. Kraus became a tutor in the house of Count Kayserling, no doubt through Kant's great influence in that family. In 1780, though only twenty-seven years old, he was appointed professor of practical philosophy in the university, and from this time he was a colleague of Kant, and was frequently in his company.

While in some respects the teacher and pupil were remarkably alike, they were as unlike in others. Kraus, like his teacher, was very conscientious in meeting his engagements, and was prompt and punctual. Respecting dress their contrast was marked, Kraus being as negligent as Kant was careful. Through his teacher's influence he was induced to adopt the Kantian diet, and from dinner to dinner he took nothing but water. Kant, who was very economical and provident, advised Kraus to lay aside two hundred thalers annually, but he was careless respecting money as well as his apparel. As a rule, Kant was strict in demanding compensation for his lectures, though he permitted some poor students to hear them gratis. He said that by neglecting to pay, the students "become spendthrifty and unscrupulous; if they neglect and cheat their teacher, they will also learn to cheat other persons. The hearer of lectures who is obliged to pay for them, is in this way made more conscientious, and is always impelled to be industrious; but he who, through careless indulgence, interferes with the success of the private lectures, brings the university itself into a miserable condition, for no one in the world is willing to sacrifice his powers for nothing." Kraus, on the other hand, was careless about the pay of students. Once he gave private instruction in mathematics to two young men, for which each was to pay him forty thalers. When the course was finished, he said to one of them, who is called a thorough Kantian and a conceited echo of the words of the metaphysician, "I advise you, Mr. L., to abandon mathematics altogether, since you have no mind for it; from you I shall accept no pay." From the other, who had learned something, he accepted the money. On his own income, as well as that of the other professors, a suggestive remark is made by him: "Whoever devotes himself to the University of Königsberg takes the vow of poverty."

Professor Kraus was a laborious and successful scholar, and said that his ardour in the study of mathematics helped him to resist temptations. Like his teacher, he never married. Both were brilliant and spirited conversationists; but while Kraus laughed heartily, Kant scarcely ever laughed. "Even when by telling funny anecdotes he made all laugh who heard him, he remained serious." At the university they were the opposite poles, the one developing his strength in speculative, the other in practical philosophy. In religion their differences were very marked. Instead of ridiculing worship, Kraus declared that his religion consisted in two things, namely in worship and in doing good. A friend said of him, "His heart was full of piety, without any admixture of fanaticism. In his last years he probably stood on a higher stand-point than Kant for judging of the true nature of religion." There was in his case a beautiful blending of profound thought and extensive scholarship with a devotional spirit. Professor Kraus did not adopt the speculations of his teacher, and he vigorously opposed the mania which possessed many of the professed disciples of the Critical Philosophy. Quite a number on whom but a few rays of the system had fallen, imagined themselves to be wholly illuminated and enveloped by its light, and looked on other knowledge as contemptible in comparison with their *à priori* wisdom. But in spite of the folly of professed Kantians and the difference in the stand-points of the speculative and practical philosopher, Professor Kraus was attached to Kant himself. Not only was he, for awhile, the daily dinner-guest of the great metaphysician, but they also frequently met each other in society. They usually sat near each other, were about the same size and equally lean, and their brilliant conversation excited general admiration. Professor Kraus repeatedly gave up his journeys during vacation for the sake of remaining with Kant. A nobleman asking him to spend a vacation with him at his country-seat, he declined on the ground that if he accepted the invitation Kant would be left without a guest. At another time he wrote to the same gentleman, "I do not know how I can leave my father, Kant;" and at another, "I must spend this vacation with my old teacher, Kant."

For some unknown reason, however, Kraus at length resolved no longer to be Kant's guest; and one day when Lampe came as usual to invite him, he requested not to be invited any more, but assigned no reason. He had, indeed, often complained that the long time spent at the table was not agreeable to him; there must, however, have been other reasons which he was unwilling to communicate. Their philosophical differences may have contributed to the estrangement, especially since both were very positive in their views, and neither could well bear contradiction, a spirit which increased with age. Kant was deeply grieved by the refusal of Kraus to dine with him; he related the fact to his guests with some feeling, and discussed with them the probable grounds of the refusal, but could come to no definite conclusion. His feelings towards Kraus did not change on account of this withdrawal from his table. "He still continued to speak of the talents of Kraus with unusual esteem, and even with enthusiasm of his almost unparalleled learning; and just as little did Kraus let it appear publicly that their confidential friendship had cooled in a marked degree. Kraus still gave expression to his high appreciation of Kant, but in a manner less pronounced than formerly." Kant made more effort than Kraus to restore the former intimate relation, and in the course of time the latter also endeavoured to come nearer his teacher again; but he never spoke as frankly of his high esteem for his teacher as Kant did of his regard for him; they, however, treated each other cordially in company. Kraus was his guest on Kant's last birthday, and he continued to visit him during his feebleness, and entreated the customary guests of the philosopher not to forsake him now that he could no longer do anything to entertain them. The news of Kant's death greatly affected him; and on the day of the funeral Wasianski introduced him to Kant's sister. Deeply moved, he seized her hand to kiss it; she resisted, but tried to seize and kiss his hand, which he prevented; they then fell into each other's arms, and wept for the sake of the departed friend and brother. Kraus survived Kant several years, and died August 25th, 1807. After the death of the great philosopher, he spoke admiringly and affectionately of his teacher, benefactor, colleague, and friend, and showed his devotion to Kant's memory by always attending the celebration of his birthday.

There were many other friends of the metaphysician, some of whom are, however, so little known that nothing of interest can be said of them, and there may have been others whose names have not even been recorded. In the following pages, especially under the head of Kant's Correspondence, an opportunity will be given to indicate the philosopher's relation to some of his other friends.

CHAPTER VIII.

KANT'S AUTHORSHIP.

Subjects of his works—Pre-critical period—Book on the Emotion of the Beautiful and the Sublime—Prevalent systems of Philosophy—Leibnitz-Wolfian system—Popular Philosophy—Sentimentality—Descartes—Locke—Newton—Berkeley—Hume—First Metaphysical Dissertation—Literary activity, 1756-63—Dreams of Ghost-seers explained by Dreams of Metaphysics—Letter to Moses Mendelssohn—Period of silence—Correspondence with Lambert—Inaugural Dissertation—Sensation and Understanding—Time and Space—Letter from Mendelssohn—Letters to Herz—Labour on the "Kritik"—Changes in the plan of the work.

An account of Kant's books, and a full view of his metaphysics, belong rather to the history of philosophy than to a biography, for which they would require entirely too much space and too much abstract discussion. Nevertheless his authorship was so essential a part of his life that a reference to its most important features should not be omitted. Where a system contains so many works, and is so rich in thought, as Kant's, it is far more difficult to limit the discussion to a few pages than to yield to the temptation to quote extensively from the profound thoughts which constitute the Critical Philosophy. The following sketch aims only to throw some light from the works on the author, and to incite to the study of the books themselves and their valuable commentaries.

In examining his authorship according to subjects, we find that Kant wrote on mathematical, physical, metaphysical, æsthetical, theological, moral, and miscellaneous subjects. (93) His works not merely cover a wide domain of thought, and include the most important of the sciences, but they also aim to give the fundamental principles of all science and a critique of all thought. He never wrote on philology, his favourite study in the gymnasium. His first five publications, 1747-55, are mathematical or physical. During the next fifteen years, till 1770, discussions on these subjects still appear, but they are short, and the most important works are metaphysical, though he also published brief discussions on theology, morals, and æsthetics. Between the Inaugural Dissertation, in 1770, and the "Kritik," which appeared in 1781, we have only a few short and unimportant articles from his pen. With the publication of the "Kritik" a new period in Kant's authorship is introduced, that work making an epoch in his literary labours as well as in philosophy; nearly all his works written after 1781 belong to metaphysics, theology, morals, or æsthetics.

From what is known of Kant's life, and by following the order in which his books appeared, we can determine the subjects which occupied his attention in different periods. His preference for the Latin classics, under the influence of Heydenreich, yielded to mathematics, physics, and metaphysics, under the influence of Knutzen and Teske in the university, though metaphysics was still kept in the background. The impulse which he received in the university was followed by Kant while a family tutor and also a few years afterwards. Then he manifested a decided preference for metaphysics, to which he devoted years of absorbing and intense application. This is followed by a more practical period, when religion and morality, in which everything culminates, are made specialities. These periods, of course, cannot be sharply defined, since different subjects often engaged his attention at the same time; in general, however, it may be said that his authorship had a mathematical, a physical, a metaphysical, and an ethical period.

The first twenty years of his authorship belong to the pre-critical period, during which Kant occupies essentially the position of Professor Knutzen, namely, the stand-point of the dogmatic school of the Leibnitz-Wolfian philosophy, yet strongly influenced by the English natural philosophers, especially Newton, and also by Descartes, Locke, and Berkeley. Owing to the study of Hume, a brief sceptical period followed the dogmatic. About the year 1769 he broke entirely with the old metaphysical systems, of which he had long been suspicious, and which for years he had severely criticized; and from this time he began the development of his own peculiar system, the Critical Philosophy, which culminated in the "Kritik" of 1781. But even before 1769 we find suggestive hints which were forerunners of the philosophy that is peculiarly Kantian. While he remained true to the great principles of the Critical Philosophy to the end of his life, ([94]) and maintained its spirit in the works which followed, he strove especially to gain a firm basis for morality and religion, and hence we find that after 1781 great prominence is given in his works to the moral as well as the critical elements.

Many of his literary efforts were intimately connected with his labours in the university, and some of his books which were published late in life, such as his "Anthropology," "Logic," "Physical Geography," and "Pedagogics," consisted of his lectures, while others contained largely the results of his preparations for his academic work. The "Kritik" is an exception, being the product of study independent of his lectures, neither did he ever use its contents, as a whole, in the lecture-room, nor make it the basis of his instruction, as was done by many professors in different parts of Germany.

The prominent characteristics of Kant's mind are seen to best advantage in his books, which are an embodiment of his spirit as well as a depository of his thoughts. Taking all his books, we are struck with the mental breadth revealed by the variety of the subjects, with the extent of his learning, the profundity and fertility of his mind, his power of abstraction, and his freshness and originality. The ceaseless activity of his mind is seen by the great number of his books, which also reveal a constant mental growth, so that various stages of progress are distinctly marked. Sometimes his works followed each other in quick succession, and the amount of fresh, deep, and original thought in them is astonishing; yet many of his literary projects were either interfered with or wholly prevented by his academic labours and by indisposition, and old age overtook him when he was still full of plans for new undertakings. After a work had been published, he generally paid little attention to it, and rarely mentioned it, treating it as something with which he was done, and devoting his time and energies to the production of a new book.(95)

There is only one of his books which can be placed in the department of belles-lettres, namely, the small volume of 1764, on "The Emotion of the Beautiful and the Sublime." It is neither profound nor remarkable for new thoughts; but it gives us aspects of the philosopher which are unusual in his books, and more than any other of his publications reveals those qualities which made him so great a favourite in society. The book itself interests us less than the characteristics of the author which are revealed in its pages. It is descriptive rather than speculative, and psychological rather than metaphysical; in its value for æsthetics, as well as in its influence, it is far inferior to the "Critique of the Judgment." It abounds in antitheses, especially in those which indicate the difference between the beautiful and the sublime, and contains suggestive comments on authors and on national characteristics.

In the first period of his authorship Kant was regarded as a master of good style; and on reading this book we are not surprised that the students requested him to deliver lectures on German style, and that the Government proposed to appoint him professor of rhetoric and poetry. Many of the sentences are short, yet weighty with compressed thought; all is clear, much is beautiful, and free scope is given to the imagination. Between this and his later metaphysical works there is a striking contrast, which is not wholly accounted for by the difference in the subjects; it seems that his philosophical speculations spoiled his style. The sentences in his metaphysical works are often long and complicated, with numerous parenthetical clauses; the subject under discussion is dropped, side-issues are introduced, then the main thought is again resumed; the regular progress in the development is hindered by breaks which make the connexion difficult, and there are numerous repetitions. Much of the obscurity is, of course, due to the difficulty of the subjects and the unusual character of the investigations; but aside from these considerations, the style is such as to render some of these books exceedingly difficult and certain parts almost unintelligible. It must, however, be remembered that the German language had not yet attained its present stage of perfection, that it was comparatively new in philosophy, and that it needed development in metaphysical terms, though this of course does not explain the fact that his earlier style was better than later in life. It is a pleasure to turn from his heavier works to this one which has much that is attractive; though we may dissent from many of its views, especially, as already indicated, those on woman. We are delighted with the life and freshness of the thought, with the striking contrasts, with the fine distinctions, with the anecdotes and the humour. While generally we see Kant as he delved in metaphysics, we see him here as he played in literature.

A few quotations will help us to form a conception of the popular Kant. Contrasting the beautiful with the sublime, he says, "The emotions excited by the sublime strain the faculties more and weary them sooner than those aroused by the beautiful. One can read a pastoral poem longer continuously than Milton's 'Paradise Lost,' and De la Bruyère longer than Young. To me it looks like a fault of the latter, as a moral poet, that he continues too uniformly in a sublime tone, for the strength of the impression can be renewed only by contrast with softer passages." Tragedy arouses the emotion of the sublime; comedy that of the beautiful. "The sublime excites; the beautiful charms." "The sublime must always be great; the beautiful may, however, be small." "The night is sublime; the day is beautiful." Other contrasts are the following, though not found exactly in this order: "The understanding is sublime; wit is beautiful. Great heroism is sublime; cunning is little, but beautiful. Sublime qualities inspire esteem, but beautiful ones inspire love. Many a person is esteemed too much to be loved. The hero of Homer is terribly sublime, while Virgil's hero is noble. It is beautiful to be communicative, but thoughtful silence is sublime." In a striking sentence he condenses the contrast between the beautiful and the useful: "What a pity that the lilies do not spin!" Many passages are pithy, as when he says, "An insipid person, when conceited, is a fool." Among the striking characteristics which he gives of the different nations, this passage on the difference between English and French wit occurs: "In England, original wit produces heavy gold, which under French hammers is beaten out into thin sheets and spread over a great surface."

Having already considered Kant's earlier mathematical and physical works, we turn from this entertaining book to his metaphysical writings, in which our interest mainly centres, and of which the great "Kritik" attracts us most. In grouping his books, this one should be made the centre, and the others should be considered in their relation to this work;

especially is Kant's own development till the production of the "Kritik" interesting.

The philosophy prevalent in Germany when Kant became a teacher in the university was the Leibnitz-Wolfian system. Leibnitz, whose philosophical views were scattered through his works without being formed by him into a system, was a dogmatist in the Kantian sense, since, without preceding criticism, he held that by means of thought we can attain knowledge beyond mere phenomena. Believing that between thought and reality there exists a pre-established harmony, he of course held that a criticism of thought is not necessary in order to determine its relation to existence. While in this respect he differs so materially from the results of the Critical Philosophy, we find that on an important point Kant's earlier works agree with him. While Descartes and his followers held that motion is able to account for all material changes and manifestations, Leibnitz aimed to introduce the organic element into natural science by means of his monads which, as living forces, are everywhere at work in nature. Kant already in his earlier works also distinguished between the mechanical forces and the organic powers in nature, and emphasized the latter much more than was usually done by writers on physics in his day.

About 1730 the Wolfian philosophy began its almost universal reign in Germany. Wolf had taken the profound but scattered thoughts of Leibnitz and worked them into a system, a process by means of which these thoughts themselves were somewhat modified. The Leibnitz-Wolfian system rested on principles which were taken for granted, and on them superstructures were reared by means of mathematical demonstrations. This method was not merely applied to science and philosophy, but also to theology, morals, and the daily affairs of life. In the pulpit, as well as the university, this method gained the ascendancy, and in social circles the conversations were interlarded with logical formulas. In its efforts to reduce everything to demonstration, it introduced a new scholastic pedantry into philosophy, a lifeless mechanism which exalted the form at the expense of the substance, and which imagined that its conceptions were synonymous with the reality of things. Claiming to give apodictic certainty, it became the veriest dogmatism.

Wolf also aimed to give to morals a basis independent of religion, so that those who rejected religion would still be bound by morality. Thomasius, too, had tried to vindicate for ethics a foundation independent of religion. Wolf declared that "human actions are in themselves good or bad, and are not made so by the will of God; hence, even if it were possible for God not to exist, and for the present order of things to continue without Him, still the free actions of men would be either good or bad, just the same as if there were a supreme moral Lawgiver."

Imposing as Wolf's mathematical method might at first appear, its emptiness was soon discovered. Its triumphs had been the more easy and the more complete, because it found in its way nothing but a modified Aristotelianism in the form of an effete scholasticism, or else a complete chaos of philosophical opinions. Even though Wolf's system could not long satisfy deep minds, it succeeded in introducing a confident tone and a comfortable ease in philosophy. As the truth was imagined to lie on the surface, its discovery was thought to be easy; there was accordingly a lack of earnest wrestling with the fundamental principles of knowledge and the deepest problems of life. A popular philosophy began to prevail which was simply the product of ordinary or common sense; it was shallow and too easily satisfied, drew its conclusions too readily, and gave a fatal facility to the whole work of philosophizing. This spirit was encouraged by the prevailing tendency to popularize philosophy, in order to make it a commodity of the people instead of an arcanum of the schools. The deep and perplexing problems which occur to speculative minds in all ages, which lie at the basis of all thinking, and which no supposed solution has succeeded in finally settling, were then regarded as settled, and frequently they were disposed of in a superficial manner. Under the circumstances, the more earnest and profound minds lost confidence in the prevalent philosophy, and metaphysics was treated with contempt. Tieftrunk, a cotemporary of Kant, says of metaphysics, "One could hardly devote himself to it without subjecting himself to the suspicion of empty speculation, and without being exposed to the derision of wits." And another cotemporary says, "The deepest investigations had degenerated into empty words and fruitless speculations, at which intellectual men, and those who desired to be regarded as such, laughed." ([96])

There was, in connexion with this popular philosophy, a tendency to a reflection which turns everything into emotion. It was a sentimental age, over which Rousseau, Wieland, and kindred spirits, exerted great influence. This sentimentality is a characteristic of much of the German, as well as of the French, literature of the second half of last century. Parallel with this ran the critical spirit, negative in its results, and hardly conscious of what it wanted except to destroy. In religion there was general confusion. Great names were derided and estimable things were degraded; it was an iconoclastic age, and it was frivolous in its destruction. French Encyclopedists, Voltaire, and Frederick the Great, gave tone to the age; and French materialism, English deism, and German illumination, were popular. System and definiteness and certainty were as much needed in the religious and moral chaos as in philosophy. It was, in fact, a fermenting period in all the departments of thought; and in the development through the crises there was the general doubt, confusion, and perplexing uncertainty, which usually precede an epoch.

While the Leibnitz-Wolfian philosophy was dominant, we find that other systems received attention and are repeatedly mentioned by Kant. His "Kritik" in a measure closes the metaphysical development up to that time, and starts a new process of philosophical speculation. In considering this work, other systems should be taken into account, at least so far as they immediately relate to Kant and the "Kritik." The English and French were superior to the Germans in philosophy, and English philosophers, in particular, were popular in Germany. Not till the "Kritik" appeared could German metaphysics be regarded as equal to the English; and it is to be attributed directly to the influence of this work that the Germans have become so pre-eminent in metaphysical thought.

The new spirit introduced into philosophy by Bacon,

which turned the mind away from the useless speculations of scholasticism to observation and the laws drawn therefrom, animated Locke and his school, as well as Newton and his followers. While the inductive method of Bacon affected physical science most, the influence of Descartes was more directly metaphysical; and instead of substituting the study of physics for scholasticism, Descartes began a new metaphysical development. Beginning with doubt, he introduces the critical element, and turns the attention of the mind on itself, in order to make it give the authority for its thoughts and processes. He questioned the evidence of the senses, and even the mathematical axioms and the demonstrations built upon them. But whatever a man may question, behind all his doubts is the consciousness that he thinks; if, however, he is conscious, he must surely exist, and thus doubt itself is an evidence of existence. Hence the celebrated formula, "Cogito, ergo sum." In this we have, according to Descartes, a basis which is absolutely certain.

Every effect must have an adequate cause, a rule to which our ideas are no exception. Now we find in our minds the idea of a Supreme Being; ([97]) what is the origin of this idea? It cannot be the product of our own minds, for it is greater than we are. God Himself is the only adequate cause of this idea of Himself in our minds. But how did He communicate it? Our idea of God cannot have been given to us through the senses; therefore it must be innate.([98]) Descartes, however, has another proof of the existence of God, namely, the ontological one: the very idea of the most perfect Being implies the existence of that Being, for existence is a necessary attribute of such an idea; it could not be the idea of the most perfect Being unless that idea itself involves existence. He therefore thinks that God cannot be thought, except as existing.

In Descartes' system the fact of God's existence is of the utmost importance, and on it his entire philosophy rests. The idea of God involves that of truthfulness, as He could not be God without being truthful; but if He is truthful, then He must also have so made man that his ideas do not deceive him, must have created him so that he may see the truth. By this circuitous method Descartes at last finds a guarantee that our minds are made for the truth, and not to deceive us. From this there is but one step to the conclusion that whatever we clearly and consistently think must also have reality; or thought corresponds with existence. Hence the principle of Descartes, that whatever is distinctly and consistently thought concerning a thing is true of the thing itself.

Kant rejected his evidence for the existence of God, and with this the whole system fell. With all the criticism in the beginning of his system, Descartes is, in Kant's estimation, a dogmatist, since he accepts the existence of God without satisfactory proof. As far as the relation between our thoughts and real existence is concerned, Descartes' view of God's truthfulness and the pre-established harmony of Leibnitz amount to the same thing. After his critical period began, Kant could no more accept the philosophy of Descartes and his followers in France than he could that of Leibnitz and his disciples in Germany.

On turning to the English philosophers, a striking similarity is found between the general aim of Locke's

"Essay on the Human Understanding" and of Kant's "Kritik;" so much is this the case that the aim of the "Kritik" might be given in the language of the Essay. Locke says that it was his purpose "to examine our own abilities, and to see what objects our understandings were and were not fitted to deal with." He proposes to investigate "the nature of understanding," and he seeks "to discover the powers thereof, how far they reach, to what things they are in any degree proportionate, and where they fail us;" and he wants men to be more cautious about meddling with things beyond their capacity. These and similar expressions of Locke give exactly Kant's aim in his "Kritik;" but the beginning, the method, and the whole development of the two books, are totally different.

While Locke denied the existence of innate ideas, whether speculative or moral, he did not regard the mind as wholly passive or merely receptive, as seems to be implied in comparing it with "white paper, void of all characters;" but he attributed to it reflection, which compares and arranges the impressions, and draws conclusions from them. Experience is not merely the beginning but also the source of all our ideas. This experience is twofold, namely, that which we gain through the senses, and that which results from observing the operations of our own understandings, better called reflection. How is the empty mind furnished? Locke answers, "From experience; in that all our knowledge is founded, and from that it ultimately derives itself." Sensation is the means of experience from external objects, and reflection is the inner sense. "External objects furnish the mind with the ideas of sensible qualities, which are all those different perceptions they produce in us, and the mind furnishes the understanding with ideas of its own operations." The understanding forms complex ideas by uniting the simple ones given in experience.

That Kant was considerably influenced by Locke is evident from his numerous references to him; but in his earlier years, at least, he was much more indebted to Newton. This is not only seen in his work on cosmogony, but also in his first metaphysical dissertation, which aims to show that metaphysic is not in conflict with the natural philosophy of Newton. Locke's influence began later.([99]) While it may be impossible to trace the direct influence of Newton on the "Kritik," indirectly it was great. Kant originally stood on the mathematical and physical basis of the English natural philosophers, especially Newton; the influence thus exerted early in life was a potent factor in forming his mental habits, and in leading him to determine to make metaphysics as definite and as certain as the mathematical and physical sciences. It should be remembered that in becoming a metaphysician, Kant did not abandon his early mathematical and physical basis, but only enlarged it by the addition of metaphysics.([100])

Locke did not draw from his empiricism its legitimate consequences as fully as did some of his French and English followers. The sensationalism and empiricism which followed were met by another extreme, namely, the Idealism of Berkeley. Like Locke, he started with experience as the source of all knowledge; but he held that in sensation we have no direct knowledge of things themselves, but only of impressions made on our own minds. All our knowledge is, therefore, concerned only about these impressions, and does not at all deal with objects which are without us. Having then no knowledge except of that which occurs within us, how do we know that anything outside of us exists? Is not that which I regard as an external world, merely a creation of my own mind? May it not be the result of the influence of the Divine Spirit on the finite mind? Berkeley opposed to materialism the proposition, that the spiritual or the mental is the only reality. And surely, if our knowledge consists only of the individual impressions which are somehow made on our minds, Bishop Berkeley's view is rational, and his Idealism is as legitimate a conclusion from Locke's philosophy as materialism is. While Kant persistently denied the idealism attributed to the first edition of the "Kritik," and opposed the conclusions of Berkeley, he saw that the arguments of the idealistic philosopher could not be met by empiricism, and also agreed with him that we have no direct knowledge of things external to us, but only of the impressions made on our minds.

While materialism and idealism stood helplessly opposed to each other on the same basis, Hume, seeing the unsatisfactory character of both systems, became a thorough sceptic. He stands on the same basis as the systems which he rejected, namely, on Locke's sensationalism, admits no *à priori* knowledge, and declares that we cannot go beyond experience, since that is the only authority on which principles can be based. The essence of mind, as well as of matter, is unknown to us; both are known only from their effects or from the impressions which they make on us. Like Locke, he aims to confine the understanding to the subjects within its reach, namely, to experience, and he wants to check the tendency to give a loose rein to the imagination under the plea of philosophical speculation. He, accordingly, regards a scepticism which checks wild speculation as beneficial. Aside from matters of fact, he regards the relation of ideas to one another as the proper subjects for the investigation of reason. Algebra, geometry, and arithmetic deal with the relations of ideas to one another, not with real objects, and their truthfulness is self-evident; but judgments pertaining to reality are not so evident. Hume discusses especially those based on the conception of cause and effect. He views the category of causality as not obtained from the things themselves, as not a product of perception; we presuppose it without any demonstration of its validity. What we call causation is merely a habitual observance of a succession of the same phenomena, from which we conclude that there must be some necessary connexion between them, as that of cause and effect. But this conclusion is invalid, and we have no reason to believe that in reality any thing corresponds with this imagined connexion. What we regard as a real connexion is, according to Hume, a mere conjunction. We know nothing of the passing of what is called cause over into what is called effect; and we can know nothing of the supposed connexion between the two. The fact that we have never observed a change in the succession of events, is no evidence that there will be none in the future. Our faith in causality is still more shaken when we reflect that at different times and by different persons the same events have been ascribed to various causes.

Hume's scepticism is radical in its effects. It reduces our knowledge to isolated perceptions, and to the relation of ideas as in mathematics. A science of nature is impossible; at best, only probability, not science, is within our reach. Not only are we ignorant of external objects and of mind, except so far as their impressions on us are concerned, but also of their laws and of the connexion of phenomena. Besides, this scepticism also affects the deepest interests of religion and morality.

The hints here given are essential for understanding the influences to which Kant himself was subject, and which had a direct effect on the development of the Critical Philosophy. There were, of course, many other prevalent philosophical views which influenced him, as well as his system. Even if, in general, he did not make the systems of his predecessors subjects of special and thorough study, and misapprehended the views even of his favourite Hume, he was in the habit of seizing their fundamental principles and most pregnant points, and of subjecting them to the crucial tests of his criticism. In Hume it was the attack on causality which arrested his attention, and gave the direct impulse which led to the production of the "Kritik." Hamann wrote, "It is certain that without Berkeley there would have been no Hume, just as without the latter there would have been no Kant." And the Critical Philosopher himself frequently refers to Hume, of whom he had a very exalted opinion. In his Introduction to the "Prolegomena," referring to Hume's attack on causality, he says, "I freely admit that it was David Hume's reminder which, many years ago, first aroused me from my dogmatic slumber, and gave my investigations in the field of speculative philosophy a new direction." In meditating on Hume's problem, he found that the conception of causality was not the only one by means of which the mind conceives things to be connected; and he saw that it was but one of the categories which really involve the whole of metaphysics. He sought for all these categories, believed that he had discovered them, and concluded that they are not drawn from experience, as Hume thought, but that they are products of the pure understanding. In the "Kritik" he states that Hume's attack on the pure reason made a complete investigation of that reason necessary; but while the "Kritik" was occasioned by Hume's scepticism, Kant aimed at something deeper and broader than merely to meet Hume's attack, and he includes the entire domain of reason in his investigation.

Kant speaks in higher terms of Hume than of any other philosopher. He admired the finish of his style, his subtlety, and his caution; and in his "Kritik" he calls him "the cold-blooded one," who was peculiarly adapted to balance arguments. The fact that Hume undermined the proof of God's existence, Kant attributes to the desire to advance reason's knowledge of self and to make it more modest. He calls him "the celebrated David Hume," and "the geographer of the human reason," who thought that he had disposed of questions lying beyond experience by placing them beyond the horizon of reason; and he asserts that Hume was probably the most ingenious of all sceptics, and that, beyond question, he was the most distinguished philosopher who produced a scepticism which made a thorough testing of the capacity of the reason a necessity.

His praise of Hume is, however, not unconditional. Kant regarded him as chiefly worthy of note because he showed the unsatisfactory character of the sensational philosophy, proposed great problems, and gave impulses which were calculated to lead to their solution. He did not go deep enough; as Kant says, he struck a spark without kindling a fire. Hume continued in his scepticism; but the impulse which he gave led Kant from dogmatism, through scepticism, to criticism.(101) In his "Kritik," Kant speaks of this as the natural process for reason, declaring that its first stage, which marks the period of its childhood, is dogmatic; the second is sceptical, and indicates caution on the part of the judgment which has been taught by experience; but a third stage is necessary, that, namely, which belongs only to the matured reason. This is the stage which does not merely investigate the facts of reason, but reason itself *à priori*, according to its whole capacity and its ability to attain pure knowledge. This is the critique of reason, by means of which not merely limits, but *the* limits of reason are demonstrated, and not merely ignorance in one thing or another is proved, but with respect to all matters beyond the reach of knowledge. "Scepticism is thus a resting-place for human reason, where it can reflect on its dogmatic wanderings and can take a survey of the field it occupies, in order to be able henceforth to choose its way with more safety; but it is not a dwelling-place for constant abode, for this can be found only in perfect certainty, either of the knowledge of objects themselves, or of the limits within which all our knowledge of objects is confined." He says that the sceptic is the schoolmaster unto the dogmatic reasoner, leading to a healthy criticism of the understanding and reason. Here Kant evidently gives a hint respecting the process through which his own mind passed. When his faith was shaken in the Wolfian dogmatism, he could not rest in Hume's scepticism, but was impelled to master it and pass beyond it to certainty. The "Kritik" was the product of this impulse.

It is probable that the metaphysical dissertation of 1755 is the only one of Kant's works on metaphysics which was written before he was brought under the influence of Hume. Its statements are clear and precise, and its criticisms are fearless, the names of Leibnitz and Wolf forming no exception; but the youthful boldness bordering on presumption, found in his first book, appears less prominently here, and he does not thrust his antagonism to great names in the foreground. The fact that the dissertation was to be read before the philosophical faculty, and was liable to be attacked in the discussion of its various points, may have moderated its tone. With all his independence of thought, Kant in this production proves himself a disciple of Wolf's school, and it would be difficult to find in it even hints of the characteristic thoughts of the "Kritik," which appeared twenty-six years later.

But from the very beginning of his authorship Kant was dissatisfied with the prevalent philosophy, and in his first book he says, "Our metaphysic, like so many other sciences, is really only on the threshold of thorough knowledge. God only knows when it will pass over this threshold. It is not difficult to see its weakness in many of its undertakings. Prejudice is often found to be its strongest proof. Nothing is more to blame for this than the prevailing disposition of those who seek to enlarge human knowledge. They would like to have an *extensive* philosophy; but it is desirable that it should also be *deep*." This dissatisfaction runs through all his earlier metaphysical works; he criticized the easy and frivolous method of philosophizing, and was convinced that a revolution in metaphysics was necessary.

Many of the steps which led to the production of the "Kritik" can be traced in Kant's metaphysical works and in his letters. From 1756 till 1762 he published only a few short essays. During this time he was occupied in preparing and delivering his numerous lectures; this was also the period of the Seven Years' War, which was unfavourable for authorship in Königsberg. In 1763 he investigated the problem of causality, stating it very much like Hume, "How can I understand that because something is, therefore something else also is?" He does not solve this problem, but says, "I have reflected on the nature of knowledge, and shall, at some time, give at length the results of these contemplations. Until that time, those whose presumptuous knowledge recognizes no limits will pursue their method of philosophizing, to discover how far they can progress in the investigation of such questions."([102]) From this it is evident that he is approaching the critical problem. Kant sees difficulties which others have either overlooked or else expected to solve without going back to first principles. He is an investigator who wanders considerably in his search; but he occasionally catches glimpses of what he seeks, and slowly feels his way, in order to find the road which leads to the desired object. There are limits to our knowledge, and he thinks that he is on the way to their discovery, and promises to give the results of his contemplations in the future, a promise which was fulfilled in the "Kritik;" but it would be a mistake to imagine that he had already either seized the problem as given in the "Kritik," or that he had discovered the method of solution which he gave in that book.

If he still follows the thread of the Wolfian philosophy here and there, he frequently finds it broken or comes to knots which he cannot untie. His course is beset with difficulties; where others trip along lightly over even ground, he says that he sees Alps rise before him in his investigations. His task is so difficult because he is so critical and his aim so profound; he wants to get behind all the philosophical results already attained and to probe things to the bottom. In the same year, 1763, he says, "Metaphysic is, without doubt, the most difficult of the human sciences; but none has ever been written;" and he speaks of the bottomless abyss of metaphysic, which he calls "a dark ocean that is shoreless and without light-houses, where one must do as a seaman on an untraversed sea, who, as soon as he anywhere sets foot on land, examines his passage to see whether unobserved currents in the ocean have not turned him aside from his course, in spite of all the care his seamanship could possibly exercise."([103]) In the same book he also attacked various proofs of the existence of God, admitting only one kind as satisfactory, namely, a form of the ontological argument; his rejection of the other proofs excited attention and aroused considerable opposition.

Kant early penetrated more profoundly the nature of metaphysic than his contemporaries, and this made his aim, method, and results, so different from those of other philosophers of the day. Instead of regarding it as the aim of metaphysic to build on the generally admitted principles of knowledge, he thought that it should first of all investigate those principles themselves, and determine how far they are reliable and fit to constitute the foundation of knowledge. While others were intent on going forward without looking back, he wanted to go back to the very beginning and lay an immovable basis, in order that he might then go forward with safety. For understanding the aim of all his speculative work, a remark made before he was forty is significant, showing how profoundly he already at that time grasped the idea of metaphysic: "Metaphysic is nothing but a philosophy of the first principles of our knowledge." The problem of philosophy, as he apprehended it, deeply interested him, and he wrestled with it persistently, in spite of his slow progress towards its solution; and three years later he declares that he is in love with metaphysic, though he can rarely boast that the object of his affection has shown him any favours.

Philosophers were so much occupied with their conceptions, that they did not stop seriously to consider whether any reality corresponded with them. Instead of grappling with the difficult problem of the relation existing between a conception and its object, philosophers often identified thought with being. Kant, however, showed that the fact that an object is conceivable, does not prove its existence, but only the possibility of that existence. The question of the existence itself can be determined only by investigating the source or sources of our knowledge of objects. (104)

How steadily Kant was progressing towards the "Kritik" is evident from his book of 1766, entitled, "Dreams of a Ghost-seer explained by Dreams of Metaphysics." It is aimed specially at Swedenborg, but gives significant hints on all kinds of fanaticism, and severe thrusts at the dreamers in metaphysics. In it we find a union of profound speculation with playful humour. Next to the Inaugural Dissertation of 1770, this book is the most important for understanding that development of Kant's mind which led to the formation of the Critical Philosophy. He already classes Wolf among the philosophical dreamers, and regards him as a man who built with but little material that was furnished by experience, and for this reason freely used surreptitious conceptions in rearing his structures; and he regards Crusius as a man who constructed a system out of nothing, by means of the magic power of a few sentences about the thinkable and the unthinkable; and both of these philosophers he calls builders of air-castles. He sees that a crisis in philosophy is at hand, is sure that the dreamers will soon awake, after which philosophers will be able to dwell together in the same world of thought; his basis for this hope is in "certain omeus which have for some time appeared on the horizon of the sciences." With ghost-seers he has no patience, and he is an enemy of fantastic notions of every kind. He says, "I do not know whether there are spirits; yes, what is more, I do not even know what the word, spirit, means." And he adds, "The attempt to make serious efforts to explain the whims of fantastic persons makes a bad impression, and philosophy thereby excites the suspicion that it is found in bad company." Kant wants ghost-seers to be treated as candidates for an asylum.

Some of the conclusions of the "Kritik" are anticipated by this book on dreams. However boastful the assertion may seem, he thinks that he has finally established the fact that, while we may have *opinions* respecting spirits, we can *know* nothing about them. And he makes the significant declaration, that our philosophical doctrine concerning spirits may be complete and final, but only "in a negative sense, since this doctrine fixes with certainty the limits of our knowledge, and convinces us that the various manifestations of life in nature, and their laws, are all that we can know; but that the principle of this life, that is, the spiritual element which we suspect but do not know, never can be conceived positively, because for this there are no data in our entire experience; and this philosophical doctrine produces the conviction that we must be content with negations respecting the conception of anything so different from all objects of sense. But the very possibility even of such negations rests neither on experience, nor on arguments, but on mere invention, to which reason, deprived of all help, takes refuge." Thus he thinks that he has already so far determined the limits of reason as to be justified in asserting, that we can understand only phenomena, and their laws, but not what lies back of them, a conclusion whose demonstration is found in the "Kritik." So confident is Kant that he has finally settled that we can know nothing about spirits, that he says, "Henceforth I lay the whole subject of spirits, which is an extensive domain of metaphysics, aside as completed and settled. In the future, it shall no more concern me. While I thus limit the plan of my investigations, and entirely reject some altogether useless inquiries, I hope to be able to use my weak powers more advantageously for the consideration of other subjects. It is mostly in vain to apply the small measure of one's talents to all kinds of airy projects. Prudence, therefore, dictates that in this, as well as in other cases, our plans should be adapted to our capacities, and that we should limit ourselves to the mediocre, if we cannot attain what is great."

Since questions about spirits are idle, the reasons for or against their existence can "hardly determine anything respecting the future state of the upright. Neither has the human reason the wings which will enable it to part the high clouds which conceal from us the mysteries of the other world; and to the curious who try to discover these mysteries, the simple but very natural advice may be given, that it would probably be more advisable to wait till they get there." We know that we are related to beings like ourselves, by means of physical laws; but we cannot determine whether we are related to beings by other than natural laws. The heart contains precepts which should be followed for their own sake, and Kant decidedly opposes the utilitarian view of virtue, which really loves vices, but avoids them for the sake of obtaining a reward hereafter. The hope of the future may exist in a heart which still cherishes vicious inclinations. "But there probably never lived a righteous soul which could bear the thought that death is the end of all, and whose noble disposition did not rise to the hope of the future. Therefore it seems more proper for human nature and for the purity of morals, to base the expectation of a future world on the emotions of a good soul, than inversely to base the goodness of the soul on the hope of another world." Kant also argues in favour of a *moral* faith, which may be raised above all the subtleties of reasoning and which alone can lead a man directly to attain the true end of his being.

The two possible methods of knowledge, which play so prominent a part in the "Kritik," namely, the *à priori* and the *à posteriori*, are also discussed in this book. Kant says that some teachers of natural science claimed that all knowledge must begin with the latter method, and in following this rule they imagined that they "caught the eel of science by the tail;" but they soon discovered that this method was not philosophical enough, and that in adopting it they came to subjects which they could not explain. Other scientists began *à priori* with the highest principle in metaphysics; "but in this there is a new difficulty, namely, that one begins, I know not where, and comes, I know not whither, and that the reasoning will not reach experience." Instead of meeting and forming one system, it was found that the metaphysical conceptions and experience ran parallel with each other; and it seemed as if the philosophers had agreed among themselves to let each one begin and end where he pleased, and to reach at last just the conclusion he desired.

Metaphysics aims to solve problems respecting the hidden qualities of things; but the hopes excited are often disappointed in the solutions given. There is, however, another aim of metaphysics, namely, to determine whether a question can be solved, and to indicate the relation of problems to experience, on which our judgment must at all times be based. Referring to the second aim, namely, the determination of the solvability of problems, he says, "In so far metaphysic is the science of *the limits of human reason.*" This is significant for the view it gives of Kant's apprehension of the sphere of metaphysics. What he here defines as a province of metaphysics, he a few years later pronounced its propædeutics, and not a part of the system itself; but in his old age he seems again to have returned to a conception of metaphysics similar to that given in 1766.

If he has given no new views in this book, Kant claims that he has, at least, destroyed illusions, and that vain knowledge which inflates the understanding and holds the place which might be occupied by the teachings of wisdom. "Like Democritus, we formerly wandered about in empty space, whither the butterfly wings of metaphysic had taken us, and we entertained ourselves with spirits. Now that the styptic power of self-knowledge has drawn together the silk wings, we find ourselves again on the low ground of experience and of the common understanding. We are fortunate, indeed, if we regard this as our assigned place, which we can never leave with impunity, and which also contains all that is necessary to satisfy us so long as we confine ourselves to the useful." No bounds should be fixed to the desire for learning except the limits of knowledge; but from the innumerable problems which arise, it is the part of wisdom to choose those whose solution is important. In the course of time, science becomes modest and suspicious, and it says, *How many things there are which I do not understand!* But when reason, taught by experience, becomes wisdom, it says cheerfully, as Socrates did amid the goods of a fair, *How many things there are which I do not need!* What can I know? What do I need? These are the two questions to which reason and wisdom demand an answer; and the answer to them should be the limit of the sphere in which philosophical inquiry moves. There is here, as so often in his works, a union of the speculative and the practical interests; and if Kant makes any distinction in the importance of the two, it is in favour of the practical; for it is the matured reason which he pronounces wisdom, and this it is which limits itself to the useful amid the comprehensible problems. "In order to choose rationally one must first know what can be dispensed with and what is impossible. Science at last determines the limits fixed for it by the nature of the human reason. All bottomless plans, which may in themselves not be unworthy, but which lie beyond the sphere of men, flee to the limbus of vanity. Metaphysic will then become something from which it is now pretty far removed, and what would least of all be expected from it, namely, *the companion of wisdom.* For so long as faith in the possibility of attaining such remote knowledge exists, wise simplicity will in vain declare that such undertakings are useless. The pleasure which attends the increase of knowledge is likely to appear to be a duty, and it easily regards intentional and planned contentment within limits, as stupid simplicity which opposes the ennobling of our nature. In the beginning, questions pertaining to the spiritual, to freedom, to predestination, to a future state, and the like, arouse all the powers of the understanding; and on account of their importance, these subjects draw the mind into the contentions of a speculation which indiscriminately subtilizes and decides, asserts or contradicts, according to what seems most probable. But when the investigation is converted into philosophy, which judges its own processes, and does not merely understand objects, but also their relation to the human understanding, then the limits are drawn more closely, and those landmarks are fixed which never again permit the investigation to leave its peculiar territory. Some philosophy was necessary in order to learn the difficulty of comprehending a conception which is usually treated as very easy and as an every-day affair. A little more philosophy removes still farther this phantom of knowledge, and convinces us that it lies altogether beyond man's horizon. For in the relation of cause and effect, of substance and action, philosophy at first aids in untangling the complicated phenomena and in reducing them to simpler conceptions. But when the fundamental relations have at last been discovered, the work of philosophy is at an end; and it is impossible for reason to comprehend how anything can be a cause, or can have force, since these relations must be drawn solely from experience." Kant proceeds to show that it is impossible for the mind to understand how anything can bring about something that is different, that is, can be a cause. "That my will moves my arm, is no more comprehensible to me than if some one were to assert that the same can hold back the moon in its course; there being only this difference, that I experience the former, but I have never experienced the latter. I recognize in myself changes as in a subject which lives, namely, thoughts, choices, and the like; and since these operations differ from those which constitute my notion of a body, I naturally conclude that there is within me an immaterial and enduring being. But whether this can think without connexion with the body, can never be determined by reflection on this being, of which we have a knowledge only from experience."

These extracts show how rich this book on Dreams is in germs which were developed in the "Kritik." The prevalent metaphysic is vague and dreamy; it must be changed *in toto* if it is to rest on a firm basis; the limits of the reason must be determined, and speculation must be confined to them; consistent thought is no evidence that outside of the mind there is an object corresponding with it, but experience is the only sure evidence of existence; the whole domain of spirits and of a future life lies beyond the sphere of science; reason limits us to the knowable, wisdom to the useful: these and numerous other thoughts and hints are forerunners of Kant's *chef-d'œuvre*, which was wrought out after fifteen years more of severe toil.

A letter to the popular philosopher, Moses Mendelssohn, also written in 1766, gives additional evidence of his intense absorption in the contemplation of metaphysical problems. He regards, as he says in this letter, the metaphysics of the day with aversion and even with hatred. The welfare of the whole human race, he thinks, depends on metaphysics; for this reason he is grieved that it has so degenerated as to be useless and even injurious. The time has come when dogmatism must be destroyed, and when a sceptical method is necessary to free the minds of men from their fictitious knowledge. Since experience teaches us nothing respecting spiritual beings, the question is whether *à priori* anything respecting them can be determined? It cannot be proved that there are spiritual forces at work, neither can it be disproved; and Kant says in this letter, that if one were to attack the possibility of Swedenborg's dreams, he himself would undertake to defend that possibility. The question to be decided is, whether we can know anything of the nature of the soul that will enable us to determine its relation to matter as well as to beings of its own kind. Kant in this letter, as well as in the book, shows that he is deeply impressed with the fact that the reason has limits, and that he is intent on their discovery.

From 1766 until the appearance of the "Kritik," in 1781, there is a long silence, broken only by a few brief articles, and by the Inaugural Dissertation of 1770, which he was obliged to present in order to become a professor. As Kant had let the public hear from him frequently, this silence was ominous and naturally caused surprise. Lavater, the celebrated physiognomist, wrote to him in 1774, "Are you dead to the world? Why do so many scribble who cannot write, while you, who can do it so well, do not write? Why are you silent in this *new* period, and why do you let no whisper be heard? Are you asleep? Kant —no, I will not praise you; but do tell me why you are silent, or rather tell me that you will speak." The philosopher, no doubt, explained his silence, but his answer is lost. In Lavater's second letter, written in the same year, we find a reference to the "Kritik," seven years before its appearance. Lavater, who was a Swiss, wrote, "Together with many of my countrymen, I am eagerly awaiting your 'Kritik of Pure Reason.'" ([105]) Kant had probably written that he needed time to mature his thoughts, and Lavater says that he will curb his desire for the appearance of the "Kritik," if Kant believes that the work will be made more perfect by delay, and adds, "Thousands of authors do not carry their work to that decisive point which makes an epoch. You are the man to do this. Penetration, learning, taste, and that *human* element which so many authors lack, and which the prevailing criticism does not think it worth while to consider, characterize your writings to such an extent that I expect more from you, in this respect, than from any one else."

This period of protracted literary silence, when he was brooding over the problems of the "Kritik," is the very time when we want most of all to learn the processes going on in his mind. Fortunately his correspondence gives us glimpses of them, especially that with the philosopher and mathematician, J. H. Lambert. It was begun in 1765, by Lambert, who desired to secure Kant's co-operation for the improvement of metaphysics, and suggested that to this end they communicate to each other their thoughts on the subject. Wolf, he thinks, knew how to go on, but not very well how to begin; yet, "if any science should be followed methodically from the very start, it is metaphysics." It will not do to begin with endless analysis; the beginning should be made by means of synthesis, according to Euclid's method. Lambert expects much from Kant, whose mode of thinking he finds very similar to his own.

Kant answered with unusual promptness the letter of the celebrated man, who, he thought, could aid him more in his investigations than any one else; he accepts his proposal and proceeds to give an outline of his speculations. For years, he says, he has held his philosophical speculations in every conceivable light, in order to discover sources of error and to study the method of mental procedure, and he thinks that at last he is sure of the method which must be pursued to escape the illusion that a valid conclusion has been attained, which must, however, afterwards be rejected, and the steps already taken must be retraced. Since the discovery of this method, he at once sees, from the very nature of the investigations in hand, what he must know to solve a particular problem, and he also sees what degree of knowledge is determined by that which is given. The result is, that the conclusion is often more limited than is usual, but, at the same time, it is more definite and more sure. He intends to give all the thoughts referred to here, in "The Peculiar Method of Metaphysics," on which subject he had intended to have a book ready by the next spring, but he deferred the matter because he did not yet have all the illustrations which he needed; before publishing this work he, therefore, proposes to prepare some smaller books, namely, "The Metaphysical Principles of Natural Science," and "The Metaphysical Principles of Practical Philosophy." ([106])

In this letter he also states that the time has come when the old metaphysic, with its endless movement in circles, must perish, and he says, "You are right iu complaining of the eternal dalliance of the witlings, and of the tedious garrulity of the writers of the prevalent fashion who have no other taste than to talk about taste. But it seems to me that this is the euthanasia of false philosophy, since it dies with silly sports; it would be far worse if it, engaged in profound but false speculations, were to be buried with the pomp of a severe method. Before a genuine philosophy can arise, it is necessary for the old metaphysic to destroy itself; and as decomposition, which always takes place when a new product is to appear, is the most complete destruction, and as there is no lack of good minds, therefore the crisis in learning inspires me with the hope that the long-desired revolution in the sciences is no longer very distant."

From Lambert's reply, early in 1766, it is not only evident that his conception of metaphysics was very profound, but also that, in some respects at least, he was on the same track as Kant. Instead of hasty generalization, he wants the introduction of a more critical method which will limit the investigation to the knowable; and instead of being content with hypotheses which delay the discovery of truth, he thinks it better to acknowledge our ignorance; and instead of the complex in knowledge, he thinks that the simple should be sought, and believes that Locke was on the right track for its discovery. Comparing mathematical with metaphysical knowledge, he calls attention to the indefiniteness of the latter; when, for instance, mathematicians enter a field till then cultivated by metaphysicians, they are obliged to undo all that the latter have done, and, as a result, philosophy itself is brought into contempt.

Kant, with his usual neglect of his correspondence, did not write again till 1770, when he sent a letter, and also his Inaugural Dissertation, to Lambert. This letter contains a hint which justifies the conclusion that in 1769 the method of the "Kritik" had its birth.

"For about a year I flatter myself that I have attained that conception which I have no fear that I shall ever change, though I may expand it, by means of which all kinds of metaphysical questions can be tested according to sure and easy criteria, and by means of which it can be decided with certainty how far their solution is possible." But ten years more were still necessary to develop and fortify this method. Kant refers in this letter to various literary plans, all of which were, however, deferred till after the completion of the "Kritik." During the winter of 1770-71, he proposes to investigate "pure moral philosophy," in which no empirical elements are found, and also to systematize his "Metaphysics of Morals;" but this book did not appear till fifteen years later. Then he wants to submit to Lambert his "Essays on Metaphysics," assuring him that he will not let a single proposition stand which Lambert's judgment does not find perfectly evident; "for if it cannot get this approval, then the aim to found this science on principles altogether unquestionable is a failure." A book from him with this title never appeared; but it is probable that he intended to publish the critical thoughts thus far developed, in a book entitled "Essays on Metaphysics." He also states that he intends to give a preparatory treatise, whose design is to be the preservation of metaphysics proper from all admixture of sense.

Lambert, replying immediately, criticized the view of time and space given in Kant's Dissertation, and claims that, instead of being mere subjective conditions of knowledge, they also have objective reality. For some time he had tried to form a league of scholars to work out metaphysical problems according to a common plan, and to publish the results; but he was discouraged, because he saw from the catalogues that everything else was being pushed aside by belles-lettres, though he cherishes the hope that there will be a return to the profound sciences. It was his desire to make Kant a prominent member of this learned league.

As Lambert had begun, so he also ended this interesting correspondence. Kant never submitted the proposed Essays, and Lambert did not live to see the "Kritik." He died in 1777, at the age of forty-nine. Kant was waiting to let his thoughts ripen before submitting them to his friend, after whose death he wrote, "I had some ideas of a possible improvement in metaphysics, which I desired to mature in order to send them for criticism and development to my deeply penetrating friend. All the hopes which I had based on so important a help vanished at the unexpected death of this extraordinary genius." He had expected much from a union of Lambert's efforts with his own for the production of something reliable and complete; while he does not now despair of accomplishing this, he regards it as more tedious and more difficult since he is deprived of the assistance of so great a mind.

This correspondence is but one of the many evidences that the speculations of Kant were timely, and that the "Kritik," however striking the contrast between it and other works of the period, was really a product of the age. Other deep thinkers, beside Kant, felt the need of a change in metaphysics; and Lambert at least was pursuing a track which was similar to that which led to the Critical Philosophy. Numerous historical threads are seen in the literature and tendencies of the age, all of which run to the "Kritik."

The Inaugural Dissertation of 1770, "On the Form and Principles of the Sensible and the Intelligible World," is of the utmost importance in tracing the development of the "Kritik." While heretofore the spirit and the tendency of Kant's writings have chiefly interested us, it is different with this Dissertation. It was presented to the philosophical faculty when he became professor of logic and metaphysics, and we naturally look for a positive statement of his metaphysical views. As he discusses the sense and the understanding, we expect to learn definitely his view of these faculties. Philosophers, at that time, generally made the distinction between the two a difference in degree, not in kind; one of quantity, not of quality. It was thought that the objects of both are the same, but that in sensation these objects are presented to the mind with less clearness than in the understanding. But, according to Kant, the understanding does not differ from the sense in the degree of clearness with which it presents objects, but there is a difference in kind.([107]) Sensation is the receptivity of the subject which enables it to receive impressions from external objects; the understanding is the ability of the subject to represent to itself that which, according to its very nature, cannot be an object of the senses. The two, therefore, have different objects, and Kant says, "The object of the senses is the sensible; but whatever contains nothing except that which can be understood only by the understanding, is the intelligible. In the schools, the former was called by the ancients *Phenomenon*, the latter *Noumenon*." Sensation gives only representations of things as they seem to be; but the understanding gives representations of things as they are. He also indicates the difference in the origin of the objects of sense and those of the understanding. While sensation receives its impressions from external things, the understanding receives its objects neither from these nor from the sensations, but they are the product of the understanding itself. To the latter, for instance, belong all moral conceptions, which are not learned from experience, but originate in the understanding. Kant thus makes a real distinction, in origin as well as in kind, between the perceptions of sense and the conceptions of the understanding, and says, "I fear, therefore, that Wolf, who held that the difference between that which is perceived and that which is a product of the understanding is only logical, brought the celebrated investigations of antiquity respecting the nature of phenomena and noumena into oblivion, to the great disadvantage of philosophy; for in turning the attention away from this investigation he has frequently directed it to mere trifles."

The "Kritik" itself must be studied in order to see the far-reaching consequences of this distinction between these two faculties. Kuno Fischer says, "The difference thus established between sensation and understanding is the first insight of the critical philosophy." Already in this dissertation Kant assigns to each faculty its own world, and the distinction which he makes, gives him a new definition of metaphysics. In 1766 he defined it as the philosophy of the first principles of our knowledge; now he defines it as the philosophy which contains the principles of the use of the pure understanding. (108) The science preparatory to metaphysics is the one which teaches the difference between the knowledge obtained through the sense, and that obtained through the understanding; and this dissertation is an essay to give the propædeutics to metaphysics.

There are no empirical elements in metaphysics; therefore its conceptions are not to be sought in sensation, but in the nature of pure understanding. While Kant rejects the doctrine of innate ideas, he holds that the conditions for the production of the objects of the understanding are in the understanding itself, and that its activity need but be properly aroused in order to produce its conceptions; the very laws of thought will evolve them. These conceptions are, therefore, acquired, being learned by observing the activity of the mind; and they are such as possibility, reality, substance, cause, and the like, with their opposites or correlatives. They do not inhere in any sensible representations, are not elements of such representations, and therefore cannot possibly be abstracted or drawn from them. But if not produced by sensation, they must be the product of the mind itself.

More remarkable than this distinction between sense and understanding, is Kant's peculiar view of time and space, given here for the first time; a view which plays so conspicuous a part in his philosophy, which met with so much opposition when first announced, and which has been the subject of a long controversy that is not yet ended. Only two years before the dissertation appeared, he had declared that space is not merely an object of thought, but also something external to the mind; (109) at that time, therefore, the theory of time and space contained in the Critical Philosophy was not yet formed. But in this dissertation it is given with unmistakable clearness, and it is interesting to examine the first statement of this important theory. Respecting time, his first proposition is, "The notion of time does not arise from the senses, but is presupposed by them;" he thus rejects the prevalent view that our notion of time is drawn from experience, namely, by observing the series of events or things following one another. Before we can get a conception of things as existing at the same time or successively, we must first have the notion of time itself. In fact, all our conceptions of things occurring in time presuppose the notion of time; therefore this notion, instead of arising from experience, must precede our knowledge of things in time.

"Time is nothing objective, nothing real, no substance, no accident, no relation; but it is a subjective condition which, from the very nature of the mind, makes it necessary to co-ordinate all things according to a certain law, and it is a pure intuition." While time is only an imaginary thing (*ens imaginarium*), it is nevertheless absolutely necessary as a condition for the perception of objects. It is a primitive and original perception. Time is absolutely the first formal principle of the sensible world; (110) for sensible things can be perceived only either simultaneously or successively.

His theory of space and its relation to perception is similar to that of time. His first proposition is, that the notion of space, like that of time, is not drawn from experience. We cannot perceive an object except as in space; therefore the possibility of the perception of external objects presupposes the notion of space, and, consequently, this perception cannot create that notion. Only what is in space can affect the senses; space itself cannot.

His second proposition is, that, like time, space is an individual perception which includes all spaces within itself, not under it as the general includes the particular. ([111]) Several spaces are only parts of one immeasurable space; therefore the parts of space are not related to space itself as species and genus, but simply as parts to a whole.

His third proposition is, that the notion of space is a pure perception, for it is a single perception, not one compounded from experience; it is the ground-form for the perception of all external objects.

Fourth proposition: "Space is nothing objective and real, is no substance, no accident, no relation; but it is subjective and ideal, and emanates from the nature of the mind according to an unalterable law; it is, so to speak, the form for the co-ordination of all that is experienced from without."

In his last proposition Kant states that while space is merely imaginary, it nevertheless contains real truth in relation to all sensible things, and is the basis of all knowledge respecting the external world; for objects can appear to the senses only by means of that power of the mind which co-ordinates the experiences according to an unalterable law implanted in its nature. We can perceive an object of the senses only according to the original axioms of space and the conclusions drawn from them. The notion of space, like that of time, is, accordingly, the condition for the perception of all sensible objects. (112) And the notion of space, as well as of time, is learned from the action of the mind, and is not in any way drawn from objects. (113) While thus Kant does not make the notions of space and time innate, the law according to which the mind acts, and from which they arise, is of course innate.

Academic dissertations generally receive but little attention, and that may be a reason why this significant one did not excite more interest. Nor was the abstract nature of the discussion calculated to attract many readers. Evidently the fact was not appreciated that there were germs in Kant's dissertation which need only be developed and applied in order to produce a revolution in metaphysics. But there was at least one mind which suspected that its author had in reserve a whole system, of which he now gave only hints. Moses Mendelssohn read the dissertation with great pleasure, as he states in a letter to Kant; though, on account of the weak state of his nerves, he was hardly able to grasp anything so profoundly speculative. However, he had the acuteness to see that it was the forerunner of a new system, and wrote to Kant, "One sees that this little book is the result of very long meditation, and that it must be viewed as part of a whole system which is peculiar to the author, and of which he is willing at present to exhibit only a few specimens. Even the apparent obscurity of some parts leads the skilful reader to suspect that there is an entire system which is not yet presented to him. In the meanwhile, it would be to the advantage of metaphysics, which now, alas! has so degenerated, if you would not withhold too long your present supply of meditations. Life is short; and while one still cherishes the hope of improving it, how soon the end approaches! And why do you so greatly fear to repeat what has already been said before you? In connexion with the thoughts peculiarly your own, even the old always appears in a new light, and gives views which were not thought of before. Since you possess in a high degree the talent of writing for many readers, it is to be hoped that you will not write exclusively for the few adepts who are eager only for what is new, and can guess from the half-said what yet remains concealed."

Mendelssohn has been regarded as a forerunner of Kant, and there is no doubt that in some respects he prepared the way for him. He himself found that some of Kant's views were similar to his own, which, as he says in this letter, were given in a book which was in press before the dissertation was received, but he did not think them so profoundly developed by himself as by Kant. The letter, however, decidedly opposes the view of time given in the dissertation, and claims that it is both the subjective condition of perception and something that is objective.

Eighteen months after the Inaugural Dissertation appeared, Kant wrote a long letter to Dr. Marcus Herz, in Berlin, in which he gives a view of his speculations at that time, stating that he has already made considerable progress in determining the difference between the sensible and the intelligible in morality, has considered quite satisfactorily the principles of the emotions, of the taste, and of the judgment, and their influences as seen in the agreeable, the beautiful, and the good. He has also planned a work which might be entitled, "The Limits of Sense and Reason," which was intended to have both a theoretical and a practical part. The theoretical section was to discuss, first, phenomenology in general; secondly, the nature and method of metaphysics: the practical section was to discuss, first, the general principles of feeling, of taste, and of the sensualistic desires; secondly, the first principles of morality. From this it is evident that the contemplated work on "The Limits of Sense and Reason," which never appeared, was intended to discuss subjects which were afterwards treated in his three critiques. Kant mentions as a neglected point, which he is investigating, the relation of perception to the object perceived. The question he has been considering is, whether in our perception we have only a product of the influence of the object on our senses, or whether the mind itself produces the perception? The conclusion which he has arrived at is, that neither the one nor the other is the case, but that there is an object external to our minds, and that there are also categories of the understanding, and that in our perceptions both co-operate. How then does it happen that our minds have conceptions which harmonize with the objects? He admits that the answers given to this question always leave some obscurity in the mind respecting the harmony existing between the understanding and the objects of the sense.

The sources of the intellectual conceptions must be known by him who wants to understand the nature and the limits of metaphysics. Kant had accordingly, as he states in this letter, tried to bring all the conceptions of the pure reason under the head of certain categories, and he thinks that he has already succeeded, essentially, in doing this; and he is now ready to give a "Kritik of Pure Reason," he says, which contains the nature of theoretical as well as practical knowledge so far as it is only intellectual. He expects to work out and publish within three months the first part of this "Kritik," discussing the sources, method, and limits of metaphysics; after that he proposes to work out the pure principles of morality. So intently is he engaged in considering these problems that he wants to think of nothing else profoundly.

While Kant has already found the name for his great work, it is evident that he has not yet formed the plan on which it was finally constructed. The three months became three times three years, all of them spent in intense application. In 1776 he wrote to Herz that he had been much censured for inactivity, and yet he had never toiled more systematically or more continuously. The letter states that, instead of publishing something for the sake of temporary popularity, as he might do, he is engaged on a work by means of which he hopes to gain a permanent reputation. For this he has already thought out the material, and it is only necessary for him to work it over; when it is finished he expects to have a clear field, and to engage in work which will be only a pleasure. Whoever understands the nature of the task he had undertaken will not think Kant's declaration strange, that obstinacy was necessary to pursue persistently such a plan as his, and that the difficulties had frequently tempted him to engage in easier and more agreeable work; but he was saved from yielding to this temptation by overcoming the obstacles and by the consideration of the importance of the subject. As the whole field of reason must be examined in order to accomplish his aim, experience cannot help him. The letter states that he wants to determine, according to reliable principles, "the whole compass of reason, its departments, its limits, its entire contents;" and he desires so to mark the boundaries that in the future one may know with certainty whether he is on the basis of reason. In order that this may be accomplished, he thinks that an entirely new science of reason is necessary, in the construction of which nothing already existing can be used. He expects to finish the work in the summer of 1777, yet has his fears that he may be disappointed: fears which were well grounded, for, as he says, he was constantly subject to indisposition.

The letters of this period give some idea of the enormous amount of labour which the "Kritik" cost its author. Repeatedly he thought that it was nearly done, when he found that the work again grew on his hands. "I do not think," he says, "that many have attempted to plan an entirely new science and have also completed it;" and he thinks that Herz cannot imagine the amount of time and labour required for the accomplishment of this. He, however, hopes to give philosophy an entirely different direction, one which will be more advantageous to religion and morality; and he also hopes to give it a form which will attract mathematicians, and make them regard it worthy of their attention.

Kant's correspondence also indicates that he frequently changed his plans. When the book was already in press, he wrote to Herz that the "Kritik" "contains the results of all kinds of investigations, which began with the ideas which we discussed under the title of the Mundi Sensibilis and Intelligibilis," referring to his Inaugural Dissertation. At other times he expected to limit the contents much more. It may surprise some that at any time Kant regarded such a "Kritik" as lying outside of the sphere of metaphysics; but this significant passage occurs in a letter written to Herz in the winter of 1774-75: "I shall rejoice when I have finished my transcendental philosophy, which is really a critique of pure reason. I shall then work on metaphysic, which has only two parts, namely, the metaphysic of nature and that of morals, of which I expect to publish the latter first; and I already rejoice over it in anticipation." At this time, therefore, he held the view which he also held for years after the "Kritik" appeared, that it was only the preparation for metaphysics; nevertheless he regards it as belonging to transcendental philosophy. His letters and books, together with his last manuscript, show that his view of metaphysic was subject to numerous changes.

That the plan of the work should have been subject to many alterations is not strange, especially when the many years required for its development are considered. The subjects discussed were held in every light, and they were the burden of his thoughts during his recreation as well as in his study. Kant himself informed Borowski that the plan of the "Kritik" was made during his promenades on the way named after him, "The Philosopher's Walk." While his own letters show with what absorbing attention he was devoting himself to the work, Hamann's letters of 1779 and 1780 also speak of him as still incessantly engaged on it. Those who marvel at the contents of the "Kritik" should remember that it embodies the results of twelve years of the intensest efforts of Kant's great intellect.

CHAPTER IX.

AUTHORSHIP CONTINUED.

Publication of the "Kritik"—Hamann's impressions of the book—Difficulties of the work—Defects and excellencies—Aim—*À priori* and *à posteriori* knowledge—Analytic and synthetic judgments—Transcendental æsthetics—The Categories—The reason—Charge of idealism—Das Ding an Sich—God, the soul, freedom, immortality—Ontological, cosmological, and physico-theological proofs of God's existence—Result of the "Kritik"— "Prolegomena" — "Metaphysical Principles of Natural Science"—"Critique of the Judgment"—Conflict of the faculties—Last manuscript.

KANT made arrangements in December, 1780, for the publication of the "Kritik." The publisher, Hartknoch, lived in Riga, but the book was printed in Halle. Professor Kraus, speaking of Kant, says, "He asked nothing for his 'Kritik.' Hartknoch, of his own accord, however, gave him four dollars a sheet, and Kant regarded the money received from Hartknoch for every new edition as a present." The professor also states that Kant had offered the book to Hartung, a publisher in Königsberg, who, however, refused to undertake the work, because the author had frankly told him that he had his doubts whether the book would pay expenses. Kant expected the "Kritik" to appear at Easter, 1781; but it was delayed until the summer of that year. It was dedicated to the Cabinet Minister, Von Zedlitz, who had shown such marked favour to Kant, and was a great admirer of his works.

As the printing of the book progressed, the publisher, who was a friend of Hamann, sent advance sheets to him, as well as to Kant. In his letters Hamann gives his impression of the parts as they appeared, and these are the first notices we have of the work. When the first sheets came, he wrote, humorously, that he had prepared himself with an ounce of Glauber's salt to digest them. To the publisher he wrote on April 8th, 1781, that he had received the first thirty sheets on the 6th, and that on the next day he had devoured the whole, but that he lost the thread of the discussion in the chapter on the Interests of the Reason. "I should think that the book would no more be in want of readers than Klopstock's 'German Republic' is in need of subscribers. I skipped a few sheets, because theses and antitheses were on opposite pages, and I found it difficult to keep hold of the double thread in a rough copy. . . . According to human probability, it will attract attention and will be the occasion of new investigations, revisions, et cetera. But there will probably be few readers who can master its scholastic contents. The interest grows with the progress of the discussion, and there are charming oases after one has long been wading in the sand. Altogether, the work is rich in prospects and in leaven for new fermentation both within and without the circle of philosophers." What he has read makes him eager for the completion of the work, so that he may read the whole.

The advance sheets taxed Hamann's powers to the

utmost, and on April 21st he wrote to Herder, "As an old hearer of Kant, you will probably understand him better. . . It seems to me that the whole tends to a new organon, new categories, and not so much to a new scholastic construction as to sceptic tactics." And he adds, "I am anxious to learn how you feel when you read the Kantian 'Kritik.' I have said *sapienti sat* to the transcendental twaddle about the legal or the pure reason; for it seems to me that in the end all tends to sophistry and empty verbiage."(114) He thinks that the size of the book corresponds neither with the size of the author nor with the idea of pure reason. Again he wrote to Herder, "I am curious to know your view of Kant's masterpiece. . . . He deserves to be called the Prussian Hume. It seems to me that his whole transcendental theology tends to an ideal of entity. With respect to space and time he is, without knowing it, more fanatical than Plato in the intellectual world." Hamann, who was a great admirer of Hume, prefers him to Kant, and says, "Hume is always my man, because he at least ennobles the principle of faith, and has received it into his system. . . . Hume's dialogues close with the Jewish and Platonic hopes of a coming prophet; Kant is rather a cabalist who makes an Eon into a Divinity in order to establish mathematical certainty, which Hume, geometry excepted, limited rather to arithmetic."

Hamann expected the last sheets of the book in the beginning of June, but on the 19th they had reached neither him nor Kant. Finally, he wrote to Herder, August 5th, that a week ago he had received a bound copy of the "Kritik." This fixes July, 1781, as the time of its appearance.

It seems that Hamann had been requested by Kant himself to review some of his writings, and he published a review of his book on the Beautiful and the Sublime. He had also prepared a review of the "Kritik" for a paper in Königsberg, but was afraid to publish it, lest he might wound his sensitive friend. Though an admirer of Kant's speculative and analytical powers, he could not adopt his philosophy as a whole. While seeing much in it to admire, there was also much which seemed to him one-sided or defective. For the people in general he pronounced it "too abstract and too precious." Owing to its high ideals, he thought the book might be called Mysticism as well as the "Kritik of Pure Reason." He told Kant that he liked his work, "all except the mysticism." Kant, who had a dread of everything of the kind, and had aimed to put an end to it by means of this book, was astonished, and could not imagine how mysticism could have gotten into the book. To Hamann this was evidence that, without knowing it, all philosophers are fanatics.

Hamann thought that, for the sake of mathematical demonstration, the "Kritik" ignored too much the heart, intuition, and faith. His later views of the book were not more favourable than the first impressions, and he wrote: "It seems to me that the step from transcendental ideas to demonology is not far." In a letter to Jacobi he makes this statement: "The ambiguity of the word 'reason' tends altogether to Jesuitical chicanery. For the world, I cannot understand how two men like Kant and Euler can smoke out of the same pipe, and can practise so gross a deception for the purpose of burdening their adversaries." Hamann sees sophistry in the "Kritik," regards the book as prolix and calculated to mislead. When Kant's "Basis of the Metaphysics of Morals" appeared in 1785, Hamann wrote that, instead of the pure reason, there is here a new fiction of the brain and a new idol, namely, the good will, and adds, "Even his enemy must admit that Kant is one of our keenest minds; but alas! his acuteness is his evil demon, just as Lessing's was his; for a new scholasticism and a new papacy are the two Midas' ears of our age." In his opinion, the "Kritik" is often suspended on a logical spider-web; but he also said, years after the work appeared, "Pure reason and a good will are still words to me whose meaning my understanding cannot grasp."

The difficulties to which Hamann referred have been experienced by all the readers of the "Kritik" and Kant himself was aware of their existence. To Mendelssohn he wrote, that the work was the product of at least twelve years of thought, but that he had written out the whole in four or five months, hurriedly, as it were, paying the closest attention to the substance, but less to the style, and also making but little effort to render the book easy for the reader. Kant admits that this makes the work difficult; still, he does not regret that he completed it in that way; for if the work had been longer delayed for the purpose of making it more popular, it might not have appeared at all. Its lack of perspicuity, he thinks, can be remedied in the course of time. He states that he is already too old to give, with uninterrupted effort, completeness to an extensive work, and, at the same time, with file in hand, make each part round, smooth, and graceful. While he had the material for the explanation of every difficult point, he says that in writing out the book he did not want to be obliged to attend to this matter; he hopes to do this in the future, when different parts of the book are attacked and explanations are made necessary. Then, he says, when one has worked out a system and has become familiar with its thoughts, he cannot easily guess what in it may to the reader seem obscure, or indefinite, or not sufficiently proved.

The various letters written by Kant while the "Kritik" was in process of preparation confirm his statement to Mendelssohn respecting his great care with reference to the contents, and also reveal the hopes which were centred in the work; and in his "Prolegomena" he states that he carefully weighed every sentence. Not only did it take years to put the book in a shape to satisfy him, it frequently took a long time and great care before he could satisfy himself respecting a single sentence. While pleased with the work as a whole, Kant regarded some parts as prolix and therefore obscure.

The mere mechanical labour of writing a book so large as the "Kritik" in four or five months must have been quite a task. In writing it "hurriedly," as he said he did, the style naturally suffered, the more so because Kant neglected that and devoted his attention to the substance. Complaints respecting the difficulties of the work are heard from scholars, as well as from the general reader. While some persons lay down the book, despairing of ever mastering its contents, others totally misinterpret it, and publish their misinterpretations as Kant's doctrines. His own disciples have engaged in bitter disputes as to the meaning of the master's words, and there have been striking differences among the Kantians as well as among the Hegelians. Many of the difficulties of the "Kritik" are largely due to the nature of the subjects discussed, to the abstract character of its thoughts, and the novelty of the method. Kant states, in the Preface, that it was impossible to adapt the work to popular use, and that it was intended for adepts in science who did not so much need explanations, which he had therefore given less frequently than would otherwise have been the case, lest the book might become too large. He also believed that difficulties have their attractions, since their solution by the reader serves to flatter his vanity.

The multitude of subjects discussed, and the wealth of the profound thought, embarrass the student and add to the difficulty of following the author.([115]) Some of the most important terms are used in different senses. That there are not merely parts which it is difficult to harmonize, but that there are actual contradictions, is now generally admitted. A thought is introduced, dropped, then taken up again; numerous secondary matters are discussed, and side-issues are introduced, while the main thought is held in abeyance. The introduction of apparently extraneous matter seems to confirm Kant's statement that the work "contains the results of all kinds of investigations."([116]) There is often a confusing prolixity where the importance of the subject makes a short, clear, and definite statement particularly desirable. Some things are repeated so often, either in the same or similar phraseology, as to become tedious; and at times the amount of material carried along in an argument is so great that the process of reasoning is almost buried under its weight; and when the conclusion is finally reached, it is exceedingly difficult to test its correctness. Whilst one almost despairs of mastering the separate parts, what shall be said of their relation to each other and their complete synthesis? When these facts are considered, we shall be able the better to comprehend how idealism and realism, scepticism and dogmatism, rationalism and mysticism, could attach themselves to the "Kritik." It is a rich mine with various ores and many veins; and it has often happened that persons of the most diverse tendencies have found, or imagined that they found, just the ore they sought, because each one worked only a particular vein or mistook the nature of the metal which he discovered.

But in spite of these patent defects, in which we have reflections of mental characteristics of Kant, especially of his liability to distraction, taking the "Kritik" as a whole, where can its peer be found? Has it not excellencies in which it stands without a rival in ancient as well as modern times? The work is one of the marvels of philosophical literature, on account of its subject, its aim, the comprehensiveness of its scope, its method, its profundity and novelty, the startling character of leading thoughts, the epoch it made in philosophy, the vast literature it has already occasioned and is still inspiring, and the new direction which it gave to thought. No other book of any age has had so deep and broad and abiding an influence on the metaphysical thought of Germany; and not only have men like Fichte, Schelling, Hegel, and Schopenhauer, developed their systems from germs found in the "Kritik," but science, theology, morals, and general literature, have received new impulses and new directions from this work.

When the greatness of this work is considered and its marvellous influence, it is not strange that Kant is known chiefly as the author of the "Kritik." While this work is too much the man himself to be dismissed with a passing notice, an analysis, or extended account, or a criticism of its contents, lie beyond the province of a biography, and would require a volume to be complete and valuable. Nor is this necessary, since many of the thoughts of the book have been embodied in modern philosophy, and largely even in literature; and the English reader will be able to form a good idea of its contents from translations and from accounts of it by English writers. A very general summary, descriptive rather than critical, of some of the main features of the work, must here suffice.

Kant wanted to make metaphysics a positive science. He spoke so contemptuously of the prevalent philosophy because it was so vague, built massive superstructures on mere hypotheses, and accepted, as absolute and final, great principles without demonstrating their validity. Where he found dreams, opinions, and faith, in the philosophy of the day, he wanted axioms. His hatred of dogmatism was the more intense because he himself had been subject to its dominion. Doubt has its mission, but only as the underminer of error and the guide to truth; as a system of philosophy, scepticism is a testimony of mental weakness and of despair in the search for truth. When Hume destroyed the basis of Kant's dogmatism, the critical metaphysician could not rest in the scepticism of the

Scotch philosopher, for his mind demanded axiomatic certainty. But in order that he might get an immovable basis it was necessary, first of all, to determine what the human mind can know and what lies beyond its capacities. His great aim in the "Kritik" is to find the limits of human reason. Two questions give us the problems which the book wants to solve, and it solves the first in order that it may be able to solve the second: "How do we know? What can we know?" In his answers to these questions, Kant uses much which had already been given in his previous works, especially in the Inaugural Dissertation.

With Locke he holds that, in point of time, all our knowledge begins with experience; but this fact he does not regard as evidence that experience is the source of all our knowledge. It may even be the case that what is called experimental knowledge is the result of impressions received from external objects *and* of additions made by our own minds. There is knowledge which is not drawn from experience, but is the product of the mind itself; this Kant calls *à priori* knowledge. The knowledge which is received through the senses is called *à posteriori*. *À priori* knowledge is independent of all experience; and such a sentence as this, "Every change must have a cause," is partly, not purely, *à priori*, because change is a conception drawn only from experience.

Observation is necessarily limited; it only shows that an object is in a certain state, but never that it must be so: that is, it deals with particulars, never with universals. But we have judgments which are both necessary and universal, such as the axioms of mathematics. These cannot possibly be given by the senses; hence all necessary and universal judgments are *à priori*. After defining *à priori* knowledge and showing that it is found even in ordinary minds, Kant discusses, in the third section of the Introduction, the proposition: Philosophy needs a science which determines *à priori* the possibility, the principles, and the limits of knowledge. The "Kritik" is of course intended to be this science, and the proposition gives its aim.

In the next section he discusses analytical and synthetic judgments, a subject which was by no means new, but it attained a prominence and importance in the "Kritik" such as it had never before received. Hume, in considering the same subject, had come to the conclusion that mathematical judgments are analytical, while Kant held that they are mostly synthetic. The distinction between the two kinds of judgments is of fundamental importance for understanding the "Kritik." If by the mere analysis of a subject a predicate is found to be contained in the idea of a subject, though in a hidden manner, then the judgment which declares that predicate to belong to the subject, is analytic. The sentence, "All bodies are extended," is an analytic judgment, for the conception of extension is contained in that of body, and the mere analysis of the conception of body gives that of extension. An analytic judgment, since it gives in the predicate only what is already contained in the subject, does not in the least enlarge our knowledge, but makes it clearer. If, however, I predicate of a subject something not already contained in the very conception of it, then I give a synthetic judgment; instead of merely analyzing my conception of it, I add something new to the subject. Kant again uses the illustration of a body, and says that the judgment, "All bodies are heavy," is synthetic, since the conception of weight is not included in that of body. Synthetic judgments, therefore, increase our knowledge. All analytical judgments are *à priori;* all judgments drawn from experience are synthetic, and they are, of course, *à posteriori.* But there are also synthetic judgments which are *à priori;* thus most mathematical judgments are synthetic and *à priori.* There can be no question about the truthfulness of analytic judgments, nor respecting synthetic judgments from experience. But there are ideas and principles which lie wholly beyond experience and are of the most momentous importance, —such as God and immortality. How can a knowledge of these be attained? Not by analytic judgments, nor by means of synthetic judgments drawn from experience. In all the sciences, in physics and metaphysics as well as in mathematics, there are *à priori* synthetic judgments, and a thorough test of their validity is of the utmost importance. Kant, therefore, thinks that an imperative demand is made on reason to answer this question, How are synthetic judgments *à priori* possible? ([117]) He regards this as synonymous with the question, How is knowledge by means of pure reason possible? or, How is metaphysic as a science possible?

The view of time and space found in the Inaugural Dissertation is also given in the "Kritik:" they are the subjective conditions for all experience. Whatever is observed by the senses is perceived in space, or in time, or in both; whatever is observed in our minds is perceived in time. The distinction between the sense and the understanding, found in the same dissertation, is also maintained in the "Kritik," and from it important consequences are drawn. The understanding gives the forms for all possible experience ; they are the conditions for all knowledge, which without them would be impossible. However, being mere forms of knowledge, they do not apply to things as they are in themselves, but only to phenomena. While the sense gives us objects, the understanding thinks them. In experience, therefore, two things are to be considered, namely, an object presented to the mind through the senses, and the forms of knowledge given by the understanding ; the former is the *à posteriori*, the latter the *à priori* element. Through the sense I receive an impression of heat; but when in connexion with this impression I think of substance, cause, force—as the substance of which the heat is but a manifestation, the cause of the heat, and the like—I add something which I did not get through the senses, something that is the product of my understanding and is *à priori*. All knowledge of things must necessarily have these two elements, the *à priori* and the *à posteriori*, the impression on the senses and the thought of the understanding. The sense cannot think, it can only receive impressions ; the understanding thinks, but by means of its thoughts it cannot give us real (existing) objects of knowledge, but only forms for a knowledge of the objects given by the senses. One of the first sentences of the "Kritik" also contains the conclusion of the whole investigation : that an object can in no wise be given to the mind except through the senses.([118])

In the first part of the book Kant discusses Transcendental Æsthetics, by which he designates the *à priori* science of all the principles of sensation. He discusses, under this head, space and time as the *à priori* subjective conditions of experience. As they themselves are *à priori*, so whatever gives their necessary relations is also *à priori;* and as these relations are not found by analysis, they are synthetic judgments. These relations are the subjects of pure mathematics. Geometry, for instance, deals with figures, hence with space, and Kant says, "Geometry is a science which determines synthetically, and yet *à priori*, the properties of space." Pure mathematics is both *à priori* and synthetic in its judgments. Although absolutely certain in its conclusions, it gives us no objects of knowledge, but only forms or conditions for a knowledge of existing things; it deals with space and time, and thus gives the conditions of the knowledge obtained through the senses.

As space and time are the conditions for all experience, so there are certain conditions which are necessary in order that we may think objects; and just as space and time are *à priori*, being given by the mind itself, so are the conditions necessary for thinking objects also *à priori*, being the product of the understanding; they are the forms which the understanding gives to experience. It is not by means of these forms that we represent objects to ourselves, but by means of them the understanding judges of the objects presented to the mind through the senses. If we eliminate the content of judgments and consider only the pure form of the understanding contained in them, we find that all the functions of thought in the judgments may be brought under four heads, each being again subdivided into three parts. Under Quantity, we have general, particular, and individual judgments; under Quality, affirmative, negative, limitless judgments; under

Relation, categorical, hypothetical, disjunctive judgments; under Mode, problematical, assertive, apodictic judgments. Kant calls these the logical functions of the understanding. Under the same four heads he gives the pure conceptions of the understanding "which are *à priori* applicable to objects of perception in general." These are called, after the example of Aristotle, Categories. They are—under Quantity, unity, multiplicity, totality; under Quality, reality, negation, limitation; under Relation, substance and accident, cause and effect, reciprocity; (119) under Mode, possibility and impossibility, existence and non-existence, necessity and accident. Kant regarded these categories as complete and exhaustive, as a general classification of all possible conceptions of the understanding, and he looked with the greatest satisfaction on their discovery, viewing his work in this respect as completing the imperfect table of the categories given by Aristotle.

Kant held that it is by means of these categories that the understanding connects all the impressions received through the senses. These impressions are separate, each standing alone, and sensation, which Kant views as the mere receptivity of the mind, has no means of connecting them; but the understanding, which he regards as the spontaneity of the mind, connects them. Without this connecting power there could be no judgments. By means of the categories, which are *à priori*, all the impressions are systematized, are bound together and classified; the perceptions are made conceptions, the impressions become thoughts, the individual is brought into relation with the general, and the predicate is connected with its subject. That we think by means of these categories, is not the result of peculiar experience, nor of any experience; it is a necessity inherent in the understanding. As no number of impressions in sensation can give the conception of causality, so no number of them can deprive the mind of this conception. This and all the other categories of the understanding are the original moulds in the mind; the impressions received through the senses are cast into these moulds, and the forms thus given to them constitute our thoughts of things. Our knowledge of objects is, accordingly, a union of what is given through the senses and of what is added thereto by the understanding.

The categories are applicable only to phenomena, not to objects not given in sensation. If applied to something not given in experience, as God, freedom, immortality, the mind simply reasons without an object. It may have conceptions which are perfectly consistent; but that is no evidence that any real existence corresponds with them. By means of its spontaneous activity the mind cannot discover an object existing outside of the mind. Kant's conclusion on this subject is: "Sensation, as subjected to the understanding, and as the object to which the understanding applies all its powers, is the source of all real knowledge." But while the understanding thus deals with real knowledge only when it limits itself to the objects furnished by sensation, it, on the other hand, prescribes the laws according to which we obtain a knowledge of objects. In his Preface to the second edition of the "Kritik," Kant says, "Until now it was thought that all our cognition must adapt itself to the objects; but, under this supposition, all attempts to determine anything respecting them, by means of conceptions through which our knowledge would be enlarged, proved to be a failure. Let it, therefore, be tried whether we shall not get along better with the problems of metaphysics, if we suppose that the objects must adapt themselves to our cognition, a supposition which harmonizes better with the demanded possibility of an *à priori* cognition of the same, which cognition is to determine something respecting the objects before they are presented to us. This is somewhat similar to the first thought of Copernicus, who, when he found that there was no satisfactory explanation of the movement of the heavenly bodies if he took it for granted that the whole heavenly host revolved around the observer, attempted to discover whether he would not be more successful if the observer was supposed to turn, while the stars remained at rest." Kant made a revolution in metaphysics similar to that made by Copernicus in astronomy: he made the objects of knowledge conform to the laws of the mind, instead of obliging the mind to draw its laws from the objects.

While by means of sensation we receive impressions from objects, or have perceptions; and while the understanding furnishes the conditions for connecting the perceptions, thus giving us thoughts or conceptions; Kant ascribes to the imagination the office of furnishing a picture or *schema* for a conception. But in the "Kritik" the function of the reason is of special importance. It is the faculty for ideas, using the word "idea" in the Platonic sense. Thus we have an idea of freedom, of virtue, of government, with which nothing known to us corresponds. The ideas are *à priori*, being the direct product of the reason; they are perfect types or archetypes; they are great principles, which are not fictions, but necessary products of the reason; and they transcend all experience, in which no object can be given which is an adequate representation or embodiment of the idea. This, of course, does not imply that there is no such an object, and Kant guardedly says, "We have no *knowledge* of an object which corresponds with the idea;" and he repeatedly warns against the conclusion that the limit of our knowledge is also the limit of existence. The principles given in the reason apply directly to the laws of the understanding, but not to the phenomena given in experience.

The charge of Idealism has repeatedly been made against Kant's philosophy. This has been based on his view of time and space as subjective conditions of knowledge, on his doctrine that knowledge must conform to the laws given *à priori* by the understanding, and to his conclusion that we can get only impressions from things, of which we can know nothing but their phenomena. According to the "Kritik," we cannot possibly know what is back of the phenomena, namely, the thing *per se* (das Ding an sich). Long before Fichte developed his Idealism from Kantian principles, there were persons who interpreted these views as idealistic. Kant, however, promptly met this charge in his "Prolegomena." There he defines Idealism as the system which asserts that there are only thinking beings, and that all other things which we imagine we perceive, are only appearances in the thinking being, with which nothing external to the mind corresponds. In opposition to this view, Kant says, "I, however, say, things which are objects outside of us are given to our senses; of what they are in themselves we, however, know nothing, but we know only their appearances, that is, the representations which they produce in us by affecting our senses. Therefore I, of course, admit that there are bodies external to us, that is, things respecting which it is altogether unknown to us what they are in themselves, which we know only by means of the representations of them produced by their influence on our senses, and to which we give the name 'body,' a word which therefore signifies for us only the representation of an unknown but, nevertheless, real object. Can this be called Idealism? It is, in fact, the very opposite." Kant, however, admits that his philosophy is Idealism in another sense, namely, in that it teaches that our minds deal only with phenomena, with the representations of things, but never with things themselves. If the theory which changes real things into mere representations is an objectionable Idealism, what shall we, on the other hand, call that theory which changes mere representations into things themselves? Kant's answer is, "I think it might be called a dreaming Idealism, in distinction from the former, which might be called the fanatical one, both of which I wanted to avoid by means of my so-called Transcendental, or better, Critical Idealism."

Kant therefore does not deny the existence of a world outside of us; but as in a mirror we see only reflections of ourselves, and not ourselves; so in our minds we have only reflections of objects, not the objects themselves. That we have no power of knowing what things are in themselves, is one of the clearest results of the "Kritik," and is stated with a frequency and with an emphasis which leave no room for doubt as to his meaning. Experience is the absolute limit of knowledge, and in his Preface to the second edition of the "Kritik" he says that the first use of the book is to teach us never to venture beyond the limits of experience with our speculative reason, since all that lies beyond these limits also lies beyond the province of reason. But since in experience we have only phenomena as objects of knowledge, it is evident that beyond these we can know nothing of things.

Kant does not merely destroy all hope of obtaining a knowledge of things *per se*, he also destroys all hope of gaining, by means of the speculative reason, any knowledge of God, the soul, freedom, and immortality. We have already seen the intimate union of the speculative and the practical interests in Kant, and that he gave to the latter the preference. It was a practical interest which gave the impulse to his profound speculations, and he says in the "Kritik," "The ideas of God, freedom, and immortality, are the proper objects for the investigation of metaphysics. Everything else with which this science is occupied serves only as means for the attainment of these ideas and a knowledge of their objective reality." But the "Kritik," instead of establishing the reality of these objects by means of speculation, shows that the speculative reason can learn nothing respecting them.

In discussing the sentence, "I think," Kant shows that all it implies or teaches is that I exist thinking; it does not teach us what the Ego in itself is. We know absolutely nothing respecting the nature of the soul; and if the materialistic explanation is unsatisfactory, so is the spiritualistic. But if the nature of the soul is a mystery to us, how can we know anything respecting its immortality? It cannot be proved that the soul is a simple substance, and that, consequently, it cannot be disintegrated, and cannot decrease or vanish altogether, but must exist for ever.

Theoretical knowledge, according to Kant, is that which knows that a thing is; practical knowledge, on the other hand, is that which represents what a thing ought to be. By means of the theoretical use of reason we learn *à priori* that something is; through its practical use we learn *à priori* what ought to be done. Theoretical knowledge is speculative whenever its object is such that it cannot be given in experience, or whenever it deals with mere conceptions of such an object. It is the very opposite of a knowledge of nature, which deals with objects given in experience, or with their predicates. Kant asserts that the purely speculative use of reason in theology is utterly worthless, and that in an *à priori* way the existence of God cannot be proved. And after repeatedly showing that we cannot know substances, but only phenomena and their laws, he proceeds to subject the speculative proofs of God's existence to searching criticism. These are of three kinds, ontological, cosmological, and physico-theological. Under whatever form the ontological argument may be presented, the inference that God exists is always drawn from the very idea of God; but in no case can a mere idea demonstrate the existence of an object corresponding with the idea. The reason may find it necessary to adopt such an idea for the explanation of things; this, however, is a mere hypothesis. To predicate the real existence of a corresponding object, is a synthetic judgment, which would be valid only if the object were given in experience. The idea of God may be perfect; but, Kant says, the conception of a hundred thalers may also be perfect, and yet the mere conception of so much money does not make a man any richer, neither does the mere idea of God in the least enlarge our knowledge of what really exists.

The cosmological proof differs from the ontological in this respect, that the latter is purely speculative, while the former begins with experience but ends speculatively. The cosmological argument is that every change must have a cause; if now we continually proceed from effect to cause, we shall have an endless series of the conditioned. From the conditioned the inference is drawn that there must be an unconditioned which conditions everything else, an uncaused cause of all that is caused. Yet even if it is admitted that the mind is obliged to postulate an ultimate cause and an unconditioned something for the explanation of things, that is no proof of the real existence of such a cause. The argument is really ontological, since from the mere idea the necessary objective reality is inferred. The idea of a first cause is one to which thought is driven as a refuge; but whether it is a real or an imaginary necessity for our thoughts, it does not demonstrate the existence of such a cause.

The physico-theological proof is the argument from design. The beauty and order in nature, the working or tendency towards certain ends, are regarded as evidence that there must have been an intelligent designer, just as from the existence of a house we infer that it had an architect. Kant, however, says that in order to prove that nature had such a designer, it would be necessary to prove that things *per se* (substances, of which we know nothing) cannot work so beautifully and harmoniously, unless they are the product of the highest wisdom. As the cosmological argument was seen to rest on the ontological, so Kant shows that the physico-theological rests on both the cosmological and the ontological. According to the physico-theological argument, the inference is drawn from the beauty and order of the universe that they must have an adequate cause. This cause is supposed to be a Being who possesses all perfections. By analyzing the argument, however, we find that it amounts to this: the beauty and order seen in nature are effects; these effects have an adequate first cause which is perfect and unconditioned (cosmological argument); and because I am obliged to conceive such a cause in order to explain phenomena, therefore an object corresponding with this idea of a first cause also exists (ontological argument). As both the ontological and the cosmological proof have been found unsatisfactory, of course the physico-theological one, which rests on them, is also invalid. But even if it could be proved that the substances, the things *per se*, cannot of themselves work beautifully and harmoniously, that would not prove the existence of an all-wise and almighty Being. It would only prove that there is an Architect of the universe, whose power is limited by the nature of the material he uses, but it would not demonstrate the existence of a Creator to whom everything is subject. In order to prove that such a Creator exists, it would be necessary to demonstrate that matter itself is conditioned.

Already in discussing the antinomies of pure reason,

Kant had come to a conclusion similar to that attained by testing the arguments for God's existence. On the following points, he says, we can determine nothing speculatively, "Whether the world had a beginning and is limited in space; whether anywhere, and perhaps in my thinking self, there is an indivisible and indestructible unity, or nothing but what is divisible and destructible; whether I am free in my actions, or, like other beings, am controlled by nature and destiny; finally, whether there is a highest cause of the world, or whether the things in nature, and their order, are the ultimate objects with which our contemplations must stop."

After his demonstration that speculatively we cannot demonstrate the existence of God, Kant shows that it is equally impossible to prove that there is no God. "The same arguments which prove the impotence of the human reason with respect to the establishment of the existence of the highest Being, also suffice to prove the insufficiency of all assertions against this existence. For whence will one, by means of pure speculative reason, obtain the knowledge that there is not a highest Being as the source of all things?"

While in the dogmatic systems there are rational psychology, rational cosmology, and rational theology, which presuppose that the soul, the cosmos, and God, are not mere ideas, but real objects which can be treated as subjects of rational knowledge, Kant shows that they are mere ideas of the reason, and that it is impossible to determine speculatively whether a real object corresponds with them. No corresponding object being given in experience, the speculative reason must treat them as mere ideas, and a rational science of psychology, cosmology, and theology, is impossible.

This conclusion was by no means new. The same result was attained by Hume; and Thomasius and others had declared that the objects of religion are matters of faith and cannot be demonstrated. But in the metaphysics of the day they were generally treated as either self-evident or demonstrable, or both, and on this supposition elaborate speculative systems were built. Kant not only proved that, as far as speculative knowledge is concerned, these systems are baseless fabrications, but he proved it so rigorously, with such mathematical definiteness and conclusiveness, and so often, that, if his premises are admitted, there is no escape from the conviction that the matter is finally settled. His thorough criticism destroyed the dogmatism of metaphysicians on these subjects.

If now metaphysic deals with God, freedom, and immortality, then it is evident from the "Kritik" that this science must be a failure, since this work proves that, speculatively, we can know nothing about them. Every argument in favour of their existence is met by an equally valid one against it. We can know nothing except mathematics and what is given in experience; that is, we can know phenomena and their laws, but besides and behind them absolutely nothing. In the "Prolegomena" the following is given as the result of the whole "Kritik:"—"That our reason, by means of all its principles, never teaches us anything *à priori* except objects of possible experience, and even of these nothing except what can be known in experience." Since the substance is altogether beyond the reach of our minds, our knowledge is doomed to move in a world of mere appearances.

The tendency of the "Kritik" is to humble man greatly, to check wild speculations in metaphysics, and to concentrate the attention of philosophers on the things which are within the reach of knowledge. If the supersensible lies beyond the limits of reason, then more attention will, naturally, be paid to the positive sciences. There is no doubt that, instead of promoting idealism or even metaphysics, the "Kritik" is rather calculated to promote the study of the natural sciences and mathematics, and that the Critical Philosophy, in this respect, ends where Bacon began.

However, what Kant takes with one hand he gives back again with the other; for what he denies to the speculative reason, he vindicates as the sphere of the practical reason. While, on the one hand, the "Kritik" is negative and destructive in its results, it is, on the other, positive and constructive. Kant believes it necessary for man to elevate himself above the sensible, and he thinks that something must necessarily be *postulated* as absolute and infinite, and as the cause of all finite things. We cannot understand what or how this is; therefore it is not an object of science, and it is not, strictly speaking, knowledge; but it is a necessary, though inexplicable, presupposition. Where the speculative reason is impotent, there the practical reason prescribes laws which are absolute, and these are based on the supposition of the existence of God and freedom. The practical reason does not, indeed, give any speculative knowledge, nor knowledge which can be used speculatively;

its domain is purely practical; nevertheless, its postulates are such as to give a basis on which moral faith can rest; and for all practical purposes this basis is absolute.

Kant does not regard it as a serious loss that it has been proved that by means of speculation we can know nothing of God and freedom and immortality. On ordinary minds the speculative arguments never had any influence. There are still arguments left which can be used and which give us moral certainty. Reason finds it necessary to accept the law that in animals no organ, no power, no impulse is in vain, but that everything is perfectly adapted to some purpose. Can it be that man is the only exception to this law? In him we find talents, impulses, and particularly a conscience, which are not merely adapted to use in this life, but which often lead a man to deny himself here with a view of fitting himself the better to become a citizen of another world; in other words, Kant recognizes in man faculties which do not have full scope for exercise here, which are adapted to another sphere, and which point to something beyond this life. If means are adapted to ends, as we are firmly convinced that they must be, then these powers within us, and the consciousness of a certain limitlessness of the possible increase of our knowledge, and the impulse to seek this increase, remain as incontrovertible arguments in favour of immortality, in spite of the fact that we can neither comprehend its nature, nor give a speculative demonstration that we are immortal.

Kant declares that we do not need a knowledge of the existence of God, of freedom, and of immortality;

yet they are urged on us by our reason, which has a presentiment of them and a deep interest in them, and which enters on a course of speculation to discover them, though they constantly flee from it. This proves that reason is constituted with reference to these objects, and they are the problems of what may be called pure philosophy. Hence if the speculative reason cannot discover them, they must belong to the province of the practical reason. As our faculties point to immortality, so all moral laws point to freedom and to God. If there is no freedom, then there is no morality; if there is no God, then virtue, which deserves a happiness which it does not receive here, is deceived, since there will be no one to give it, in another life, the happiness which it merits. Repeatedly and emphatically, Kant shows that, practically, we must believe in God, freedom, and the immortality of the soul, and that if these are fictions, then our nature is so constituted as to deceive us. He is anxious to check empiricism, as well as speculation, in their denial of the basis of religion and morality; and he shows that they become dogmatic and transcend the limits of reason whenever they deny the existence of objects beyond experience. And so anxious is he to secure a place for morality and faith, that he says, in the Preface to the second edition of the "Kritik," "I was obliged to destroy knowledge, in order to make room for faith." And while he destroys the useless speculations which try to prove the existence of objects not given in experience, he also expects the "Kritik" to destroy the roots of materialism, fatalism, atheism, pernicious scepticism, anaticism, superstition, and idealism.

Although Kant's moral and religious views are considered in the next chapter, it is necessary to give their basis in the "Kritik" more fully than is done in the preceding general outline. He thinks that in giving to our reason the character it possesses, the aim was moral, not speculative. The three problems of God, of freedom, and of immortality, have this peculiar significance, that they show us *what is to be done* if the will is free, if there is a God, and if the soul is immortal. That the will is free, is a matter of experience; it may, consequently, without anything further, be regarded as settled. ([120]) The problems which therefore remain are: "Is there a God? Is there a future life?"

The three questions on which the interest of the speculative as well as the practical reason is concentrated are the following: "What can I know? What ought I to do? What may I hope?" The first is purely speculative, and Kant thinks that he has exhausted all possible answers to this question. The second is purely moral, and may belong to pure reason; but as it is not transcendental, it does not belong to the "Kritik." The third question may be put in this form, "If I do what I ought, what may I hope?" It is practical since it deals with conduct, and theoretical since it concludes that something exists because certain things ought to be done, something which determines the ultimate aim of conduct. This is therefore a question which can properly be considered in the "Kritik."

There are purely moral laws which determine *à priori* what ought to be done; and their commands are absolute, without regard to empirical motives, such as happiness. The moral judgment of every person acknowledges this imperative. There must therefore be possible a system of what ought to be done, and the principles of the pure reason which determine this have an objective reality in their practical and moral application. The answer to the question, "What ought I to do?" is this, "Do that which will make you worthy of being happy." The question then arises, "If by means of my conduct I am made worthy of being happy, shall I attain the happiness which I deserve? In the exercise of its theoretical as well as practical functions, reason presupposes that every one has a right to expect that degree of happiness of which he has made himself worthy by his conduct. Therefore the ideas of morality and happiness are inseparably connected in pure reason. But after we have done the utmost to make ourselves worthy of happiness, we cannot expect this happiness itself to result from the nature of things, nor from the conduct itself; how then can we account for this ceaseless striving to become worthy of happiness? If there is nothing but nature, then reason cannot answer this question. This harmony between morality and happiness can be hoped for only if a highest reason, which rules according to moral law, is taken as the basis of nature. "I call the idea of such an intelligence, in which the morally perfect will is connected with the greatest happiness, and which is the source of all happiness in the world, so far as it is exactly proportioned to morality (the worthiness of being happy), *the ideal of the highest good.*" It is only in this ideal that the pure reason can find the practically necessary union between morality and happiness. Now it is evident that in this world happiness is not proportioned to worthiness; therefore we must believe in the existence of another world for the consummation of this harmony. Kant therefore draws the conclusion, that obligation as the principle of conduct, to which the reason subjects us, presupposes two things, namely, the existence of God and a future life. For, unless there is a God as the wise author and governor of the universe, there cannot possibly be the required harmony between morality and happiness. If there is no such a Being and no future life, for the compensation of virtue, then the moral laws must be regarded as empty phantoms, since the consequences, which are implied in obedience to these laws, do not follow. The moral laws, which are universally regarded as commands, cannot be such commands if they do not *à priori* connect with their rules proportionate results, and attach to them promises and threats; but they cannot attach these unless the source of the laws is a Being which is the Highest Good, for only this Being can fulfil the promises and execute the threats. If we suppose that there is no God and no future life, then the ideas of morality are, indeed, objects of approval, but they are not motives for resolutions and for the execution of the resolutions, because they do not fulfil the purpose which is natural to every rational being, and which is ordained *à priori* and made necessary by the pure reason.

Neither happiness alone, nor morality alone, but both together, the one exactly proportioned to the other, constitute the highest good. But we must be careful not to pervert their relation to each other. The moral disposition is the condition for being made partaker of happiness; but the prospect of happiness is not to be made the ground of a good disposition. If the latter were done, then the disposition would not be moral, and consequently it would not be worthy of happiness.

This is an outline of the Kantian basis of a moral theology, which he places immeasurably above the speculative, since it necessarily leads to the idea of a perfect and rational Being as the author of all things. This Being must be one; for how could we find a unity of purpose in different wills? This supreme Will must be almighty, in order that nature and its relations may be subject to it; it must be omniscient, in order that it may know the innermost purposes of man and their moral worth; it must be omnipresent, in order that it may be present to meet all the necessities required by the greatest welfare of the world; and it must be eternal, in order that at no time there may be a failure to harmonize nature and freedom, worthiness and happiness. The ideas thus practically gained by reason necessarily lead to the conclusion that there is a unity of purpose in all things. The world must be viewed as having sprung from one idea, if we are to regard it as in harmony with the moral use of reason. Accordingly, purpose is demanded in nature; and all investigation of nature receives a tendency towards a system of means adapted to ends, and in its highest development becomes physico-theology.

We thus find that for our highest interests the practical reason furnishes what the speculative cannot supply, but can at best only imagine. While the practical reason cannot make this a demonstrated dogma, it absolutely demands it as a condition for its highest purposes. Kant is extremely guarded in the use he makes of the conclusions thus drawn from the practical reason. He does not regard moral acts as obligatory because they are God's commands; but he regards them as God's commands because they are subjectively obligatory. Kant does not deduce the moral law from the existence of God; but the existence of God is deduced from the existence of the moral law. Moral theology is to be used for practical purposes only, namely, to enable us to fulfil our destiny in this world; and it is an abuse to use for speculative purposes the results obtained practically. We therefore still have every reason to be very modest. There are three stages in our convictions, namely, opinions, faith, and knowledge. The practical reason gives us only faith, not dogmas which can be regarded as demonstrated; but this faith may be so strong as to give its possessor the conviction of certainty. This certainty is not logical, but moral. Kant says, "No one can boast that he knows that there is a God and a future life; for if he knows it, he is just the man whom I have long been seeking. All knowledge (if it is an object of pure reason) can be communicated, and I should hope to see my knowledge wonderfully increased by his instruction. No, the conviction is not *logical*, but *moral* certainty; and as it rests on subjective grounds, namely, on the moral disposition, I must not even say, It is morally certain that there is a God, et cetera, but I am morally certain that this is the case."

Kant thus comes to the conclusion that the highest philosophy cannot determine more respecting the essential purposes of human nature than to attain that guidance which it is also the privilege of the ordinary understanding to attain.

In his "Kritik," Kant did not aim to give a system of metaphysics. This he says plainly in the Preface of the second edition, and in a letter to Mendelssohn he states that it was the aim of the "Kritik" to investigate the ground on which the superstructure of metaphysic was to be built. So far is Kant from believing that he gave the system itself in the book, that two years after it appeared he discussed the question whether metaphysic is possible, and declared that the conditions for producing a system had never yet been complied with, and states plainly that as yet there is no metaphysics. In the "Kritik" he gave the propædeutics to the system, while in the works following it he aimed to give metaphysics itself. Fichte, Schelling, Hegel, and also others attempted to give the system.

Kant, aware of the difficulty of understanding the book, determined, immediately after the appearance of the "Kritik," and before the public had time to give a verdict, to prepare a popular abstract of the work, so as to make its results accessible to a larger class of readers. He immediately began the preparation of this abstract, and he expected to have it ready for the press in the spring of 1782, but it appeared a year later, under the title, "Prolegomena to every Future Metaphysic which can appear as a Science." (121)

While the "Kritik" is the masterpiece of Kant, there are important works which followed the "Prolegomena," works which are interesting for their own sake, as well as on account of their relation to the "Kritik" and the application of its ideas. In 1786 he published his "Metaphysical Principles of Natural

Science," in which he discusses the laws of the phenomena of matter. The "Kritik" had shown that we can know nothing but phenomena; applying this to nature, we can, of course, understand only the manifestations of matter, not substances. In this book on Natural Science, Kant discusses the principles of motion, applying to them the four categories, quantity, quality, relation, and mode, and considers the subjects, phoronomics, dynamics, mechanics, and phenomenology. The book is only a kind of propædeutics to a metaphysical system of natural science.

According to the results of the "Kritik," the understanding gives the forms of all knowledge, and this knowledge deals only with phenomena. This limits our knowledge to nature, and a metaphysic of nature, if complete, would embrace the whole domain of the knowable. Man would thus be treated as also a product of nature. But the "Kritik" had also shown that we have moral interests, the principles of which are given *à priori*, they being the product of pure reason. While, therefore, the understanding deals with nature, the reason deals with morals. In the "Critique of the Practical Reason," and in his other works on morals and religion, Kant embodied what he regarded as the principles of reason respecting our conduct. But in thus giving the principles of nature and of morals he did not yet complete his work. One more critique was necessary, namely, the "Critique of the Judgment."(122)

The reason is the faculty which gives principles *à priori*. These principles are regulative, not constitutive. The understanding, on the other hand, gives categories *à priori*, which are the laws for all phenomena. Whatever speculative notions are not included under these laws of the understanding, are ideas (such as soul, God, freedom) which belong to the reason. Since we cannot prove that any reality corresponds with these ideas, they are, as Kant says, not constitutive; but they are regulative ideas, being guides to us in our investigation and practice. Thus by means of these regulative principles, the understanding is checked in its assumption that it has included all things in its categories, and it is also guided in its contemplations of nature to proceed according to a perfect principle.

Kant divides the faculties of the soul as follows: the faculty of knowledge; that of the emotions of pleasure and displeasure; and the appetitive faculty; or into intellect, susceptibility, and will. The intellect he divides into understanding, judgment, and reason. From the understanding proceed the laws for nature, from the reason the laws for freedom; the former is theoretical, the latter is practical. Here, then, we have the reason and the understanding strictly separated, each having its domain where it is supreme,—the reason in determining free conduct, and the understanding in giving the laws of nature. How can they be united?

According to Kant, the judgment mediates between the understanding and the reason, between nature and freedom, between the sensible and the supersensible, all of which were shown by the "Kritik" to be sharply separated. The judgment is based on the idea that there is design in nature. This design, while in nature, is nevertheless a principle of freedom, and is, accordingly, a union of nature and of freedom, or of the understanding, which gives laws to nature, and of the reason, which gives laws to freedom. It is the judgment which discovers design in nature. This design is twofold; it is viewed as applying only to ourselves, namely, as producing in us pleasure or displeasure, and the judgment deals with design in this sense under the head of taste; or design is in things themselves, and then it must be teleological, having reference to the Author of the design. In the "Critique of the Judgment" there are therefore two parts, the first discussing the æsthetic judgment, the second the teleological. It is the former which chiefly interests us, which has also had the greatest influence on literature. Kant's view of art is found mainly in this book.

What is the beautiful? It is that whose very contemplation pleases us; its very form gives pleasure. There are three kinds of pleasure, the first derived from the agreeable, the second from the beautiful, and the third from the good; but it is only in the case of the beautiful that the mere contemplation gives pleasure. The hungry man is not satisfied with a mere thought or the sight of a feast, nor the moral man with a mere representation of the good; in each case the thing itself is desired, the one to be eaten, the other to be done. But the æsthetic taste is satisfied with the mere representation of a beautiful object and with its contemplation; the appropriation of the object, or its use in any sense, is foreign to this taste. It is not use, nor appropriation, nor knowledge, which is the essence of the æsthetic; but it is a pleasure which springs solely from the contemplation of an object. In æsthetics, therefore, we have a purely disinterested emotion.([123])

Kant does not discuss beauty in objects, but only the impression which it makes on the soul, or the emotion of the beautiful. He calls the agreeable, that which gratifies; the beautiful, that which pleases; the good, that which one approves. The agreeable is for irrational animals as well as for man; the good is for all rational beings; the beautiful is only for beings both animal and rational, that is, it is for man. The beautiful is, therefore, peculiarly human.

"Beauty in nature is a beautiful object; beauty in art is a beautiful representation of an object." It is the aim of the beautiful arts to produce beauty which pleases of itself, without reflection and without use. As has already been stated, it is only in art that Kant admits any genius, and he says, "Beautiful art is the art of genius." A Newton produces a system which another can master and reproduce in his own mind—we can think his thoughts after him; but Homer cannot be imitated. "Genius is the talent, or gift of nature, which gives to art its law."

A production may be according to rules, and yet lack spirit. There are poems, histories, conversations, which are correct and instructive, but they lack spirit, the very thing which is the living element and the soul of a production. What is this spirit? It is simply the ability to represent æsthetic ideas. By an æsthetic idea Kant means that product of the imagination which inspires thought, although it cannot itself be definitely given in thought, hence language can never adequately represent it. We may say, therefore, that Kant means by the spirit of a production, the symbols of thought embodied in it, but not fully expressed; it is the suggestive element in a production. The elements necessary for the production of the fine arts are the imagination, spirit, and taste.

The times were favourable for giving this book an

influence in literature. Through Baumgarten, Lessing, Winckelman, and others, a new impulse had been given to the study of æsthetics, and Kant aimed to give the essence of the whole matter in this book. Schiller was much indebted to this "Critique of the Judgment," and he modified and used its principal thoughts in his "Æsthetic Letters" and other writings, just as he embodied many of Kant's moral ideas in his poetry. Goethe read Kant's works much less than Schiller, but he thought highly of this book. His criticism of it is, that it "discusses rhetoric admirably, and poetry tolerably well, but the plastic arts inadequately."

The last book written by Kant appeared in 1798, and discussed the conflict for supremacy between the different faculties in the universities. It is particularly interesting on account of its views of religion, and the references to his health; and frequent use has been made of it in this biography. This, however, did not end his efforts at authorship. Till near the end of his life he worked on a manuscript which has a melancholy interest for us. After completing various other literary plans, he was anxious to give a fitting close to his philosophy by the publication of still another work. As early as 1795 his friend Kiesewetter wrote to him from Berlin, complaining that the last catalogues contained no announcement of books by him, and adds, "For several years you have intended to give the public a number of sheets on the transition from your 'Metaphysical Principles of Natural Science' to physics." In 1798 Kant wrote to his friend, "My health is that of an old man who is not sick, nevertheless is an invalid who has become unfit for public official duties, but is still conscious of a small measure of strength to complete a work on which he is now engaged, with which he expects to complete the Critical undertaking and to fill up a still remaining gap, namely, "The Transition from the Metaphysical Principles of Natural Science to Physics," as a separate part of natural philosophy which must not be omitted in the system."

From Hasse ([124]) we learn that for some years Kant worked on this manuscript, that its title was to be, "The system of Pure Philosophy according to its complete idea," and that in it he discussed philosophy, God, freedom, and especially the transition from physics to metaphysics. This friend of Kant says of the manuscript, "Kant was accustomed to speak confidentially of this as his principal work, his chef-d'œuvre, and to say that it was to complete his system, that it was already finished, and needed only revision." Jachmann states, "Kant was accustomed to speak with genuine inspiration to me about his last book, which was, he declared, to be the keystone of his entire system, and would establish the validity and applicability of his philosophy." While he sometimes spoke of the manuscript as so far completed as to need only "the last file," at others he had his doubts about the matter and expressed the wish that it should be burnt after his death.

Kant adopted the old Greek division of philosophy into the three sciences, physics, ethics, and logic. The last is pure formal philosophy, since it deals merely with the forms or the necessary and universal laws of thought. The other two, physics and ethics, may be called material philosophy, since they deal with objects and their laws. The objects of which material philosophy treats, are nature and freedom, the science of the former being physics, of the latter, ethics. There are, however, both in nature and in freedom, two kinds of elements, namely, the *à priori* and the *à posteriori*, the rational and the empirical; therefore, we have both rational and empirical physics and morals.

Kant deals with the rational elements of science, his aim being to put them on an immovable basis; he discusses pure, not applied philosophy. Pure philosophy rests solely on *à priori* principles, and has no empirical elements. Pure formal philosophy is logic. But if pure philosophy deals with objects, and not merely with forms of thought, it is called metaphysics. These objects being those of nature and of freedom, we have a metaphysic of nature and a metaphysic of morals, in both of which there is simply a discussion of *à priori* principles. In order that there may be a complete system of metaphysics, it is necessary to have in it a system of nature based on *à priori* principles, and a system of morals also based on *à priori* principles. The latter Kant gave in his works on morals, but for the former he gave only the propædeutics in his "Metaphysical Principles of Natural Science." The last manuscript was, no doubt, intended to be the science of nature based on *à priori* principles, for which this book was the preparation.

After the death of Kant, the manuscript was found among his papers, and was carefully examined with a view to its publication, but it was found that there was so much confusion in the thoughts that it was altogether unfit to appear in print. Hasse says, "The idea of philosophy seems to have caused the sublime thinker much trouble, since the subject was so often crossed out and worked over." After this examination the manuscript was lost sight of for a long time; then Schubert saw it in Berlin and examined it, but did not have access to it long enough to describe it fully. It disappeared again, and all trace of it was lost until recently, when a description of it was sent to Dr. Reicke, of Königsberg.(125) From this description we learn that, in the beginning of this manuscript, Kant made great efforts to define transcendental philosophy and to give the objects of which it treats. "That definition is attempted several hundred times, at least, and the following are mentioned as its objects, God, the world, and man in the world." It bears this title, "The Transition from the Metaphysical Principles of Natural Science to Physics." There are one hundred sheets, most of them written quite legibly and without abbreviations. Besides the definitions of transcendental philosophy, the manuscript treats chiefly of subjects pertaining to physics. In different parts the same subjects are treated, Kant evidently having forgotten that he had already discussed them. Many subjects are begun, but nothing is completed; the same thought is frequently repeated; there are laborious efforts to produce system, but, instead, there is hopeless confusion and a strange mixture of thoughts. Instead of continuing the discussion of the subject under consideration, Kant seems at times to have written whatever stray thought happened to be in his mind; and on the margin and between the lines there are all kinds of miscellaneous remarks and domestic memoranda. In one place he wrote that henceforth the day of prayer ought to be called a day of repentance, and that repentance should not consist in asking for forgiveness, but in making restitution.

The manuscript gives an insight into the state of Kant's mind and the character of his intellectual occupations towards the close of his life. In his plans and in his subjects we find him intellectually great to the last. He still attempted to solve the great mysteries of mind and nature, and his thoughts continued to move in the sphere to which he had given his best energies for over half a century; but he could no longer concentrate his attention steadily on any subject. He was not able to develop a thought fully, and, still less, to unite the different thoughts into a system; and his memory was too weak to remember what he had already written. Repeatedly he attempts to wrestle with the profoundest problems of the human intellect, but is baffled in every effort at solution. The contrast between the grand plan and the feeble execution is as striking as it is sad. That the author of the "Kritik" could at any time imagine that this jumble needed only revision in order to make it ready for the press, shows how completely the great mind had lost its grasp.

His efforts to define transcendental philosophy are found at the beginning of the manuscript, and were, no doubt, made before his mind had lost the power of consecutive thought. While he had lost much of his former vigour, it is, nevertheless, an evidence of the extreme difficulty of the subject that, after devoting so many years to metaphysics and after writing the "Kritik," he should have made hundreds of futile attempts to define transcendental philosophy. Did he change his former views of the whole subject? He seems, also, to have had difficulty in determining the objects with which metaphysics deals, though he formerly thought that this had been settled by the "Kritik." God, nature, and man, are mentioned as these objects; but, unfortunately, we do not know how the great metaphysician at last viewed the whole matter. What might not have been accomplished if, with his powers unimpaired, he had been able to carry out his plan to give a complete system of pure philosophy! Then we should have had the "Kritik" as the propædeutics to the system, while his works on morals, and the work to which he devoted his last labours, would have given the system itself.

CHAPTER X.

MORAL AND RELIGIOUS VIEWS AND CHARACTER.

Importance of the subject—Freedom—Conscience a sufficient guide —Duty—The practical reason—Its primacy—The good will—Emotionless morality — Categorical Imperative — Maxims—Stoicism—Integrity—Truthfulness—Emotional nature—Basis of his theology—Postulates—Religious character of the age—Rationalism—Historical faith—History depreciated—His religion essentially morality—View of Scripture—Moral interpretation—Public and private use of reason—The Trinity—Christ—Sin—Conversion—The Church—Worship—The next world—Ministers—Influence of his rationalism—Explanation of his theology—Called to account by the Government.

KANT's Critical Philosophy receives and deserves more attention than his practical works, on account of its profundity and because it has exerted the greatest influence and determined his place in history; if, however, we want to understand the man himself, we must also consider his relation to morals and religion. The supreme importance which he himself attached to these subjects, and the light which his moral and religious views throw on his mind and heart, make it the more necessary to give them a prominent place in his biography. The fact that he did not establish morality and religion on a firm speculative basis, and that in some respects his efforts to do so reveal his weakness rather than his strength, does not in the least justify a neglect of these subjects here where the interest is not centred on the truth of the system but on the character of its author. Even when his influence is considered, his practical as well as his speculative works must be taken into the account. If the former have received less attention than they deserve, it is because men have been so dazzled by the brightness of the latter that they have overlooked his other works; just as over Goethe's literary productions men forget that he also wrote on scientific subjects. Kant's influence on morals and religion was only second to that exerted by him on philosophy. The Kantian morality filled works on ethics, was taught in the universities, was preached from the pulpits, and was potent in shaping conduct and in determining the moral tone of literature. At the close of last century and the beginning of the nineteenth, the number of Kantian theologians was legion; and Kantian theology, as well as the Critical Philosophy, forms a prominent period in German literature. It was through his marvellous power that the various anti-orthodox tendencies which flourished during the period of Illumination were concentrated into Rationalism.([126])

Kant rejected the doctrine of natural depravity, though he held that every man sins; but instead of regarding this as a consequence of an original corruption of human nature, he held that, in the case of every individual, it is the result of free choice. While we cannot understand how sin could enter the world, or how a man can pass from a state of purity to corruption, the fact of sin itself cannot be questioned. During the period of Illumination it became common to view sin superficially and sentimentally; but Kant, with his profound knowledge of human nature, had a deep view of sin, pronounced men depraved, and called the evil reigning in man radical. Nevertheless, in spite of this deep and universal prevalence of sin among men, he held that the original nature is good, and that if this nature were only properly developed, man would be morally perfect, and he says, "The germs which lie in man need only be more and more developed; for the grounds of evil are not found in the natural endowments of man. The source of evil is found in the fact that human nature is not subjected to rules. There are in man no germs except for that which is good."

In order that the development may be perfectly moral, it is only necessary to follow the dictates of conscience. "The law within us," as he defines conscience, is an infallible guide; and nothing but obedience to this can give a man dignity and worth. On this autonomy of man he places the strongest emphasis; it determines the entire character of his system of morals, and largely influences his theological views. While others laid the stress on man's freedom with reference to the creature, Kant also emphasized this freedom in man's relation to God; and as in his cosmogony he held that nature's laws, originating with God, work without the interposition of the Divine agency, so he held that conscience, originally proceeding from God, is of itself sufficient to be the guide in morals and religion. Thus man is not only free, but, as far as moral guidance is concerned, he is independent, and it is unworthy of him to subject himself to external authority in morals. While Kant regards the conscience as the gift of God, it is easy to understand why he bases morality directly on conscience, not on God. We have an immediate knowledge of conscience; by means of its activity it makes itself known directly to consciousness; but the existence of God is, according to the "Kritik," inferred chiefly from the fact that man has a conscience. The existence of conscience is for us a primitive fact, that of God is derivative. The moral law in us being the evidence of God's existence, instead of being dependent on that existence, is treated by Kant as authoritative for us if even there were no God. Whatever the ultimate ground of morals may be, for us its source is in ourselves; for conscience is an absolute law unto itself.

What is duty? Kant answers that it is the obligation to act solely from regard for the moral law; and he wants it to be perfectly pure, that is, uninfluenced by any motive whatever except regard for that law. Pure duty is its own absolute and all-sufficient motive; and the *ought*, in perfect and cold isolation, is the sole, as well as the supreme rule in morals. Nothing inspires Kant more than this idea of duty, and he becomes eloquent and enthusiastic in discussing it. He says that the two objects which fill the spirit with ever new and increasing admiration the oftener and the more continuously reflection dwells on them, are the starry heavens above us and the moral law within us. And he exclaims, "Duty! thou great, sublime name! thou includest nothing which flatters, but thou demandest subjection; neither, on the other hand, dost thou threaten anything which excites a natural aversion in the soul, nor dost thou frighten in order to move the soul; but thou only announcest a law which of itself finds access to the spirit, and in spite of itself excites reverence—a law before which all inclinations are dumb, though in secret they oppose it."

The reason having two functions, the theoretical and the practical, the former deals with knowledge, the latter with conduct.(127) In both functions the reason is *à priori*, its laws being inherent in itself and not the product of experience. Hence it is the pure practical reason (with no empirical elements) which determines *à priori* the principles of conduct, just as the pure speculative reason gives ideas. This pure, practical reason is, according to Kant, simply the free will. Speculatively we can determine nothing respecting it, but practically we must accept it as the source of conduct and the basis of morality. Without freedom there could be neither morality nor worthiness; but since men are free, their dignity requires that they should not be treated as mere means, instead of ends.

Since the reason is both speculative and practical, it is a question of the utmost importance in morals, "Which is the more important function?" We have already found the answer; but we must emphasize it, as otherwise the negative results of the "Kritik" will be likely to affect our views of his moral system. With an emphasis that is unmistakable, the speculative Kant gives the preference to the practical reason, and declares that to it belongs the "primacy." Its principles, like those of the speculative reason, are *à priori*, universal, and necessary; they, indeed, must not conflict with the speculative reason, nevertheless they transcend it, since it cannot explain these principles. If the practical were subject to the speculative reason, then its principles, which the speculative cannot explain, would have to be rejected. Even the interest of the speculative reason is only conditional, and is made perfect in its practical application. It is not the fact that man has reason which elevates him above the brute, if that reason only enables him to do for himself what instinct does for the animal; in that case reason would indicate for man no higher aim or destiny than that of the brute, but only a different way of attaining the same end. Man is elevated above the animal because he has an aim which it cannot have. Reason distinguishes between good and bad, and it can make morality the ruling purpose of life; this is man's prerogative and glory.

Kant declares that there is nothing good in the world, except the good will.([128]) Not only does he emphasize this, but he also gives it a strictly literal application to morality. The good will is one which acts purely from regard for the moral law; and this will alone, and not culture, nor endowments, nor emotions of any kind, makes a man good. An act may conform to the law without being moral; it is moral only when it is done *for the sake* of the law. If a man is honest from policy, not from regard for the law, his honesty is legal, not moral. Neither is that benevolence moral which springs from pity for the suffering, not from regard for the law, and he says in his "Basis for the Metaphysics of Morality:"—

"It is a duty to be charitable when one can; and many souls are so sympathetic that, without any other motive of vanity or selfishness, they find an inward joy in spreading joy, and they take pleasure in the satisfaction of others as far as it is their work. But I declare that in such a case these acts, however dutiful, however lovely they may be, have no real moral worth; but they are to be classed with other inclinations, as, for instance, with the desire for honour when it agrees with what is generally beneficial and dutiful, and therefore is also honourable and deserving of praise and encouragement, but not of esteem; for the maxim lacks moral worth, which does not do such deeds from inclination, but because it is a duty to do them." Kant supposes the case of a man who is so much absorbed in his own grief that the calamities of others do not touch him. If now he relieves others solely from duty, without any inclination, "only then has the deed genuine moral worth." He seems to describe himself in the following: "If nature had put but little sympathy into the heart of a person; if he, an honest man, were from temperament indifferent and cold toward the sufferings of others, perhaps because he is furnished with the special gift of patience and persevering endurance with respect to his own, and also expects and even demands the same of others; if nature had formed such a man (who would verily not be her worst product) not specially for a philanthropist, would not he, nevertheless, find in himself a source of much greater worth than that which springs from a kind temperament? Certainly. Just there the worth of that character begins which is moral and without comparison the highest, namely, the character which does good from duty, not from inclination." Not only does he want to banish all emotions, even the higher ones, from morality, but he also fails to mediate between duty and feeling; the two are separated by a gulf which he leaves fixed and impassable. Disciples and great admirers of Kant have regarded his system as defective in this respect, and could not agree with him that the noblest feelings are a hindrance to morality; and some of the Kantian moralists, especially Schiller, have attempted to mediate between the emotions and morals, and to introduce soul as well as conscience into his cold and stern and heartless morality.([129])

While in his moral philosophy everything revolves around conscience, free will, and duty, Kant also gives what he regards as the highest principle of morality and the most general rule of conduct, namely, his celebrated Categorical Imperative. It is this law: "*Act in such a way that the maxim of thy conduct might be made a general law.*"([130 a]) This law excludes all selfishness, and is in no sense a maxim of prudence or expediency; it takes into account neither results nor any possible contingencies, but it is always, and everywhere, and for every person, absolutely and imperatively, the supreme rule of action. Instead of considering only the actor, it takes all mankind into the account, and declares that the law of conduct ought to be one which I could wish every other human being to adopt; for it says, act in such a way that you could wish every one else to act in the same way. This Categorical Imperative is essentially the same as the Golden Rule in the Sermon on the Mount.

This sublime law, so free from every objectionable motive, was received with all the more enthusiasm because it was in such striking contrast with the prevalent morality. It reveals the moral grandeur in Kant himself, gives the key to his whole system of morals, and indicates the spirit of his ethics. But he is far from being satisfied with general laws; he wants rules even for the details of life, and leaves as little room for spontaneity in conduct as he does for inclination. In his works there are numerous maxims which throw light on his views as well as his life. Not only was he in the habit of making general rules and such as covered important cases, but he also made maxims for matters of minor importance. These rules were sharply defined, stood out in bold relief, and received an unusual prominence and importance. This effort to shape life, its emotions, as well as its thoughts and volitions, according to rules, was the natural result of his desire to reduce everything to method and to system. In the course of time these maxims, like the rules of grammar, were used without thinking of them. In early life he found himself liable to yield to the first impulse, whence consequences resulted to himself and others which he had reason to regret. In order to avoid such contingencies in the future, he determined to use these occasions for the formation of maxims covering those peculiar cases; these were to be his rules of conduct under similar circumstances. With his indomitable will he carried out these resolutions; and Jachmann states that he followed with unswerving firmness the maxims once adopted. "In this way his whole life, in the course of time, became a chain of maxims." Rarely can it be said with equal truth that the maxims are the man. The writer just quoted gives an illustration of the manner in which they were formed. One day, as Kant was returning home from a walk, a count who was riding in his carriage met him. He stopped, alighted, and asked him to take a drive with him, and Kant accepted the invitation. The spirited and fleet horses made the philosopher nervous. After driving over his possessions, the count proposed that they should visit a friend a few miles distant, and out of politeness Kant assented. Contrary to his usual custom, he did not reach home till ten in the evening. The whole affair was exceedingly disagreeable to him; and to avoid like occurrences in the future he adopted the rule, never again to let any one take him pleasure-riding, and to enter a carriage only when it was under his own control.([130 b]) "As soon as he had formed such a maxim he knew just what to do in similar cases, and nothing in the world could induce him to depart from the rule adopted." This determination to regulate life strictly according to rules struck his friends as one of the most marked traits of his character; and Borowski observes: "That which was properly the characteristic of Kant, according to the observation of all who knew him, was his constant effort to act, in all things, in conformity with well-matured and, in his estimation at least, well-founded principles; the effort to fix, for large and small, for important and unimportant affairs, maxims which were to be referred to constantly, and were always to be the source of conduct. These became so interwoven with himself that he acted according to them without being conscious of them." Kant himself says, "It is necessary for our whole life to be subjected to moral maxims."

Owing to his strict adherence to rules, Kant's life was remarkably even and regular, and was in an unusual degree the result of rational self-control. There is always grandeur in a life which shows itself so superior to inclination and passion and circumstances, and makes reason the supreme arbiter. Not only in

Kant's philosophy, but also in his life, there is much that suggests the sage who is immeasurably superior to creatures of circumstances; and the philosophic mood of his lonely career has justly gained admiration. He had an ideal for life, as well as for philosophy, and he was stern and severe in his efforts for its realization. But with all our admiration of the wisdom which shone in his conduct, his effort to discipline life into the grooves of his maxims also had its disadvantages. The rules which free a man from the control of his inclinations may themselves be woven into a strait-jacket, and rational principles may be carried to an extreme which makes their application irrational. The reign of maxims in Kant's case was a logical deduction from his emotionless morality; and their supremacy to an extent which suppressed impulse and spontaneity helped to rob his life of much of the warmth, freshness, and variety, which beautify even ordinary lives, and to limit it methodically to wise but cold formulas. A cotemporary said of Kant, "He has made himself a slave of his reason, and unflinchingly obeys its laws." Although this was intended as a compliment, the word "slave" is too suggestive of something else. His rules were, indeed, the result of careful reflection, often embodied much wisdom, and saved him from many mortifying experiences. But why are the emotions given if, with and besides the rules, they are to have no room for their healthy play? Impulse and inclination may be in harmony with truth and right, and may intensify all that is noblest in man; and to banish or suppress them may in some respects make a man more than ordinary humanity, but in others it will make him less. It is said that when Kant found that a maxim was no longer adapted to his condition he would change it, and thus proved that he was master of his maxims; but it is evident that they sometimes gained the complete mastery over him, and made his life restrained and rigorous, and that at last slight changes, even when necessary for his health and safety, were made with extreme difficulty. His mental, as well as his moral and physical life, was subjected to rules, and his career was marked by an almost unvarying sameness, especially in his later years. The following is an illustration of the fact that, with all his power of abstraction, his mind was much influenced by mechanical routine. After returning from his walk he was in the habit of reading till twilight. Then, in winter and in summer, he would stand before the stove and fix his eyes on a certain tower, while his mind was occupied with reflections. In the course of time the poplars in a neighbouring yard grew so high as to hide his favourite tower. This so disturbed and annoyed him that he was anxious that the trees should be topped; and the owner, to gratify him, did as he desired, thus enabling the philosopher again to pursue his meditations uninterruptedly. This story reveals a prominent characteristic of Kant, namely, the tendency to an undeviating sameness.

While he made the free and good will the essence of all morality, he nevertheless thought it necessary to prevent arbitrariness by carefully determining the course of conduct by means of rational principles. He wanted to introduce a mathematical exactness into the activity of the practical as well as of the speculative reason. His moral philosophy shows how predominant the intellectual element was in Kant. The will is the practical reason, not in any sense the heart; its elements are intellectual, not emotional; and the maxims give the intellectual grooves in which the will is to run. He says, "Many persons have no idea what they want; hence they act according to instinct and authority." Men should learn to know what they want, and this knowledge should be embodied in maxims as the laws of life. Kant treats the will as if it did not belong to the whole man, but only to the intellect; and in his morality, as well as in his speculative philosophy, the emotional element seems to have been absorbed by the intellectual. Reason, being the highest, is also the governing faculty; as it gives the principles of knowledge, so it also gives the laws of conduct; and Kant wants to make life, as well as our philosophy, rational, insisting as strenuously on conduct which has its source in the (practical) reason, as he does on a philosophy which has its source in the (speculative) reason. He regards as the true life that one which translates reason into conduct; and in this fact we find the explanation of his numerous maxims.

While, however, depreciating the emotions in general, Kant sought to attain that joy which springs from the consciousness of having done right. In a letter to Reinhold, he speaks of philosophical indifference respecting all things not in our power, and claims that the consciousness of having done our duty constitutes the real worthiness of life, and that experience teaches us that all other enjoyment, except this consciousness, is vain. According to Kant, therefore, the real grandeur and highest enjoyment of life are within the reach of all, the poorest, the humblest, and the illiterate, as well as the richest, the most exalted, and the most learned—a conclusion worthy of the great metaphysician and the sublime moralist.

Maxims, which Kant defines as laws made subjective or rules chosen as the guides of life, should be taught early in life. Authority should be exercised to lead the child to adopt them; nevertheless it should learn to appreciate them and adopt them voluntarily. Moral training must rest on them, and he says, "One must see to it that the pupil does right according to maxims, not from habit, in order that he may not merely do what is good, but because it is good; for the whole moral worth of actions consists in the good maxims." The pupil should learn the grounds of his conduct and recognize the idea of duty as its source. Kant gives directions for the training of others in which he reveals his own laws of conduct. He says that rules, not impulse, ought to determine the conduct of the young. "Moral culture must be based on maxims, not on discipline. . . . The first effort in moral training should be to form a moral character. Character consists in skill to act according to maxims. At first they are maxims of the school; afterwards they become those of humanity." When children have once adopted rules of conduct, they ought to follow them strictly. It is true, Kant says, that those are blamed who always act according to law, the man, for instance, who has a definite time for everything, as if he were regulated by the watch; yet, while such strict adherence to time may look painful, it is, nevertheless, important in the formation of character.

Laxity was altogether foreign to Kant's nature; and

as he asked no mercy of others, so he was not very merciful in his judgments. Especially was he strict in the fulfilment of promises to the letter, and in demanding that others should do the same. Soon after he became a tutor, a student promised to bring him the pay for his lectures at a certain time. When the appointed hour came, and the student did not appear, Kant was restless and greatly displeased, telling two friends who were present, that it was not for the sake of the money but because a definite promise had been given; and every fifteen minutes he would again speak of the fact that the young man did not appear. When he made his appearance, a few days later, he received a severe rebuke; requesting permission to take part in a disputation which was to occur soon, Kant refused, saying, "You might again break your word and not appear at the discussion, and thus spoil everything."

Kant associated mostly with those who had comparatively few wants, and did not come in contact with the great sufferings of humanity; it is not strange, therefore, if his sympathies were but little developed. His wonderful power of will in controlling his own sufferings, his great endurance, and his successful conflict with poverty and difficulties, led him to expect of others similar power and triumphs; and he looked with a degree of contempt on those who failed. If he depreciated the sympathies which Christianity particularly develops, he cherished sentiments worthy of the noblest of the old Roman heroes, and there is a grandeur in his stoicism. It seems as if we hear a Spartan voice when he says, "A man must never weep other than magnanimous tears. Those which he sheds in pain, or on account of misfortune, make him despicable."[131] The same spirit breathes in his maxim, "Crying and moaning in physical pain are unworthy of you, especially if you are conscious of being yourself the cause of the pain." The nature of his studies and the character of his life must be taken into consideration in judging of his relation to others. Rink, who knew him well, says, "His world was in his study; and even when he had observed men with a sharp eye, he transferred the results of his observation to the school, and judged others as severely as he did himself. In doing this, he naturally overlooked the impossibility of appreciating the stand-point of others as fully as his own, or as one at least believes that he appreciates his own, so that the severity supposed to be just may easily degenerate into slight injustice. And thus, I believe, it may be explained that Kant, when he once believed himself justified in forming an unfavourable opinion of any one, seldom or never changed it." And he also says, "The isolated life which Kant had always lived, together with his limited wants, led him either entirely to overlook much in the life of other persons, or else at least to under-estimate it. Otherwise, I am convinced, it would be possible to relate many more noble deeds of him than can now be done."

In spite of the severity of his principles and the efforts to suppress his emotional nature, his life furnishes numerous examples of genuine kindness, and at times he was even tender. Kant was better than his principles, in this respect, and his heart sometimes transcended his philosophy. It may seem to be a contradiction, but the testimony of his friends makes it evident that, in spite of his maxims, which excluded impulse, and of his cold morality, he remained child-like; and though he was not able to place himself on the stand-point of the masses, he repeatedly proved that he could be moved by the needs of others. He was not an impulsive or sentimental philanthropist, and (though the statements on this point are contradictory) the most reliable testimony declares that he could not tolerate beggars; still, he won many hearts by his good and kind deeds.

Kant has justly been admired for his uprightness and his sterling integrity. He not only taught the Categorical Imperative, but he also strove to conform his life to it, and he was above petty meanness and selfishness. He made strenuous efforts to attain the strictest morality in his dealings with others, and his life was singularly free from injustice and immorality. "Kant lived as he taught," was said of him while still alive, and since then it has been repeated frequently, and efforts have not been wanting, on the part of devout disciples, to ascribe to his doctrine and his life a perfection which the unbiased critical student may fail to find; but the very extravagance of the praise heaped on Kant shows what a profound impression his exalted character made on some of his contemporaries. Though he did not attain his own ideal of perfection, his earnest desire and even anxiety to do so are worthy of all commendation; and he deserves enthusiastic praise who so loved duty as to declare, "Whoever will yet propose to me a good deed in my last moments, him will I thank."

Truthfulness was regarded by Kant as the cardinal virtue, and on it he laid the strongest emphasis. He brought this trait from his early home, in which this virtue reigned, and where his father was most careful to inculcate it. Kant esteemed lying inexpressibly base. His usual strictness is seen in his very definition of a lie,—whatever is announced as true when one knows that it is false, and whenever a man announces as certain that of which he is not certain. In his "Pedagogics" he speaks of truthfulness as the fundamental and most essential trait of character, and says, "A man who lies, has no character at all; and if he has anything good, it emanates only from his temperament;" and he also says, "Lying makes a man an object of general contempt, and is one of the means of robbing him of that regard and confidence which each person should have toward himself." So strict is he in demanding truthfulness, that he will tolerate no deviation, not even in the extremest cases. There were others who advocated the view that in dealing with persons we must take into account the question whether they are entitled to know the truth. Kant, however, claimed that truthfulness is a duty which I owe myself, irrespective of my relation to others; and he held that we have no right to deceive even the murderer who seeks to take the life of our friend.

Truthfulness was a prominent trait of his own character. In his researches, his aim was the truth in its purity; hence his dread of prejudice and his long and profound investigations to find a firm basis for knowledge. His friends make special mention of his strict adherence to the truth, and Borowski's testimony is, "He was reliable and truthful in every word, and taught me, while yet a youth, with solemn earnestness, to be reliable and truthful and candid, just as he was and continued to be." To this general rule, Borowski himself found a single exception, which will, however, be mentioned in considering Kant's religious views.([132])

He, of course, made a distinction between truthfulness and candour, and held that, while a man ought always to be truthful, he need not tell all he thinks or knows, but must be his own judge of the extent of his frankness. There may be many reasons for withholding facts or convictions from the public, and perfect frankness might be a great evil.([133])

His aversion to flattery and to unmeaning compliments was but a reflex of his love of truth. The fact that empty and ostentatious ceremonies and fulsome praise were so common in society, made it the more a duty to oppose them vigorously. He disliked the parade of titles, and usually omitted his from the title-page of his books. After he had attained to years of maturity, he found extravagant compliments in dedications disagreeable, though in his first attempt at authorship he was guilty of the very thing he afterwards so severely censured.([134]) With his views of the dignity of man, he could only look on everything like cringing as degrading, and it was one of his maxims, "Do not become a servant of men; do not let others, with impunity, trample your rights under foot." He placed a high estimate on self-respect and self-confidence, and opposed all that tended to lower them; hence the importance which he attached to the feeling of independence, individually as well as politically.

That moral perfection which some of his eulogists ascribed to him, Kant himself would have been the first to disclaim. With all his self-confidence, and with all the purity of his motives, he knew full well that he was human; and he was too keen an observer of self not to see some of the failings which those who were intimate with him did not fail to discover. Profound and learned as he was, and earnestly as he strove to do his duty, his isolated student-life, his limited experience, and his predominantly intellectual development, were certainly not calculated to make him great-hearted. He placed the speculative and the practical reason upon the throne: and in speaking of his intellectual greatness and of his moral grandeur, rare praise can be bestowed on him without danger of flattery. The heart was not his domain; in the emotions his sphere was limited; many of the affairs of humanity were altogether foreign to him, while others touched him only externally. The breadth of sympathy developed by personal suffering was unknown to him, and he was a stranger to the emotions fostered by family ties. When we look at his character as a whole, we admire its moral earnestness and even sternness, its sincerity, and its general excellence; but he himself was too suspicious of the emotions to desire to inspire any enthusiasm with reference to his own heart.

Kant's moral severity was in marked contrast with the prevailing laxity. The undermining of faith in Germany had prepared the way for the contagion of French frivolity. In their thirst for happiness, men lost sight of the claims of morality, or sought to make them minister to their ruling passion. The low tone of morals made the sublime height of Kant's ethics the more conspicuous. The prevailing views may have led him to make his morality the more stern and to exclude from it all emotion, so as the more successfully to reject all endæmonism. But Kant himself brought in happiness again as necessary for the realization of the highest good.

The religious as well as the moral views of Kant are based on the results of the "Kritik," and they rest solely on the practical, not on the speculative reason. We are conscious of our freedom; we cannot go behind this fact, nor is it necessary. "*You can, for you ought*," an expression which is often used by him, settles the matter; the fact that there is an *ought* implies freedom, without which there could be no responsibility. Speculatively, freedom itself is an insoluble mystery; but whatever the immediate causes of moral conduct may be, its ultimate source is the spontaneity of the actor.

This primal and indisputable fact of man's freedom is the basis of Kant's theology, as well as of his ethics. Conscience, which rests on this fact, demands perfection, namely holiness; but that is not attainable in this life. Since, however, it is demanded of us, it must also be practicable, and Kant again uses the argument, "You ought, therefore you can." But since holiness is not practicable here, it must be in another life where there is an eternal progress toward the realization of this ideal. The highest good, of which the perfect conformity of the disposition with the moral law is the first condition, is therefore possible only if there is another life; and the immortality of the soul is the first postulate of the practical reason.

But the realization of the highest good, namely, the perfect harmony between moral worthiness and happiness, or the bestowal of happiness according to desert, cannot be accomplished by nature, nor by virtue itself;

and yet our nature demands that our happiness should be proportionate to our virtue. Therefore it can be accomplished only in another world, and by a Being not subject to nature, but which can reward according to moral desert, namely, God. The existence of God is therefore the second postulate of the practical reason.(135)

Kant declares that these postulates must not be used speculatively, as, for instance, to account for the origin of the world and of design in nature, though the existence of God would be the most satisfactory explanation of these problems. He is extremely cautious in the application of these postulates, and insists that they can be used only for practical purposes, but for these, he thinks, they are entirely sufficient.

Both in laying the foundation of rational theology and in building a superstructure on it, we find that Kant went his own way. Not that he is free from the influences of the age; but he sought to master and concentrate its various tendencies, and he gave them a new basis and a new direction. After turning with aversion from the religious influences of his youth, he still found many tendencies in the age which were anything but congenial to his rationalizing spirit. On the one hand, he found religious extravagance and fanaticism, and some of his severe expressions against the religion of the day are probably aimed at this tendency; on the other, there was religious as well as moral indifference, or even decided hostility towards religion. The age demanded tolerance, fraternity, humanity, reason; and many of their apostles sought the promotion of these objects with a passion which made them intolerant and fanatical. The old forms of faith were looked upon as fetters; the preaching of the times neither satisfied the restlessness of the age nor met the demands of reason; orthodoxy became hateful, because it was regarded as narrow and intolerant, and as lacking the fraternal and humane spirit. English deism and French naturalism found a congenial soil among men of culture in Germany, and Illumination became the watchword of literature. Kant felt the influence of these tendencies, and in his religious views the effect of English deism and of Lessing's rationalizing efforts is clearly seen. When we consider the influence of the English natural philosophers on his early life, it is not surprising that there are traces of deism already in his cosmogony. It is natural that his fondness for Hume should subject him to the religious, as well as the philosophical influence of the sceptical philosopher. Among the French authors, Rousseau's influence was especially powerful. In considering Kant's religious views, it should be remembered that he lived in the age of Voltaire and of the French Encyclopedists; that literature was predominantly sceptical; that the reaction against a religious dogmatism, which had often been narrow and oppressive, had made Frederick II. and Joseph II. popular heroes of tolerance; and that instead of a religion based on revelation and on doctrines transcending reason, there was a cry for religion based on common sense. The age which hailed with delight Lessing's "Nathan the Wise," had no taste for dogma or for orthodoxy.

To form a correct estimate of Kant's theology and of his originality in its development, we must view him as he stands amid the fermentations of the age, both receiving its leaven and also, in turn, giving it new leaven. While in many respects his religious views were a product of the age, he was too profound and too earnest to treat religion with the flippancy which was the fashion among many of his contemporaries. He viewed religion as involving too many interests of humanity for such treatment; and there were in him moral and religious aspirations, developed no doubt by Pietism, which demanded satisfaction, and made religion to him a serious matter. Kant places much emphasis on the demands of our nature, and frequently refers to them, and he could not regard as satisfactory any system which fails to meet them. The frivolous, irresolute Voltaire, swinging like a pendulum between deism and materialism; the sentimental deism of his favourite Rousseau; and the scepticism in which Hume seemed content to rest, could no more satisfy the needs of his deep nature than could the shallow and illogical Illumination of Germany, which labelled its heterogeneous and chaotic mass of opinions "Common Sense." Kant saw that in many cases this latter tendency might with more propriety be called vulgar sense; and he wanted something which transcended this, namely rationality. The tendency also lacked the moral earnestness which he sought. It applied historical criticism, which had received a great impulse from Semler, but it was chiefly negative in its results; Kant shifted the ground from history to reason, and from historical to rational criticism. While there was much similarity between his religious views and the prevalent English deism, he went deeper, and made conscience, duty, and morality more stern than was usually the case with deists; but the chief difference consisted in this: that while they rejected the possibility of revelation, Kant maintained that a revelation may be possible, and he made an effort to attach his religious views as closely as possible to the New Testament; and though the similarity is generally only that of the terminology, he claimed that his theology was the essence of the teachings of that book. Whatever analogies there may be between his views and the systems mentioned, none of these names designate his theology, which he himself called Rationalism. In the Kantian sense, this means that reason is the source and interpreter of religion, and therefore the final appeal in theology.

Some of his definitions are significant and will help us to understand his own position. He who regards natural religion as the only one that is obligatory, may be called a rationalist. If he denies the possibility of a supernatural revelation, he is called a naturalist; if he admits its possibility, but declares that for religion it is not necessary to know and accept a revelation, he may be called a pure rationalist; but if he regards faith in it as necessary for the universal religion, he may be called a pure supernaturalist. Kant himself was a pure rationalist. As the very name implies, a rationalist is one who moves within the limits of the reason, and regards its light as sufficient for a knowledge of religious truth and for practical guidance.([136]) But just because he confines himself to the limits of human knowledge, he will never deny the possibility of a revelation, nor its necessity as the divine means for the introduction of the true religion, because these are subjects concerning which reason determines nothing. The admission which Kant thus makes respecting the possibility of a divine revelation, is, however, of no practical value, for he declares that even if one had been given, it would be impossible to determine that it is a supernatural revelation. "Even if God did speak to him, man could never know that it was God who spoke. It is utterly impossible for man to recognize God with his senses, to distinguish Him from objects of sense, or to know Him by any marks whatever." A revelation would be valuable only because it gave truth sooner than reason, which can, however, discover the same in the course of time —one of the many views in which Kant agrees with Lessing. He does not admit that a revelation gives any doctrines which are above reason, for his principle, that all the doctrines of religion must be rational, excludes all super-rational doctrines.

It is one of his favourite notions that a rational religion is the only one which can be general, and for this reason he repeats the statement so often. He thinks that a religion which rests on revelation should always tend more and more to become rational; and that, in the course of time, the church which is based on a revelation should be able to dispense altogether with historical faith, and will do so when it has become a rational church. Indeed, he declares that it is the most senseless thing imaginable to make a faith based on history the condition of salvation; and he repeatedly treats the historical element in religion as unworthy of notice. He says, in a letter to Jacobi, that the question whether reason, in order to get the idea of theism, could have been aroused only by something taught in history, or only through an inscrutable supernatural influence, is merely of secondary importance, since it refers solely to the origin of this idea. "For it may be admitted that, if the Gospel had not first taught the general moral laws in all their purity, reason until now would not have apprehended them so clearly; though, since they are here now, it is possible to convince persons of their correctness and validity by means of mere reason." He depended so wholly on reason, and on *à priori* constructions, that his depreciation of history is characteristic, and in religion, he thinks, it can be dispensed with altogether. The Church, which is based on historical faith, he calls the Church Militant, which will become the Church Triumphant by becoming rational. The leading-strings of holy tradition and its associations—such as statutes and observances, which in their day did good service—can be dispensed with, in the course of time, and at last they even become fetters. Kant regards these things as intended for the childhood of humanity, and as not adapted to the age of manhood. When this manhood is attained, the law, "which each one gives himself," becomes his guide. This law must not, however, be regarded by man as merely his own, but also as that of the Ruler of the world, who reveals it through the reason. Kant, of course, degrades the statutes and ceremonies of the Church by making them valuable only as aids to the immature and weak; but he was far more tolerant than some of the freethinkers of the day, who were revolutionary, and aimed to destroy the Bible, the Church, and every vestige of worship. He held that the transition from a religion resting on revelation and historical faith to rational religion, is not to be accomplished by an outward revolution, but by means of rational convictions. The faith of a church may be tolerated as a vehicle or servant of reason; in other words, in its most perfect development revealed religion becomes rationalism. ([137])

As faith and revelation thus culminate in rational religion, which can almost dispense with the former and wholly with the latter; so Kant at last lets all religion culminate in a morality in which the religious element is reduced to a minimum. This is evident from his whole theology and even from his division of religions. He claims that all religions may be divided into two classes—those which seek the divine favour, and the moral religion or the religion of a good life. According to the former, man flatters himself either that God can make him eternally happy without becoming a better man, by forgiving his sins, or, if this is not possible, that God can make him better without any effort on his own part except to pray for it; but since, before an omniscient Being, praying is nothing more than wishing, it can accomplish nothing; for if it could be done by mere wishing every person would be good. This division degrades all religions which have a cultus; and it is taken for granted that a religion cannot at the same time have a cultus and be thoroughly moral. But this separation of worship from morality is as characteristic of him as the attempt to let morality absorb religion. Kant puts Christianity into the second class, declaring that it is the only public moral religion which has ever existed, a religion which inspires the hope that whatever more is needed than man himself can supply will be granted from above. He thinks that it is not essential for man to know what aid God gives, but that it is necessary for him to know what he must do in order to make himself worthy of divine help.

So often and emphatically does Kant represent religion as essentially morality, that his view in this respect is of the utmost importance for understanding his theology. He bases religion more on conscience, of whose existence we are immediately conscious, than on God, whose existence is only mediately known; it rests mainly on the ideas of freedom and responsibility, and consists rather in what man can do for himself than in what God does for him; its principal factor is therefore man, not God; and it is quite natural that, with these views, the supremacy should be given to the moral element in religion. Kant says, "In substance—that is, with regard to its object—religion does not in the least differ from morality, for it deals with duties in general." The idea of God, he holds, is not to inspire worship, but moral conduct. "In religion, all depends on the actions." His idea of the true church is that of an "ethical community," as he calls it, which is based solely on morality, and has neither symbols nor cultus; and he wants everything in religion to have only a moral aim. "Religion is that faith which places the essence of all reverence for God in the morality of man;" and the religion which fails to do this he pronounces heathenism. "If reverence for God is the first aim to which virtue is subjected, He is made an idol, that is, He is regarded as a Being whom we dare not hope to please by means of a moral course in this world, but whose favour we hope to gain by means of adoration and flattery; then religion is idolatry." It is very evident that Kant did not believe in a religion which unites the strictest morality with the highest reverence and purest worship. He brings in God as only a moral help, and as necessary to secure for man that happiness which he deserves; and, as far as morality is concerned, God could be dispensed with, since man has in himself a complete moral basis and the only moral law that exists for him. The "ought" is really independent of God; but, on the other hand, on it our faith in God rests. Kant's religion differs too little from his ethics to require the divine Being as its centre or its essence. After postulating the existence of God, he makes Him almost useless, except so far as He may be necessary to supplement morality by rewarding it with happiness. The God of Kant inspires no love and no worship; indeed, he would pronounce Him an idol if He did.([138])

Kant is as anxious to exclude from man's relation to God all emotion as he is to eliminate all inclination from morality. He regards the command of Scripture, to love God supremely and the neighbour as one does himself, as in perfect harmony with a morality that is really loveless. Love to God, he says, as an affection is impossible, because He is not an object of the senses; on the other hand, love to man is, indeed, possible, but it cannot be commanded; "for no man can love any one at the command of another. Therefore it is only the practical love which is meant in that summary of all laws. In this sense, to love God signifies to do all His commands gladly; and to love the neighbour signifies to perform gladly all duties toward him." Perhaps this statement more clearly than any other indicates the difference between the Kantian and Christian morality. While the latter demands absolute obedience to duty, it also regards God and man as persons, between whom a personal relation, especially that of love, is possible; and it requires a state of heart which both loves and obeys. Kant, however, lays the emphasis on obedience for the sake of the law; he seems to be afraid of giving prominence to the personal element, just as he is afraid of the introduction of heart into morality and religion. His ultimate aim is a character that is purely moral for morality's sake; while Christianity aims to develop a personality that is loving, trustful, hopeful, and holy.

Admitting, as he did, that a revelation might be possible (though reason cannot settle definitely whether it is), he was not prepared to reject the Scriptures altogether; but as he made reason and conscience the supreme and only guides in religion, he could place no high estimate on anything which claimed to be a revelation. The Bible, he thinks, may continue for a long time to be the authentic religious guide of the masses; but it is not needed by those whose reason and conscience are fully developed.([139]) For the existence of the Church it is necessary, since this institution contains many weak persons; but for the existence of religion, the Bible is not necessary. Of the Old Testament he had a low opinion, and he spoke of Judaism as not at all a religion, but as merely a political institution. The laws of Judaism he pronounces laws of force merely, which apply only to the outer conduct, and not at all to the moral purpose; and he states that even the Ten Commandments are intended "absolutely" only for external conduct, and not at all for the heart.(140) He places the moral character of the New Testament inestimably higher than that of the Old, and seeks to attach his views to his interpretation of the essence of its teachings.

Kant's recognition of Scripture is purely a matter of expedience. The state needs the Bible to control the people; the masses need it, in order that they, having weak consciences, may recognize their duty; and the philosopher finds it a convenient vehicle for conveying to the people the faith of reason. Were it rejected, it might be difficult, if not impossible, to put in its place another book which would inspire as much confidence. Kant's principles of course led him to deny that the Bible is authoritative in matters of religion, or that it is of itself a safe guide in morals. It is not held by him to be valuable for the sake of its doctrines and what may legitimately be inferred from them; but its value consists in the fact that, owing to the confidence of the people in it, reason can use it to interpret into Scripture its own doctrines, and can thus make it the means of popularizing rational faith. If any one imagines that the aim of the interpretation is to obtain the real meaning of Scripture, he is no Kantian on this point; that book is simply to be used as a help for moral reflections and applications, without inquiring into the meaning which the writers themselves may have intended to convey, for about this Kant does not care. He claims that it was the aim of the sacred writers to make better men, and that the historical, which contributes nothing to this end, is in itself altogether a matter of indifference, and one can regard it as he pleases.

All the ingenuity of Kant is exerted to answer the

question, "How shall the Scriptures be interpreted?" Repeatedly, emphatically, and with various illustrations, he teaches that the interpretation should be such as to make Scripture harmonize with the practical reason, and that its sole aim is to get moral rules and impulses. The theoretical passages which transcend reason can be interpreted in the interest of the practical reason; and all the passages which are in conflict with this reason must be so interpreted. The preacher must make every passage of Scripture which he uses minister to some moral purpose; and if a moral sense is not found in the passage itself, one must be interpreted into it or forced upon it; and he argues so strenuously, persistently, and prolixly in favour of this rule for the very purpose of making passages the vehicles of teachings which they do not contain. Sometimes it may be necessary to draw from a passage the very opposite of that which it seems to teach. This method of using Scripture is, he thinks, perfectly honest so long as we do not assert that the sense which we interpret into the symbols and sacred books is really intended to be conveyed by them, but say nothing about it, and only assume the possibility of so understanding them. For instance, if passages of Scripture make faith itself meritorious, "then they must be interpreted as if the moral faith, which improves and elevates the soul by means of reason, were meant." Only when the Scriptures are interpreted to suit our moral purposes are they valuable; otherwise they are "practically empty, or even obstacles in the way of the good. And only then are they practically *authentic;* that is, God in us is Himself the interpreter." According to Kant, therefore, this interpretation gives the real will of God, and he says, "That God who speaks through our own (moral, practical) reason is an unerring, universally understood interpreter of His word, and there absolutely cannot be any other (for instance, a historically) authenticated interpreter of His word, because religion is purely an affair of reason." And Kant calls his rule of "moral" interpretation, "The only evangelical, biblical method for the instruction of the people in the true, inner, and universal religion."

This hermeneutical rule was first announced in 1793, in the book entitled, "Religion within the Limits of mere Reason;" and in 1798 he found it necessary to explain the rule. He then declared that it might be demanded of the interpreter, whether he was interpreting authentically or doctrinally; if the former, then he must explain the sense of the writer; if the latter, then he can put into the passage under consideration his own rational views, whether found there or not. He still calls this art of interpretation, "Hermeneutica sacra."

Surprising as it may seem, there were many rationalistic theologians who adopted this rule; and in an age when many ministers found their convictions in conflict with the Scriptures, it was very convenient. There were, however, other theologians who saw in it a sacrifice of principle to expediency, and who thought it would be more honest boldly to reject Scripture than to profess adherence to it and yet reject its real teachings. Men like Eichhorn, Noesselt, Storr, and many others, protested against the rule in the interest of truth as well as out of regard for Scripture. Not only was the honesty of the rule questioned, but it was also seen that it opened the way for every one to put his own supposed moral views, however irrational or fanatical they might be, into Scripture; and there was no sufficient reason why the Koran or some other book might not, under certain circumstances, be made the basis of religion, since the Scripture is not the only work which ministers can use as a depository for their moral ideas.

Even before he announced this hermeneutical rule he advocated a distinction between the official or public use of reason and its private exercise,(141) which is not less strange than his moral interpretation of Scripture. He says, "A minister is bound to instruct his catechumens and members according to the creed of the church he serves, for it is on this condition that he has been accepted. But as a scholar he has perfect freedom; yes, it is even his calling to communicate to the public all his carefully considered and beneficial thoughts respecting the faults in that creed, and he should also publish plans for the better organization of religious and ecclesiastical affairs. There is in this course nothing which can burden the conscience. For what he teaches by virtue of his office, as the agent of his church, that he teaches as something respecting which it is not in his power to give instruction as he thinks, but he should teach what he is commissioned to do in the name of another. He will say, 'Our church teaches this or that doctrine, and these are the proofs it uses.' He will draw all the practical lessons for his congregation from dogmas which he himself cannot subscribe with a full conviction of their truth, but which he can teach, since it is not altogether impossible that truth may be concealed therein; at all events, there is in them nothing which opposes inner religion. For if he believed the latter to be the case, then he could not perform his work conscientiously; he would have to abandon his office. The use which a minister makes of his reason before his congregation is only a *private use*, because this is always a family gathering, however large it may be; and respecting it, he, as a minister, is not free and dare not be, for he executes a foreign commission. On the other hand, as a scholar, who through his writings speaks to what is, properly speaking, the public, namely, to the world, he is a minister in the *public use* of his reason, and he has unlimited freedom to exercise his reason and to speak in his own name; for that the spiritual leaders of the people should themselves be dependent, is an inconsistency which would tend to make inconsistencies eternal."

That the same reason can have its public and its private use, and can be so different in its teachings, and even contradictory; that in the one case it is free and speaks in its own name, and in the other it is not free, but speaks in the name of another; that the minister may teach one thing in the pulpit, and yet in books teach something else—this certainly is a strange doctrine for a strict moralist. It puts the preacher on a level with a political ambassador who is supposed to represent the views of another, whatever his own may be. Kant evidently had such a view of the office of the ministry, a view which may have been promoted by the union of church and state. According to the modern and more independent position of ministers, his rule respecting the public and the private use of reason puts expediency where principle should reign supremely.

Though he interpreted Scripture so as to make it harmonize with the practical reason, Kant made a constant effort to clothe his religious ideas in biblical language. He thinks that the doctrine of the Trinity has no practical value whatever, and that it is a matter of no significance whether there are three or ten persons in the Godhead, since both views are equally inconceivable and equally useless. Nevertheless he holds that the practical reason requires faith in God: first, as the Almighty Creator of heaven and earth, that is, viewed morally, as the Holy Lawgiver; second, as the Preserver of the human family, or as a Gracious Ruler and Moral Maintainer of the same; third, as the Administrator of His own holy laws, that is, as the Righteous Judge. Kant believes that God wants to be served in these three aspects, and that the idea of a trinity of persons in the Godhead is not an inappropriate representation of God's threefold relation to us as moral beings.

For Kant, Christ has significance only as an idea, and this idea he constructs according to his view of the demands of reason. The section, in his book on Religion, in which he discusses this subject is headed, "The Personified Idea of the Good Principle." He claims that the only thing which could have made the world an object of the divine counsel and which gives an aim worthy of creation, is humanity in its entire moral perfection. The man who alone is pleasing to God "is in Him from all eternity;" that is, this man as an idea and as the aim of creation is in the divine mind—God has a conception of such a being; this ideal being is, therefore, not created, but is God's only begotten Son. Since all things are created for this perfect, ideal man, he is the Word (the Logos) by whom "all things were made; and without Him was not anything made that was made." This perfect man is the reflection of God's glory; in Him God loved the world; and only in Him and by accepting His views can men become the children of God. In the whole discussion of the subject this perfect man is viewed by Kant as a mere ideal of humanity; and He is the Son of God in the sense that this ideal had its birth in the divine mind. For the sake of this idea the world was made, and for this reason it may be said that by this ideal man all things were made.

This idea of moral perfection, called Christ by Kant, is the prototype of perfect purity, and is placed before us as an ideal which each person ought to strive to realize. The idea itself, "which reason presents to us for imitation," can give us the power necessary for this imitation. But since we are not the originators of this idea, and as it has taken root in man when there is no possibility of our understanding how he could be receptive for such an idea, "it is better to say that this prototype came down to us from heaven, namely, that it became incarnate." The union of this ideal of perfect humanity with man may be regarded as a condescension on the part of the Son of God, if this divinely inclined person, who, being holy, was not obliged to undergo suffering, is viewed as nevertheless taking upon Himself the greatest suffering for the benefit of the world. We cannot conceive of this ideal of humanity otherwise than under the idea of a man who not only performs every duty and promotes good to the utmost, but who also, in spite of the greatest temptations, is ready to submit to all suffering, even to the most disgraceful death, for the welfare of the world and even for His enemies; for it is only when we conceive of a power as in conflict with difficulties and temptations, that we get an idea of its greatness.

In this discussion Kant forcibly proves his confidence in the miraculous power of a mere idea. He regards this as Christ's significance for man: by practical faith in this Son of God (or in this perfect idea of man) a person may hope to be acceptable to God and to be saved; that is, as Kant explains it, he who is conscious of such a moral purpose as to be able to believe confidently that under similar temptations and sufferings he would be true to this prototype of humanity, and he alone, has the right to regard himself as an object not unworthy of the divine favour.

Kant proceeds to show that this "idea" has its practical value in itself, and that it exists in our conscience. "We ought to be like this idea, and therefore we can be like it," again closes all further discussion. And he thinks that it must be possible to give an example of such a perfect being, for according to the requirements of the inner law every one ought to give a realization of this ideal. If now a person with such a divine disposition had come at a certain time, as it were from heaven to earth, and had given in doctrine and in life the example of a man acceptable to God; and if thus he had brought to the world an inestimably great blessing in the form of a revolution in the human family: still, we should have no reason to regard him otherwise than as a man naturally conceived, though this does not deny, absolutely, that he might have been a man conceived supernaturally. But the latter view is of no practical value, since the prototype of the example given by such a person must always be sought in us; and the very presence of this idea in us is itself incomprehensible enough, so that it is not necessary, besides the supernatural origin of this idea, to regard it as having been incarnated in a particular person. Indeed, Kant thinks that the exaltation of such a holy one above all human weaknesses would rather militate against the practical application of the idea, since it could not be the model for our imitation.

In order that the Gospel may be of practical value for all times, Kant thinks that its history is of no significance, and that the popular representations which it gives must be deprived of their mystical garb so that we may get at the underlying ideas. The spirit and the rational ideas in that Gospel are for the whole world and for all ages, and each one can see in the picture, or in what he puts into it, his own duty.([142]) The ideas which Kant finds in the life of Jesus which are of significance for each person, are as follows:—That there is absolutely no salvation for man except in the personal reception of genuine moral principles into the disposition; that this reception is opposed by our own perversity, which nothing can conquer but the idea of the moral goodness in its purity, with the conviction that this goodness is the end for which we were originally created; when this idea of moral goodness has once been fully taken into the disposition, we are to have confidence "that the gates of hell cannot prevail against it;" and that the characteristic mark or the evidence of the possession of this idea is the good life. He closes the whole discussion with the remark, that such an effort as he has made to find the ideas of reason in Scripture is not only proper but also a duty.

For Kant, therefore, Christ has significance only as a mere idea, namely, the ideal of perfect humanity in the divine mind. He valued history too little to attempt seriously to account for the historical origin of this idea, or to investigate the relation of the historical Christ to the account given in the gospels. The moral teachings of Christ he valued highly as an aid to reason, and he states that they are sufficient to establish Christ's authority, whatever the real history may be; in other words, he regards the moral truths of the Gospel as alone significant. Kant thought that he found in the New Testament itself authority for the use which he made of Scripture, and he says that Christ did not appeal to other laws, such as those of the Old Testament, because they are true; but that this was merely an accommodation to the prejudices of the people, in order that the rational religion which Christ taught might be made more palatable to them. Whether Christ gave what might be called a divine revelation, cannot be determined, he thinks, for we have no criteria by which to judge such a revelation. Nor can it be proved that any event is a miracle, simply because we do not understand the powers of nature enough to know what transcends their limits. Kant declares that it is possible that the person of the teacher of the only religion valid for all mankind was a mystery; that His appearance on earth, His removal from the same, His life and His sufferings, were all miracles; and that even the history which is to confirm all these miracles is itself a miracle, namely, a supernatural revelation. But this must rest on its own merits ; for us it really has no significance. We may, indeed, still value the garb which served to introduce the idea which is now indelibly impressed on every soul and needs no miracle ; but a confession of faith in these historical ducuments is not necessary. While he thus treats the historical account of Jesus as of no significance except as a shell into which the practical reason puts the kernel, his whole argument tends to destroy faith in the historic person of Jesus as given in the Gospel, treating the account itself as something whose truthfulness it is not worth while to investigate. Of the institution of the Last Supper he speaks as "a sad intercourse," and as looking like a formal farewell, indicating no speedy return ; and "the complaining words on the Cross give expression to a disappointed aim (namely, to bring, during his life, the Jews to the reception of the true religion)." The account of the Resurrection and Ascension he can use only as an embodiment of the idea of the beginning of another life and the entrance into the place of happiness, that is, upon communion with all that is good. When Jesus promises to abide with His own for ever, that only means that the ideal of humanity, which Christ gave and which is acceptable to God, shall abide with His disciples to the end of the world. The historical Christ is in reality not needed for morality ; but as the Gospel exists, He can be used for moral purposes.([143])

While Kant idealized the account of the Fall, and denied natural depravity, he nevertheless, as we have seen, admitted the reality of sin. Its essence consists neither in sensuality nor in a corruption of conscience.

There are two opposite tendencies in man: a conscience which impels him to seek the good, and an impulse to selfishness. One or the other of these must be supreme, and depravity consists in perverting the proper relation between the two, namely, in the subordination of the conscience to self-love. Therefore sin, whose beginning is always a free choice, but inexplicable, is selfishness as the supreme law of conduct.

In order that he may overcome sin and become good, man needs a radical change or conversion. This change from evil to good can no more be explained than can the transition from a state of purity to sin; but since the moral law demands that we become better, therefore we must also be able to do so. This conversion is wholly man's work, and the Christian doctrine of grace and faith in conversion has no place in the system. Kant says that we can know nothing about the influences of grace, and that, consequently, the idea can neither be used speculatively nor practically. While the deeds of a man are always imperfect, Kant supposes that God takes the good intention for the good deed, and that he who has a good disposition may cherish the belief that God accepts him. This is, of course, a mere supposition, but it is all the assurance which Kant gives.

His most serious difficulty, however, consists in this: although a man may have formed a good disposition, he was sinful before; how then is the debt of the past to be paid? Sin is an infinite violation of the law, and it therefore seems as if its result ought to be endless punishment. The debt contracted is not like a pecuniary debt, which one man can pay for another. The old man did not pay it; the new man is, as it were, a new being, and cannot assume the debt owed by the old man—yet divine justice must be satisfied. Somehow, therefore, the debt must be paid in the process of conversion. But Kant's whole discussion of the matter is confused and unsatisfactory, and at last he admits, and distinctly states, that man has no claim to be regarded as just, and that he is accounted righteous as a matter of grace.

His discussion of the Church is characterized by great bitterness, partly owing, no doubt, to his experience with the censors in Berlin. He says that the strait gate and the narrow way, leading to eternal life, is the good life; but the wide gate and the broad way is the Church. Not that the Church itself is to blame for this; but it is the broad way because attending church, confessing its creed, and celebrating its ordinances, are held to be the means for becoming acceptable unto God.

His aversion to formality in religion was partly due to the tendency of the times to value forms for their own sake, and he went so far in his opposition to this spirit as to reject all religious observances. He spoke contemptuously of all acts of worship; and all efforts to please God otherwise than by means of a moral life he pronounced fetichism. And he declared that between the degraded Wogulite who in the morning places the paw of a bearskin on his head with the prayer, "Do not kill me," and "the sublimated Puritan and Independent in Connecticut," there is, indeed, a great gulf as far as the manifestations of their faith are concerned, but there is none in principle, they belonging to the same class in that respect. This class consists of those who place their divine service in that which does not make men better, namely, in faith in statutory dogmas or in the observance of certain ceremonies. Kant pronounces it fetichism to regard any religious observances, however few they may be, as necessary. Holding such views, it is not surprising that for many years he never attended church, and observed no religious usages whatever. When a new rector of the university was inaugurated, the professors marched in procession to the cathedral, to attend religious services; but unless he himself was the rector, Kant, instead of entering, passed by the church.

He did not like the singing in the churches, and pronounced it mere bawling. In prayer, whether private or public, he had not the least faith; and in his conversation as well as writings he treated it as a superstition, and held that to address any thing unseen would open the way for fanaticism. Not only did he argue against prayer, but he also ridiculed it, and declared that a man would be ashamed to be caught by another in the attitude of prayer.(144) It is the custom of Germans to stand at table while asking the blessing; if any one of his guests prepared to say grace, he would interrupt him by urging him to sit down. In 1802 Hasse said one day, "This is the day set apart for repentance and prayer." Kant at first ridiculed the matter, but afterwards admitted that such a day might be useful in leading persons to think of their sins.

But while in principle Kant views prayer as fetichism, his estimate of expediency should not be forgotten. He says, "The existence of God is not proved but postulated, and it can be used only for that purpose for the sake of which reason was obliged to postulate it. If now a man thinks to himself, 'If I pray to God it can in no way injure me; for if He does not exist, then I have a supererogation of good works; but if He does exist, it will help me;' this prosopopœia is hypocrisy, since we must suppose in prayer that he who offers it is perfectly convinced that God exists. Therefore it happens that he who has already made great progress in goodness ceases to pray, for sincerity belongs to his principal maxims; and for this reason, also, those who are found praying are ashamed." Kant here makes the existence of God so problematical as to put prayer to Him out of the question. The reason did not postulate the existence of God for the purpose of prayer; therefore the idea of His existence does not justify prayer. But while he is certain that prayer has no efficacy whatever, except its influence on the men offering or hearing it, he nevertheless says, "In public addresses to the people, prayer may be retained, since it may really be of great rhetorical effect and may make a deep impression, and because in addressing the people one must speak to their sensuousness, and must let himself down to them as much as possible." ([145])

These are the essential elements of the religious views which the philosopher cherished till the close of life. Thinking it contemptible for any one to become devout in the weakness of old age, he declared that this should never be the case with him; and he kept his promise, for during his greatest weakness and with death staring him in the face, there was a remarkable absence of all religious expressions. It is self-evident that his faith could not be very cheerful, nor his hopes bright. His mind left many questions unsettled, questions concerning which souls of a deeply religious nature long for firm assurance. It is not strange that the faith which he built on his own postulates varied somewhat with his moods. While the close of his life was anything but cheerful, he seems generally to have been calm respecting religious subjects. His emotional nature does not appear to have asserted itself sufficiently to express any earnest longing for eternal life. The other world was not one of his favourite topics of conversation, and he himself followed the rule which he laid down for others,—not to attempt to pry into the secrets of the other world, but to wait for the solution of its mysteries till we get there. Sometimes, however, the other life was mentioned in his conversations. Some one said to him that it would be difficult to get an opportunity, in the next world, to converse with him, since he would be so much occupied with the company of the wise of ancient and modern times. Kant answered that if he met his servant Lampe there, he would rejoice and exclaim, "God be praised, I am in good company!" On July 2nd, 1803, while in a depressed mood, he said, "I cannot last long; I become weaker every day." Hasse then asked him what he expected of the future life? At first he evaded the question, and then answered, "Nothing definite." At another time he said respecting the next life, "Of that state I know nothing." And once he exclaimed, "Eternity! between thee and here a great gulf is fixed."

He did not cherish a high regard for clergymen; but the same must be said of his views of physicians and jurists. If the ministers had been purely moral teachers, instead of proclaiming doctrines which he regarded as beyond the limits of reason, he would have been more favourably disposed towards them. If, however, they were excellent men, their calling did not deprive them of his esteem, and several preachers were among his guests; and when in old age he became helpless, he committed himself and all his affairs into the hands of a clerical friend.

The fact that Kant deprived religion, aside from its moral elements, of all significance, as well as his personal attitude towards the Church, greatly grieved some of his friends. His great authority in philosophy added weight to his theological views, especially since his work on Religion appeared when his fame was at its height. His biographer Borowski says, "From my heart I wish that Kant had not regarded the Christian religion merely as a necessity for the state, or as an institution to be tolerated for the sake of the weak (which now so many, following his example, do even in the pulpit), but had known that which is positive, improving, and blessed in Christianity." Some of his disciples in philosophy also accepted him as their religious authority, and the same writer expresses the wish that "the beardless youth and idle babblers, who in a hundred less significant things do not know the right hand from the left, did not appeal to Kant's views respecting Christianity." There were some to whom the very fact that he held such views was a sufficient guarantee of their truth; and many also adopted his religious opinions who had neither his moral earnestness nor his outward respect for existing institutions. There were those who accepted his negative views, and carried them to an extreme which he would have deprecated, and committed excesses in his name for which he could not be held responsible. At one time it was reported that a band of fifty theological students, who professed to be Kantians, were open mockers of religion. Hamann states that one of them became a tutor in the family of a nobleman, and advised his pupil to reject, as priestly twaddle, all he had learned from his minister respecting religion, and to commit himself henceforth to the moral guidance of his tutor. The affair created considerable excitement, and was at last brought before the consistory. The tutor admitted the truth of the charges brought against him, and with four of his ilk signed a declaration that neither morality, nor sound reason, nor public welfare, could exist in connexion with Christianity. Such openly destructive tendencies were wholly foreign to Kant, whose hope was in the silent power of ideas. But while he did not seek such a result, he was anxious to exert a strong influence on religion. Not only was the ultimate aim of his speculation moral, but he also lectured on natural religion, and was especially desirous that theological students should be among his hearers, as he hoped by means of these lectures to produce a lasting reformatory effect.

In taking a general survey of his theological opinions, it should be remembered that he discusses the whole subject of religion as a philosopher who places himself wholly on reason, and aims to move strictly within its limits. His early religious training, the religious character of the age, his mathematical mind, his disregard of the historical element, and his depreciation of the emotional nature, must be taken into the account.([146]) Above all, the extent of his knowledge of the subject under discussion should be considered. Although he subjected theology to severe criticism, he did not make it a subject of careful study; and this fact alone can explain some of his strange views respecting theology, especially the Scriptures, which are found in his book on Religion. The suspicion arises that his reliance on *à priori* constructions relieved him of the necessity of attaining that knowledge of the subject which many regard as essential for its thorough discussion. After speaking of the universal character of his learning, Borowski says, "Theological investigations only, of whatever kind they might be, especially exegetics and dogmatics, he never touched." He neglected even the works of Ernesti and Semler, which excited much attention at that time. His studies and occupations were such that he could not be a theologian; and the writer just quoted, speaking of his theological attainments, says, "Really, his knowledge in this department did not extend beyond the dogmatic lectures of Professor Dr. Schulz, which he heard in 1742—1743. . . . Many will probably find the story remarkable, that Kant, before he published his work on 'Religion within the Limits of Reason,' carefully read one of our oldest catechisms, namely, the 'Basis of Christian Doctrine,' which appeared in 1732 or 1733. This explains the strangeness of many expressions in the book, and his evident inclination to adopt, for his theological views expressed in the work, the terminology and exegesis prevalent during the years mentioned." In the latter part of his life, according to Borowski, he read scarcely anything in theology, except some works on Church History. In the funeral oration on Kant, his colleague Wald said, "He was, however, entirely ignorant of the new investigations of Semler, Ernesti, Noesselt, and others. His theological knowledge scarcely reached to 1760. What he had formerly learned at school from the catechetical instructions of Dr. Schulz and finally in his dogmatic lectures, was and continued to be his entire knowledge of positive religion. No wonder that respecting it he judged thus and not otherwise." ([147]) But while his neglect of the study of the subject explains some of his strange views, it cannot be denied that his theology is interesting, in that it shows what so great a metaphysician regarded as settled by reason respecting natural religion. And whatever may be thought of his theology and his ethics, it must be admitted that there is much in them that is rich and profound, and worthy of serious thought; and his moral and religious views, as well as his metaphysical works, may give the impulse to new constructions. That these views are final could be claimed only by him who is ignorant of the developments in ethics and religion since Kant's time.

The religious opinions of our philosopher were too revolutionary in their character not to excite opposition. During the reign of Frederick the Great there was no danger that the Government would interfere with their promulgation; but a marked change occurred when Frederick William II. ascended the throne. His minister, Woellner, exerted great influence over him, and used it against the tolerance which had prevailed under the reign of his predecessor. In July, 1788, soon after Woellner became the Minister of Religion, an edict was published which bound the teachers of religion to adhere strictly to the confessions of the Church; and another, which appeared a few months later, placed the press and all home and foreign literature in Prussia under censorship. Three men after Woellner's own heart—Hermes, Woltersdorf, and Hillmer—were appointed in 1791 as a committee to execute these edicts, and the churches and schools were placed under their supervision. Even before his book on Religion appeared, Kant had been an object of special vigilance, and it is said that an unsuccessful effort had been made to induce the king to forbid the publication of works by him in the future. The war with France, the home of sensualistic philosophy and materialistic atheism, increased the vigilance of the Government, and in quick succession edicts followed each other which aimed at the suppression of all writings against the Christian religion. The reaction against the liberal policy of the preceding king reached its height about the time when Kant's "Religion within the Limits of Reason" appeared. The first part of the book, on "Radical Evil," had previously appeared as an article in a Berlin monthly, in April, 1792. The second article, entitled, "The Conflict of the Good Principle with the Bad for the Dominion over Man," was intended for the same monthly, and had been submitted to the Berlin censors, who, however, refused to permit its publication. When the publisher inquired for the reason of this refusal, which, according to the published decree respecting the censorship, he had a right to know, he was informed that another instruction was on hand which the censor followed as his law, but whose contents he refused to make known. When Kant was informed of this procedure he was greatly incensed. Determined to publish his views, he submitted the rejected article, and, in fact, the entire contents of his volume on Religion, to the theological faculty in Königsberg, with the request that they should decide whether the censorship of the book belonged to them or to the philosophical faculty. They decided that it belonged to the philosophical faculty, which, having examined the manuscript, gave the permission for its publication. The volume appeared in 1793, consisting of the article which had already been published, of that rejected by the Berlin censors, and of two other articles. The bitterness manifested toward the Church in the last article of the book may have received much of its inspiration from the course of the censors.

Hermes, the principal censor, was very strict, and was watching for opportune occasions to increase the vigilance and severity of the censorship. A friend in Berlin wrote to Kant, "You see, we are under hard taskmasters, and Hermes himself told my publisher that he was only waiting for peace to publish several cabinet decrees which were lying in his desk."

The publication of his book on Religion, in spite of the rejection of the second part in Berlin, was of course calculated to arouse still more opposition to Kant; and the contents of the book were such as to embitter the censors and those who agreed with their religious views. The work excited the more attention because it was regarded as giving the theology of the Critical Philosophy. In 1794 Woellner, in the name and at "the special command" of the king, wrote to Kant respecting the religious views promulgated by his lectures and writings, making special reference to his recent book on Religion, and charging him with distorting and degrading many of "the principal and fundamental doctrines of the Sacred Scriptures and of Christianity." For this Kant is to render an account to the Government, and he is warned not to promulgate similar views in the future. In his reply, Kant gave an account and a defence of his course with reference to theological doctrine, and at the close of his letter he says, "As far as the second point is concerned—not to be guilty in the future of a distortion and degradation of Christianity similar to that of which I am accused—I think it safest, in order to forestall the least suspicion in this respect, as your Royal Majesty's most faithful subject to declare solemnly, that henceforth I will refrain altogether from all public discussion of religion, whether natural or revealed, both in lectures and in writings."

After the king's death Kant regarded himself as released from the promise which he had made in this letter, and as again at liberty to express his religious views publicly. While some blamed him for having made the promise, regarding it as showing a lack of moral courage, others now censured him severely for publishing his religious views after the king's death, regarding this act as a violation of his pledge, and he was charged with duplicity. His own explanation of his conduct is, that he was very careful in choosing the expression, "as your Royal Majesty's most faithful subject;" and that he chose it for the very purpose of regaining his former freedom, if the monarch receiving the promise should die before him; for under the following king he would no longer be the subject of Frederick William II., to whom he made the promise. But if it was prepared, as Kant says it was, with very great care and with this mental reservation, then it is evident that it was intended to make the king and the censors think that he meant one thing by the promise, while Kant himself really meant something very different. Every one who read it without Kant's explanation would naturally regard it as a promise to remain silent on the subject in the future. If neither the promise itself, nor the later explanation which Kant gave of it, reveals a heroic nature, it should be taken into account that Kant was already old, that such conflicts with the authorities were exceedingly disagreeable to him, and that he laid much stress on obedience to the law and submission to the existing authorities.([148])

CHAPTER XI.

INFLUENCE OF KANT.—ADVOCATES AND OPPONENTS OF THE CRITICAL PHILOSOPHY.

Early popularity as a teacher—Spread of his reputation—Neglect of the "Kritik"—Its sudden popularity—Poems on Kant and his philosophy—Pilgrimages to Königsberg—Enthusiasm of disciples—Influence of works following the "Kritik"—Fanaticism of Kantians—Opposition: Hamann, Kraus, Herder—Silence amid abuses—Influence of Kantism at home and abroad—Honours—Subsidence of the excitement—The return to Kant.

It is of course impossible to form an exact estimate of Kant's influence on metaphysics, literature, and thought in general. There was a time when his philosophy had gained a power which seems almost fabulous, and when its author was regarded by many of his disciples with a reverence which bordered on adoration. This great fame, the reward of long and severe toil amid difficulties, was the crown of his old age. While his reputation in the last decade of the eighteenth century has scarcely a parallel, it becomes the more remarkable when we reflect that it was a tribute to profound thoughts lying beyond the usual sphere of literature and even of philosophical research —thoughts which silently, without the aid of a school or persons of influence or any other favourable external circumstances, worked like leaven in the intellectual world, and wrought a marvellous revolution in thinking.

When Kant became a teacher, his local reputation for scholarship was already so great as to crowd his lecture-room. The character of his instruction rapidly increased his reputation, made him the most popular lecturer in the university, and attracted to his auditory many who were not students. During his earlier years he stood in more intimate relation with his students than afterwards; he sympathized with their aspirations, took an interest in their intellectual, moral, and social welfare, and exerted on many a direct personal influence. The popularity gained as a teacher was increased by his authorship, and long before the "Kritik" appeared he had gained an extensive and enviable reputation, though he could not have been called celebrated.

In the learned and governmental circles of Berlin he attracted attention by means of his contest, in 1763, for the prize offered by the Academy of Sciences; and about the same time he was, as he himself said, "introduced to the public" through some reviews of his books by Moses Mendelssohn. Thus, already before he became a professor, he had won distinction as an instructive and inspiring lecturer, and as a profound, original, and genial writer. His reputation as a philosophical thinker was materially increased by his Inaugural Dissertation of 1770, but its influence was confined to a limited number of scholars. The first eleven years of his professorship did not add to his reputation as an author, since he published no books during this period; but what he had previously written was of such a character as to excite great expectations. Still, before the "Kritik" appeared his books had not created a general impression that a reformer in philosophy had arisen. In 1779, two years before the publication of the "Kritik," Professor Kraus was in Göttingen on a visit. In the company of several of the professors of the university, he made the remark that Kant had a manuscript in his desk which would one day cost the philosophers hard work. The professors smiled at the statement, thinking that this could hardly be expected from a *dilettante* in philosophy. And although he was highly esteemed in Königsberg as a scholar, before the "Kritik" was published, his reputation in his native city was based less on his profound metaphysical speculations than on several courses of popular lectures. Only after that work had given him celebrity abroad did he become generally esteemed at home as a deep thinker.

Even after the "Kritik" appeared it attracted little attention for several years. Immediately after its publication, Hamann wrote, "Kant intends to publish a popular epitome of the 'Kritik' for the laity." It soon became evident that philosophers as well as the laity needed a "popular epitome;" indeed, compared with Kant, the professional philosophers of the day might generally have been classed with the laity. But the "Prolegomena," published in 1783, did not make Kant's master-piece popular.

Besides his own popular abstract of the "Kritik,"

other efforts were made to bring its contents before the public. The first notices and reviews of the work were, however, not favourable, and philosophers in different universities spoke of it disparagingly; it was evident that they had either failed to read or to understand the book. A popular exposition of the contents of the work was published in 1784, by Professor Schultz of Königsberg, with which Kant was so much pleased that he not only pronounced it a correct commentary of his philosophy, but also referred persons to it who desired an explanation of the "Kritik." Still the Kantian philosophy excited little attention. This neglect is not wholly attributable to the inherent difficulties of the book. The study of metaphysics had fallen into contempt; and soon after the "Kritik" appeared Kant complained that that subject was greatly neglected by scholars, and was no longer placed among the profound sciences, and he thought the appearances indicated that speculative philosophy was about to perish. The learned were devoting themselves to the study of the useful sciences, and the great revival in literature made the department of belles-lettres so prominent as to push speculative works into the background. These various causes led to the neglect of the "Kritik," and two years after its appearance the author spoke of the silence with which the book had been received by the learned public. In 1784 Hamann wrote, "The 'Kritik of Pure Reason' is beginning to stir and to ferment;" but the time for its success had not yet come. Kant's book on "The Basis of the Metaphysics of Morality," appearing in 1785, directed new attention to the author, and may have had some influence in preparing the way for the success of the "Kritik." For five or six years after the work appeared it seemed doubtful whether it would achieve any marked success, and at the end of this time there were about as many voices against it as in its favour. In 1786-87, K. L. Reinhold published a series of letters on the "Kritik," in a popular literary journal, and these, more than anything else, introduced the work to the attention of the literary public. In 1787 a second edition of the book appeared.(149)

All at once the work now became popular, and the praise was as loud and fulsome as at first the silence had been profound. The literature of the day began to teem with Kantian ideas, with discussions of the new philosophy, and with the praises of its author; and these were not confined to literature, but are also found in the correspondence of the day, and they were frequently the topics of conversation. An enthusiasm was aroused which was all the more remarkable because it was occasioned by a cold and dry metaphysical work—an enthusiasm which in its zeal threatened to overwhelm all opposition, which became contagious and carried with it others than professors and students, scholars and literary men. High officials in Berlin would lay aside the weighty affairs of state to consider the "Kritik," and among them were found warm admirers of the work and its author. Merchants unaccustomed to severe study took up the book, read it with absorbing interest, and became professed disciples of the Königsberg metaphysician. A friend wrote to Kant from Brunswick, in 1787, that the letters of Reinhold had created a great sensation there, and had aroused the liveliest interest in his system;

and he declared that though he was so far from Königsberg, he was surrounded by the Kantian philosophy. Even while travelling, men would read the book, and this correspondent states that in the Hague he had found a man all alone in his room, in a hotel, absorbed in the effort to master the "Kritik." This is but a sample of the interest excited by the book when its popularity began. Not only in private social circles, but also at table in public houses this new philosophy and its author were eagerly discussed. Nor was the interest in it confined to the men; women also took up the book, racked their brains over its contents, sought explanations of its mysteries, and professed to be disciples, as well as admirers of Kant.

Significant voices were still heard against the Kantian philosophy, and it met with decided opposition in every stage of its progress to victory; but shortly after its popularity began it was spread all over Germany, and within ten years after the "Kritik" appeared its author was on the pinnacle of fame. It would not have been strange if he had received the quiet and profound admiration of scholars; but the popular applause bestowed on him is rather such as is accorded to military heroes or favourite party leaders than to metaphysicians or even to literary men. Many looked on him as a kind of universal oracle who could authoritatively decide important questions even outside of the domain of metaphysics. So great was the popularity of this philosophy, that it was held responsible for results of which it was innocent, and to it even the most absurd influences were attributed. Thus, Professor Reuss, of

Wurzberg, felt it incumbent on him, in 1792, to prove that the French Revolution did not spring from the Kantian Criticism.(150) On the other hand, there were disciples who wanted it to be made the law for everything, who desired science, philosophy, literature, governments, religion, and life, to be conformed to its principles; and it was thought that even postal affairs should be regulated according to the new transcendentalism.(151)

From the universities it soon drove the remnants of the philosophy of Wolf and Crusius, and it became the prevalent system in Catholic, as well as Protestant institutions; it is claimed that it gained even more ground in the former than in the latter. Besides Königsberg, it was taught in the universities of Erlangen, Jena, Halle, Leipzig, Göttingen, Würzburg, Mayence, Heidelberg, Ingolstadt, Erfurt, Bamberg, Dillingen, and other places; indeed at the beginning of the last decade of the eighteenth century, lectures on the "Kritik" were delivered in all the universities of Germany. It was also taught in cloisters; and in many cities where there were no universities, lectures on it were delivered before mixed audiences.

The Critical system and its author became so celebrated that their praises were frequently sung by poets, who strove to compensate for the lack of poetic worth in their verses by an admiration which was boundless. The students, ever ready to do him honour, repeatedly celebrated him in song; and soon after his death a number of poems on Kant were composed by students, professors, and others. A few years before his decease, 348 Latin hexameters, celebrating the merits of the author of the "Kritik," were published in Königsberg. These words occur in the poem: "Et lux e densis oriatur tanta tenebris." ([152]) It is not strange that Kant was sung by poets; but the attempt to turn his metaphysics into verse is almost too much for human nature to bear; yet such an effort was actually made, and the result was published in 1794. The whole was prefaced by an ode "To the Founder of the Critical Philosophy." ([153]) The verses following this ode bear the titles: "Time and Space, the Pure Forms of Sensation;" "Methodology;" "To the Reason;" "The Highest Principle of Morality;" and other equally felicitous poetic inscriptions. Even if these and other verses on Kant lack poetic inspiration, the enthusiasm which they display is an evidence of the wonderful influence of the philosopher on his contemporaries.

The obscure and isolated Königsberg became the centre of philosophy, and Kant was so celebrated that his fame was burdensome on account of the correspondence and the visits of which he became the victim, though in many respects the calls he received were as gratifying as they were complimentary. He attracted many students to the city, who crowded his lecture-room, and many who were not students came solely to see him and to receive the benefit of his counsel and instruction. Among those who made pilgrimages to Königsberg was Reuss, Professor of Philosophy in Würzburg, who one day entered his room with the remark that he had come 160 miles (German) to see Kant; no small undertaking in those days of slow and difficult travel. His bishop (Catholic) had aided him in defraying the expenses of the journey.

Another Professor of Philosophy, Memel, of Erlangen, came to Königsberg for the same purpose. Count Purgstall made a journey all the way from Vienna to visit Kant, and then, full of enthusiasm over what he had seen and heard of the thinker, he went to Copenhagen and gave glowing descriptions of his visit. The wife of a Danish cabinet minister wrote, "We had very definite accounts of Kant last summer. A young Count Purgstall, from Vienna, made a pilgrimage to Königsberg, and then came to us. We listened to him with great pleasure, because he had often seen the philosopher of Königsberg and came to us from him with shining countenance, like Moses from Mount Sinai." ([154]) The tutor of the Prince of Brunswick sought to make a similar pilgrimage, but was prevented; he, however, secured manuscript copies of Kant's lectures on morality and anthropology, and used them in instructing the prince.

It is almost incredible that any man should have been the object of such tributes of praise as were bestowed on Kant, the more so when the nature of his metaphysics is considered. The enthusiasm which he aroused was in strange contrast with his own aversion to all extravagant feeling. A certain mania seems to have taken possession of many of his admirers, so that not merely to his philosophy but also to its author perfection was ascribed. "He lived as he taught," was echoed and re-echoed. The Kantian Criticism had apparently deprived men of the power of criticism, and the "Kritik of Pure Reason," of the exercise of reason. Those who called Kant the Master of Philosophy, the Hercules among thinkers, the modern Socrates, the German Plato and Aristotle united in one person, were very moderate. One wrote, "God said, Let there be light; and there was—Kant's philosophy." Among his most ardent admirers was Professor von Baggesen, of Copenhagen, a literary character of some repute at that time on account of his writings both in Danish and German. In common with many others, he saw in the Kantian philosophy the salvation of the world. In a letter to his friend Erhard, he calls Kant "our philosophical Messiah," and states that he intends to visit Königsberg solely for the purpose of seeing "the second Messiah." Afterwards he wrote that he had been obliged to abandon the project of visiting Königsberg to see "our Messiah." He also wrote, "Next to Christ, this man interests me most of the living and the dead."

The glory of the "Kritik" was reflected on the works of Kant which followed it, and all of them appeared in large editions. When his books on morality and religion were published, they were regarded as part of the Critical system, and shared its popularity. Kant was lauded as the saviour of religion and morality, and some regarded him as the improver and perfecter of the Christian religion. In the universities, as well as in the churches, rationalism became prevalent, and by means of lectures and sermons it was spread among students and the masses. Morality, with the Categorical Imperative as its Golden Rule, became the watchword of the pulpit; and God, freedom, and immortality, the trinity of rationalism, were the favourite dogmas. Creeds and the cultus, as well as the Scriptures, were now to be conformed to the Critical Philosophy and its religion and morality. A Reformed minister declared that the Kantian morality surpasses that of Christianity. Reinhold, who more than any one else had promoted the popularity of the "Kritik," wrote to Erhard, one of Kant's most intimate friends, "Kant's book on Religion has given me the indescribable comfort of being able to call myself openly, and with a good conscience, a Christian." Many others accepted Kant's construction of Christianity, by means of his rule of moral interpretation, as the Christian religion itself. Erhard was so thoroughly a Kantian that he said, "I am, as it were, a Pietist in the Kantian philosophy; I can regard nothing in it as orthodox except what Kant himself has written." And he also says, "Kant's book on Religion satisfies me wholly," and he speaks of "Christianity as purified by Kant." In another letter he gives his views more fully. Pestalozzi had sent him a manuscript to criticize, and he altered it considerably; the alterations were accepted by the author, and Erhard writes of him, "He says that the changes I had made were entirely in accordance with his views, for he, too, is convinced that Christianity, according to its essence, was never introduced, never will be, never can and never should be, since it is fanaticism incompatible with the needs of men. Only from a few passages can the morality which it teaches be interpreted as pure and excellent; but to these, other superstitions and fanatical passages are directly opposed again. We will speak of this matter soon. I regard Christian morality as something which has been falsely imputed to Christianity; and the existence of Christ does not at all seem to me to be a probable historical fact." These were the views of a man who not only regarded himself as wholly a Kantian, but who also wrote to Kant, "I can call myself yours as truly as if you were my real father." Another pupil and enthusiastic admirer of Kant, named Kiesewetter, lectured on his philosophy in Berlin. He found it expedient to make it appear that Christianity and the Critical Philosophy harmonize, but states that he felt it exceedingly difficult to steer between the Scylla of antagonism to Christianity and the Charybdis of hypocrisy. To Kant he wrote, "I assure you, dearest Professor, that at times I am placed in situations in which I need all possible caution, on the one hand, not to become untruthful, and on the other, not to reveal my views and injure myself." Some agreement between the Christian and the Critical system he thinks possible, and he appeals to Kant to aid him with suggestions. "I am convinced that it could at least be made evident that the fundamental principle of your moral system harmonizes well with the doctrines of the Christian system, and that if Christ had heard and understood you, he would probably have said, "That is what I meant to teach with my command, Love God, et cet." The philosopher Reinhold assured Schiller, that in a century Kant would have the reputation of Jesus Christ. In some quarters it became quite common to draw a paralled between the author of the Critical Philosophy and the Founder of the Christian religion.

Kant's "Kritik" was intended by its author to put an end to all extravagant opinions. Henceforth there were to be no more dreams of ghost-seers, metaphysicians, and enthusiasts; instead of dream-land and the spirit-world, men were now to walk on the solid earth, with their eyes open, and guided by the light of reason, but with their hearts mostly closed. Philosophy, morality, and religion, were henceforth to be cold and stern, mathematically exact, and very proper. The result looks like irony; instead of cold propriety, a new fanaticism appeared which seemed to be but the revenge of human nature for the effort to suppress its feelings. Neither in his lectures nor in his books did Kant aim merely to inculcate certain doctrines which were to be accepted by disciples, without further investigation, as truth. "It is probable that few teachers have so often and so earnestly warned against this as Kant did; yet it is probable that he had more followers who echoed his opinions without testing them than any one else. Certain it is that he did not want them. To think for oneself, to investigate, to stand on one's own feet, were expressions which were constantly recurring."(155) But instead of accomplishing what Kant desired, a spirit of blind devotion, which fanatically advocated a system not understood and often grossly perverted, characterized many of the disciples of Kantism during the period of its greatest dominion. The folly and extravagance are, of course, to be ascribed mainly to those who did not fathom the depths of that philosophy; but the same spirit is seen in Reinhold, in Fichte while yet a Kantian, and in many others who claimed to be the true followers of Kant and authentic interpreters of his system."(156) His professed disciples differed respecting the interpretation of his philosophy, each claiming to be a correct exponent of the views of the master. Bitter contentions occurred in the school itself, and many and great abuses were committed in the name of Criticism. Those who were opposed to this philosophy attacked it severely, exposed the folly of its followers, and added to the philosophical confusion.([157])

Among the opponents of the system were some of the most eminent men of the day; but their first opposition was overwhelmed by the tide which for awhile swept everything before it and resisted all efforts to produce an ebb. The popular philosophers opposed Kant because he introduced reason instead of common sense as the criterion of truth; many of the advocates of illumination opposed him because he rejected their endæmonism; others, who wanted the Bible to be wholly renounced, objected to him because he was willing to retain that book in religious instruction; and the evangelical theologians or supernaturalists, as they were called to distinguish them from the rationalists, were opposed to his subordination of Scripture to reason, to the subjection of religion to the position of a handmaid of morality, and, in fact, to his entire theology. Men like Storr, Flatt, Döderlein, Reinhard, entered the lists against him. Schleiermacher must also be placed among the opposition, though his influence only began to be felt towards the close of Kant's life; his theory of the relation of the emotions to religion was diametrically opposed to Kant's view, and he became the most potent opponent of rationalism. The adversaries of the Critical Philosophy subjected it to the severest criticism, exposed its weak points and the abuses made of the system by its friends. The ebb did come, and the reflux was as marked, if not as sudden, as the flow had been. For every ardent admirer of the Kantian philosophy there was an equally ardent opponent; but for extravagance the professed Kantians retained the palm.

Here we must consider the relation of scholars to Kantism chiefly from a personal stand-point, namely, so far as it affected Kant himself. Among his personal friends, as we have seen, there were zealous advocates of his system; but there were others, some of them in Königsberg, who as decidely rejected it. Hamann opposed Kant's moral and religious views more emphatically than he did his metaphysics. According to Kant, religion consists in what we do to gain the divine favour, namely, in a moral life; according to Hamann, it consists in what God does for us. In his letters, which contain numerous allusions to Kant, he expresses the highest regard for his intellect, and praises the "Kritik" as a great work, but often speaks slightingly of the Critical Philosophy.([158])

But Hamann's opposition was less significant than that of Professor Kraus. The latter was a systematic thinker, the former was not; and Kraus was far more intimate with Kant than Hamann. He had been a pupil of the great philosopher, was his colleague, and at one time his daily guest. While a great admirer of his teacher, he thought for himself. Kraus had fine speculative powers, and Kant spoke of him in the most complimentary terms, regarding him as one of the greatest minds the world had ever produced, and he did not hesitate to compare him with Kepler. In his old age he said to a friend, "Of all men whom I have known in my life, I have found no one with such talents to comprehend all things and to learn all, and yet in every affair to stand as admirably and eminently as our Professor Kraus. He is quite an unparalleled man."

The influence of such a mind in favour of his Criticism would have been especially gratifying to Kant. Kraus, who was a superior mathematician, did not condemn speculation, but he objected to the efforts of those who made it the source of all knowledge, and he opposed the flagrant abuses of philosophy because they were deleterious to the advance of learning. The conduct of many professed Kantians disgusted him, and he vigorously assailed their transcendental madness. In his lectures he spoke with warmth and even with bitterness against the modern metaphysic, which he described as useless, and thought worthy of banishment from the universities. It was in the midst of the abuses of the Kantian system that he said, "What I desire and expect from philosophy is, indeed, according to the prevalent opinion, something quite strange, namely, the improvement of the human race and the purification of the mind. It seems to me something monstrous that there should be any fixed philosophy, one named after a man, as, for instance, the Kantian philosophy." He spoke of the "Kritik" as jugglery, and preferred the more practical English and also the older German systems, especially the Leibnitz-Wolfian. While he spoke with admiration of metaphysic when it occupied what he regarded as its proper sphere, he could not tolerate the metaphysicians "who either tried to hide the insipidity of their notions behind a web of an incomprehensible bombast, or else expressed their really deep thoughts as obscurely before the public, by whom they wished to be understood, as if they needed to shun the light of day." He was enraged at what he called the idolatry "of the coarse goblin, the Kantian philosophy;" he held that this system ought to be studied, but that the aim of the study should be to enable men the better to stand on their own feet. "It grieved him when such a system became the occasion for young men, who had scarcely grasped the primary conceptions of logic, to talk vaguely about philosophy in general, without making any application of it to life and the commonwealth." And the statement is made that "in his lectures he never permitted an occasion to pass without giving his pupils the advice, by all means first of all to gather a fund of knowledge concerning realities before hearing philosophical lectures."

While the course of Hamann and Kraus shows that in its very home the Critical Philosophy met with decided opposition even from Kant's personal friends, their antagonism has less historic significance than that of J. G. von Herder. Of all Kant's students he was probably the most brilliant, and in literature he became the most celebrated. If the three most eminent names of Eastern Prussia, during the second half of last century, were required, few, if any, would hesitate to mention Kant, Herder, and Hamann. When Herder was Kant's pupil, the philosopher formed great expectations respecting him; and Herder's forty-five volumes on theology, religion, literature, art, poetry, history, and philosophy, show that the teacher's estimate of his abilities was well founded. He deserves an honourable place in literature beside Goethe, Schiller, and the other distinguished men with whom he associated in Weimar, then the German Athens, and is worthy of the characteristic inscription on his tomb, "Light, Love, Life."

There had been much ardour in Herder's attachment, while a student, to his favourite teacher, and this inspired Kant with the hope that he would use his talents and influence to advocate the Critical Philosophy; but in this he was disappointed.(159) Herder, impressible as he was, was too original, too much Herder, to become the disciple of another. Whatever he learned he worked over into his own peculiar texture and gave it the stamp of his individuality. While with his friend Hamann he was a great admirer of the philosopher's intellectual powers, he also, like Hamann, never became an advocate of his system; in fact, this warm admirer of Kant became one of the most decided, most active, and most bitter opponents of Kantism. Both Kant and Herder were original, learned, and great, but they had their failings; both were very tenacious of their peculiar views; both had bright literary hopes, and were ambitious; and both were very sensitive. Their early relation as teacher and pupil, their warm attachment, and the high regard of each for the other's abilities and attainments, should have made them friends for life; but a coldness, and even bitterness, sprang up between them, which form a painful contrast with their former friendship. Herder professed to attack the system and its blind advocates, not the author; but in assailing the philosophy, he was not only unnecessarily severe, but he also cast considerable blame on Kant himself, who keenly felt the violent opposition of him whom he had been specially desirous of securing as an adherent.

Herder's literary reputation made him a central figure in the war waged against the "Kritik;" but less for this reason than on account of his personal relation to our philosopher is the matter here considered. Kant's review of one of Herder's books—apparently favourable, and yet with a slighting air and a vein of satire—wounded the sensitive author, and probably made him more bitter in his attacks on the Kantian philosophy, but it does not wholly explain his opposition. Herder was the apostle of Humanity, a word which he was constantly using, and whose broad signification, including all the interests of man, characterizes his entire being and tendency. The whole of humanity deeply interested him, also the world with its realities so far as related to man. The Critical system was too cold for him, ignored the heart too much, and put *à priori* speculations where he wanted historical facts. As he sought the richness and variety of the tropics, he felt cold and solitary and lost in an Iceland, notwithstanding its sublimity. On the other hand, Kant could not appreciate Herder's fiery imagination, nor the warm heart whose glow is felt in all his works. Where he demanded reason, he often found fancy; hence the enthusiasm in Herder's books and the luxuriance of his style were an offence to the Critical Philosopher. Intellectually they were antipodes.

Herder was the president of the Uppor Consistory in Weimar, and his sad experiences in the examination of candidates for the ministry, as well as in many other instances, gave him an opportunity of seeing the destructive influences of men who were advocates of the Kantian system, especially those connected with the University of Jena, which was one of the centres of this philosophy, and where Reinhold was professor. At first Herder exonerated Kant himself from blame, and attributed the abuses to the arrogance and misunderstanding of the system on the part of his blind followers; but afterwards, when he saw that Kant did nothing to check the abuses, he censured him also. Before the culmination of the furor occasioned by the new philosophy, he defended Kant against the abuses of his disciples. Herder regarded his works as calculated chiefly to fix the limits of thought, to purify the sciences, and to test the power of the mind; and not as intended to exhaust the sciences or to give the contents of all knowledge. He thought the Kantian zealots made the mistake of imagining that in these works they had that knowledge itself, of which the great philosopher aimed to give only the boundaries. Herder therefore exclaims, "If the outline is taken for the substance, the frame for the picture, the vessel for the contents; and if one then imagines that he has gathered all the treasures of knowledge, what a mistake, what an abuse!" Acknowledging that Kant's works were admirable as a preparation for philosophy, he was not willing to admit that they gave to philosophy a completeness and perfection which could not be transcended—a view which for many Kantians was entirely too moderate.

When, however, men began to swear by the words of the master without understanding them, and when the zealots disputed fiercely with each other as to which one understood Kant aright, then not only Herder but many others also became indignant because no one made a serious effort to check the confusion. Germany had suddenly been aroused by Kant from its metaphysical slumber and dreams; but the awakening was followed by a wild intoxication. A hint of this has already been given; but one must study the sources of the history of the last fifteen years of the eighteenth century in order to form a just conception of the confusion, the contradictions, the criminations and recriminations, the intolerance and arrogance, prevalent among the professed followers of the Kantian philosophy. Herder, in the literary centre of Germany, saw many evidences of this madness, and says that the intolerance with which the Kantians, "seated on their universal tribunal, speak, condemn, praise, and reject, has become as disgusting to the healthy part of Germany as it must be averse to the tolerant nature of the author of this philosophy and to his thoughtful love of the truth. To aim, by means of fire and sword, scorn and derision, to introduce a Critical Philosophy which emphatically disclaims all intention of preaching dogmatism, is the most miserable despotism." Of Kant's works he writes, "They will remain. Their spirit, even if embodied in other forms and clothed in other words, will, in substance, continue to work and to live. It has already accomplished much, and its influence is seen in almost every department of human investigation. Through Kant the mind has received a new impetus, not merely to sift the old, but also (which is the principal aim of philosophy) to give a systematic arrangement to the sciences which are peculiarly human." But while thus praising Kant, Herder was unwilling to have the claims of other philosophers ignored, and he opposed those who spoke of the Kantian system as wholly new and original, and said of its author, "Surely, his most presumptuous admirer will not claim that everything in his works is new. In this case it is not proper, as has often been done, to place all the philosophers of antiquity on their heads in order that the latest may alone stand on his feet." Herder claimed that much of what Kant taught had long ago been said in other words, and that for many things in the Critical Philosophy the way had been prepared by men like Hume, Rousseau, and Lambert. He says, "Kant's 'Kritik' so deeply affects the minds of the present because the way for it had been so well prepared, and because it was able to bring to light a thousand existing but obscure notions.(160)

Herder's opposition to this philosophy became more decided when he perceived the increase of its abuses, and found that some of its advocates opposed the Christian religion in its name. After Fichte had declared in Jena, "In five years there will be no more Christian religion; reason is our religion," even some theological professors were led astray. Theological students, examined by Herder, gave impertinent answers, and a talented young man wrote an article against marriage, and at the same time urged the Consistory to give him an appointment as a pastor. Sacred things were ridiculed, and Christianity was treated as a superstition. Herder then wrote his "Metakritik" and "Kalligone" against the Critical Philosophy. Anxious that Kant should do something to check the abuses of his system, he said, "I will arouse Kant, by means of my writings, to declare himself respecting the perversion of his philosophy." The bitterness of his tone in opposing this system, he explained as follows: "The Kantian philosophy is to be regarded as a ferment; stupidity took the leaven for the dough. Hence this indescribable abuse. It is little of Kant that he, who knows better, leaves men in their error, and sacrifices truth to the vanity of having established a school. Time will reveal the truth in this matter. In my position, it was my duty to speak against the injurious effects of this philosophy as loudly as I have done; I wanted to excite the Kantians so that they might hear me. A book in a milder tone would have been without effect altogether."

These extracts indicate Herder's relation to Kant and to Kantism, especially as this appeared at Jena and Weimar; and they also give us a picture of the times. The Kantian philosophy had taken men by storm, and many thought that it was final. Herder saw that it swept everything before it, and he said, "The century or the decade is drowned in the Kantian subtlety of words. A new man will arise and that deluge will subside. At present it seems to be in vain for me to contend with it; only let holes be made now, through which the water may run when its time comes." This testimony of an enemy shows what a mighty power this system had become.

Kant was deeply pained by Herder's course. The prominent position of Herder in Weimar, his great influence in literature, and his former relation to Kant, made it all the harder for the aged savant to bear his merciless attacks. To the question, "Whom did Kant esteem most among his opponents?" Borowski replied, "Certainly none; least of all Nicolai and the great Herder. Of most of them he took little or no notice. He rarely read what was written for or against him." And Hasse says of Kant, "Against Herder he spoke almost passionately, declaring that he wanted to be dictator and was anxious to make disciples."

The best disciples of Kant were not those who

adopted his system without criticism, pronounced it absolute and final, and aimed to transmit it as finished and unchangeable to future generations. Such were the Kantian dogmatists and fanatics, who based their claim to be true disciples on the fact that they blindly accepted the words of the master and abused all others who did not do likewise. There were, however, others who subjected the "Kritik" itself to severe tests and tried to develop its well-established principles, while rejecting the rest; and although decried as false disciples by unconditional Kantians, they have promoted that philosophical development which it is the glory of Kant to have started. That men perverted his system certainly cannot dim that glory, and it would be foolish to make him responsible for the folly and extravagance of his followers. But was not his failure to check them blameworthy? Why was he silent amid the abuses of his philosophy on the part of his disciples? That he was aware, to some extent, of the disputes among his disciples, and of the confusion and offence created thereby, is evident from his own letters; and publicly, through the press, as well as privately, through letters, earnest appeals were made to him to give such explanations of disputed points as would end the wrangling about the sense of his philosophy; and it was also hoped that he would do something to check the arrogant claims of many of his adherents. By his opponents Kant's silence was attributed to selfish motives, particularly to the desire to found a school; and it was claimed that if the love of truth animated him, he would certainly break the silence, restore harmony, and disown the abuses of his professed disciples. While, therefore, some persons were loudly extolling his merits, there were others who as bitterly denounced his course in these disputes; and those who blamed him for his silence were not confined to the opponents of his system.

If we place ourselves in Kant's position, we shall find that there was much to excuse that silence, even if it cannot be wholly justified. Although he was aware that there were abuses, he could hardly have known their full extent. Not only was Königsberg isolated, but he himself withdrew more from society as old age advanced. His favourite reading, as we have seen, was not philosophical literature, and he rarely read what was written for or against his system, and greatly disliked controversy. Those in his own city who were in more immediate contact with the world could see the abuses better than he did; and in a literary centre, such as Weimar, they were far more apparent than in Königsberg. Then it should be remembered that Kant was anxious to complete his various literary projects, and was devoting his energies so exclusively to them as to neglect other matters; and even after devoting all his time and energies to his literary plans, he had to leave one of the most important unfinished, as his last manuscript shows. Besides, he was really unable to enter and master thoughts and systems foreign to his own, and his friends would read on the philosophical disputes of the day and then give him their views. The whole conflict, therefore, lay largely beyond the sphere of the thoughts of him whom it concerned most. Kant's physical and intellectual condition was such, at this time, that he found it necessary, for the sake of his health and mental labours, to avoid excitement. For some years before his death he was really unfit to enter the controversy, and he declared that he must leave to others the explanation and defence of his system.

In a letter to Reinhold, in 1788, Kant gives a hint of his feelings respecting the controversy occasioned by his philosophy, though at that time it was only in its beginning. In speaking of the dissensions among those who reject the "Kritik," he says that it is only necessary to watch them quietly, and perhaps take notice occasionally of the principal errors, but otherwise to pursue one's plan uninterruptedly, and to cherish the hope that in the course of time everything will move along in the right track. This implies confidence that the discovery of truth would be the result of the contentions. That Kant had a degree of satisfaction in the disputes occasioned by the "Kritik," is true. A year later he wrote to Reinhold, "In reality, the general excitement occasioned and still promoted by the 'Kritik,' together with all the alliances formed against it (though its opponents disagree and will continue to do so), can only be agreeable to me, for by this means interest in the subject is maintained. Then the perpetual misinterpretations and perversions give occasion to make the expressions, here and there, which might lead to a misunderstanding, more definite; consequently, I fear nothing in the end from these attacks, even if they are treated with silence." He hoped that the conflict would keep the subject prominently before the public until the truth finally triumphed, which for Kant meant the victory of his system.

The temporary excitement occasioned by the "Kritik" was, indeed, an evidence of Kant's influence, but it was only the foam and the waves on the surface of the great deep. On thoughtful minds, on literature, on universities and other institutions, he produced an effect which was deep and broad and lasting, and it may safely be said that no other factor in modern German literature has been so potent as his philosophy. Often where it is hardly apparent, this influence is deepest and most universal, because it is the influence of principles which determine foundations as well as superstructures. So thorough and general was the revolution in thought which Kant produced, that scholars were obliged to take sides for or against his philosophy, or else to subject the "Kritik" itself to severe criticism, and winnow the chaff from the wheat. Every philosopher since his day, whatever else he might neglect, has been constrained, first of all, to determine his relation to Kant; and even when other philosophers temporarily obscured the name of Kant, they really began with him and largely built upon his system. While others prepared the way for the "Kritik," that work contains the seed from which German metaphysic sprang. The effort necessary to master its contents made the book a discipline for thinkers, a test of their speculative powers, and the means of strengthening their intellects. The epoch in thought, which it created, contains the most eminent names in modern metaphysics, and Rosenkranz says, "With the exception of the history of Greek philosophy from Anaxagoras to Aristotle, the history of philosophy furnishes no example of such rapid development of speculation as that produced by those well-matched heroes, Kant, Fichte, Schelling, and Hegel." Wald affirmed in his funeral oration, that Kant had effected a greater revolution in metaphysics than Newton had accomplished in physics.

From the hundreds of other evidences of the broad and deep influence of the Critical Philosophy, only the testimony of a few cotemporaries can here be given. One writes concerning Kant's principles, "I found these principles, especially the moral ones, in nurseries, in schools, in the shops of mechanics, among soldiers, at the desk both of the merchant and of his clerk, in the temple of the Christian, and in the synagogue of the Jews." (161) Bouterwek says, "No other German author of the eighteenth century ruled with such imposing authority over superior minds; no other writer found among his opponents so many admirers; and there was not another who so powerfully affected all the sciences, and also the moral tendency of German mental activity, as Immanuel Kant." Another cotemporary declares, "In a short time the new philosophy exerted an almost magic influence on all the sciences, and gained friends and adherents even among the classes which did not devote themselves to science at all, or, at least, not to metaphysics. It aroused a spirit of thorough philosophic inquiry in Germany, of which the age would not have been thought capable; and it contains such an inestimable wealth of ideas and opinions, that until now only a small part of this material can be regarded as having been appropriated, and from it new germs of knowledge may yet be developed in the remote future." (162)

Kant's fame spread to foreign lands during his life, but the influence of his philosophy outside of Germany was very limited. Although French journals mentioned his name and referred to his system, the Critical Philosophy was not introduced into France till in 1801, when Charles Villers began the publication of a work on the subject, of which, however, only the first volume appeared, the demand probably not being sufficient to justify the completion of the whole. The disturbed state of that country was, no doubt, largely the occasion of this neglect of the great German metaphysician. Although its principal thoughts were also discussed in other French philosophical works, his "Kritik" made but little impression on France. More attention was paid to it in the Netherlands. The Critical Philosophy was taught in Amsterdam by Paul Van Hammert, who in 1792 issued a compend of this system, and in 1796-98 published a work on it in four volumes. In 1802 the "Kritik" was translated into Dutch.

As early as 1795 an effort was made by F. A. Nitzsch to introduce the Kantian philosophy into England. He had studied under Kant, and had a good knowledge of his system, on which he probably delivered the first lectures and published the first book in the English language. To Professor Kraus, who was his friend, we are indebted for a description of his first lecture in 1795. "All through London Nitzsch had sent circulars announcing a course of lectures on the perceptive and reasoning faculties of the mind, according to the principles of Professor Kant. In this prospectus, of which he sent me a copy, he offered, in order to secure confidence in his proposition, to deliver three lectures gratis, and to answer all the London philosophers who, after hearing him, might propose objections. When, on the 3rd of March, in this year, at 8 p.m., Nitzsch for the first time entered the lecture-room, he found, what the equipages at the door had led him to expect, a multitude of aged lords, ministers, young scholars, and finely dressed ladies. For an hour and a half he read the first part of his introduction, which had been well prepared, and was apparently received favourably; but scarcely had he finished when a discussion of two whole hours arose, during which he was obliged to defend his position. In this he succeeded well; and the result of this and the two following lectures was that his whole course of thirty-six lectures, which had been announced for three guineas, was successful. He completed it a few weeks ago with honour, and in this month of October will begin a second course. In the meanwhile he is having an abstract of his lectures published by subscription." ([163])

Professor Kraus received his account from Nitzsch himself, who seems to have had sanguine expectations which were not realized. He was not successful in his effort to introduce the Critical system into England, and Borowski says, "Nitzsch was laughed at in London." Dr. A. F. M. Willich made a similar attempt, which was also unsuccessful. ([164]) In 1797 and 1798 John Richardson published two books in England on Kant's Philosophy, but they also failed to excite an interest in the subject.

Kant's fame crossed the sea, and became known in America during the philosopher's life. An encyclopedia published in Philadelphia, in 1798, contains the following: "It is certain that Professor Kant of Königsberg has gained a great reputation by means of his original view of the intellectual and moral powers of man, and that the philosophers of Germany are as devotedly attached to him as the natural scientists are to Newton, or the scholastics to Aristotle. The

Kantian philosophy is therefore a subject which cannot be omitted from our encyclopedia." ([165]) In Russia, Italy, Sweden, Denmark, and other countries, Kant was also known. A letter from Bishop Lindblom, in Sweden, addresses him, "Vir omnibus titulis major," and calls him "Princeps philosophorum."

In spite of his great reputation, Kant was the recipient of comparatively few honours from learned bodies, and he made no parade of those which he did receive. He was a member of the Academy of Sciences in Berlin, and also of that in St. Petersburg, and he was invited to become a member of the Academy of Sciences in Sienna, and to take part in its work; he had been proposed as a member of the National Institute of Sciences in Paris, but his death occurred before his election. All these honours were conferred on him after the "Kritik" appeared.

The excitement created by the new philosophy was too intense to last, and already before the death of its author all parties were disposed to view it more calmly and more critically. Fichte's Idealism was an effort to develop some of Kant's principles and to supersede his philosophy in part, if not to supplant it altogether. It attracted much of the attention which had hitherto been bestowed on the Critical Philosophy; and while it introduced a new element of confusion and discord, it also did much to effect a more critical investigation of the principles of the "Kritik." Some who had been warm advocates of the Kantian Criticism now forsook it, among them Reinhold, who had done so much for the popularity and defence of the "Kritik." Within four months after Kant's death

Bouterwek wrote that the Kantian intoxication was over, and that there was danger that the prevalent tone would so depreciate his intellect as to put it on a level with ordinary minds. There were at that time enthusiastic followers of Fichte, just as there had been and still were of Kant. Their treatment of the Critical Philosopher is evident from a remark of the writer just quoted, "It is well known that the youths of the new school of Idealism speak of Kant as only a Philister."

Soon other philosophers arose and gathered disciples, and Schelling and Hegel became the metaphysical heroes. Kantian principles were, however, still powerful, and many who had been trained in the Critical Philosophy occupied important positions of trust during and after the wars with France; but this philosophy gradually lost its adherents, till at last Kant was neglected.([166]) But about thirty years ago a revival of the study of Kant began, and since that time the Kantian literature has grown to such vast proportions as to suggest a parallel with the close of last century. Naturalists, as well as metaphysicians, and, in fact, scholars of every class, favour a return to Kant, and regard the renewed study of the "Kritik" as the condition for a new start in philosophy; and philosophers again speak of themselves as Kantians, which, of course, does not mean that they follow Kant implicitly. Many thinkers want to start with him; they adopt some of his conclusions while rejecting others, and favour especially his critical method. Some of those who are ready to take his name, differ from him materially on important points. ([167]) The conviction is universal, that he must be used critically, in order that he may be transcended. "The Return to Kant," which has become the watchword of philosophers, wants to make him the starting-point, so as to enable philosophy to attain that goal which is a matter of hope, but not yet of realization. The revival of the study of Kant, the hopes centred in the Critical Philosophy by scholars in various departments of learning, the numerous recent editions of his "Kritik," and the vast literature on this work, are among the most significant indications of the deeper tendencies of German thought.

CHAPTER XII.

CORRESPONDENCE AND CORRESPONDENTS.

Small number of Kant's letters—Numerous correspondents—Lambert—Moses Mendelssohn—Herz—Erhard—Maria von Herbert—J. G. Fichte—Kiesewetter—Jung Stilling.

When we consider Kant's literary activity of more than fifty years, we are surprised to find that so few of his letters, only about seventy in all, are extant. That there are no more is partly accounted for by the fact that he neglected his correspondence; then, all of his earlier letters and many of the later ones have been lost. In his letters Kant discusses metaphysics, and refers to his literary labours and personal affairs; but we look in vain for that confidence, intimacy, and affection, which are common in the correspondence of friends. Many of the letters written to him remained unanswered, others were neglected for a long time. Nor was he careful to preserve the letters received, and he is said not to have left among his literary remains a single letter of his learned correspondence. After he had become celebrated, he received so many communications that they were an annoyance and a burden to him, and one of his biographers says, "In his last years he received many letters, from many places, and had to pay much postage, which greatly displeased him. Once he said to me that celebrity causes much trouble. Continuous correspondence, properly speaking, he probably had with no one." His fame brought him letters from Holland, Sweden, England, France, Switzerland, Austria, and other lands, as well as Germany. Many of his correspondents revealed an unbounded confidence in him, and treated him as an oracle. Some of them sought a solution of intellectual and moral difficulties, while others asked advice on subjects which did not interest him; he was requested to distribute lottery tickets, to secure subscribers for publications, to read and criticize essays, and to do other things which were both disagreeable and robbed him of precious time. A medical professor in Halle wrote to him repeatedly, in the name of several members of the medical faculty, to inquire whether he regarded vaccination as moral or immoral, a question much discussed at that time. A count in Silesia, who called one of Kant's books on morals "*my* compend," wrote to ask him whether it would be morally right to have the lady vaccinated whom he expected soon to marry. "Do let me know as soon as possible what the (moral) law says." The annoyance, much augmented by the fact that so many letters were not prepaid, at last became so great that he was on the point of resolving not to accept any letters unless he recognized their authors by the handwriting or seals.

Kant's letters have already been so extensively used in this biography that little more need be said of them. The two which were written to Lambert are long and weighty, and have been found valuable in tracing the Critical idea; they are the most profound of his entire correspondence, and their style is similar to that in his metaphysical works. J. H. Lambert was an automath who, in spite of great obstacles, became one of the most prominent German scholars of the day, and it was said that from Leibnitz till his time there had not been a more learned man in Berlin. He was eminent in mathematics, physics, astronomy, and metaphysics, and in analytical power was probably not surpassed by any of his cotemporaries.([168]) He never met Kant; but the fact that each had published a work on cosmogony led to a correspondence which extended from 1765-70. Not only had they written on the same subject, but their cosmological views, formed independently of each other, were remarkably alike; their specialities were also the same, and both were mathematical as well as metaphysical. Lambert had a very exalted opinion of Kant, and says in his first letter, "You, sir, have looked with a keen astronomical eye into the firmament, and have investigated its depths and the order prevailing therein." Kant also had a very high regard for Lambert, who at that time was the more celebrated of the two; and he speaks of the remarkable agreement with himself in method, which he had frequently noticed in his works, and declared that Lambert was that philosopher with whom, of all men, he had the greatest similarity in thought. They had agreed to co-operate in metaphysics, and expected much from this union of effort; but this hope was frustrated by the early death of Lambert.

From Kant to Moses Mendelssohn we have four letters, chiefly on learned subjects, written between 1766 and 1783. The correspondence of these two men is peculiarly interesting from the fact that one was the most popular of the "Popular" philosophers, while the other was the most eminent of the speculative. As Mendelssohn had gained celebrity long before Kant, he did his speculative friend good service by introducing him favourably to the literary public by means of notices of his works. The fact that both had contended, in 1763, for the prize offered by the Berlin Academy of Sciences for the best dissertation on "The Evidences of the Metaphysical Sciences," led to a correspondence between the two philosophers. While Mendelssohn admired the metaphysical depth of Kant, the latter admired Mendelssohn's popular elements, especially the clearness and elegance of his style, saying, "There are only a few so fortunate as to be able to think for themselves and put themselves in the place of others, who, at the same time, can present their thoughts so appropriately. There is but one Mendelssohn." And to his pupil and friend, Dr. Marcus Herz, Kant wrote respecting Mendelssohn, "To have here in Königsberg such a man as a permanent and daily companion—one with so gentle a spirit, such good-humour, and so clear a head—would give my soul that nourishment of which I am here wholly deprived."

Mendelssohn had received an enthusiastic account of Kant from Dr. Herz, who gratefully mentioned his indebtedness to his teacher for the instruction received, and particularly for the personal influence exerted by him during their friendly intercourse. In writing to Kant, Mendelssohn says of Herz, "He has a clear understanding, a regulated imagination, and a certain subtlety of mind which seems to be peculiar to that people.(169) But what a good fortune it was for him that these natural endowments were so early led in the way of truth. How many who did not have this good fortune were left to themselves in the immeasurable region of truth and error, and have been obliged to consume their valuable time and their best powers in a hundred vain attempts, so that they lacked both time and strength to pursue the road which they found at last after much experiment? If only before my twentieth year I had had a Kant!" When Kant sent him his Inaugural Dissertation, Mendelssohn wrote his views respecting it to the author, stating that he would not have ventured to criticize it so freely had not Herz assured him that Kant would not find fault with such frankness. "Rare as this trait is among imitators, it is frequently a characteristic of those who think for themselves. He who has himself experienced how difficult it is to find the truth, and to convince himself that it has been found, is always more inclined to be tolerant towards those who differ from him."

Kant's last letter to Mendelssohn speaks of the "Kritik," and he desires the opinion of his correspondent on the following points: first, whether his views of analytic and synthetic judgments are correct; second, whether it is true, as the "Kritik" asserts, that *à priori* we cannot judge synthetically of anything except the formal condition of a possible experience; third, whether the last conclusion of the "Kritik" is legitimate, namely, that all possible speculative *à priori* knowledge does not extend beyond objects of possible experience. Kant suggests, as still undecided, an important question: how it happens that reason is impelled to go beyond its proper sphere—a question whose solution, he thinks, is not very difficult. These points, suggested by Kant two years after the "Kritik" appeared, involve the fundamental doctrines of that book. Can it be possible that he had any doubts respecting these problems? We are not able to state why he desired Mendelssohn's suggestions on them.

In 1777 Mendelssohn visited Königsberg, met Kant, and heard some of his lectures. Writing to Herz, Kant says, "Yesterday Mendelssohn did me the honour to attend two of my lectures, *à la fortune du pot* as one might say, for the table was not prepared for so eminent a guest." Their personal intercourse drew the two eminent men nearer each other, but neither that nor their correspondence seems to have had any influence in assimilating their philosophical views. A few years after the "Kritik" appeared, Mendelssohn, in introducing a young man to Kant, wrote, "Without other recommendations, every youth who strives to get wisdom recommends himself to you." Having heard the rumour that Kant intended to visit Pyrmont, for the sake of his health, and expected to pass through Berlin, he says, "You would find open arms in Berlin and also many an open heart; and among others, you would find a man who is your admirer, without being able to follow you. For many years I have been dead to metaphysics. My nervousness forbids all severe application, and in the meanwhile I occupy myself with less difficult labours, some specimens of which I shall have the pleasure of sending you. Your 'Kritik of Pure Reason' is for me a criterion of my health. As often as I imagine that I have gained some strength I read in this nerve-destroying work, and I am not altogether hopeless of mastering it in this life." But he did not master it, the difficulties of the book being too great for him; he, however, consoled himself with the reflection that his loss was not very serious. He wrote to Eliza Reimarus, "It pleased me to learn from Mr. Rudolph that your brother does not think much of the 'Kritik of Pure Reason.' For my part, I must admit that I do not understand it; therefore it is a satisfaction to know that if I go hence without understanding this book, I shall not lose much."

While these two leaders of the rising and waning schools of philosophy had much in common, their stand-points were too different to enable them to appreciate each other. Their philosophic friendship, for it never was anything else, was based on their mutual interest in philosophy, not on similarity of views. Mendelssohn, the last eminent representative of the popular "Common Sense" philosophy, could not understand Kant; and the herald of the philosophy of Reason could not esteem highly the school which the Jewish philosopher represented, and which the Kantian Criticism was intent on destroying. Hamann says of Kant, "He regards Mendelssohn's lectures as a system of illusion; they are to him similar to Mendelssohn's description of a lunatic."

Nineteen letters from Kant to Dr. Marcus Herz, a much larger number than to any other person, have been published. They were written from 1770-97, and like those to Lambert and Mendelssohn, they belong to the most interesting period of Kant's life; besides the scholarly subjects discussed, they contain numerous personal references and allusions to miscellaneous affairs. In tracing the genesis of the "Kritik" they have been found very important. Herz was one of Kant's favourite students, and in one of his letters the philosopher distinguishes him among his pupils for that noble gratitude which so many lacked, and says, "What can be more comforting, when one is about to leave this world, than to perceive that he has not lived in vain, since some, if only a few, have been developed into good men." From another letter to Herz it is evident that Kant did not desire to have his correspondence published. Speaking of the proposed publication of Moser's correspondence, and of his own letters to him, he says, "I also pray earnestly that my letters, which were never intended for publication, may be entirely omitted."

Dr. Herz, after completing his studies at Königsberg, resided in Berlin, where he practised medicine, and also delivered lectures on logic and metaphysics before mixed audiences, Minister von Zedlitz being one of his hearers; his practice, however, gradually drew him away from philosophical studies. He had considerable influence, and used it to spread the fame of his beloved teacher in the capital. His exceedingly beautiful and cultured young wife, Henrietta Herz, made her brilliant drawing-room the resort for the literary luminaries of Berlin, and men like Schleiermacher, the Schlegels, and the Humboldts, delighted to frequent her house; and the favourite of Kant was eclipsed by the glory of this German Recamier, as she, who probably surpassed the French original, has been called.

Of the correspondence with Dr. J. B. Erhard, two of Kant's letters, written respectively in 1792 and 1799, and quite a number of Erhard's, have been preserved. The relation of this correspondent—who was both a philosopher and physician—to Kant is a good illustration of the influence of the metaphysician over young men. Erhard addressed him for the first time in 1786, when twenty years old, calling him his "most honoured teacher and friend"—teacher by means of his books, for he had never seen him. Erhard acknowledges that it was to his influence that he was indebted for strength "not to be frightened by the mists of prejudice, nor to be misled by the glitter of dogmatism, but to be secure against the darts of the philosophers *à la mode,* and able to penetrate to the light of genuine philosophy." From Mendelssohn he had received his first impulses to reflection, then he became a devout Wolfian, and determined to do his utmost to fortify that philosopher's position; and he states that he took up the "Kritik" with more bitterness than he had ever felt toward any other book, and began to read it with a view of refuting it; but instead of this result, the bold young man was made, by the "Kritik," a devoted Kantian. His purpose in writing was to learn whether some arrangement could be made for him to study under Kant in Königsberg. Such an arrangement was made, and he formed for his teacher the warmest attachment, which lasted during life. Of his stay in Königsberg he says, "Here I enjoyed blessed days in my intercourse with Kant. The manner in which I spoke of his books seemed to surprise him. I asked of him no explanations, but only thanked him for the joy which his works had given me, and spoke to him no word of flattery. This ease in understanding him, which found expression in my conversation, at first seemed to make him doubt whether I had read his works; but we soon understood each other, and were mutually agreeable companions." He was greatly encouraged by Kant's friendship, and it was certainly very flattering; in few of the great man's letters is his attachment so marked as in those to Erhard. Of course, we must not expect him to be prompt in replying even to this warm friend, and in his first letter he apologizes for delaying his answer a whole year. Kant pleads their friendship as an apology for this delay, since so many other letters required attention, from whose authors he could not expect such leniency; but he gives as another reason, the conviction that all his time, when well, should be devoted to finishing his books, a work in which he does not like to be interrupted. His regard for Erhard is evident from this statement, "Why did not fortune so order it that the man whom, of all who ever visited our region, I would like most for daily companionship, might be brought into more intimate relationship with me?"

Erhard's enthusiasm for Kant began with the reading of the philosopher's works; and there were many similar cases, one of which is related by Erhard. Writing from Göttingen to Reinhold in 1791, he says of a young student in that university who possessed extraordinary mathematical talents, "He heard of Kant in 1787, and, in spite of the warning of the bigots of the Church here, he began to read his books, and became in the strictest sense a Kantian. I believe that he would die for Kant."

In Erhard's correspondence a Miss Maria von Herbert is frequently mentioned, and it is probable that it was through his influence that she became one of Kant's correspondents. Kant's letter to her is lost, but the three which she wrote to him are preserved.

They reveal a morbid disposition and sad life, and also give some conception of the age and of Kant's influence. Her first letter, sent in the spring of 1792, through Erhard, who was a friend of her brother, is a wail of despair, and begins, "Great Kant! I appeal to thee, as a believer does to God, for help, for comfort, or for counsel to prepare me for death. The evidences of a future existence were made sufficiently clear to me in thy works; hence I take refuge to thee now." She had been deeply affected by his books; but while giving her the hope of immortality, they did not furnish the strength she needed to battle successfully with this life. Erhard informed Kant, who had become interested in her through her letter, that the rock on which she had been wrecked was "romantic love." "In order to realize an ideal love, she committed herself to a man who abused her confidence; and again, in the interest of this same ideal love, she made a confession of the affair to her second lover." She was devotedly attached to the second lover, who was a man of superior endowments; for awhile she had kept from him the story of her first love and its termination, though there had been nothing immoral in that relation. Finally, goaded by her conscience, she revealed the secret, and as a consequence lost his affection, but received the promise that he would remain her friend. This did not satisfy her ardent nature, and the loss of his love brought her to the verge of despair, so that in her letter to Kant she says, "My heart breaks into a thousand pieces. I should have ended my life before this if I had not read so much of your works; but I am restrained by the conclusion which I had to draw from your theory, namely, that I ought not to take my life on account of my sorrows." The powerful influence exerted on her by his books prompted her to make this earnest appeal to Kant to put himself in her place, and either to give her comfort or else to doom her. "Geben Sie mir Trost oder Verdammung." Neither his moral works nor his "Categorical Imperative" had helped her. "My reason forsakes me just when I need it most. I adjure you to give me an answer; if you do not, your conduct will not be in harmony with your proposed 'Categorical Imperative.'"

It would be exceedingly interesting to learn how the cold philosopher met a case like this, for he answered her passionate appeal; and her second one, dated January, 1792, is in reply to his lost letter. Her second letter is very long, and makes it apparent that the deepest gloom had immovably settled on her soul. Every object had lost its charm, so that study, activity, and life itself, had become almost intolerable; ill-health made her misery the greater, and her sole desire is to shorten this useless existence, in which each day has an interest for her ("who am young yet") only because it brings her nearer the end. She appeals to Kant to remove the "intolerable emptiness" of her life; and if she improves sufficiently with his help, she intends, several years hence, to visit Königsberg, but wants him to promise in advance that she may visit him. "Then you must tell me your history, for I would like to know to what kind of a life your philosophy has led you, and whether it was not worth your while to take a wife, or to devote yourself with your whole heart to some one, and whether it was not worth your while to propagate your likeness." She closes with these words: "Would that I were God, and could reward you for what you have done for us!"

This strange letter of the noble lady, with its familiar tone and its disposition to pry into the secrets of his life, and especially into the reasons of his single state, must have shocked him. She was young and ardent; he was cold and nearly seventy. Of course he did not answer this wild epistle. Nevertheless she wrote again, in the beginning of 1794, addressing him: "Highly honoured and most devotedly loved man!" She thanks him for his book on Religion, and says that she had already found his "Kritik" quite satisfactory, but that it did not render unnecessary the works which followed. The sentimental tone of the former letter is also found in this one, and she says, "Gladly would I command the course of nature to stand still, if I could only be assured that you would complete for us what you have begun; and gladly would I attach my future days to yours, in order to find you in this world at the end of the French Revolution." She has become more calm, but is not yet reconciled to life, and she thinks that from a selfish point of view a longing for death is natural to every pure reason, and that only in view of morality and friendship can one who has the strongest desire for death be willing to prolong life. It was still her purpose to visit him with the friend who had been her lover; but she never saw Kant. With this letter the correspondence ended, and he probably never heard of her again.

A few months after Kant's death she committed suicide. She had carefully arranged all her affairs, and on the last day of her life gave a *déjeuner*, at which she seemed to be very cheerful, and then she disappeared. Her brother had defended suicide in her presence, with the thought of which she had been familiar for many years; and in the papers left by her she appeals to the brother's justification of her course. The editor of her letters says, "It is possible that Kant's life kept her from the horrible act which she threatens in all three of her letters." ([170])

A peculiar interest attaches to Kant's relation to J. G. Fichte, and in the beginning of their acquaintance there is a touch of the romantic. Fichte came to Königsberg when twenty-nine years old, in 1791, when many others were attracted thither by the fame of the great metaphysician. With all the zeal of his ardent nature he devoted himself to the study of the Kantian philosophy. He also visited Kant, who, however, did not receive him with any marked attention; and he attended some of his lectures, in which Fichte was disappointed, since Kant had lost much of his former life and spirit, and delivered them in a drowsy manner. But for Kant himself he had the greatest respect, and he resolved to enter into as intimate relation with him as possible. About the middle of July, Fichte began to write his "Critique of all Revelation," which he finished in a little more than a month. On the 18th of August he sent the manuscript to Kant, with a letter, in which he says: "I came to Königsberg to become acquainted with the man whom all Europe honours, but whom in all Europe few men love as I do. I called on you. Not till afterwards did it occur to me that, without the least proof that I was worthy of it, it was presumption to claim the acquaintance of such a man. I could have had letters of recommendation. I desire only those which I myself write. Here is mine." He requested Kant's opinion of the manuscript, and again called on him on the 23rd, when the philosopher received him with marked cordiality. He had read only a part of the manuscript, but from that he formed a favourable opinion of the whole. Kant entered into no philosophical conversation with him; but for the answer to his questions and doubts he referred him to the "Kritik" and to Court-preacher Schultz. Fichte at once visited this commentator of the "Kritik." A few days later he dined with Kant, and found him very agreeable and entertaining.

Fichte's letter to Kant reveals the same spirit and independence which are so marked in his patriotic "Addresses to the German Nation." In order to understand his relation to Kant, it should be remembered that he was imaginative and enthusiastic, as well as self-reliant and heroic, and that he was eloquent, as well as philosophical. His letter contains this passage: "Your greatness, excellent man, has, with all imaginable grandeur, this peculiarity, this likeness to Divinity: that one can approach it with confidence." On other occasions he manifested a similar enthusiasm for the revered Kant, whom he, at that time, regarded as the ideal philosopher. Once he was present while the guests at a table, in a hotel in Königsberg, were discussing the immortality of the soul. A captain, who was especially pronounced in his doubts, appealed to Kant's authority, declaring that he would not have claimed mere probability for the doctrine if it was settled beyond all question. Fichte was not acquainted with the disputants, but he listened to the conversation with deep interest, and said abruptly to the captain,

"You have not read Kant." He then took part in the discussion, claimed that Kant had given invincible arguments in favour of immortality, and proceeded to give some of his moral proofs.

Through his protracted stay in Königsberg, Fichte became involved in pecuniary embarrassment, and in his strait he appealed to Kant to lend him money to enable him to return home. The aged philosopher had inspired him with confidence, and he wrote him a frank statement of his need, and made a modest and most touching but, at the same time, honourable and even noble appeal for help. The letter was dated September 2nd, and Fichte's journal says: "On September 3rd I was invited to Kant's house. He received me with his usual frankness, informed me, however, that he had not yet come to a conclusion respecting my letter, but that for the next two weeks he could do nothing for me. What lovely candour!" Three days later he was there again. Kant had, evidently, become interested in the man whose manuscript revealed extraordinary ability, and he thought that by means of this production the author might be relieved of his pecuniary difficulties. Fichte had requested him to alter whatever he did not approve; but Kant erased only one line, the dedication to himself, which read, "To the Philosopher." During this visit he urged the author to sell the manuscript to a publisher, and thus secure the needed funds. He himself declined to lend him the money, but he made an effort to secure a publisher. That same afternoon, while taking a walk, Kant met Borowski, and his first words were, "You must help me, must help me quickly to get a name and bread for a breadless young man.

Your brother-in-law (Hartung, the publisher) must be favourably inclined toward him; use your influence to get him to publish the manuscript which I will send you this day yet." But the relief was not secured by the sale of the manuscript; Fichte was, however, appointed tutor in the family of the Countess of Cracow, to whom Kant had recommended him.

Fichte's essay—"Critique of all Revelation"—was published, and in connexion with its appearance we have a striking illustration of the difficulty and uncertainty of literary criticism. The book appeared anonymously, and with surprising unanimity the critics and reviewers pronounced it a work of Kant. He had already published three Critiques, and his disciples recognized this as his fourth. In his enthusiasm, Von Baggesen called "the author of the four Critiques" "the Messiah of Philosophers." This general verdict respecting the authorship was the more flattering to the author because Kant's fame was at its zenith, and Fichte was unknown. The human mind is, however, subject to sudden and wonderful transformations. Kant felt it obligatory on him to publish a statement that he was not the author, but that the book was the production of a young candidate for the ministry. After this declaration, those who examined the book of course saw at once, from its style and matter, that Kant could not have written it, and they wondered how such a mistake could have been possible!

After Fichte left Königsberg he became one of Kant's correspondents. His letters from Cracow show that his warm attachment to Kant continued, and he professed to love him above all men. From Berlin he wrote to him: "In yonder world, the hope of which you gave to so many who had none, and to me also, I shall surely know you, not by your physical characteristics, but by your mind." He speaks of him as the man whom he honours "unspeakably;" and from Zürich he wrote: "No, great man, highly important to humanity! your works will not perish; they will bear fruit, and will bring about a new intellectual flight in the human family and a total regeneration of principles, views, and constitutions. . . . . What must it be, great and good man, to have such emotions as yours at the end of one's earthly career! I acknowledge that the thought of you shall always be my genius to impel me not to leave the scene of activity without having blessed humanity." He regards Kant as the man who has made the last half of the eighteenth century for ever memorable with respect to the progress of mankind.

The extraordinary reputation which Fichte suddenly gained by means of his book secured for him a call to the University of Jena. He was thirty-one years old at the time, just the age at which Kant became a tutor in the University of Königsberg; but, while the latter toiled for fifteen years as a tutor, Fichte was at once made professor in ordinary of philosophy. Soon after he went to Jena he wrote to Kant, giving expression to his disgust at the prevalent tone in philosophy, lamenting that amid the philosophical pretensions it was difficult to get a calm hearing, and still more difficult to secure thorough investigation and impartial criticism.

This is not the place to follow Fichte's interesting career—the charge of atheism made against him in

Jena, and his flight to Berlin as a place of refuge; his patriotic addresses in this city, in the presence of French bayonets; his literary activity; and his death, in 1814, from a fever contracted while waiting on the patients in a hospital. An account of the termination of his friendly relation to Kant must not, however, be omitted.

When Fichte went to Jena, that university, more than Königsberg even, was the centre for the advocacy and the spread of the Critical system. But he soon developed some of the Kantian principles and formed his own Idealistic philosophy as found in his "Wissenschaftslehre." To Jacobi he wrote in 1795: "You are well known as a realist, and I suppose that I am a transcendental idealist more strictly than Kant; for he still admits a manifoldness of experience, but I assert in plain terms that even this is produced by us, by means of a creative power."

Fichte claimed that he had given the system of philosophy, for which the "Kritik" gave only the propædeutics; this alienated and incensed Kant. Writing to Tieftrunk, in 1798, Kant speaks of the "Wissenschaftslehre" as prolix, and says that it would interfere too much with his work to read the book, which he knew only through a review. Though this review was exceedingly favourable, he himself did not form a favourable opinion of the book, and was desirous of learning Tieftrunk's views of the work, and of its impressions on others in Halle.

Although Kant depended wholly on others for his knowledge of Fichte's system, he nevertheless concluded that he ought to repudiate all sympathy with its peculiar views. Accordingly, he published a declaration in 1799, that he regarded the "Wissenschaftslehre" as a system which is wholly unreliable; and that the assumption of Fichte that he, Kant, wanted to write only the propædeutics to transcendental philosophy, not the system itself, was inexplicable to him. Such an intention, he says, could never have entered his mind, since in his "Kritik" he himself praises pure philosophy as the best characteristic of that "Kritik." He also speaks of deceitful, so-called friends, who meditate our destruction, and quotes an Italian proverb, "God protect us against our friends; against our enemies we can protect ourselves." Speaking of the Critical Philosophy, he says that, owing to its ability to satisfy the reason theoretically as well as practically, no change awaits it through emendations or through the influence of another system, however much opinions may change; but that the system of the "Kritik," resting on a perfectly secure basis, is for ever established, and is indispensable to all future ages for the highest purposes of humanity.

Fichte replied in the same journal in which this declaration had been published, in the form of a letter addressed to Schelling. He appealed to the fact that Kant, in his last letter to himself, had stated that, on account of the weakness of old age, he now gladly left to others the subtlety of theoretical speculations, and found it advisable to devote himself wholly to the practical. Fichte therefore claims that Kant's own letter is an evidence of his inability to judge of the speculations of others, and thus shows what his public declaration respecting his (Fichte's) system is worth, and adds: "I did not regard it as persiflage, but could well think it seriously meant, that Kant in his old age, after a toilsome life, should regard himself unable to enter speculations altogether new." Instead of following Kant or any one else, he says, "The venerable man eight years ago gave me different advice, which I prefer to follow,—always to stand on my own feet."

Kant's declaration was certainly unfortunate, for it was understood to repudiate a system which he knew only through the representations of others. The statement that the "Kritik" was intended to give the system of transcendental philosophy, and not merely the propædeutics to it, is equally unfortunate, since it is in conflict with his own statements in the "Prolegomena," in the Preface to the second edition of the "Kritik," and also in his letters. But Kant's intellectual condition was already such as to make him less responsible for his utterances than formerly.

Fichte, like Herder, from both of whom Kant had expected so much as disciples, became a powerful agent in destroying the supremacy of the Critical Philosophy. Kant's published declaration shows how deeply he felt grieved at Fichte's effort to transcend his system. From Borowski we learn that he sometimes spoke bitterly of Fichte; and from Hasse, that he so disliked Fichte and his school, that his guests did not dare to mention them in his presence.

Among Kant's favourite pupils was Professor J. G. C. Kiesewetter. He went to Königsberg about 1788, being sent and pecuniarily aided by Frederick William II., for the purpose of thoroughly studying the Kantian system. After completing his studies at Königsberg he lectured on that philosophy in Berlin. His letters throw considerable light on Kant's influence in that capital during the last decade of the eighteenth century;

and his acquaintance with men in high positions gave him special facilities for learning the relation of the Government to Kant.

Kiesewetter is another illustration of the remarkable fascination exercised by Kant on the minds of some of his pupils. He writes to his teacher as the man who "has my whole heart, and whom I love above all others. Never without the deepest emotion do I think of the happiness I enjoyed in my intercourse with you, and very often I recall the past. Would that I could once tell you wholly my feelings toward you, and how much I appreciate that for which I am indebted to you! . . . I shall never forget what I owe you; I shall always honour you as my second father. I heartily beseech you not to deny me your friendship in the future, and to grant me the privilege of occasionally writing to you, thus to recall the oral communications I had with you, which formerly made me so happy."

This correspondent lived with the cabinet minister Count von Schulenberg, was the tutor of the princes Henry and William, and was well acquainted in official circles. To the Chancellor von Hoffmann, who was a warm admirer of the philosopher, he was required to speak for a whole hour about Kant. Von Zedlitz and other men in high places, Woellner included, spoke in high terms of Kant and his philosophy. Kiesewetter used his position to cultivate enthusiasm for his beloved teacher. He was indebted to the Baroness von Bielefeld for his appointment as tutor to the princes; and she was also his pupil, for he lectured to her on anthropology and taught her Kantian philosophy. To Kant he wrote, "What will you say when I tell you that a beautiful young lady, for that the Baroness von

Bielefeld is, ventures to enter the mysteries of your system, and that she has had explained to her, and actually comprehends, the difference between analytic and synthetic judgments, between knowledge *à priori* and *à posteriori*, and your theory of space and time? Still more will you be surprised when I inform you that she does not study philosophy for the purpose of making a show of her attainments, for she is modest beyond all description, and one does not shine at our court by means of philosophy; and it will surprise you to learn that she neglects none of her duties on account of the study of philosophy."

In these letters of Kiesewetter to Kant there is a strange mixture of Kantian philosophy, extravagant expressions of friendship, information about personal matters and government officials, court-gossip, and Teltow turnips. These small and superior turnips, which grew near Berlin, were greatly prized by Kant, and his friend was careful to forward them to him regularly. Once he sent instructions from his mother, through Kant, to the cook on the best method of preparing this delicacy. The philosopher at one time reminded him of the turnips, and in response he wrote, "Do not think that without your letter I should have forgotten you. The turnips had already been ordered, and I make it a law unto myself to provide for you this domestic necessity every year." He wants Kant to inform him whether they are to his taste. Indeed, Kant's interests included much beside abstract philosophy, and the publisher of these letters says, "It is evident that these Teltow turnips, and the literary and political news, which play so prominent a part in these fifteen letters, were as highly prized by Kant as the fact that Kiesewetter remained true to the Critical Philosophy."

It is not strange that philosophical minds should have been greatly attracted and stimulated by the "Kritik;" but it is surprising that this book, which was intended to check religious enthusiasm, should have won the admiration of a man like Dr. H. Jung, commonly called Jung Stilling. He wrote to Kant that the explanation of the "Kritik" by Schultz had given him such calmness as he had never before experienced. He had also read the "Kritik" itself, and the "Critique of the Practical Reason," and everywhere he found apodictic truth. In his enthusiasm, he exclaims, "God bless you! you are a great, a very great instrument in the hand of God. I do not flatter. Your philosophy will effect a far greater, a more general, and a more blessed revolution than Luther's Reformation; for as soon as a man has well apprehended the 'Kritik of Reason' he sees that no refutation is possible. Your philosophy must, consequently, be eternal and unchangeable, and its beneficial influences will lead the religion of Jesus, so far as it aims only at holiness, back to its original purity. All the sciences will become more systematic, more pure, and more certain; and legislation, in particular, will gain extraordinarily." He desires Kant's views on legislation, and closes as follows: "How peacefully, how full of blessed expectation you can approach the evening of your life! May God make it cheerful and full of anticipations of a joyful future! Farewell, great, noble man! Your true admirer, Dr. Jung."

Kant had made preparations to answer this letter, and a paper was found in his handwriting which treats of the principles of legislation. Among other things, Kant wrote, " The universal problem of civil association is, to unite freedom with a constraint which harmonizes with universal freedom and promotes its preservation."

CHAPTER XIII.

OLD AGE AND DEATH.

Sad life—Early symptoms of old age—Interference with literary projects—Close of his lectures and literary labours—Relation to the Academic Senate—Wasianski assuming control of his affairs—Loss of memory—Visitors—Undeviating uniformity—Change of servants—Method of retiring—Exercise—Approach of spring—Sleeplessness—Last birthday—Failing sight—His sister—Strange notion of the atmosphere—First sickness—Efforts to rob him—Loss of conversational power—Longing for death—Extreme feebleness—Death—Funeral—Mementoes—Will—Kant Society—Monument.

DURING the evening of Kant's life the shadows gathered rapidly and enveloped him in deep gloom. The broad scholar, the profound metaphysician, the genial, humorous, and brilliant companion, and the man with an iron will, lost the power of consecutive thought and became helpless as a child. His life, as a whole, was a sad one, in spite of his intellectual pleasures and his great fame. The poverty, obscurity, and sensitiveness of his youth; the self-denial and struggles of his early manhood; his mental conflicts; the pain caused by the bitter attacks on his philosophy; the opposition to his religious views, especially that of the Government; the defection of pupils and disciples from his system; the absence of all the cheering influences of family ties; his real isolation and solitude, in spite of the host of admiring friends, are the dark outlines of the picture of his life. Of inspiring faith and enthusiastic hope there is scarcely a trace, and, in reality, his religion was as emotionless practically as it was in theory. His position, his mode of life, and his habits, deprived him, in a marked degree, of the ordinary enjoyments, the pleasures of company alone excepted; but he was generally calm and even stoical, and cherished the heroic virtues too much to moan over his lot. On the other hand, his rare intellectual joys and his delight in moral contemplations relieved the dark outlines; and the solitude of his bachelor home was cheered by the presence of his chosen and delighted guests. But he could not always live on the sublime heights of his speculation, or on the snow-peaks of his morality; and his social pleasures were not his life, but only episodes. Life to him was toil, and his recreations were only the means for exercising the elements in his nature not already exhausted by toil, and of fitting him for new exertion. However unsatisfactory to exalted minds the ordinary routine of life may be, he who leaves the beaten track will find his journey rough and difficult, and will experience that an unusual course has unusual pains, though it may also have exquisite pleasures. Looking at Kant's life as a whole, we are prepared to hear one of his friends and biographers say, "Who has not read in his writings, and which of his friends has not heard him say frequently, that he would not be willing, for any price, to live his life over again on condition of living from the beginning just as he had done?" His life, especially the later years, had so little attraction, that he admitted that if the choice were given to him between a life after death similar to this and annihilation, he would not hesitate to choose the latter.

In old age the sadness deepened, while his few joys diminished and then vanished altogether. The former exhilaration of his mental powers and the buoyancy of his spirit were gone ; his faculties became so weak that he could not continue his usual occupations, and he lost all interest in passing events. By means of careful attention to his body, by extreme regularity and simplicity, and through the great power of his will over his physical state, he had succeeded in preserving his weak constitution in a tolerable degree of health till old age ; and by successfully practising the art of prolonging life, he had extended his beyond the period of its enjoyment; and at last the resolute will lost its power and the mind its grasp, he sank into utter helplessness, and existence itself became a burden.

The relaxing of Kant's intellectual powers began comparatively early, and there were marked traces of the effects of old age when he was only sixty-five. In 1789 he wrote to Reinhold that age with it weakness was making itself sensibly felt; and two years later he wrote to him again, "About two years ago my health underwent a sudden revolution without any apparent cause, and, excepting a cold of three weeks, without any real sickness." He states that his appetite has suffered, and though he has neither physical weakness nor pain, yet his disposition for mental labour is changed, and even the reading of his lectures is thereby affected. He could now perform mental work only two or three hours in the forenoon, then he became sleepy, no matter how well he had slept the previous night; after these few hours of continuous labour he could work only at intervals. This state was beyond the control of his will, and in order to accomplish his labours he was obliged to wait for favourable moods. "It is, I think, nothing but old age, which obliges the one sooner and another later to cease work, but which to me is the more unwelcome because I believed that I was about to see the accomplishment of my plan."

The early appearance of the symptoms of old age was, no doubt, partly caused by his frail physical condition, and by his excessive mental labours, he himself being suspicious that it was in part attributable to his philosophical speculations. He thought it not strange that the metaphysician, who has to strain his attention in order to keep it fixed on the thoughts under consideration, should become an invalid sooner than others. During the preparation of the "Kritik" he suffered much from indisposition, and it is probable that this work largely contributed to the early exhaustion of his powers, a result not at all surprising when the long, continuous, and exceedingly laborious effort necessary for the completion of that work is considered. ([171]) His intense mental application seems to have worn his brain till the power of recuperation was gone.

His powers began to fail when he still had numerous literary projects, and the desire to use every available moment to finish them led him to defer less pressing matters, such as the claims of friendship and the writing of letters. In 1794 he wrote that though subject to indisposition, he regarded himself as pretty well for a man of seventy, but that he had inexplicable difficulty in entering into the thoughts of others and forming a definite and critical view of their systems. A year later, in speaking of the development of the Critical Philosophy, he says, "My age and the physical inconveniences connected therewith make it necessary for me to leave to my friends all further development of this science, and to use my little remaining strength for the appendices of the same, which are still in my plan, though I can work at them but slowly."

Kant had on hand materials for numerous literary works, and he was anxious to prepare them for publication; but he found that the debility of old age interfered seriously with his projects, though he made everything else subservient to them. When he was seventy-four, it was his turn to be rector; but his weakness and the desire to devote all his time to his literary labours induced him to decline the position. Not only his letters, but also the important books which he published at this time, show that he must have worked very hard, in spite of his difficulties. His "Metaphysics of Morals," in two parts, embracing the metaphysical principles of law and those of virtue, appeared in 1797. During the winter of 1796-97 he laboured constantly in preparing works for the press, and as a consequence of overwork his mind and body suffered greatly, and in various parts of Germany it was reported that he was dead. After this his debility was more marked. For a number of years before this time his lectures had lost much of their former life, and for a year or two he had delivered only public ones; these he also closed in the summer of 1797. The commencement of his last course, in the spring of that year, was delayed on account of his feebleness; and when he was ready to begin it, the occasion was treated as an academic festival: the students formed a procession and marched to his house, in order to manifest their joy that he who for forty-two years had been the pride of the university was once more able to resume his lectures.

The last book written by him was published in 1798, on the "Conflict of the Different Faculties in a University;" in the same year his "Anthropology," consisting of his lectures on that subject, appeared; afterwards he himself published nothing except a few short prefaces to the books of others. His "Logic" appeared in 1800; his "Physical Geography," in 1802; and his "Pedagogics," in 1804,—all edited by friends, at his request.

After closing his lectures he had no official duties in connexion with the university except as member of the senate, which was composed of the ten oldest professors. On account of their age and feebleness, he and another member no longer attended the meetings, and it was proposed to appoint two other professors as substitutes, so as to secure a full attendance. Kant regarded this as an infringement on his rights, and in July, 1798, he wrote an emphatic protest, claiming that, when necessary, the votes of the absent members could be obtained, as had been the custom, by sending to their homes. This last document of Kant in reference to his relation to the university indicates his spirit and determination to maintain his rights. Finally the matter had to be appealed to the Government, which, in the name of the king, decided in his favour.

In business affairs Kant lacked that independence which was so striking a characteristic in his intellectual pursuits. During the life of Green, that gentleman attended to the loaning of his money; Lampe and the cook attended to his household, though he himself kept a close supervision over his domestic affairs; and he had friends enough to aid him whenever necessary. In extreme old age he found the management of his affairs burdensome, and therefore gave it into the hands of his friend, the Rev. E. A. C. Wasianski. He had been one of Kant's students, became his amanuensis in 1774, and afterwards officiated as pastor in Königsberg. For ten years he had not come in contact with the revered professor, when they met again in 1790, at a wedding, and after that time he was frequently Kant's guest. He was a good scholar and, which was of special importance in his later relation to his teacher, he possessed unusual mechanical skill. Although Kant had no predilection for preachers, Wasianski had his entire confidence, and he felt greatly relieved when this friend undertook the direction of his affairs. One day Kant said to an acquaintance, "You cannot imagine how agreeable it is to have a friend to whom one can commit all his domestic affairs with the conviction that he will attend to them as if they were his own." Wasianski proved himself worthy of this confidence; he visited Kant daily, and sometimes repeatedly on the same day, was very judicious and kind, but firm, took great pains to make his noble charge as comfortable as possible, and, in spite of the difficulty of his position, he succeeded in managing everything to the satisfaction of the philosopher and his friends. He wrote a valuable account of Kant's old age, telling his story in a simple but affectionate manner, and giving many interesting details of his decline and death; and it is mainly to him that we are indebted for whatever is known of Kant's last years.

Being accustomed to observe his condition very carefully, Kant was painfully conscious of his increasing physical and mental weakness. In 1799 and afterwards, he repeatedly said to his guests, "Gentlemen, I am old and feeble; you must regard me as a child." Feeling the need of more sleep than formerly, he continued still to rise at five, but retired earlier, at first a few minutes, then at nine, afterwards at five o'clock. His walks were gradually shortened, and he became so feeble that one day he fell and was unable to rise till aided by two ladies who hastened to his assistance; after this experience he abandoned his out-door exercise. So weak did he become, that he sometimes sank to the floor while attempting to walk or stand in his room. Occasionally he fell asleep in his chair, and once his head fell forward and his cotton nightcap caught fire from the lamp on the table; but on awaking he had the presence of mind to take it off, throw it on the floor, and stamp out the fire.

When he was seventy-eight, the great weakness of his memory was one of the most striking evidences of increasing mental debility. Events of recent occurrence were now forgotten, while those of former years were still well remembered; and he would frequently repeat himself, relating the same things a number of times in a day. While heretofore he had been in the habit of using the blank parts of letters and envelopes, and other small pieces of paper, for learned notes, he now used them for memoranda of the most ordinary affairs, in order to avoid repetitions, and to promote variety in his conversation. These papers accumulated so rapidly that it became difficult to find what he wanted; Wasianski therefore made little blank books for this purpose. In one of these, each of which lasted about a month, he wrote five times, "The name of my barber is Rogall." He also made memoranda of the news of the day, the names of persons whom he desired as his guests, the dishes to be prepared, also whatever particularly interested him in the conversation of friends, hints on natural science, accounts of travel, politics, and similar things. The repetitions show how soon he forgot what he had written, and many trivial things were noted. Once he wrote, "June, July, and August are the three summer months." Strange that, while these notes were intended to help his memory, he once wrote the very thing he wanted to forget, probably to remind him that it was to be forgotten; thus, after dismissing his old servant, he made this memorandum, "The name of Lampe must now be entirely forgotten." But notes of an intellectual character are also found in these little books, indicating that the powers of his mind were not wholly extinct.([172])

After he became famous, Kant received numerous calls from strangers who visited Königsberg. Being regarded as one of the sights of the city, many who had no interest in science called on him from mere curiosity. Such visits had always been disagreeable, and in old age they became a great annoyance. He felt that he could no longer interest visitors with his conversation, and he did not like to have them witness his infirmity; therefore those who requested to see him were generally refused, but some were so persistent and brought such influence to bear that he could not well deny their request. Persons admitted into his presence were asked to make their visit very short.

He would generally receive them standing, leaning against his table, in a surly mood; and to the compliments paid him he would answer, "What do you see in me, an old, emaciated, frail, weak man?" Among those who were determined to see him was a young Russian physician who, when admitted into Kant's presence, seized his hands and kissed them, to the great embarrassment of the philosopher, who was no friend of such demonstrations. The Russian afterwards sent his servant to inquire about Kant's health, and also whether he was pecuniarily provided for in his old age; and he begged for a scrap of paper with some of his writing, as a memento. Such a piece of paper was found and sent; when delivered to him, he seized it with joy and kissed it, and in his enthusiasm he pulled off his coat and vest and gave them to the bearer. When Kant heard of the matter he thought it strange conduct; nevertheless he felt a degree of pleasure in the fact that he was held in such reverence.

The extreme regularity to which he had accustomed himself became more excessive and unyielding in his old age, when the rules which he had so long and so faithfully observed had become so much a part of himself that even the slightest necessary deviation became difficult and painful. He wanted things done "at once," as he was accustomed to say, and the least delay seemed a long time and greatly annoyed him. He was induced now to take coffee after dinner, and if it was not ready at the desired moment he became very impatient. When told, "It will be brought immediately," he would answer, "Yes, *will be;* there's the rub, that it is yet to be brought." Sometimes he would exclaim, "Well, I can die waiting, and in the next world I shall drink no coffee;" or he would go to the door and call, "Coffee, coffee!" At last, when he heard the servant coming with it, he would say exultingly, in sailor's language, "I see land." He had accustomed himself to such an undeviating uniformity that "if the shears or his penknife lay a few inches out of their usual place, or if their accustomed position was changed, it would disturb him; and a disarrangement of larger objects, such as a chair, or an increase or decrease of their number, troubled him greatly, and would attract his eye until the old order of things was entirely restored."

Wasianski found his position peculiarly trying on this account, especially as it became necessary to introduce material changes for the invalid's comfort and safety. Kant was desirous of submitting wholly to the judgment of his friend, and to be led as a child, and once he said to him, "Dearest friend, if you think a matter advantageous to me, and I do not; if I regard it as useless and disadvantageous, nevertheless if you advise it, I will approve and accept it." And it was with this distinct understanding that Wasianski consented to take charge of him and his affairs. But it was one thing to resolve and promise, and another to execute; and he was so set in his ways that he found it exceedingly difficult to be faithful to his promise, and sometimes his friend had to insist peremptorily that the measures which he regarded as necessary should be adopted.

One of the most serious changes in the home of the philosopher occurred in February, 1803. Lampe, who understood perfectly his master's peculiarities, and knew how to adapt himself to them, had become so intemperate and rude that he was no longer fit to wait on Kant, who was then most in need of his services. A memorandum of the philosopher, written about this time, reads, "Mr. Jensch, criminal counsellor, is to be asked how my drunken servant can be discharged." After he was dismissed, Kant found it very trying to adapt himself to the presence of the new servant, although he was far superior to Lampe. On the first morning after Lampe's discharge, Wasianski thought it advisable to be present when Kant arose, so as to make everything comfortable for him. The philosopher was excessively worried, for he missed his old servant, and was confused by the presence of the new one. No other person but Lampe had prepared his table for him, or knew just how it should be arranged; at last Kant himself placed everything as he wanted it, when his friend proposed to join him in taking a cup of tea and smoking a pipe of tobacco. To this he assented; but it was evident that something still annoyed him. Finally, Kant requested his friend to seat himself where he could not be seen, since for more than half a century no one had ever been present with him when taking his tea. Wasianski complied with his request, the new servant withdrew, and then all was right.

Kant retained his delicacy of feeling to the last. He had been in the habit of calling his servant by his family name. That of the new one was Kauffmann, the German for "Merchant;" but as he invited two merchants to dinner every week, he thought it might not be agreeable to them if he designated the servant by his surname in their presence, so he called him by his baptismal name, John.([173])

At first, after dismissing Lampe, he liked to have his guests remain with him while he retired, which he did now immediately after dinner. It was thought that Lampe had made an assault on him while retiring; that this had made him fearful, and that he desired the presence of his friends to give him the feeling of safety. Even trifles in his conduct were regarded as significant and worthy of remark, since they indicated characteristics of the man whose fame filled Germany. Numerous details are given of this period which must be omitted; there is, however, an account of his method of retiring of which some things are so characteristic as to be worthy of mention. When he divested himself of his clothing, it was done strictly according to rule, and he would permit no one to do for him what he could do himself. After taking off his wig, whose bag generally hung forward and almost on his breast, and which he was continually throwing back, he would draw his coat to the elbows, and unbutton his vest, and his servant would pull them off. There was a certain routine which was not allowed to be varied, and every article of clothing had to be removed in a particular way, at a particular time. The cravat he himself removed and laid carefully in its old folds, then gave it to the servant, who was waiting with a piece of paper into which to wrap it, and to put it precisely in its appointed place. "Neither in this case nor in that of the hat was any deviation allowed." When its turn came, the old but very regular watch was by Kant himself drawn from his pocket and hung on a nail between the barometer and thermometer, so as to have the indicators of the time and the weather together and convenient for observation. The act of putting on the night-clothes was performed with equal regularity and method. In summer one, in winter two night-caps were worn. A cloth was wrapped around his neck; it was first neatly smoothed and then the servant was obliged to be very careful, while putting it on, not to let it become wrinkled. His toilet for the night completed, he would take some pills; but this was an act which he did not want his friends to see, because, he said, his posture was altogether too peculiar.

Showing his extremely wasted body while undressing, he would say softly and sadly, "Ah, gentlemen! You are still quick and young; but look at my wretchedness! If you are once eighty years old, you will be just as weak and helpless as I am. . . . I cannot live much longer; but I shall leave the world with a pure conscience and with the cheerful consciousness of having intentionally done no one a wrong or an injury." When Hasse asked him with reference to his heart, "But how will it be if it is not right under the left button-hole?" Kant answered, "Then restitution, reparation, and compensation must be made, in order, as far as possible, to make it right and repair the fault."

As he had not been out of the house for a long time, he was induced in the spring of 1802 to enter his garden in order to get some fresh air and exercise. Everything there was strange to him, and he could not comprehend the fact that it was his garden and was next to his house; he declared that he did not know where he was, said that he felt as if on a desert island, and was anxious to enter the house again. After this he was occasionally taken out driving; but the time, even if very short, seemed intolerably long, and the change from his accustomed mode of life and the weariness were too much for him. He had, in fact, lost all idea of the measure of time, so that a few minutes seemed very long, and he called the short drives "excursions," sometimes "journeys," or even "long journeys." These airings might have been less wearisome if nature had not lost all attraction for him. When told that spring was approaching, that the sun was getting warmer and the buds were appearing, he would answer coldly, "Surely, that is the case every year." There was only one event in connexion with the return of spring which interested him, namely, the fact that it would bring back a certain little bird which sang in his garden and before his window. If the little songster delayed his coming, he would say, "It must be very cold on the Appenines." In the spring of 1803 he listened in vain for its cheerful song, and repeatedly said, in a disappointed, melancholy tone, "My little bird does not come."

His nights were often sleepless and tormented with horrible dreams. Frequently he wanted the presence of his servant, who at the ringing of the bell would immediately hasten to his room; but Kant, having no notion of time, never waited for his appearance, but arose and tried to walk. Owing to his great weakness, this gave occasion for many falls, which were, however, generally followed by no more serious results than some blue marks. Wasianski, fearing that they might prove serious, thought it necessary for his servant to sleep in his room; Kant, however, objected because he was not accustomed to it, and insisted that he could not sleep in the presence of another, though he finally yielded to the determined counsel of his friend.

His last birthday, April 22nd, 1803, was celebrated as a festival. His intimate friends had been invited, and he looked forward to the occasion with joy; but when the day came he took no pleasure in the entertainment, and was annoyed by the noise of the conversation of the large company. On this day he wrote in a memorandum-book, "According to Scripture, the days of our years are threescore years and ten; and if by reason of strength they be fourscore years, yet is their strength labour and sorrow."

In the autumn of 1803 his seeing eye became very weak, and his room had to be darkened. Prior to this time he had been able to read even fine print without glasses; now he was obliged to stop reading the papers and to cease writing; at last he could not even write his name. Whatever he used had to be placed immediately before him, and he depended more on the sense of touch than on that of sight. This new deprivation greatly distressed him, and he often sighed heavily.

There was also a marked increase of weakness during the same autumn. Once, in the absence of his servant, he was wounded by a fall, and blood flowed freely over his face and down his back. It was therefore thought advisable to bring his widowed sister, Mrs. Theuer, into the house, to assist in taking charge of him. As her presence at first disturbed him, she took her place behind his chair; after he was accustomed to her, and had been the recipient of her kind services, he was pleased to have her about him. She attended him kindly and faithfully to the end.

Even in his old age, and while very weak and frequently indisposed, he was not really sick till near the close of life; and as late as 1802 he said, "I have all the four requisites of a healthy man: a good appetite, good sleep, good digestion, and painlessness. I have never been sick, have never had a physician, and hope never to need any. That I am becoming so infirm probably arises from a revolution in the strata of the air which occurred several years ago; when this changes and all moves along again as usual, I may recover." For years he complained of a pressure on his head, sometimes speaking of it as a kind of cramp of the brain, which interfered greatly with his intellectual activity. In 1796 there had been an unusual mortality among cats in Basle, Vienna, Copenhagen, and other places, which was ascribed by a learned paper to the electric condition of the atmosphere. Not only did Kant adopt this view, but he also explained the peculiar feeling in his head, which began at that time, in the same way. "Even the sickness of other persons was now also attributed to this cause, with the exception of those of whom he knew that they took beer, which he never drank, and which he regarded as itself a sufficient cause of sickness and death. Now he ascribed nearly everything to the electricity of the atmosphere; and the sky might be perfectly clear or in any measure cloudy, it was equally regarded by him as an indication of that state of the air which was dangerous to life or at least injurious to health. Only from a change in the atmosphere did he expect convalescence." He thought he had noticed peculiar appearances in the clouds, which were caused by electricity; and that these electric phenomena were the cause of his ill-health, was a notion to which he clung with such tenacity that no amount of argument could change his opinion.

Kant's first real sickness occurred on October 8th, 1803. Being very fond of English cheese, he had eaten an unusual amount of it on the 7th, and the next morning, while led by his sister, he suddenly sank to the floor, and was unconscious, appearing as if he had been struck by apoplexy. In about an hour consciousness returned; but for the first time in his life he was confined to his bed for several days. On the 12th Wasianski dined with him, and resisted his earnest entreaties to be permitted again to partake of the cheese.

About this time two efforts were made to rob him, both by women. Once, when he was alone in his room, a gentle tap was given at the door of his study and a well-dressed woman entered. At this unexpected and unusual visit Kant sprang up. This surprised her, as she had thought him too weak to stand; but she had presence of mind enough to ask quietly for the time of day. Taking out his watch and holding it more firmly than usual, he answered her question. She thanked him and turned to leave, but had scarcely closed the door when she again opened it, saying that his neighbour, whose name she mentioned, desired to set his watch by Kant's, and had sent her to ask the loan of it for that purpose. The refusal to let her take his watch along was given with such force and decision that she at once left.

Another woman desired to see him about a matter which she wanted to talk over with him alone; but Kant referred her to Wasianski, who recognized her as a notorious character who recently, under threat of violence, had extorted money from a lady. She informed him that her aim in calling on Kant was to demand of him a dozen silver spoons, and some gold rings, which, she claimed, her husband had pawned to him against her will; in case she could not find them, she was willing to accept their equivalent in money. Wasianski threatened her with imprisonment; but after she had been frightened, and had promised never to enter Kant's house again, she was permitted to depart.

At the close of 1803 Kant was unable to write his name, and was so blind that he could not find an object immediately in front of him. He was too much accustomed to have guests for dinner, to deprive himself of their presence now; but after his attack of illness, the life and cheerfulness at the table were gone. He would still begin the conversation as formerly, though feebly, indistinctly and disconnectedly It was his desire that there should be talking; but as he had long been the leader and the inspiration of the table-talk, he was not pleased to have his guests now talk to each other and not to him. "As he was now weak and hard of hearing, it was not possible to converse with him; therefore he generally spoke alone, his subjects usually being the nature of the food, dark reminiscences of the past, and his recent sickness. His old friends knew how to turn his attention to reminiscences of earlier times, respecting which his memory was still faithful." After he had been at table about half an hour he became so weary that he had to be led to his room. As he gradually became still weaker, only his older acquaintances were invited. His sentences were usually broken and incoherent, so that even his intimate friends could not understand him, and he found it difficult to grasp the meaning of simple sentences addressed to him; but occasionally he had more lucid intervals and was in good spirits. Even after his illness, when he could no longer converse about ordinary affairs, he, who had spent his life in scholarly pursuits, was occasionally able to speak on learned subjects, such as physical geography, physics, and chemistry. On the Monday before his death, when he had lost all interest in the conversation of his friends at table, Wasianski proposed that they should speak on learned affairs, declaring that he was sure Kant would take part in the conversation, which the others questioned. When a question on a scholarly subject was proposed, he gave a brief but lucid answer.

There are numerous details of this period, all of which present pictures which are calculated to move us with the deepest compassion. The profound philosopher and brilliant companion had long ceased to exist; and even the ruin gave no idea of the majestic greatness which had departed. It is not surprising that he longed for death and said, "Life is a burden to me; I am tired of bearing it. And if this night the angel of death were to come and call me hence, I would raise my hands and say, God be praised." Sometimes he would add, "Yes, if an evil demon sat on my shoulder and whispered in my ear, 'You have made men unhappy,' it would be otherwise." His moral purposes remained unshaken, and he determined to bear whatever burdens might be placed on him. Suicide he regarded as cowardly, and cowardice he despised. The name poltroon was, in his estimation, a designation of extreme baseness, and he said, "I am no poltroon; I have strength enough yet to take my life, but this I regard as immoral." His abhorrence of suicide was so great that he declared that it was not easy to find anything more contemptible, and he thought one ought to spit in the face of him who took his own life.

At last he frequently failed to recognize his most intimate friends, even Wasianski, his sister, and his servant. He became so feeble that he could hardly sit in his arm-chair, though supported by pillows. The lowest possible degree of physical weakness seemed to have been reached on February 3rd, 1804, when all his energy was apparently gone. After this he took, properly speaking, no food. Yet there were occasions when he exerted his will to an extraordinary degree. On this very day a professor of the university, who was his physician and friend, called; he had been very kind and attentive, and had refused all compensation for his services. Kant arose from his chair when he entered, offered him his hand, and uttered some incoherent sentences, which Wasianski interpreted to mean that Kant wanted to express his gratitude to the physician for his great kindness in calling, especially since his position as rector of the university made it difficult for him to spare the time. Kant said that was what he meant. He almost sank down from weakness, and was urged by the physician to be seated, but he still hesitated. Wasianski intimated that Kant's refinement would not let him sit until the physician had first taken his seat. The professor at first doubted whether this was the reason; but he was convinced of it when he took his seat and Kant did the same; and he was almost moved to tears when Kant, with great effort, said, "The feeling of humanity has not yet left me."

On the same day a few friends, as usual, were his guests, though he could eat nothing. Wasianski and another friend were with him at dinner on Sunday, February 5th; he was, however, so weak that he was unable to sit upright, and he sank together in his chair. On the next day he took no part whatever in the conversation, and his eyes stared; on the 7th there were three guests at table, but Kant was in bed. Wasianski was the only guest on the 8th; Kant, indeed, came to the table, but he ate nothing and hurried to bed. The daily meetings of friends for so many years around that hospitable board, with their delightful associations, their intellectual feasts, their wit, humour, and anecdotes, were over. Kant became unconscious on the evening of the 9th; he was conscious the next morning, but not the remainder of the day. He was restful on the 11th, but speechless; in answer to Wasianski's question, whether he recognized him, Kant gave him a kiss. On Sunday morning, the 12th of February, some water was given him; after quenching his thirst, he said, "It is well." These were his last words. Early on that morning he had stretched out his body at full length, and he remained in that posture till death. As the clock struck eleven on that Sunday forenoon he quietly breathed his last, in the presence of his sister, his nephew, Wasianski, another friend, and his servant. He was two months and ten days less than eighty years old. It was not sickness but marasmus which consumed his strength, and Wasianski says, "His death was not a violent act of nature, but simply a cessation of life."

The news of his long-expected death spread rapidly through the city, and all classes felt the loss of their most celebrated citizen. "The day was so clear and cloudless that few of the kind occur in Königsberg in a period of twenty years; only a small cloud hovered in the zenith over the azure of the sky. A soldier on the Schmiede Bridge is said to have called attention to it with the remark, 'See, that is Kant's soul flying heavenward.' This was regarded as an evidence of the knowledge which even the common people had of Kant, and of their idea of the purity of his soul, which, they thought, was at once taken up to the pure ether." A letter written from the city the day after his death, says, "Königsberg has lost one of its noblest inhabitants. His faithfulness, his kindness, his uprightness, and his sociability, will long be subjects of painfully-precious remembrance for all who were intimately acquainted with him." (174)

His body was so dried up that it seemed to be scarcely more than a skeleton, and its appearance created universal astonishment. Years before his death he spoke humorously of his emaciated condition, and said that he had attained the minimum of muscular substance; but at the time of his death he was still more emaciated, and his muscles had disappeared to such an extent that his body almost seemed like that of a mummy.

His head was shorn, and a mould of it was taken. He had expressed the desire not to have his body exposed to the gaze of the curious, and had written a paper respecting his funeral, requesting to be buried quietly, early in the morning, his remains to be followed only by his guests. As Wasianski had, however, represented to him the difficulties of such an arrangement, Kant left the whole matter to his judgment. The remains were kept for sixteen days, and the desire to view them was general; day after day multitudes came to see for the last time the little that was mortal of the immortal Kant.

On the 28th of February, one of the finest days of winter, the funeral took place amid unusual solemnities. The streets through which the procession passed had been cleared of snow, and the city authorities had issued an appeal to the people to show proper respect for the funeral of the man who, on account of his teachings and life, was so eminently worthy of regard; but the inhabitants of Königsberg esteemed the illustrious services of Kant too highly to need this official recognition of his eminence and worth to inspire them with a proper respect for his memory. At three in the afternoon the body was borne by students from the house to the cathedral, which was also the university church, where the services took place. His sister and nephew were the only relatives present; among the chief mourners were between twenty and thirty of his guests and more intimate friends. Headed by a detachment of soldiers, there was a long procession, consisting of the professors and students, the governor of the province, numerous civil and military officers, the ministers of the city, and many other persons of all ranks and classes from Königsberg and the vicinity. Solemnly, amid the tolling of all the church bells, the procession moved through the crowds which lined the streets, to the cathedral, where the curator of the university, the rector, the senators, and other high officials and dignitaries received the body. The church was illuminated with hundreds of wax candles. The coffin was placed on a catafalque in front of the altar. At the head stood a marble bust of Kant; at the foot were two inverted torches; at the sides eight silver lamps were burning; and on the altar lay the principal works of the great philosopher. The coffin bore the inscription, "Cineres mortales immortalis Kantii." The solemn services consisted of a dirge and two addresses, after which the remains were placed in the Professors' Vault beside the cathedral.

There was a strong desire to secure mementoes of the great Kant. His silver hair was braided into rings and sold; and the demand for these souvenirs was so great, that one of his biographers suspects that there was a miraculous increase of his hair, as in the case of relics of saints, and that more was sold than ever adorned his head. At the sale of his effects, trifles, such as a tobacco-pouch, in itself worthless and used probably for twenty years, brought large sums. The three-cornered hat which he was accustomed to wear in his study, and which had done service for twenty or thirty years, was sold for a high price to an Englishman.

His money and property amounted to 21,539 thalers. In addition to his regular salary, he had received the fees of the students who heard his private lectures, and there had also been an income from the sale of his books. The revenue from his works, however, began late, namely, after the success of the "Kritik" was established; before the appearance of this work his books were, probably, published mostly at his own expense. His early struggles with poverty had taught him frugal habits; his wants were limited, and he valued money too highly to waste it. He was very economical, some thought excessively so; but he was not miserly. He was provident, and was anxious to secure a competence, so as to be independent. Debt he carefully avoided, and he said that a rap at the door never gave him anxiety lest there might be a creditor there. As his money accumulated, it was judiciously put at interest for him by his friends. It was in this way that he secured a competence and also the means to help his relatives, and was able to leave a considerable sum at the time of his death.

His business manager and executor, Wasianski, received 3076 thalers; Professor Gensichen inherited his library and 500 thalers; his aged cook, who had been in his service for many years, received 666, and Kauffmann, his last servant, 250. Kant had ordered that 3500 thalers should be set apart, so as to secure for his childless sister, Mrs. Theuer, one hundred thalers annually; the remainder of the interest, forty thalers, was to be given to Lampe. The rest of his money he willed to his nephews and nieces, and their descendants, who were also to receive the 3500 thalers after the death of Mrs. Theuer and Lampe.

In order to perpetuate his memory, a Kant Society was formed in Königsberg at the suggestion of Dr. Motherby. The first members consisted of the more intimate acquaintances of the philosopher, the number who assembled being rarely more than twelve or eighteen persons. They met on Kant's birthday, at first in his house, afterwards in some other public place. The dinner on such occasions was made as much as possible like those given by Kant; it was a plain meal, with a pint-bottle of red or white wine before each guest. An address on Kant's life, character, works, or philosophy, was delivered by the presiding officer or "Bean-King," as he was called from the manner of his appointment. At every celebration a cake was eaten, in which a bean was hid; and the member who took the piece with the bean became the Bean-King. As the personal friends of Kant died, others who had attended his lectures or were attached to his philosophy were selected to fill the vacancies, but the number was limited to thirty. In 1846 only three of the original members were present, and the last of the founders of the Society died in 1848. Many of the addresses delivered before the Society, which still exists, have been published, and are an important contribution to the Kant literature.

In 1809 Kant's friend, Scheffner, formed the plan of converting the Professors' Vault, which was no longer used as a place of interment, into a walk. A gallery, 136 feet long and fifteen wide, was constructed and Kant's remains were placed in the eastern end. Over the main entrance were inscribed the words, "Stoa Kantiana," and a marble bust, by Schadow, was placed over the grave. On April 22nd, 1810, Kant's friends met to celebrate his birthday. After an address by the philosopher, Professor Herbart, they proceeded to the grave and unveiled the bust; subsequently it was, however, removed for protection to the university.

For some years Kant's grave was entirely neglected, and it was described as desolate and almost forgotten, and some even questioned whether his remains were there. Repeated efforts have been made since 1873 to secure the money necessary to make the tomb of Kant worthy of his great name, and these have finally been crowned with success. During the

Centennial of the "Kritik," in the summer of 1881, a monument in the form of a beautiful chapel was completed and dedicated to his memory, and in it his remains were deposited.

APPENDIX.

1. In order to avoid too frequent reference to authorities, I here mention the most important books used in the preparation of this volume.

Three biographies of the first importance were published by intimate friends of Kant: Borowski's "Darstellung des Lebens und Charakters Immanuel Kant's," 1804; Jachmann's "Immanuel Kant geschildert in Briefen an einen Freund," 1804; and Wasianski's "Immanuel Kant in seinen letzten Lebensjahren," 1804.

Two other friends contributed important facts in books which appeared about the same time; Rink's "Ansichten aus I. Kant's Leben," and Hasse's "Merkwuerdige Aeusserungen Kant's."

A not very reliable, anonymous biography was published in 1804, entitled, "I. Kant's Biograpie, Leipzig, O. Weigel." This work was to comprise four volumes, but only two appeared. Another anonymous book, printed in the same year, was named, "Aeusserungen über Kant, seinen Charakter und seine Meinungen. Von einem billigen Verehrer seiner Verdienste." Professor J. D. Metzger, of Königsberg, was discovered to be the author. Another anonymous book of the same period bore the name, "Fragmente aus Kant's Leben."

In 1842 Professor F. W. Schubert published the best biography of Kant in the German language; it is found in vol. xi. of Kant's works edited by Rosenkranz and Schubert.

In 1860 Dr. R. Reicke issued a small book styled, "Kantiana." It contains a funeral address on Kant, delivered April 23rd, 1804, by Professor Dr. Wald, of Königsberg, and much other valuable material from the university library of that city.

The journals published in Königsberg, the "Preussiche Provinzialblätter," "Neue Preussische Provinzialblätter," and "Altpreussische Monatsschrift," contain many valuable articles on Kant.

Much of the literature cotemporary with Kant, such as journals, letters, biographies, and other books, has been found serviceable. The principal authorities not already named are mentioned in the following notes. Diligent search has been made for everything calculated to throw light on the life of Kant; and hundreds of volumes have been used to which no special reference is necessary, but the consultation of which was important for understanding Kant's life and works and the age in which he lived. For the great thinker's views I am indebted chiefly to his own works; in some cases I used his own editions; in others, those of Hartenstein, and of Rosenkranz and Schubert; and I also made use of Tieftrunk's edition of his smaller works.

Very naturally numerous traditions respecting Kant have, in the course of time, become current, especially in Königsberg. Among these are two stories of attempts to murder him, one by an insane butcher, and another by an escaped prisoner. As these are based on no reliable evidence, and are wholly unworthy of credence, no reference is made to them in the text.

2. In 1762, 550 vessels landed at Königsberg; in 1773, 861. The exports consisted chiefly of grain, wood, and flax; the imports were mostly colonial wares, manufactured articles, and wines. In 1784 and 1792 the yearly exports amounted to over four million thalers, though generally they amounted to two and a half or three millions about that time. In 1795-6 the income for excise, duty, and licences, exceeded that of any other city in the kingdom, amounting to 554,559 thalers. There were 143 officers to attend to this business.

3. The principal authorities I have used on Königsberg are: Faber: "Königsberg in Preussen;" "Neue Preussische Provinzialblätter," 1854, 197; "Jahrbücher der Preussischen Monarchie," 1804, vol. ii. 270; and "Altpreussische Monatsschrift," vol. i. 353.

4. Immanuel changed the name from Cant to Kant. This change is accounted for by a story which indicates his sensitiveness. A boy teased him by saying that the C in his name should be pronounced like a *Z*, so that Cant would become Zant. This induced him to write it Kant. In the catalogue of the gymnasium which he attended, the name is spelt in five ways: Cant, Candt, Cante, Kant, Kandt. Reicke, "Kantiana," 46, 47.

5. Reicke: "Kantiana," 5.

6. Rink: "Ansichten aus I. Kant's Leben," 13.

7. "Neue Preussische Provinzialblätter," 1852, 2, 81.

8. "Martin Knutzen und seine Zeit," von Benno Erdmann, 34.

9. The term *Pietistic* was applied to the school by its enemies as a term of reproach, and they spoke of it as the Pietistic seminary or the Pietistic inn. Kant relates that while he was a pupil, a young loafer one day entered the room of Schiffert, and in a spirit of ridicule asked, "Is this the Pietistic school?" Schiffert had him soundly whipped, after which he sent him away with the remark, "Now you know where the Pietistic school is." Hasse: "Merkwürdige Aeusserungen Kant's," 36.

10. "Pietism must therefore not yet have degenerated into fanaticism, and the discipline of the school cannot have been so fearfully severe as some ungrateful pupils—it had many more who were grateful—have at times represented." Wald's address, in Reicke's "Kantiana," 6.

11. Ruhnken, a fellow-pupil of Kant, wrote to him as follows: "Anni triginta sunt ipsi, cum uterque tetrica illa quidem, sed utili tamen nec pœnitenda fanaticorum disciplina continebamur." Rink: "Tiberius Hemsterhuys und Ruhnken," 267.

12. "Streit der Facultaten," Ros. and Schub. vol. x. p. 313.

13. Article by A. Rogge, Altp. M. 1878-79.

14. Biedermann, "Deutschland im 18. Jahrhundert," ii. 3, 679.

15. From the spring of 1758 to that of 1759 the total income was only 3665 thalers. For one thaler twenty-five hours of instruction were given. N.P.P.B., 1853, 241. Cunde, who was there at the same time as Kant, had twenty-three teachers in three and a half years. As soon as the candidates for the ministry received an appointment as preachers, they left and other teachers took their place. "The scholars in Prima had to submit to three teachers in philosophy." Do. 250.

16. Rink: "Hemsterhuys und Ruhnken," 80, 81.

17. In the summer of 1731 there were 443 students, of whom 219 were theological, 125 juridical, 37 medical, and 62 philosophical. In the winter 1731-32 there were 442, of whom 208 studied theology, 89 law, 47 medicine, 28 cameralistics, and 70 belonged to the philosophical faculty. P.P.B., 1832, 279. In 1744, at its second centennial celebration, it is said to have had 44 professors and 1032 students, of whom 992 were Lutheran, 21 Reformed, 13 Catholic, and 6 belonged to the Greek Church. N.P.P.B., Neue Folge, vol. ix. 172. I think this a mistake, and suppose the author simply added the number of students in summer and winter, and thus counted most of them twice.

18. Arnoldt: "Historie der Königsberger Universität," vol. ii. 183.

19. "The chairs were occupied mostly by men with no scientific reputation; the lectures were delivered in strict scholastic formulas, partly yet in the Latin language; whatever was necessary as a preparation for the examination ordered by the state was taught in meagre dictations; the students were trained to empty formalities for spiritless discussions; and owing to the isolated position of the university, no intellectual inspiration was spread by it over the land." N.P.P.B., 1854, 198.

20. See on this whole subject, "Martin Knutzen und seine Zeit," by Benno Erdmann, to which I am chiefly indebted for these facts.

21. His principal metaphysical book, "Systema causarum efficientium," passed through two editions; his "De immaterialitate animi" was translated into German; and a book on the "Defence of the Christian Religion," which was aimed chiefly at English deism, passed through five editions. Eminent cotemporaries speak highly of him, and Hamann says, "I was a pupil of the celebrated Knutzen."

22. N.P.P.B., 1854, 202.

23. Reicke, 50.

24. In the biographical sketch prepared by Borowski and reviewed by Kant, the statement occurs that several attempts had been made by Kant to preach in the country; but another person being preferred in an appointment to a school for which he had also applied, he abandoned the thought of entering the ministry. Kant crossed out this part of the sketch; for what reason Borowski, who says that the statement is nevertheless true, did not know. To another friend Kant declared that he had once prepared a sermon on a certain text; but that may have been before he left the university. Kant's studies at the university, and the statement of Heilsberg quoted in the text, lead to the conclusion that he was not preparing for the ministry. Borowski must have been mistaken, a view also taken by Benno Erdmann, in his "Life of Knutzen," 133, note. Kant's lack of sympathy with Pietism, religious doubts, and his preference for other studies than theology, were probably his main reasons for failing to comply with the wish of his parents and his benefactor, Dr. Schulz.

25. "Gedanken von der wahren Schätzung der lebendigen Kräfte und Beurtheilung der Beweise, deren sich Herr Leibnitz und andere Mechaniker in dieser Streitsache bedient haben, nebst einigen vorhergehenden Betrachtungen, welche die Kraft der Körper überhaupt betreffen."

26. "Kant here appears altogether as an adherent of that freer tendency of Wolfianism to whose most decided advocates Knutzen belonged. That he is governed everywhere in the most essential points by the spirit of the Leibnitz-Wolfian doctrines, is evident from every paragraph of this book." "Life of Knutzen," 143.

27. Biedermann, ii. 1. 522. Forty thalers is here given as the annual pay.

28. N.P.P.B., 1854, 203.

29. "Allgemeine Naturgeschichte und Theorie des Himmels, oder Versuch von der Verfassung und dem mechanischen Ursprunge des ganzen Weltgebäudes nach Newton'schen Grundsätzen abgehandelt."

30. Privatim docentes, professores extraordinarii, and professores ordinarii. For the first, called by the Germans Privat-Docent, I use the word tutor. From a tutor in private families the term is always sufficiently distinguished by the context.

31. "Meditationum quarundam de igne succincta delineatio."

32. "Principiorum primorum cognitionis metaphysicæ nova delucidatio."

33. "Metaphysicæ cum geometria junctæ usus in philosophia naturali."

34. "Thus the forty-five year old Kant, who in 1763 had received the second prize from the Berlin Academy of Sciences; who already in 1764 had been designed for an ordinary professorship by the cabinet; and who in 1769 had received an honourable call to an ordinary professorship in another university, was not permitted in this year to announce his lectures to the students in the official catalogue." N.P.P.B., 1846, 459.

35. N.P.P.B., 1854, 206.

36. This gives us as the subjects of his lectures, mathematics, physics, logic, metaphysics, physical geography, a critique of the proofs of the existence of God, optimism, fortification, pyrotechnics, anthropology, encyclopædia of the philosophical sciences, pedagogics, moral philosophy, and natural theology. Every professor in ordinary in the philosophical faculty was obliged to lecture in turn on pedagogics, which accounts for Kant's lectures on this subject.

37. Altp. M., xvi. 610.

38. Though he became most eminent as a metaphysician, his metaphysical lectures were never the most popular, not even among the students. They were very dry to many; and already in 1759, four years after Kant began his lectures, Hamann wrote that it was difficult to follow him. Hamann's works, vol. ii. p. 445. Kant knew

very well that his lectures were difficult for beginners, and he publicly advised his students to prepare themselves for his lectures by first hearing those of Professor Poerschke.

39. The lectures were published in 1798, the last work which he himself published. Even in book form they retained their popularity, and the fourth edition appeared in 1833.

40. Altp. M., xvi. 607.

41. Schubert, 41. This was written after Kant had criticized one of Herder's books, and there was already some alienation between the teacher and pupil.

42. "Herder's Leben," von Carolina von Herder, 60.

43. N.P.P.B., 1848, 291.

44. The subjects on which he lectured after he became professor were: logic, metaphysics, natural law, moral philosophy, natural theology, physical geography, anthropology, and pedagogics.

46. "Untersuchungen über die Deutlichkeit der Grundsätze der natürlichen Theologie und der Moral. Zur Beantwortung der Frage, welche die Königl. Akademie der Wissenschaften zu Berlin auf das Jahr 1763 aufgegeben hat."

47. "De mundi sensibilis atque intelligibilis forma et principiis."

48. Dr. W. G. Kelch, "Ueber den Schädel Kant's," gives the result of his examination of the head immediately after death. When the remains of Kant were removed to the Chapel in 1880, C. Kupffer and F. Bessel Hagan examined the skull with the most minute care. They give a full description of their investigations in "Archiv für Anthropologie," Braunschweig, vol. xiii., Aug. 1881, in an article entitled, "Der Schädel Immanuel Kant's."

49. Dr. Bohn, Altp. M., vi. 611, regards this as a light podagra.

50. Bouterwek; "I. Kant," 48, 57.

51. "Von einem neuerdings erhobenen vornehmen Ton in der Philosophie," 1796.

52. "Träume eines Geistersehers erläutert durch Träume der Metaphysik," 1766.

53. While his "Kritik" contains many evidences of his analytical powers, and of nice distinctions, it would be difficult to find a more striking instance than in his "Logic" where he follows the various steps in observation, and distinguishes the different kinds of knowledge. R. and S. vol. iii. pp. 236, 237. First the object is represented by the senses; secondly, it is represented consciously, *percipere;* thirdly, it is compared with other objects, and is known, *noscere;* fourthly, it is known consciously, *cognoscere: noscere* applied

to animals also, *cognoscere,* only to man; fifthly, to understand a thing, *intelligere ;* sixthly, to get an insight into things by means of reason, *perspicere;* seventhly, to comprehend a thing, to understand it *à priori, comprehendere.*

54. Schlichtegroll's "Nekrologie," 1797, vol. i. p. 286.

55. Hamann to Jacobi, Sept. 22, 1785.

56. Hamann, Nov. 20, 1785.

57. On Kant's political views, see an article by Schubert, in Raumer's "Histor. Taschenbuch," vol. ix. In 1795, on the occasion of the recognition of the French Republic by some of the European powers, Kant published his pamphlet on "Eternal Peace." The edition of 1500 copies was exhausted in two weeks.

58. One of these on Dr. Lilienthal, Professor of Theology, who died March 17, 1782, is as follows :—

"Was auf das Leben folgt, deckt tiefe Finsterniss;
Was uns zu thun gebührt, des sind wir nur gewiss.
Dem kann, wie Lilienthal, kein Tod die Hoffnung rauben,
Der glaubt, um recht zu thun, recht thut, um froh zu glauben."

59. Bouterwek, pp. 20—22.

60. "Versuch über die Krankheiten des Kopfes," 1764.

61. N.P.P.B. vi. p. 13. Rink, p. 137.

62. Herbart, in "I. Kant's Gedaechtnissfeyer zu Königsberg am 22 April, 1810."

63. "Hamburger Correspondent," March 7, 1804. Schubert, 141.

64. Altp. M. xvi. 612. The account was written in 1795.

65. One friend says, "He read unusually much, especially physical, historical and anthropological writings ; most of all, accounts of travel." Another says, "He liked accounts of travel best of all. He seldom read philosophical books, not even those written for or against him." Reicke, 15, 16. "Men, people, natural history, physics, mathematics, and observation were the sources whence he drew the materials for his lectures and conversations." Do. 17.

66. Reicke, 56.

67. Adamson, "Lectures on the Philosophy of Kant," 25.

68. Hasse, 7—9.

69. Jachmann, 174, mentions another strange fact. Kant was very fond of snuff; but at times there was so little moisture in his body that he could not take it. Thinking that more moisture was necessary for his system, he would drink a quantity of water daily in order to supply it. In his study he would keep his handkerchief lying on a chair in order that he might occasionally be obliged to get up.

70. N.P.P.B., iv. 22. Heine also speaks of Kant's merciless, sharp, unpoetical, cold honesty, and draws a parallel between him and Robespierre. "We find in both the same talent for suspicion, the difference being that one uses it against thought and calls it criticism, while the other uses it against men and calls it republican virtue. In both we find the type of the Philister in the highest degree—nature had designed them to weigh coffee and sugar, but destiny wanted them to weigh other things, and placed on the scales of one a king, and on the scales of the other God . . . . And they gave the correct weight." Of course a frivolous spirit like Heine could not appreciate Kant. What would Kant have said of Heine!

71. N.P.P.B., vi. 9. This strange occurrence led Hippel, a friend of both, to write a short comedy, entitled, "Der Mann nach der Uhr oder der ordentliche Mann."

72. Altp. M., xvi. 608. The count speaks of his face as having something lively, fine, and friendly about the mouth, which cannot be reproduced in a hard copperplate. Of his reception he says, "He received me cordially, said much, naturally talked most of trifles, joked very wittily, and made some quite original remarks about fanaticism, and especially about learned ladies and their diseases."

73. He had become so accustomed to guests that it seemed at last as if he could not get along without them. Hasse, 50, relates that at one time he was obliged to eat his dinner alone; but it was so painful to him that he wanted his servant to go into the street and bring to him whomsoever he might find, as he must have company.

74. In his "Anthropology" he says, "If a young, inexperienced man enters a company (especially where ladies are present) surpassing in brilliancy his expectations, he is easily embarrassed when he is to begin to speak. Now, it would be awkward to begin with an item of news reported in the paper, for one does not see what led him to speak of that. But as he has just come from the street, the bad weather is the best introduction to conversation." He several times says essentially the same thing, a kind of repetition of which there are other examples in his works.

75. "Kant's Werke," Rosenkranz und Schubert, vol. iv., Preface. Kant had a copy of the book so bound that every alternate leaf was blank. The pages of these blank leaves, and in many instances also the margins of the printed pages, were covered with closely written notes.

76. N.P.P.B., vi. 291.

77. Jahrbücher d. Preuss. Monarchie, 1799, 194.

78. Jachmann, 101. Borowski says, "I never saw him with his relatives, his brother only excepted."

79. Wasianski says that Kant did not like to see his relatives about him, not because he was ashamed of them, but because he could not converse with them to his satisfaction. But Hasse, 39, and Billiger Verehrer, 17, give a less favourable view. It is repeatedly stated that his higher education separated Kant from his relatives; and it is evident that he did not want to associate with them, whatever his reasons may have been.

80. In his "Anthropology" he says, "As far as learned women are concerned, they use their books somewhat like their watches, namely, to carry them in order that it may be seen that they possess them, though their time-pieces generally stand still or are not regulated by the sun."

81. Even now similar opinions are common in Germany, and may be heard in cultivated society. In 1877 an address was delivered before the Kant Society in Königsberg, on Kant's views of woman, and the speaker declared them to be his own convictions concerning woman's culture and mission, and he thought it to be specially important to make them known at this time, when the influences, especially from Russia and America, tend to break through the limits fixed by nature for woman's intellectual attainments. The address is published in Altp. M. xiv. 593.

82. Borowski, 149.

83. Rosenkranz (Kant's Works, vol. xii. p. 269) says that Kant has frequently and bitterly been charged with degrading marriage, since he makes its essence to consist in the sexual relation of husband and wife. He pronounces Kant's views "barbarous," and says that it may be regarded as an apology that Kant, as a bachelor, could have no experience of the depth and intimacy of the marriage relation. His views of marriage are found in his "Rechtslehre," his "Anthropologie," and his book on "The Emotion of the Beautiful and Sublime."

84. "Ich selbsten, mit Erlaub zu sagen,
Ich selbsten habe keine Frau."

85. "Die Regel bleibt: Man muss nicht freien,
Doch excipe, solch wuerdig Paar."

86. Reicke, 12. Altp. M. xvi. 608. This lady afterwards married, and she frequently boasted that Kant had been in love with her. She was twenty-two years younger than Kant.

87. N.P.P.B., vi. 15.

88. Jachmann, 77—82, makes the conversation refer to the

American Revolution. But Kant and Green were acquainted long before that time, and as early as 1770 Hamann dedicated a translation to Green, speaking of him as "the friend of our Kant." Schubert, 53. Jachmann's account must therefore refer to some other circumstance than that revolution.

89. N.P.P.B., 1853, 165. The article is on Immanuel Kant and George Hamann.

90. Scheffner wanted him to explain some parts of his writings; but Hamann answered that this was impossible, since much which he had taken into the account while writing had escaped his memory. "Life of Scheffner," 207. He himself admitted that he could not master systems, and says that it was his province to deal with "crumbs, fragments, whims, and notions." Letter to Lindner, October 12th, 1759. In this letter he speaks of Kant as the little magister whom he loved and esteemed very much, and already at that time he calls him "the little Socrates."

91. Schlichtegroll, 1801, i. 303. Another writer says, "Hippel's life and character were full of peculiarities and contradictions. With a clear, enlightened mind, he manifested a spirit of fanaticism and an inclination to superstition; with strong passion and sensuousness, he had a devotion bordering on bigotry and an ardent zeal for virtue; he cherished a friendship which was almost enthusiastic, and yet was reticent towards his friends; he was imperious and severe, and yet, at the same time, cheerful and refined; he was an enthusiastic admirer of nature and simplicity, and yet was inclined to etiquette and to avarice; he appreciated the excellencies of woman in general, and also the marriage relation, and yet he had a decided antipathy to wedlock; his moral principles were disinterested, and yet in his conduct he manifested the most striking egotism. Brockhaus' "Conversations-Lexicon," article Hippel.

92. "Das Leben des Prof. C. J. Krauss," von J. Voigt, 27.

93. There are more books on philosophical than on other subjects. In all there are about seventy or eighty writings of Kant, of which very many are short dissertations, reviews, or newspaper articles. In Hartenstein's edition of Kant's works, there are eight large volumes; in Rosenkranz and Schubert's, ten are devoted to his works, one to his letters and life, and one to an account of his philosophy. In Kirchmann's edition there are eight volumes, with one supplementary volume.

94. This is true, at least, as far as the great results of that philosophy are concerned. In his second edition of the "Kritik," Kant made many changes; but he claimed that they pertained only

to the style and the argument, not to the thought. But Schopenhauer claimed that Kant had also changed the thought materially, that he had done this intentionally, cowardly, and dishonestly. As to the exact nature of the changes the commentators differ, some claiming that the declaration of Kant is correct; others, however, as stoutly asserting that the substance of the first edition is materially changed in the second, of which the following were all a reprint. The whole subject is discussed by Benno Erdmann, in his "Kant's Kriticismus." It is the second edition which has made the greatest impression on literature, and is generally cited. Recent editions of the "Kritik" usually give Kant's second edition, Hartenstein and Benno Erdmann at the same time indicating its variations from the first. Rosenkranz, however, gives the first edition.

95. "He had his plan, wrote his book, made a cheap contract with his publisher, and then quietly awaited the result, though, as his replies indicate, he was by no means indifferent to reviews." Mundt's "Dioskuren," vol. ii. p. 24.

96. "Berlinische Monatsschrift," 1804, 279.

97. Descartes repeatedly speaks of God as "Substantia infinita." He distinguishes God as the infinite Substance, whose cause is in Himself, from all other substances, which are finite and are caused by God. The latter substances are of two kinds, matter, whose essence is extensive, and spirit, whose essence is thought. Spinoza's pantheism is based on the idea of God as substance. But this view seems to have had no influence on Kant.

98. Descartes held that there are three sources of ideas: some are innate, others come from the objects they represent, and others are fictions which the mind itself produces.

99. Kuno Fischer (iii. 169), speaking of Kant's writings during the first decade of his authorship, says, "Kant is evidently more inclined to oppose Leibnitz than Newton. He places himself on the standpoint of the English natural philosophy, passes from this to the English philosophy of experience, which established the principles according to which Newton had projected his system: he went from Newton to Locke and Hume."

100. Newton's indirect influence on the "Kritik" must be regarded as a potent factor. Professor A. Riehl, in his book, "Der Philosophische Kriticismus," thinks that the spirit and the method of the mathematical natural sciences were the patterns according to which Kant's method was formed. He holds that Newton's natural philosophy was as powerful as Hume's scepticism in determining the character of Kant's "Kritik," and says, "I believe that I can show that

the natural philosophy of Newton had no less an influence on the origin of the Critical Philosophy of Kant than Hume himself." It would perhaps be more correct to say that Newton's influence was directed chiefly to the formation of his method of thinking, while Hume gave the direct impulse which led to the development of the "Kritik."

101. We cannot tell exactly when Kant was aroused from his dogmatic slumber by Hume, but it was probably not many years after he became tutor in the university. Fischer thinks it must have been about 1760. iii. 178. In 1759 Hamann wrote a letter to Kant, in which he speaks of "the Attic philosopher Hume who, in spite of all his errors, is a Saul among the prophets." It was about this time, also, that Kant spoke of Hume in his lectures.

102. "Versuch den Begriff der negativen Grösse in die Weltweisheit einzuführen."

103. "Der einzig mögliche Beweisgrund zu einer Demonstration für das Dasein Gottes."

104. Tieftrunk, in his Preface to the edition of Kant's smaller works, says, "Men were accustomed to give an account only of what was contained in their conceptions." Kant then put the question, whether these are conceptions of real objects, or whether they are mere fictions of the mind?

105. "Dörptsche Beiträge," iii. 102. The letters are written from Zürich. He asks Kant, whether in his "Kritik" he is going to say that the present criticism could hardly be more remote than it is from the critique of pure reason; also, whether he will say "that all our wisdom is folly until we fix all our observations more on man; that we constantly err so greatly because we seek outside of ourselves what is within us; that it is absolutely impossible to understand the inner nature of a thing, and that we can understand only the relation of objects to our needs; and that all occupations, writings, meditations, reading, are folly and childishness unless they are definite means for satisfying human needs?" These letters are an evidence that Kant was already known beyond the borders of Germany years before the "Kritik" appeared.

106. The first work mentioned was never published by Kant, the thoughts he intended to give in it were probably developed and embodied in the "Kritik." A man who had heard that Kant intended to write on this subject, changed it a little and published a work on it. A book on the second subject appeared twenty years after he wrote this letter. Under the third title he published nothing, but the thoughts intended to be given under that head probably appeared in his "Critique of the Practical Reason," or in his other moral works.

107. Already in 1762 Kant spoke of the understanding as the logical faculty, or the faculty for knowing, in his book, "Die falsche Spitzfiudigkeit der vier syllogistischen Figuren."

108. "Philosophia autem prima continens principia usus intellectus puri est metaphysica."

109. "Von dem ersten Grunde des Unterschiedes der Gegenden im Raume." 1768.

110. "Tempus itaque est *principium formale* Mundi sensibilis absolute primum."

111. *Conceptus spatii est singularis repreesentatio* omnia *in se* comprehendens, non sub se continens notio abstracta et communis."

112. "Spatium itaque est *principium formale Mundi sensibilis* absolute primum."

113. "Sed ab ipsa mentis actione, secundum perpetuas leges sensa sua coordinante, quasi typus immutabilis, ideoque intuitive cognoscendus."

114. Writing to Herder, Sept. 15th, 1781, he calls the "Kritik" "Sancho Panza's transcendental philosophy."

115. A Latin translation of the "Kritik" was made, and Kant complained that he could not understand it. Hamann glories in this fact, and says, "It serves the author right to experience the difficulty of his readers.

116. His aim in the "Kritik" was to make the book very comprehensive, and he says in the Preface to the first edition, "I venture to say that there is not a single metaphysical problem which is not solved here, or for whose solution at least the key is not given."

117. Kant thinks that the very existence of metaphysics depends on the answer to this question, and in his "Prolegomena" he says, "All metaphysicians are therefore solemnly and legally suspended from their occupations until they have satisfactorily answered this question : How are synthetic judgments *à priori* possible ?"

118. He says that without sensation no object would be given, and without the understanding none would be thought. "Thoughts without content are empty; perceptions without conceptions are blind." "The understanding perceives nothing, the senses think nothing. Knowledge can only arise from the union of both. Nevertheless we dare not for this reason confound their functions, but we have great reason to separate and distinguish each carefully from the other. Therefore we distinguish the science of the rules of sensation in general, that is, æsthetics, from the science of the rules of the understanding in general, that is, logic."

119. Kant calls this "Gemeinschaft (Wechselwirkung zwischen

dem Handelnden und Leidenden)." The difficulty Kant experienced with the categories is evident fram his statement in the Preface that they cost him the most trouble.

120. "The question respecting transcendental freedom pertains only to speculative knowledge, which we can set aside as altogether a matter of indifference when we are concerned about the practical." Rosenkranz says that he not merely laid the greatest stress on the practical element in his speculation, but he even undertook to root out metaphysics. N.P.P.B., iv. 13.

121. "Prolegomena zu einer jeden künftigen Metaphysik, die als Wissenschaft wird auftreten können." It is the first book he published after the "Kritik." As it popularizes the main thoughts of that book, it should be read before the "Kritik," since it will greatly facilitate the understanding of that difficult work.

122. "Kritik der Urtheilskraft," 1790. His definition of judgment is, "Urtheilskraft überhaupt ist das Vermögen, das Besondere als enthalten unter dem Allgemeinen zu denken."

123. Kant says respecting the pleasure derived from the agreeable, the beautiful, and the good, "It may be said of these three kinds of pleasure, that the taste for the beautiful is alone an uninterested and free pleasure. For no interest, neither that of the senses nor that of the reason, compels approval."

124. Hasse, 22. In a letter to Professor Schütz, 1785, Kant already speaks of "The Metaphysic of Nature," and says that the "Metaphysical Principles of Natural Science"—a book completed that summer—is a preparation for that work.

125. This is published in Altp. M., i. 742.

126. His principal works on morals and religion followed his "Kritik," and were based on its conclusions. On morals his most important works are, "Grundlegung zur Metaphysik der Sitten," 1785; "Kritik der praktischen Vernunft," 1788; "Die Metaphysik der Sitten," 1797, in two parts, of which the first discusses the metaphysical principles of jurisprudence, and the second, the metaphysical principles of virtue. His principal work on religion is, "Die Religion innerhalb der Grenzen der blossen Vernunft," 1793; the last book he published also treats of religious subjects, but, as a rule, merely repeats the views given in the other book. The title of his last book is, "Der Streit der Facultäten," 1798. In many of his other works moral and religious subjects are also discussed.

In the first book on morals he discusses the highest principles of morality, namely, the Categorical Imperative. As the "Kritik" is the propædeutics to all philosophy, so the second book on morals, the

"Critique of the Practical Reason," is the propædeutics to all moral philosophy, and it discusses the problem of the freedom of the will. The third book discusses the principles of morality in general, and contains the system.

127. The question asked by the speculative reason is, What can I know? That asked by the practical reason is, What ought I to do? In his "Logic" (Rosenkranz and Schubert, iii. 186), he, however, says that philosophy deals with four questions, namely, What can I know? What ought I to do? What may I hope? What is man? "The first question is answered by metaphysics; the second by morality; the third by religion; the fourth by anthropology. Really, however, all this might be treated under anthropology, since the first three questions are all related to the last."

128. "Es ist überall nichts in der Welt, ja überhaupt ausser derselben zu denken möglich, was ohne Einschränkung für gut könnte gehalten werden, als allein ein guter Wille." The will, according to Kant, is the character. It is not to be judged by what it accomplishes, but by itself, by its volitions. Man is a lawgiver unto himself, and his own being imposes obligations upon him. He is his own authority, and prescribes his own rules of conduct.

129. Bouterwek, 117, says, "Let it be remembered that no so-called feeling-philosophy found an entrance into Kant's cold understanding, and that all sentimentality, even the noblest, was disagreeable to him." Rink, 99, says that a physician wrote to Kant in 1794: "My dear Professor! Mr. Kant's rational faith is a faith entirely free from all hope. Mr. Kant's morality is a morality *entirely free from all love.* The question now arises, Wherein does Mr. Kant's faith differ from the faith of devils? And in what respect does Mr. Kant's morality differ from the morality of devils?" In other letters the same twitted him on the lack of the emotional element, and in one he says, "Animals have no reason. The absence of reason is the cause why animals cannot rejoice that there is a God, and that God is so gracious as He is. But it is a mystery to me what the cause can be that my rational brother, Immanuel Kant, *cannot*, or *will not*, rejoice, just as well as I do, that God is as gracious as He is."

130*a*. Kant states this celebrated law repeatedly and in different language, but its essence is always as given in the text. "Ich soll niemals anders verfahren, als so, das sich auch wollen könne, meine Maxime solle ein allgemeines Gesetz werden." "Handle so, als ob die Maxime deiner Handlung durch deinen Willen zum allgemeinen Naturgesetze werden sollte."

130*b*. For the relief of constipation a physician advised him to take a pill daily. After awhile he found that this was not enough, and another physician advised him to take two. But Kant, reflecting on the matter, concluded that the increase might go on indefinitely, and therefore resolved never in his life to take more than two pills a day, a rule which he could not be induced to break, except perhaps in old age, when he was feeble and yielded to the advice of others.

131. "The Emotion of the Beautiful and the Sublime." Rosenkranz and Schubert, iv. 431. On a blank leaf of this book, Kant wrote: "It is not necessary to sympathize with others in natural misfortune, but it is necessary to sympathize with them when suffering from injustice." Rosenkranz and Schubert, xi. 1, 221.

132. In N.P.P.B., 1848, 14, it is said, "In his last years his conscience troubled him, because at one time, in order to decline a disagreeable invitation, he pretended to be already invited for the time designated."

133. Hippel (Schlichtegroll's "Nekrologie," 1797, vol. i. p. 281) says, "Kant often says that if a man were to say and write all he thinks, there would be nothing more horrible on God's earth than man." In a letter to Mendelssohn, April 8th, 1766, Kant wrote, "Much that I, indeed, think with the clearest conviction and to my great satisfaction, I shall never have the courage to say; but I shall never say anything that I do not think."

134. It would be difficult to find a dedication in which there is a more diffuse use of complimentary terms than that of Kant's first book. Dr. Bohlius was a friend of the family, and seems to have shown them, and particularly Kant, some kindness. To him the book is dedicated, and he is addressed: "Hochedelgeborener Herr, hochgelahrter und hocherfahrner Doctor, insonders hochzuehrender Gönner!" In the brief dedication of less than a page the dedicatee is five times addressed "hochedelgeborner." The close of the dedication declares that Kant remains, with constant high esteem, "Hochedelgeborener, hochgelahrter und hocherfahrner Herr Doctor, insonders hochzuehrender Gönner, Ew. Hochedelgebornen verpflichtester Diener. Immanuel Kant."

135. Before his "Kritik" appeared Kant used various arguments to prove God's existence. In his Cosmology, 1755, he uses the argument from design and says, "If one does not wilfully oppose all conviction, he must be convinced by such irresistible reasons." In 1763 he used the ontological argument in "Der einzig mögliche Beweisgrund zu einer Demonstration für das Dasein Gottes." In his Inaugural Address, 1770, he argues in favour of God's existence from the unity in nature, and he says that his view is not very

different from that of Malebranche, namely that "we see all things in God."

With his "Kritik" he ends all speculative proofs of the divine existence. But it should be remembered what he said in 1766 in his Träume; "Common sense often sees the truth sooner than it understands the reasous by means of which it can prove or explain it." And at another time he said, "It is absolutely necessary to be convinced of the existence of God; but it is not necessary to demonstrate it."

136. How purely he makes religion rational is evident from his definition of religious faith in his "Streit der Fakultäten," 287. Religious faith is "one which can be developed from each person's reason." Not the ideal reason of humanity, nor the divine reason, but the reason of each individual is thus made the source of his religion, and is treated as if absolute. Page 290 he says that religion can be an object of reason only, and that all the principles of religion must be dictated by reason. And 299 he says, "For ecclesiastical faith historic learning is necessary; for religious faith only reason." Reason, as the sole arbiter in all things, was the watchword of Kant, as well as of the age in which he lived.

137. In "Was ist Aufklärung?" published in 1784, he says that Aufklärung or enlightenment is the departure of man from the state of immaturity for which he is himself to blame. This immaturity is inability to use one's understanding without the guidance of another." "The motto of enlightenment is, "Have the courage to use your own understanding." Laziness and cowardice are the causes why men who should be independent in thought still remain dependent, a fact which makes it so easy for others to be their leaders. "It is so comfortable to remain dependent. If I have a book which thinks for me, a pastor who is my conscience for me, a physician who chooses my diet, et cet., then I need not trouble myself." Perfect independence is Kant's aim in religion as well as in thought: independence of history, of the Church, and, in fact, of everything except reason.

138. This conclusiou is drawn from a careful study of all his religious views, and others have been forced to the same conclusion. Rosenkranz says, "It is true that Kant fell into the one-sidedness of absorbing religion in morality." "Kant's Werke," xii. 202. And he also says, "If now religion is entirely absorbed by morality, then the relation of mau to God as a *personal* Being ceases. He may believe in God; morality does not forbid this. But it is

superfluous. It is not necessary. Conscience is his God. The most essential thing is the conception of the highest good, of the categorical imperative, of the maxim," 253. Even Feuerbach's view finds a basis in "Religion," 257, note, where it is declared that each man makes himself a God and must do so. In his "Kritik" he first destroys all hope of a speculative proof of the existence of God; then, after he postulates His existence, he destroys the speculative use of that existence; and even practically He is only of secondary significance. That God is a person and sustains personal relations to man, is not made practically real.

139. Less than a year before his death he said, "Were not the Bible already written, it would probably not be written any more." Hasse, 27.

140. Such declarations are simply amazing, especially when one reads in Exodus xx. as part of the commandments, "And showing mercy unto thousands of them that *love me, and keep my commandments.*"

141. In his short treatise, "Was ist Aufklärung?" 1784.

142. It is only necessary to develop Kant's hints in order to get the views of Strauss in his "Leben Jesu." But there is this difference, that Kant uses the gospels chiefly for the purpose of putting or finding moral ideas there, while Strauss views them chiefly as the product of religious ideas; Kant finds moral hints there, Strauss, myths; Kant is more purely rational, Strauss wants also to account for the history.

143. Without having formed a clear conception of what the historical Christ really was, Kant sometimes spoke in favourable terms of Him as if he regarded Him highly. Owing to his moral philosophy, Kant was repeatedly compared with Christ; but this he himself did not favour, declaring that in comparison with Him he was only a bungler.

144. One of his maxims was, "To kneel or prostrate himself on the earth, even for the purpose of symbolizing to himself reverence for a heavenly object, is unworthy of man."

145. In 1788-91 Kant gave his friend Kiesewetter a number of small articles, from which this extract and the preceding are taken. R. and S. xi. 1, 269.

146. Jachmann, 117, says that if ever a man's religious views were cold declarations of reason, and if ever any one excluded all emotion from his religious acts, this was so in Kant's case.

147. Wald, in Reicke, 14. The same says that Kant did not succeed in theology "because he lacked the best knowledge of

biblical philology and criticism." 16. Rink, 27, also speaks of his neglect of the study of theology, and attributes his religious views to his early training, the character of his mind, and his lack of philological and historical knowledge.

148. Rink, 44, 45, finds it difficult to explain Kant's conduct in this matter, but supposes that when Kant wrote the letter he had no idea he would outlive the king, and made no mental reservation; but that, when the king died, he really believed that he had made such a reservation as he afterwards declared he had done. Borowski, 125, 126, regards this case as an exception to Kant's general rule, never to deviate from the strict truth. If Kant's own statement of his mental reservation is correct, then the explanation given in the text is the most charitable construction possible. Some have, of course, justified Kant's conduct in this matter. It should be remembered that he himself held that, while one must always speak the truth, he must himself be a judge as to how much of what he knows or thinks shall be said. It was about the time he made the promise to the king that he wrote on a paper found among his effects, "Recantation and denial of one's convictions are base; but silence in a case like the present is the duty of a subject; and if all one says must be true, it is not for that reason also a duty to speak openly all truth." Schubert, 138.

149. Rink says that for the first six years the "Kritik" excited no attention; and the publisher is said to have been ready to consign the first edition to waste paper—statements which are hardly credible. When the new chapel erected to Kant's memory was dedicated, June 19, 1881, Dr. J. Walter, Professor of Philosophy in Königsberg, delivered an address, in which he said that those who criticized the work during the first two years after its appearance had not studied the book, indeed had scarcely read it; that the third year more voices against it were heard, such as Eberhard in Halle, Platner in Leipzig, Tiedemann in Marburg, Lossius and others; and that advocates and opponents were about equal in numbers in 1786 and 1787, after which the former gained and the latter lost strength. About the year 1788 the success of the "Kritik" was established, and from this time its marvellous influence became general.

The third edition of the "Kritik" appeared in 1791; the fourth, in 1794; the fifth, in 1799; the sixth, in 1818; the seventh, in 1828, all a reprint of the second edition.

150. Raumer's "Historisch. Taschenbuch," 9, 557.

151. Nicolai, "Ueber meine Gelehrte Bildung," 76.

152. Their author was Hieronymus de Bosch. Either the same or another wrote :—

> "Non sic Hugenii memorent inventa Batavi,
> Nec sic Newtoni veneretur et Anglia nomen,
> Lavoisieri referat nec Gallia laudes,
> Doctrinam quam tota tuam Germania, Kanti!"

153. These lines occur :—

> "Du trugst die Fackel bis in den Grund
> Des Denkvermögens, und die Natur erschrak,
> Als tief in ihrer finstern Werkstatt
> Plötzlich Dein Licht ihr entgegenstrahlt."

Most of these facts are given in Altp. M. xv. 377, in an article entitled "Verse Kant's und über Kant."

154. Letter to Erhard, Nov. 10, 1795. Found in "Denkwürdigkeiten des Philosophen und Arztes Johann Benjamin Erhard." By Varnhagen von Ense.

155. Borowski, 187. In closing his account of Kant's life, this writer says, "Would that the numerous disciples, readers, and friends of Kant, would never carry to excess their veneration for him, the most humane and the most modest of philosophers!"

156. Schiller's words were intended for those disciples of Kant who were mere echoes of his opinions :—

> "Wie doch ein einziger Reicher so viele Bettler in Nahrung
> Setzt! Wenn die Könige baun haben die Kärrner zu thun."

157. Kant's warmest friends deplored the abuses of his philosophy and his name. Erhard wrote to Nicolai, Dec. 13, 1798, that he and Baggesen had years ago planned a satire on the philosophical confusion. The title was to have been, "The One Thing Needful, or the Council of Philosophers; a Transcendental Drama." Forty cotemporaries had been chosen as the characters of the play, and the number who should be included in such a satire had greatly increased, Erhard thought, when he wrote that letter. Jensch wrote to Kant, May 22, 1796, that he had written a work on the whole of his philosophy, and desired his opinion of it. He appealed in this book to Kant to settle the disputes of his pupils as to what his opinions are, by declaring authoritatively his views. In the letter he says, "I have made so free, amid the vexatious contentions of your other pupils and partisans, which are disagreeable to all Germany, as to make the appeal to yourself and to your judgment, without any importunity."

158. In a literary dispute, Jacobi hoped that Kant would take his side. Hamann wrote to him, April 9, 1786, "Do not depend

on our critic, nor need you do so. He is, like his system, no rock, but sand, in which one soon becomes weary of going farther. . . . Do not let Kant's neutrality disturb you. All my indebtedness to him . . . shall not keep me from writing as I think; I fear for myself no envy or ambition respecting his fame. I have already had many a hard conflict with him, and sometimes have evidently been in the wrong; nevertheless he has always been my friend. Neither will you make him your enemy if you give the truth the honour it deserves and which you have already bestowed on it. You must expect every systematist to think of his system as the Roman Catholic does of his only church."

159. When Hartknoch, Kant's publisher, was on a visit to Weimar, in 1783, Herder inquired about Kant, and received this answer: "I will tell you confidentially that Kant believes that you are the cause why his 'Kritik of the Reason' did not meet with the reception which he expected." Herder answered, "It never occurred to me to intrigue against any one, least of all against Kant. It is true that I do not relish his 'Kritik,' and that I do not like his style; but I have neither written anything against it, nor have I induced any one else to do so. Of this you may assure Kant." Herder's Life, by his widow, ii. 220. Two years after this, Kant published a review of Herder's "Philosophy of the History of Humanity," in which Herder thought he saw evidences of bitterness towards himself, and he regarded it as proof that Kant was displeased because he did not publicly praise his books, 223.

160. 'Life of Herder,' ii. 240—245. These views probably belong to the year 1790.

161. Anonymous Biography, published by Weigel, ii. 241. On page 239, the same writer states that he once met a former pupil of Kant who spoke with the greatest enthusiasm of his rare talents and his excellent character. "He showed me how this philosophy must affect all the sciences and all men, and that through it a change in the national mode of thinking was unavoidable. 'Friend!' he finally exclaimed, 'if this system, united with the philosophy of Socrates and the properly-understood Gospel of Christ, does not ennoble the human family, I shall despair of the much praised capacity of my race for culture,'"

162. Stäudlin, "Geschichte und Geist des Skeptizismus," 1794, ii. 269.

163. There is a book in the Berlin Royal Library which is probably the one meant. Its title is, "F. A. Nitzch, late Lecturer of

the Latin language at Köuigsberg. A general and introductory view of Prof. Kant's Principles concerning Man, the World and the Deity. London, 1796." The next book on the Kautian philosophy in the English language in that library, is one by Thomas Davies, 1863, which was printed in Göttingen. The catalogue of that library gives the titles of 151 works, some comprising a number of volumes, devoted exclusively to Kant's philosophy. They are in the German, Latin, English, and French languages, and some of them have appeared in a number of editions. There are, of course, thousands of other works which discuss that philosophy, such as histories of philosophy, and works in all departments of science, morals, and religion. Of these 151, only five are English; three of these are since 1871, and are by David Rowland, Edward Caird, and Robert Adamson.

164. "Elements of the Critical Philosophy." B. A. F. M. Willich. London, 1798.

165. "Encyclopædia or a Dictionary of Arts, Sciences, and Miscellaneous Literature." The extract is from the Preface, which promises a summary of Kant's philosophy in a supplementary volume. As I have not the original, the text gives a translation from a German translation in Reicke, 16.

166. Prof. Dr. Julius Walter, in his address "Zum Gedächtniss Kant's," 1881, says that amid the events of the day Kant's death was scarcely noticed in Germany, and continues: "Die Schule besteht zwar in einzelnen Vertretern bis in das zweite, dritte, ja vierte Jahrzehnt noch fort; aber die Diskussion der kantischen Lehren, die eine Fortbildung derselben bezweckte, tritt mit dem neuen Jahrhundert in augenfälliger Weise zurück. Nur wenig Schriften, einzelne verlorene Dissertationen beziehen sich direkt auf Kant; so dass die Stille der ersten Decennien die Behauptung der neuen Koryphäen nur zu sehr zu bewahrheiten schien, die Philosophie Kant's sei ein überwundener Standpunkt. . . . Als die Schule Hegel's auf der Höhe ihrer Entwicklung stand, um das Jahr 1840, war von kantischer Philosophie nur noch in so fern die Rede, als etwa dieses oder jenes System zu anderen in Gegensatz trat und hierbei sich auf Kant zu berufen Gelegenheit nahm. Während die benachbarten Nationen allererst schüchternen Muthes sie gründlich kennen zu lernen beginnen, ist sie in Deutschland scheinbar vergessen." 26, 27.

In 1851 Rosenkranz made a statement (N.P.P.B. xi. 160, 162) respecting the schools to which the professors of philosophy in Germany at that time belonged. Twenty-nine of these professors in

Prussia were classified as follows: One Platonist, two Aristotelians, one historico-critical, one scholastic, two Guentherians, four Kantians, three eclectics, three Herbartians, two followers of Schelling, and ten Hegelians. In the rest of Germany there was not a single Kantian professor of philosophy, and in Königsberg there had not been one for twenty years.

167. Probably few could be found in Germany who would be willing to go as far as an English admirer of Kant, who says, "What Kant has done no one need do over again." Caird on Kant's Philosophy, 125. Many more will be ready to agree with Schubert, who said in Königsberg (P.P.B., 1833, 13), "It would be a disgrace to attempt to belittle Kant in the place where the sublime thinker lived. But to make his philosophy final now and for ever, could only be the notion of a Kantian who, since Kant is to be exonerated from all despotism in the dominion of mind, would arouse to indignation the honourable shade of the Renewer of philosophy."

168. In his Life by Huber, 21, it is said, "In physics, mathematics, astronomy, and philosophy, he deserves one of the first places. In these, the highest sciences, his name is placed beside those of Newton, Euler, Herschel, and Kant."

169. Mendelssohn and Herz were both Jews. But the views of the former were so liberal that Lavater hoped he might convert him to Christianity. His efforts, however, were delicately but decidedly resisted by Mendelssohn. This led Lessing to write his "Nathan the Wise," in which Nathan represents Mendelssohn.

170. For these letters see an article by F. Sintenis, on "Maria von Herbert und Kant," Altp. M. xvi. 270. The close of last century and the beginning of this was a strange era of suicide in Germany, especially among young women, a tendency partly represented and partly promoted by "The Sorrows of Young Werther." Sintenis says that this era began with Miss von Lassberg, in 1788, and ended with the unfortunate Louise Brachmann, in 1822. The brother of the above-mentioned Maria was another warm admirer of the "Kritik." His disposition was much like that of his sister; he suffered greatly from ill-health, was extremely melancholy, and between his high moral ideas and his real life there was a strange contrast. To Erhard he wrote, October 7th, 1804, of his sister: "She left this world a heroine." And speaking of another world, he says, "Whether there is another, the wisest want to know speedily." He ended his own sufferings by suicide, March 13th, 1811.

171. In Altp. M. ix., Professor Dr. Bohn has an article on Kant's

relation to medicine, in which he expresses the opinion that Kant's condition, late in life, cannot be attributed to old age or senility, but thinks that at that time the brain must have been diseased. The disease, he thinks, was one discovered some years ago as an inflammation of the inner surface of the membrane of the brain, "Pachymeningitis iuterna," 616.

172. After Kant's death several thousand pieces of paper, such as he had used for notes of lectures, outlines to be used in preparing his books, memoranda, aud the like, were found. Of the blank books prepared for him by Wasianski some were given as mementoes to friends, and some were sold at high prices for collections in England. Many of these papers are preserved in the University Library in Königsberg.

173. In his gratitude to this servant for his kindness, he would sometimes call him his companion, his protector, or his friend. But he tolerated nothing which he regarded as unjust or indiscreet. He noticed that this servant took snuff from his snuff-box; and immediately he offered to give him a florin a month more, in order to put an end to this community of goods.

174. "Hamburger Correspondent," 1804, March 31st.

THE END.

Bedford Street, Strand, London, W.C.
March, 1882.

Macmillan & Co.'s Catalogue of Works in the Departments of History, Biography, Travels, Critical and Literary Essays, Politics, Political and Social Economy, Law, etc.; and Works connected with Language.

HISTORY, BIOGRAPHY, TRAVELS, &c.

ADDISON.—ESSAYS OF JOSEPH ADDISON. Chosen and edited by John Richard Green, M.A., LL.D., Honorary Fellow of Jesus College, Oxford. 18mo. 4*s.* 6*d.* (Golden Treasury Series.)

ALBEMARLE.—FIFTY YEARS OF MY LIFE. By George Thomas, Earl of Albemarle. With Steel Portrait of the First Earl of Albemarle, engraved by Jeens. Third and Cheaper Edition. Crown 8vo. 7*s.* 6*d.*

ALFRED THE GREAT.—By Thomas Hughes, Q.C. Crown 8vo. 6*s.* (Biographical Series.)

ANDERSON.—MANDALAY TO MOMIEN; a Narrative of the Two Expeditions to Western China, of 1868 and 1875, under Colonel E. B. Sladen and Colonel Horace Browne. By Dr. Anderson, F.R.S.E., Medical and Scientific Officer to the Expeditions. With numerous Maps and Illustrations. 8vo. 21*s.*

APPLETON.—Works by T. G. Appleton:—

A NILE JOURNAL. Illustrated by Eugene Benson. Crown 8vo. 6*s.*

SYRIAN SUNSHINE. Crown 8vo. 6*s.*

ARNOLD (M.)—ESSAYS IN CRITICISM. By Matthew Arnold. New Edition, Revised and Enlarged. Crown 8vo. 9*s.*

ARNOLD (W. T.)—THE ROMAN SYSTEM OF PROVINCIAL ADMINISTRATION TO THE ACCESSION OF CONSTANTINE THE GREAT. Being the Arnold Prize Essay for 1879. By W. T. Arnold, B.A. Crown 8vo. 6*s.*

ART.—THE YEAR'S ART: A concise Epitome of all Matters relating to the Arts of Painting, Sculpture, and Architecture, which have occurred during the Year 1880, together with Information respecting the Events of the Year 1881. Compiled by Marcus B. Huish. Crown 8vo. 2*s.* 6*d.*

THE SAME, 1879—1880. Crown 8vo. 2*s.* 6*d.*

ATKINSON.—AN ART TOUR TO NORTHERN CAPITALS OF EUROPE, including Descriptions of the Towns, the Museums, and other Art Treasures of Copenhagen, Christiana, Stockholm, Abo, Helsingfors, Wiborg, St. Petersburg, Moscow, and Kief. By J. Beavington Atkinson. 8vo. 12*s.*

3.82, 5,000.

BAILEY.—THE SUCCESSION TO THE ENGLISH CROWN. A Historical Sketch. By A. BAILEY, M.A., Barrister-at-Law. Crown 8vo. *7s. 6d.*

BAKER (SIR SAMUEL W.)—Works by Sir SAMUEL BAKER, Pacha, M.A., F.R.S., F.R.G.S.:—

CYPRUS AS I SAW IT IN 1879. With Frontispiece. 8vo. *12s. 6d.*

ISMAILÏA: A Narrative of the Expedition to Central Africa for the Suppression of the Slave Trade, organised by Ismail, Khedive of Egypt. With Portraits, Map, and numerous Illustrations. New Edition. Crown 8vo. *6s.*

THE ALBERT N'YANZA, Great Basin of the Nile, and Exploration of the Nile Sources. With Maps and Illustrations. Fifth Edition. Crown 8vo. *6s.*

THE NILE TRIBUTARIES OF ABYSSINIA, and the Sword Hunters of the Hamran Arabs. With Maps and Illustrations. Sixth Edition. Crown 8vo. *6s.*

BANCROFT.—THE HISTORY OF THE UNITED STATES OF AMERICA, FROM THE DISCOVERY OF THE CONTINENT. By GEORGE BANCROFT. New and thoroughly Revised Edition. Six Vols. Crown 8vo. *54s.*

BARKER (LADY).—A YEAR'S HOUSEKEEPING IN SOUTH AFRICA. By LADY BARKER. With Illustrations. New and Cheaper Edition. Crown 8vo. *6s.*

BATH.—OBSERVATIONS ON BULGARIAN AFFAIRS. By the MARQUIS OF BATH. Crown 8vo. *3s. 6d.*

BEACONSFIELD.—MEMORIALS OF LORD BEACONSFIELD. Reprinted from *The Standard*, with Portrait. Crown 8vo. *3s. 6d.*

BEESLY.—STORIES FROM THE HISTORY OF ROME. By Mrs. BEESLY. Extra fcap. 8vo. *2s. 6d.*

BECKER.—DISTURBED IRELAND, being the Letters Written during the Winter of 1880—1881. By BERNARD H. BECKER, Special Commissioner of *The Daily News*. With Route Maps. Crown 8vo. *6s.*

BERNARD (ST.)—THE LIFE AND TIMES OF ST. BERNARD, Abbot of Clairvaux. By J. C. MORISON, M.A. New Edition. Crown 8vo. *6s.* (Biographical Series.)

BIOGRAPHICAL SKETCHES, 1852—1875. By HARRIET MARTINEAU. With four Additional Sketches, and Autobiographical Sketch. Fifth Edition. Crown 8vo. *6s.* (Biographical Series.)

BISMARCK—IN THE FRANCO-GERMAN WAR. An Authorized Translation from the German of Dr. MORITZ BUSCH. Two Vols. Crown 8vo. *18s.*

BLACKBURNE.—BIOGRAPHY OF THE RIGHT HON. FRANCIS BLACKBURNE, Late Lord Chancellor of Ireland. Chiefly in connection with his Public and Political Career. By his Son, EDWARD BLACKBURNE, Q.C. With Portrait engraved by JEENS. 8vo. *12s.*

BLAKE.—LIFE OF WILLIAM BLAKE. With Selections from his Poems and other Writings. Illustrated from Blake's own Works. By ALEXANDER GILCHRIST. A new and Enlarged Edition, with additional Letters, and a Memoir of the Author. Printed on hand-made paper, the Illustrations on India paper, and mounted in the text. 2 vols. Cloth elegant, gilt, with Designs after Blake by FREDERICK J. SHIELDS. Medium 8vo. *£2 2s.*

BLANDFORD (W. T.)—GEOLOGY AND ZOOLOGY OF ABYSSINIA. By W. T. BLANDFORD. 8vo. *21s.*

BRONTË.—CHARLOTTE BRONTË. A Monograph. By T. WEMYSS REID. With Illustrations. Third Edition. Crown 8vo. 6*s.* (Biographical Series.)

BROOK.—FRENCH HISTORY FOR ENGLISH CHILDREN. By SARAH BROOK. With Coloured Maps. Crown 8vo. 6*s.*

BROOKE.—THE RAJA OF SARAWAK: an Account of Sir James Brooke, K.C.B., LL.D. Given chiefly through Letters or Journals. By GERTRUDE L. JACOB. With Portrait and Maps. Two Vols. 8vo. 25*s.*

BRYCE.—Works by JAMES BRYCE, M.P., D.C.L., Regius Professor of Civil Law, Oxford:—

THE HOLY ROMAN EMPIRE. Sixth Edition, Revised and Enlarged. Crown 8vo. 7*s.* 6*d.*

TRANSCAUCASIA AND ARARAT: being notes of a Vacation Tour in the Autumn of 1876. With an Illustration and Map. Third Edition. Crown 8vo. 9*s.*

BURGOYNE.—POLITICAL AND MILITARY EPISODES DURING THE FIRST HALF OF THE REIGN OF GEORGE III. Derived from the Life and Correspondence of the Right Hon. J. Burgoyne, Lieut.-General in his Majesty's Army, and M.P. for Preston. By E. B. DE FONBLANQUE. With Portrait, Heliotype Plate, and Maps. 8vo. 16*s.*

BURKE.—EDMUND BURKE, a Historical Study. By JOHN MORLEY, B.A., Oxon. Crown 8vo. 7*s.* 6*d.*

LETTERS, TRACTS, AND SPEECHES ON IRISH AFFAIRS. By EDMUND BURKE. Arranged and Edited by MATTHEW ARNOLD. With a Preface. Crown 8vo. 6*s.*

BURROWS.—WORTHIES OF ALL SOULS: Four Centuries of English History. Illustrated from the College Archives. By MONTAGU BURROWS, Chichele Professor of Modern History at Oxford, Fellow of All Souls. 8vo. 14*s.*

CAMBRIDGE.—MEMORIALS OF CAMBRIDGE. Greatly Enlarged and partly Rewritten (1851—66). By CHARLES HENRY COOPER, F.S.A. With Seventy-four Views of the Colleges, Churches, and other Public Buildings of the University and Town, engraved on steel by J. LE KEUX, together with about Forty-five of those engraved on Copper by STORER, and a few Lithographs, with Twenty additional Etchings on Copper by ROBERT FARREN. 8vo. 3 vols. 25*s.* each. Also a Large Paper Edition. The Engravings and Etchings, Proofs on India Paper. 3 vols. 4to. half-morocco, £10 10*s.* Fifty copies of the Etchings, by R. FARREN, from the "Memorials of Cambridge," proofs signed in portfolio. £3 3*s.*

CAMERON.—OUR FUTURE HIGHWAY. By V. LOVETT CAMERON, C.B., Commander, R.N. With Illustrations. 2 vols. Crown 8vo. 21*s.*

CAMPBELL.—LOG-LETTERS FROM THE "CHALLENGER." By LORD GEORGE CAMPBELL. With Map. Fifth and Cheaper Edition. Crown 8vo. 6*s.*

CAMPBELL.—MY CIRCULAR NOTES; Extracts from Journals; Letters sent Home: Geological and other Notes, written while Travelling Westwards round the World, from July 6th, 1874, to July 6th, 1875. By J. F. CAMPBELL, Author of "Frost and Fire." Cheaper Issue. Crown 8vo. 6*s.*

CAMPBELL.—TURKS AND GREEKS. Notes of a recent Excursion. By the Hon. DUDLEY CAMPBELL, M.A. With Coloured Map. Crown 8vo. 3*s.* 6*d.*

CARPENTER.—THE LIFE AND WORK OF MARY CARPENTER. By J. ESTLIN CARPENTER, M.A. With Steel Portrait. Crown 8vo. 6s. (Biographical Series.)

CARSTARES.—WILLIAM CARSTARES: a Character and Career of the Revolutionary Epoch (1649—1715). By ROBERT STORY, Minister of Rosneath. 8vo. 12s.

CHATTERTON: A BIOGRAPHICAL STUDY. By DANIEL WILSON, LL.D., Professor of History and English Literature in University College, Toronto. Crown 8vo. 6s. 6d.

CHATTERTON: A STORY OF THE YEAR 1770. By Professor MASSON, LL.D. Crown 8vo. 5s.

CICERO.—THE LIFE AND LETTERS OF MARCUS TULLIUS CICERO: being a New Translation of the Letters included in Mr. Watson's Selection. With Historical and Critical Notes, by Rev. G. E. JEANS, M.A., Fellow of Hertford College, Oxford, Assistant-Master in Haileybury College, 8vo. 10s. 6d.

CLARK—MEMORIALS FROM JOURNALS AND LETTERS OF SAMUEL CLARK, M.A., formerly Principal of the National Society's Training College, Battersea. Edited with Introduction by his WIFE. With Portrait. Crown 8vo. 7s. 6d.

CLASSICAL WRITERS.—Edited by JOHN RICHARD GREEN. Fcap. 8vo. Price 1s. 6d. each.

EURIPIDES. By Professor MAHAFFY.

MILTON. By the Rev. STOPFORD A. BROOKE.

LIVY. By the Rev. W. W. CAPES, M.A.

VERGIL. By Professor NETTLESHIP, M.A.

SOPHOCLES. By Professor L. CAMPBELL, M.A.

DEMOSTHENES. By S. H. BUTCHER, M.A.

TACITUS. By A. J. CHURCH, M.A., and W. J. BRODRIBB, M.A.

Other Volumes to follow.

CLIFFORD (W. K.)—LECTURES AND ESSAYS. Edited by LESLIE STEPHEN and FREDERICK POLLOCK, with Introduction by F. POLLOCK. Two Portraits. 2 vols. 8vo. 25s.

COMBE.—THE LIFE OF GEORGE COMBE, Author of "The Constitution of Man." By CHARLES GIBBON. With Three Portraits engraved by JEENS. Two Vols. 8vo. 32s.

COOPER.—ATHENÆ CANTABRIGIENSES. By CHARLES HENRY COOPER, F.S.A., and THOMPSON COOPER, F.S.A. Vol. I. 8vo., 1500—1585, 18s.; Vol. II., 1586—1609, 18s.

CORREGIO.—ANTONIO ALLEGRI DA CORREGIO. From the German of Dr. JULIUS MEYER, Director of the Royal Gallery, Berlin. Edited, with an Introduction, by Mrs. HEATON. Containing Twenty Woodbury-type Illustrations. Royal 8vo. Cloth elegant. 31s. 6d.

COX (G. V.)—RECOLLECTIONS OF OXFORD. By G. V. COX, M.A. New College, late Esquire Bedel and Coroner in the University of Oxford. Cheaper Edition. Crown 8vo. 6s.

CUNYNGHAME (SIR A. T.)—MY COMMAND IN SOUTH AFRICA, 1874—1878. Comprising Experiences of Travel in the Colonies of South Africa and the Independent States. By Sir ARTHUR THURLOW CUNYNGHAME, G.C.B., then Lieutenant-Governor and Commander of the Forces in South Africa. Third Edition. 8vo. 12s. 6d.

"**DAILY NEWS.**"—THE DAILY NEWS' CORRESPONDENCE of the War between Russia and Turkey, to the fall of Kars. Including the letters of Mr. Archibald Forbes, Mr. J. E. McGahan, and other Special Correspondents in Europe and Asia. Second Edition, Enlarged. Cheaper Edition. Crown 8vo. 6*s*.

FROM THE FALL OF KARS TO THE CONCLUSION OF PEACE. Cheaper Edition. Crown 8vo. 6*s*.

DAVIDSON.—THE LIFE OF A SCOTTISH PROBATIONER; being a Memoir of Thomas Davidson, with his Poems and Letters. By JAMES BROWN, Minister of St. James's Street Church, Paisley. Second Edition, revised and enlarged, with Portrait. Crown 8vo. 7*s*. 6*d*.

DAWSON.—AUSTRALIAN ABORIGINES. The Language and Customs of Several Tribes of Aborigines in the Western District of Victoria, Australia. By JAMES DAWSON. Small 4to. 14*s*.

DEAK.—FRANCIS DEAK, HUNGARIAN STATESMAN: A Memoir. With a Preface, by the Right Hon. M. E. GRANT DUFF, M.P. With Portrait. 8vo. 12*s*. 6*d*.

DEAS.—THE RIVER CLYDE. An Historical Description of the Rise and Progress of the Harbour of Glasgow, and of the Improvement of the River from Glasgow to Port Glasgow. By J. DEAS, M. Inst. C.E. 8vo. 10*s*. 6*d*.

DELANE.—LIFE AND LETTERS OF JOHN T. DELANE, late Editor of the *Times*. By Sir GEORGE W. DASENT, D.C.L. 8vo. [*In the Press*.

DENISON.—A HISTORY OF CAVALRY FROM THE EARLIEST TIMES. With Lessons for the Future. By Lieut.-Colonel GEORGE DENISON, Commanding the Governor-General's Body Guard, Canada, Author of "Modern Cavalry." With Maps and Plans. 8vo. 18*s*.

DILKE.—GREATER BRITAIN. A Record of Travel in English-speaking Countries during 1866—67. (America, Australia, India.) By Sir CHARLES WENTWORTH DILKE, M.P. Sixth Edition. Crown 8vo. 6*s*.

DILETTANTI SOCIETY'S PUBLICATIONS. ANTIQUITIES OF IONIA. Part IV. Folio, half-morocco. £3 13*s*. 6*d*.

DOLET.—ETIENNE DOLET: the Martyr of the Renaissance. A Biography. With a Biographical Appendix, containing a Descriptive Catalogue of the Books written, printed, or edited by Dolet. By RICHARD COPLEY CHRISTIE, Lincoln College, Oxford, Chancellor of the Diocese of Manchester. With Illustrations. 8vo. 18*s*.

DOYLE.—HISTORY OF AMERICA. By J. A. DOYLE. With Maps. 18mo. 4*s*. 6*d*. [*Historical Course*.

DRUMMOND OF HAWTHORNDEN: THE STORY OF HIS LIFE AND WRITINGS. By Professor MASSON. With Portrait and Vignette engraved by C. H. JEENS. Crown 8vo. 10*s*. 6*d*.

DUFF.—Works by the Right Hon. M. E. GRANT DUFF.

NOTES OF AN INDIAN JOURNEY. With Map. 8vo. 10*s*. 6*d*.

MISCELLANIES, POLITICAL AND LITERARY. 8vo. 10*s*. 6*d*.

EADIE.—LIFE OF JOHN EADIE, D.D., LL.D. By JAMES BROWN, D.D., Author of "The Life of a Scottish Probationer." With Portrait. Second Edition. Crown 8vo. 7*s*. 6*d*.

ELLIOTT.—LIFE OF HENRY VENN ELLIOTT, of Brighton. By JOSIAH BATEMAN, M.A. With Portrait, engraved by JEENS. Third and Cheaper Edition. Extra fcap. 8vo. *6s.*

ELZE.—ESSAYS ON SHAKESPEARE. By Dr. KARL ELZE. Translated with the Author's sanction by L. DORA SCHMITZ. 8vo. *12s.*

ENGLISH MEN OF LETTERS.—Edited by JOHN MORLEY. A Series of Short Books to tell people what is best worth knowing as to the Life, Character, and Works of some of the great English Writers. In crown 8vo. price *2s. 6d.* each.

I DR. JOHNSON. By LESLIE STEPHEN.
II. SIR WALTER SCOTT. By R. H. HUTTON.
III. GIBBON. By J. C. MORISON.
IV. SHELLEY. By J. A. SYMONDS.
V. HUME. By Professor HUXLEY.
VI. GOLDSMITH. By WILLIAM BLACK.
VII. DEFOE. By W. MINTO.
VIII. BURNS. By Principal SHAIRP.
IX. SPENSER. By the Very Rev. the DEAN OF ST. PAUL'S.
X. THACKERAY. By ANTHONY TROLLOPE.
XI. BURKE. By JOHN MORLEY.
XII. MILTON. By MARK PATTISON.
XIII. HAWTHORNE. By HENRY JAMES, Jun.
XIV. SOUTHEY. By Professor DOWDEN.
XV. BUNYAN. By J. A. FROUDE.
XVI. CHAUCER. By Professor A. W. WARD.
XVII. COWPER. By GOLDWIN SMITH.
XVIII. POPE. By LESLIE STEPHEN.
XIX. BYRON. By Professor NICHOL.
XX. LOCKE. By Professor FOWLER.
XXI. WORDSWORTH. By F. W. H. MYERS.
XXII. DRYDEN. By G. SAINTSBURY.
XXIII. LANDOR. By Professor SIDNEY COLVIN.
XXIV. DE QUINCEY. By Professor MASSON.
XXV. CHARLES LAMB. By Rev. ALFRED AINGER.
XXVI. BENTLEY. By Professor R. C. JEBB. [*In the press.*

In Preparation :—

SWIFT. By LESLIE STEPHEN.
ADAM SMITH. By LEONARD H. COURTNEY, M.P.
DICKENS. By Professor A. W. WARD.
BERKELEY. By Professor HUXLEY.
STERNE. By H. D. TRAILL.
SIR PHILIP SIDNEY. By J. A. SYMONDS.
MACAULAY. By J. COTTER MORISON.
GRAY. By EDMUND GOSSE.

Other Volumes to follow.

ENGLISH POETS: SELECTIONS, with Critical Introductions by various Writers, and a General Introduction by MATTHEW ARNOLD. Edited by T. H. WARD, M.A., late Fellow of Brasenose College, Oxford. 4 vols. Crown 8vo. 7*s*. 6*d*. each.

Vol. I. CHAUCER to DONNE.
Vol. II. BEN JONSON to DRYDEN.
Vol. III. ADDISON to BLAKE.
Vol. IV. WORDSWORTH to SYDNEY DOBELL.

ETON COLLEGE, HISTORY OF. By H. C. MAXWELL LYTE, M.A. With numerous Illustrations by Professor DELAMOTTE. Coloured Plates, and a Steel Portrait of the Founder, engraved by C. H. JEENS. New and Cheaper Issue, with Corrections. Medium 8vo. Cloth elegant. 21*s*.

EUROPEAN HISTORY, Narrated in a Series of Historical Selections from the best Authorities. Edited and arranged by E. M. SEWELL, and C. M. YONGE. First Series, crown 8vo. 6*s*.; Second Series, 1088-1228, crown 8vo. 6*s*. Third Edition.

FARADAY.—MICHAEL FARADAY. By J. H. GLADSTONE, Ph.D., F.R.S. Second Edition, with Portrait engraved by JEENS from a photograph by J. WATKINS. Crown 8vo. 4*s*. 6*d*.

PORTRAIT. Artist's Proof. 5*s*.

FISON AND HOWITT.—KAMILAROI AND KURNAI GROUP. Marriage and Relationship, and Marriage by Elopement, drawn chiefly from the usage of the Australian Aborigines. Also THE KURNAI TRIBE, their Customs in Peace and War. By LORIMER FISON, M.A., and A. W. HOWITT, F.G.S., with an Introduction by LEWIS H. MORGAN, LL.D., Author of "System of Consanguinity," "Ancient Society," &c. Demy 8vo. 15*s*.

FORBES.—LIFE AND LETTERS OF JAMES DAVID FORBES, F.R.S., late Principal of the United College in the University of St. Andrews. By J. C. SHAIRP, LL.D., Principal of the United College in the University of St. Andrews; P. G. TAIT, M.A., Professor of Natural Philosophy in the University of Edinburgh; and A. ADAMS-REILLY, F.R.G.S. With Portraits, Map, and Illustrations. 8vo. 16*s*.

FRANCIS OF ASSISI. By Mrs. OLIPHANT. New Edition. Crown 8vo 6*s*. (Biographical Series.)

FREEMAN.—Works by EDWARD A. FREEMAN, D.C.L., LL.D.:—HISTORICAL ESSAYS. Third Edition. 8vo. 10*s*. 6*d*.

"CONTENTS:—I. "The Mythical and Romantic Elements in Early English History;" II. "The Continuity of English History;" III. "The Relations between the Crowns of England and Scotland;" IV. "St. Thomas of Canterbury and his Biographers;" V. "The Reign of Edward the Third;" VI. "The Holy Roman Empire;" VII. "The Franks and the Gauls;" VIII. "The Early Sieges of Paris;" IX. "Frederick the First, King of Italy;" X. "The Emperor Frederick the Second;" XI. "Charles the Bold;" XII. "Presidential Government."

HISTORICAL ESSAYS. Second Series Second Edition, Enlarged. 8vo. 10*s*. 6*d*.

The principal Essays are:—"Ancient Greece and Mediæval Italy:" "Mr. Gladstone's Homer and the Homeric Ages:" "The Historians of Athens:" "The Athenian Democracy:" "Alexander the Great:" "Greece during the Macedonian Period:" "Mommsen's History of Rome:" "Lucius Cornelius Sulla:" "The Flavian Cæsars."

FREEMAN—*continued.*

HISTORICAL ESSAYS. Third Series. 8vo. 12s.

CONTENTS:—"First Impressions of Rome." "The Illyrian Emperors and their Land." "Augusta Treverorum." "The Goths of Ravenna." "Race and Language." "The Byzantine Empire." "First Impressions of Athens." "Mediæval and Modern Greece." "The Southern Slaves." "Sicilian Cycles." "The Normans at Palermo."

COMPARATIVE POLITICS.—Lectures at the Royal Institution. To which is added the "Unity of History," the Rede Lecture at Cambridge, 1872. 8vo. 14s

THE HISTORY AND CONQUESTS OF THE SARACENS. Six Lectures. Third Edition, with New Preface. Crown 8vo. 3s. 6d.

HISTORICAL AND ARCHITECTURAL SKETCHES: chiefly Italian. With Illustrations by the Author. Crown 8vo. 10s. 6d.

SUBJECT AND NEIGHBOUR LANDS OF VENICE. Being a Companion Volume to "Historical and Architectural Sketches." With Illustrations. Crown 8vo. 10s. 6d.

OLD ENGLISH HISTORY. With Five Coloured Maps. New Edition. Half-bound. Extra fcap. 8vo. 6s.

HISTORY OF THE CATHEDRAL CHURCH OF WELLS, as illustrating the History of the Cathedral Churches of the Old Foundation. Crown 8vo 3s. 6d.

THE GROWTH OF THE ENGLISH CONSTITUTION FROM THE EARLIEST TIMES. Third Edition, revised. Crown 8vo. 5s.

GENERAL SKETCH OF EUROPEAN HISTORY. Being Vol. I. of a Historical Course for Schools, edited by E. A. FREEMAN. New Edition, enlarged with Maps, Chronological Table, Index, &c. 18mo. 3s. 6d.

GALILEO.—THE PRIVATE LIFE OF GALILEO. Compiled principally from his Correspondence and that of his eldest daughter, Sister Maria Celeste, Nun in the Franciscan Convent of S. Matthew in Arcetri. With Portrait. Crown 8vo. 7s. 6d.

GALLOWAY.—THE STEAM-ENGINE AND ITS INVENTORS: a Historical Sketch. By ROBERT L. GALLOWAY, Mining Engineer. With numerous Illustrations. Crown 8vo. 10s. 6d.

GEDDES.—THE PROBLEM OF THE HOMERIC POEMS. By W. D. GEDDES, LL.D., Professor of Greek in the University of Aberdeen. 8vo. 14s.

GLADSTONE.—Works by the Right Hon. W. E. GLADSTONE, M.P.:—

JUVENTUS MUNDI. The Gods and Men of the Heroic Age. With Map. Second Edition. Crown 8vo. cloth. 10s. 6d.

HOMERIC SYNCHRONISM. An inquiry into the Time and Place of Homer. Crown 8vo. 6s.

GOETHE AND MENDELSSOHN (1821—1831). Translated from the German of Dr. KARL MENDELSSOHN, Son of the Composer, by M. E. VON GLEHN. From the Private Diaries and Home Letters of Mendelssohn, with Poems and Letters of Goethe never before printed. Also with two New and Original Portraits, Fac-similes, and Appendix of Twenty Letters hitherto unpublished. Second Edition, enlarged. Crown 8vo. 5s.

GOLDSMID.—TELEGRAPH AND TRAVEL. A Narrative of the Formation and Development of Telegraphic Communication between England and India, under the orders of Her Majesty's Government, with incidental Notices of the Countries traversed by the Lines. By Colonel SIR FREDERICK GOLDSMID, C.B., K.C.S.I., late Director of the Government Indo-European Telegraph. With numerous Illustrations and Maps. 8vo. 21*s.*

GORDON.—LAST LETTERS FROM EGYPT, to which are added Letters from the Cape. By LADY DUFF GORDON. With a Memoir by her Daughter, Mrs. Ross, and Portrait engraved by JEENS. Second Edition. Crown 8vo. 9*s.*

GRAY.—CHINA. A History of the Laws, Manners, and Customs of the People. By the VENERABLE JOHN HENRY GRAY, LL.D., Archdeacon of Hong Kong, formerly H.B.M. Consular Chaplain at Canton. Edited by W. Gow Gregor. With 150 Full-page Illustrations, being Fac-similes of Drawings by a Chinese Artist. 2 vols. Demy 8vo. 32*s.*

GRAY (MRS.)—FOURTEEN MONTHS IN CANTON. By MRS. GRAY. With Illustrations. Crown 8vo. 9*s.*

GREAT CHRISTIANS OF FRANCE: ST. LOUIS and CALVIN. By M. GUIZOT, Member of the Institute of France. Crown 8vo. 6*s.* (Biographical Series.)

GREEN.—Works by JOHN RICHARD GREEN, M.A., LL.D.:—

HISTORY OF THE ENGLISH PEOPLE. Vol. I.—Early England—Foreign Kings—The Charter—The Parliament. With 8 Coloured Maps. 8vo. 16*s.* Vol. II.—The Monarchy, 1461—1540: The Restoration, 1540—1603. 8vo. 16*s.* Vol. III.—Puritan England, 1603—1660; The Revolution, 1660—1688. With 4 Maps. 8vo. 16*s.* Vol. IV.—The Revolution, 1683—1760; Modern England, 1760—1815. With Maps and Index. 8vo. 16*s.*

A SHORT HISTORY OF THE ENGLISH PEOPLE. With Coloured Maps, Genealogical Tables, and Chronological Annals. Crown 8vo. 8*s.* 6*d.* Seventy-seventh Thousand.

STRAY STUDIES FROM ENGLAND AND ITALY. Crown 8vo. 8*s.* 6*d.* Containing: Lambeth and the Archbishops—The Florence of Dante—Venice and Rome—Early History of Oxford—The District Visitor—Capri—Hotels in the Clouds—Sketches in Sunshine, &c.

READINGS FROM ENGLISH HISTORY. Selected and Edited by JOHN RICHARD GREEN. In Three Parts. Fcap. 8vo. 1*s.* 6*d.* each. Part I.—From Hengest to Cressy. Part II.—From Cressy to Cromwell. Part III.—From Cromwell to Balaklava.

THE MAKING OF ENGLAND. With Maps. Demy 8vo. 16*s.*

GUEST.—LECTURES ON THE HISTORY OF ENGLAND. By M. J. GUEST. With Maps. Crown 8vo. 6*s.*

HAMERTON.—Works by P. G. HAMERTON:—

ETCHINGS AND ETCHERS. Third Edition, revised, with Forty-eight new Plates. Columbier 8vo.

THE INTELLECTUAL LIFE. With a Portrait of Leonardo da Vinci, etched by LEOPOLD FLAMENG. Second Edition. Crown 8vo. 10*s.* 6*d.*

THOUGHTS ABOUT ART. New Edition, revised, with an Introduction. Crown 8vo. 8*s.* 6*d.*

HEINE.—A TRIP TO THE BROCKEN. By HEINRICH HEINE. Translated by R. MCLINTOCK. Crown 8vo. 3*s.* 6*d.*

HELLENIC STUDIES—JOURNAL OF. Parts I. and II., constituting Vol. I. 8vo., with 4to Atlas of Illustrations. 30*s.* Vol. II., Two Parts with 4to. Atlas of Illustrations. 15*s.* each.

The Journal will be sold at a reduced price to Libraries wishing to subscribe, but official application must in each case be made to the Council. Information on this point, and upon the conditions of Membership, may be obtained on application to the Hon. Secretary, Mr. George Macmillan, 29, Bedford Street, Covent Garden.

HILL.—THE RECORDER OF BIRMINGHAM. A Memoir of Matthew Davenport-Hill, with Selections from his Correspondence. By his daughters ROSAMOND and FLORENCE DAVENPORT-HILL. With Portrait engraved by C. H. JEENS. 8vo. 16*s.*

HILL.—WHAT WE SAW IN AUSTRALIA. By ROSAMOND and FLORENCE HILL. Crown 8vo. 10*s.* 6*d.*

HODGSON.—MEMOIR OF REV. FRANCIS HODGSON, B.D., Scholar, Poet, and Divine. By his son, the Rev. JAMES T. HODGSON, M.A. Containing numerous Letters from Lord Byron and others. With Portrait engraved by JEENS. Two vols. Crown 8vo. 18*s.*

HOLE.—A GENEALOGICAL STEMMA OF THE KINGS OF ENGLAND AND FRANCE. By the Rev. C. HOLE, M.A., Trinity College, Cambridge. On Sheet, 1*s.*

A BRIEF BIOGRAPHICAL DICTIONARY. Compiled and Arranged by the Rev. CHARLES HOLE, M.A. Second Edition. 18mo. 4*s.* 6*d.*

HOOKER AND BALL.—MOROCCO AND THE GREAT ATLAS: Journal of a Tour in. By Sir JOSEPH D. HOOKER, K.C.S.I., C.B., F.R.S., &c., and JOHN BALL, F.R.S. With an Appendix, including a Sketch of the Geology of Morocco, by G. MAW, F.L.S., F.G.S. With Illustrations and Map. 8vo. 21*s.*

HOUSE OF LORDS.—FIFTY YEARS OF THE HOUSE OF LORDS. Reprinted from *The Pall Mall Gazette.* Crown 8vo. 2*s.* 6*d.*

HOZIER (H. M.)—Works by CAPTAIN HENRY M. HOZIER, late Assistant Military Secretary to Lord Napier of Magdala:—

THE SEVEN WEEKS' WAR; Its Antecedents and Incidents. New and Cheaper Edition. With New Preface, Maps, and Plans. Crown 8vo. 6*s.*

THE INVASIONS OF ENGLAND: a History of the Past, with Lessons for the Future. Two Vols. 8vo. 28*s.*

HÜBNER.—A RAMBLE ROUND THE WORLD IN 1871. By M. LE BARON HÜBNER, formerly Ambassador and Minister. Translated by LADY HERBERT. New and Cheaper Edition. With numerous Illustrations. Crown 8vo. 6*s.*

HUGHES.—Works by THOMAS HUGHES, Q.C., Author of "Tom Brown's School Days."

MEMOIR OF A BROTHER. With Portrait of GEORGE HUGHES, after WATTS, Engraved by JEENS. Crown 8vo. 5*s.* Sixth Edition.

ALFRED THE GREAT. Crown 8vo. 6*s.*

RUGBY, TENNESSE. Being some account of the Settlement founded on the Cumberland Plateau by the Board of Aid to Land Ownership. With a report on the Soils of the Plateau by the Hon. F. W. KILLEBREW, A.M., Ph.D., Commissioner for Agriculture for the State of Tenessee. Crown 8vo. 4*s.* 6*d.*

HUNT.—HISTORY OF ITALY. By the Rev. W. HUNT, M.A. Being the Fourth Volume of the Historical Course for Schools. Edited by EDWARD A. FREEMAN, D.C.L. 18mo. 3*s*.

HUTTON.—ESSAYS THEOLOGICAL AND LITERARY. By R. H. HUTTON, M.A. Cheaper issue. 2 vols. 8vo. 18*s*.

CONTENTS OF VOL. I.:—The moral significance of Atheism—The Atheistic Explanation of Religion—Science and Theism—Popular Pantheism—What is Revelation?—Christian Evidences, Popular and Critical—The Historical Problems of the Fourth Gospel—The Incarnation and Principles of Evidence—M. Renan's "Christ"—M. Renan's "St. Paul"—The Hard Church—Romanism, Protestantism, and Anglicanism.

CONTENTS OF VOL. II.:—Goethe and his Influence—Wordsworth and his genius—Shelley's Poetical Mysticism—Mr. Browning—The Poetry of the Old Testament—Arthur Hugh Clough—The Poetry of Matthew Arnold—Tennyson—Nathaniel Hawthorne.

INGLIS (JAMES) ("MAORI").—Works by JAMES INGLIS ("Maori"):—

OUR AUSTRLIAN COUSINS. 8vo. 14*s*.

SPORT AND WORK ON THE NEPAUL FRONTIER; or, Twelve Years' Sporting Reminiscences of an Indigo Planter. By "MAORI." With Illustrations. 8vo. 14*s*.

IONIA.—THE ANTIQUITIES OF IONIA, see under Dilettanti Society's Publications.

IRVING.—THE ANNALS OF OUR TIME. A Diurnal of Events, Social and Political, Home and Foreign, from the Accession of Queen Victoria to the Peace of Versailles. By JOSEPH IRVING. New Edition, revised. 8vo. half-bound. 18*s*.

ANNALS OF OUR TIME. Supplement. From Feb. 28, 1871, to March 19, 1874. 8vo. 4*s*. 6*d*. ANNALS OF OUR TIME. Second Supplement. From March, 1874, to the Occupation of Cyprus. 8vo. 4*s*. 6*d*.

JAMES (Sir. W. M.).—THE BRITISH IN INDIA. By the late Right Hon. Sir WILLIAM MELBOURNE JAMES, Lord Justice of Appeal. Edited by his Daughter, M. J. Salis Schwabe. Demy 8vo. 12*s*. 6*d*.

JEBB.—MODERN GREECE. Two Lectures delivered before the Philosophical Institution of Edinburgh. With papers on "The Progress of Greece," and "Byron in Greece." By R. C. JEBB, M.A., LL.D. Edin. Professor of Greek in the University of Glasgow. Crown 8vo. 5*s*.

JOHNSON'S LIVES OF THE POETS.—The Six Chief Lives—Milton, Dryden, Swift, Addison, Pope, Gray. With Macaulay's "Life of Johnson." Edited, with Preface, by MATTHEW ARNOLD. Crown 8vo. 6*s*.

JONES.—THE LIFE'S WORK IN IRELAND OF A LANDLORD WHO TRIED TO DO HIS DUTY. By W. BENCE JONES, of Lisselan. Crown 8vo. 6*s*.

KILLEN.—ECCLESIASTICAL HISTORY OF IRELAND, from the Earliest Date to the Present Time. By W. D. KILLEN, D.D., President of Assembly's College, Belfast, and Professor of Ecclesiastical History. Two Vols. 8vo. 25*s*.

KINGSLEY (CHARLES).—Works by the Rev. CHARLES KINGSLEY, M.A., Rector of Eversley and Canon of Westminster. (For other Works by the same Author, *see* THEOLOGICAL and BELLES LETTRES Catalogues.)

AT LAST: A CHRISTMAS in the WEST INDIES. With nearly Fifty Illustrations. New Edition. Crown 8vo. 6*s.*

THE ROMAN AND THE TEUTON. A Series of Lectures delivered before the University of Cambridge. New and Cheaper Edition, with Preface by Professor MAX MÜLLER. Crown 8vo. 6*s.*

PLAYS AND PURITANS, and other Historical Essays. With Portrait of Sir WALTER RALEIGH. New Edition. Crown 8vo. 6*s.*

In addition to the Essay mentioned in the title, this volume contains other two—one on "Sir Walter Raleigh and his Time," and one on Froude's "History of England."

HISTORICAL LECTURES AND ESSAYS. Crown 8vo. 6*s.*

SANITARY AND SOCIAL LECTURES AND ESSAYS. Crown 8vo. 6*s.*

SCIENTIFIC LECTURES AND ESSAYS. Crown 8vo. 6*s*

LITERARY AND GENERAL LECTURES. Crown 8vo. 6*s.*

KINGSLEY (HENRY).—TALES OF OLD TRAVEL. Re-narrated by HENRY KINGSLEY, F.R.G.S. With Eight Illustrations by HUARD. Fifth Edition. Crown 8vo. 5*s.*

LANG.—CYPRUS: Its History, its Present Resources and Future Prospects. By R. HAMILTON LANG, late H.M. Consul for the Island of Cyprus. With Two Illustrations and Four Maps. 8vo. 14*s.*

LAOCOON.—Translated from the Text of Lessing, with Preface and Notes by the Right Hon. Sir ROBERT J. PHILLIMORE, D.C.L. With Photographs. 8vo. 12*s.*

LEONARDO DA VINCI AND HIS WORKS.—Consisting of a Life of Leonardo Da Vinci, by Mrs. CHARLES W. HEATON, Author of "Albrecht Dürer of Nürnberg," &c., an Essay on his Scientific and Literary Works, by CHARLES CHRISTOPHER BLACK, M.A., and an account of his more important Paintings and Drawings. Illustrated with Permanent Photographs. Royal 8vo., cloth, extra gilt. 31*s.* 6*d.*

LETHBRIDGE.—A SHORT MANUAL OF THE HISTORY OF INDIA, with an account of INDIA AS IT IS. The Soil, Climate, and Productions; the People—their Races, Religions, Public Works, and Industries; the Civil Services and System of Administration. By ROPER LETHBRIDGE, M.A., C.I.E., Press Commissioner with the Government of India, late Scholar of Exeter College, &c. &c. With Maps. Crown 8vo. 5*s.*

LIECHTENSTEIN.—HOLLAND HOUSE. By Princess MARIE LIECHTENSTEIN. With Five Steel Engravings by C. H. JEENS, after paintings by WATTS and other celebrated Artists, and numerous Illustrations drawn by Professor P. H. DELAMOTTE, and engraved on Wood by J. D. COOPER, W. PALMER, and JEWITT & Co., about 40 Illustrations by the Woodbury-type process, and India Proofs of the Steel Engravings. Two vols. Medium 4to., half morocco elegant. 4*l.* 4*s.*

LLOYD.—THE AGE OF PERICLES. A History of the Arts and Politics of Greece from the Persian to the Peloponnesian War. By W. WATKISS LLOYD. Two Vols. 8vo. 21*s.*

LOCH ETIVE AND THE SONS OF UISNACH.—With Illustrations. 8vo. 14*s.*

LOFTIE.—A RIDE IN EGYPT FROM SIOOT TO LUXOR, IN 1879; with Notes on the Present State and Ancient History of the Nile Valley, and some account of the various ways of making the voyage out and home. By the Rev. W. J. LOFTIE. With Illustrations. Crown 8vo. 10*s*. 6*d*.

LUBBOCK.—ADDRESSES, POLITICAL AND EDUCATIONAL. By Sir JOHN LUBBOCK, Bart., M.P., D.C.L., F.R.S. 8vo. 8*s*. 6*d*.

MACDONELL.—FRANCE SINCE THE FIRST EMPIRE. By JAMES MACDONELL. Edited with Preface by his Wife. Crown 8vo. 6*s*.

MACARTHUR.—HISTORY OF SCOTLAND. By MARGARET MACARTHUR. Being the Third Volume of the Historical Course for Schools, Edited by EDWARD A. FREEMAN, D.C.L. Second Edition. 18mo. 2*s*.

MACMILLAN (REV. HUGH).—For other Works by same Author, *see* THEOLOGICAL and SCIENTIFIC CATALOGUES.

HOLIDAYS ON HIGH LANDS; or, Rambles and Incidents in search of Alpine Plants. Second Edition, revised and enlarged. Globe 8vo. 6*s*.

MACREADY.—MACREADY'S REMINISCENCES AND SELECTIONS FROM HIS DIARIES AND LETTERS. Edited by Sir F. POLLOCK, Bart., one of his Executors. With Four Portraits engraved by JEENS. New and Cheaper Edition. Crown 8vo. 7*s*. 6*d*.

MAHAFFY.—Works by the Rev. J. P. MAHAFFY, M.A., Fellow of Trinity College, Dublin:—

SOCIAL LIFE IN GREECE FROM HOMER TO MENANDER. Fourth Edition, revised and enlarged, with a new chapter on Greek Art. Crown 8vo. 9*s*.

RAMBLES AND STUDIES IN GREECE. With Illustrations. New and enlarged Edition, with Map and Illustrations. Crown 8vo. 10*s*. 6*d*.

MARGARY.—THE JOURNEY OF AUGUSTUS RAYMOND MARGARY FROM SHANGHAE TO BHAMO AND BACK TO MANWYNE. From his Journals and Letters, with a brief Biographical Preface, a concluding chapter by Sir RUTHERFORD ALCOCK, K.C.B., and a Steel Portrait engraved by JEENS, and Map. 8vo. 10*s*. 6*d*.

MARKHAM.—NORTHWARD HO! By Captain ALBERT H. MARKHAM, R.N., Author of "The Great Frozen Sea," &c. Including a narrative of Captain Phipps's Expedition, by a Midshipman. With Illustrations. Crown 8vo. 10*s*. 6*d*.

MARTIN.—THE HISTORY OF LLOYD'S, AND OF MARINE INSURANCE IN GREAT BRITAIN. With an Appendix containing Statistics relating to Marine Insurance. By FREDERICK MARTIN, Author of "The Statesman's Year Book." 8vo. 14*s*.

MARTINEAU.—BIOGRAPHICAL SKETCHES, 1852–75. By HARRIET MARTINEAU. With Four Additional Sketches, and Autobiographical Sketch. Fifth Edition. Crown 8vo. 6*s*.

MASSON (DAVID).—For other Works by same Author, *see* PHILOSOPHICAL and BELLES LETTRES CATALOGUES

CHATTERTON: A Story of the Year 1770. By DAVID MASSON, LL.D., Professor of Rhetoric and English Literature in the University of Edinburgh. Crown 8vo. 5*s*.

THE THREE DEVILS: Luther's, Goethe's, and Milton's; and other Essays. Crown 8vo. 5*s*.

WORDSWORTH, SHELLEY, AND KEATS; and other Essays. Crown 8vo. 5*s*.

MATHEWS.—LIFE OF CHARLES J. MATHEWS. Chiefly Autobiographical. With Selections from his Correspondence and Speeches. Edited by CHARLES DICKENS. Two Vols. 8vo. 25*s.*

MAURICE.—THE FRIENDSHIP OF BOOKS; AND OTHER LECTURES. By the Rev. F. D. MAURICE. Edited with Preface, by THOMAS HUGHES, Q.C. Crown 8vo. 10*s.* 6*d.*

MAYOR (J. E. B.)—WORKS edited by JOHN E. B. MAYOR, M.A., Kennedy Professor of Latin at Cambridge:—

CAMBRIDGE IN THE SEVENTEENTH CENTURY. Part II. Autobiography of Matthew Robinson. Fcap. 8vo. 5*s.* 6*d.*

LIFE OF BISHOP BEDELL. By his SON. Fcap. 8vo. 3*s.* 6*d.*

MELBOURNE.—MEMOIRS OF THE RT. HON. WILLIAM, SECOND VISCOUNT MELBOURNE. By W. M. TORRENS, M.P. With Portrait after Sir T. Lawrence. Second Edition. Two Vols. 8vo. 32*s.*

MENDELSSOHN.—LETTERS AND RECOLLECTIONS. By FERDINAND HILLER. Translated by M. E. VON GLEHN. With Portrait from a Drawing by KARL MÜLLER, never before published. Second Edition. Crown 8vo. 7*s.* 6*d.*

MEREWETHER.—BY SEA AND BY LAND. Being a Trip through Egypt, India, Ceylon, Australia, New Zealand, and America—All Round the World. By HENRY ALWORTH MEREWETHER, one of Her Majesty's Counsel. Crown 8vo. 8*s.* 6*d.*

MICHAEL ANGELO BUONAROTTI; Sculptor, Painter, Architect. The Story of his Life and Labours. By C. C. BLACK, M.A. Illustrated by 20 Permanent Photographs. Royal 8vo. cloth elegant. 31*s.* 6*d.*

MICHELET.—A SUMMARY OF MODERN HISTORY. Translated from the French of M. MICHELET, and continued to the present time by M. C. M. SIMPSON. Globe 8vo. 4*s.* 6*d.*

MILLET.—JEAN FRANÇOIS MILLET; Peasant and Painter. Translated from the French of ALFRED SENSIER. With numerous Illustrations. Globe 4to. 16*s.*

MILTON.—LIFE OF JOHN MILTON. Narrated in connection with the Political, Ecclesiastical, and Literary History of his Time. By DAVID MASSON, M.A., LL.D., Professor of Rhetoric and English Literature in the University of Edinburgh. With Portraits. Vol. I. 1608—1639. New and Revised Edition. 8vo. 21*s.* Vol. II. 1638—1643. 8vo. 16*s.* Vol. III. 1643—1649. 8vo. 18*s.* Vols. IV. and V. 1649—1660. 32*s.* Vol. VI. 1660—1674. With Portrait. 21*s.* [*Index Volume in preparation.*

This work is not only a Biography, but also a continuous Political, Ecclesiastical, and Literary History of England through Milton's whole time.

MITFORD (A. B.)—TALES OF OLD JAPAN. By A. B. MITFORD, Second Secretary to the British Legation in Japan. With upwards of 30 Illustrations, drawn and cut on Wood by Japanese Artists. New and Cheaper Edition. Crown 8vo. 6*s.*

MONTEIRO.—ANGOLA AND THE RIVER CONGO. By JOACHIM MONTEIRO. With numerous Illustrations from Sketches taken on the spot, and a Map. Two Vols. Crown 8vo. 21*s.*

MOSELEY.—NOTES BY A NATURALIST ON THE *CHALLENGER*: being an Account of various Observations made during the Voyage of H.M.S. *Challenger* Round the World in 1872—76. By H. N. MOSELEY, F.R.S., Member of the Scientific Staff of the *Challenger*. With Maps, Coloured Plates, and Woodcuts. 8vo. 21*s.*

MURRAY.—ROUND ABOUT FRANCE. By E. C. GRENVILLE MURRAY. Crown 8vo. 7*s.* 6*d.*

MUSIC.—DICTIONARY OF MUSIC AND MUSICIANS (A.D. 1450—1881). By Eminent Writers, English and Foreign. Edited by GEORGE GROVE, D.C.L. Three Vols. 8vo. With Illustrations and Woodcuts. Parts I. to XIV., 3*s.* 6*d.* each. Vols. I. and II. 8vo. 21*s.* each.

Vol. I.—A to Impromptu. Vol. II.—Improperia to Plain Song.

NAPIER.—MACVEY NAPIER'S SELECTED CORRESPONDENCE. Edited by his Son, MACVEY NAPIER. 8vo. 14*s.*

NAPOLEON.—THE HISTORY OF NAPOLEON I. By P. LANFREY. A Translation with the sanction of the Author. Four Vols. 8vo. Vols. I. II. and III. price 12*s.* each. Vol. IV. With Index. 6*s.*

NEWTON.—ESSAYS ON ART AND ARCHÆOLOGY. By CHARLES THOMAS NEWTON, C.B., Ph.D., D.C.L., LL.D., Keeper of Greek and Roman Antiquities at the British Museum, &c. 8vo. 12*s.* 6*d.*

NICHOL.—TABLES OF EUROPEAN LITERATURE AND HISTORY, A.D. 200—1876. By J. NICHOL, LL.D., Professor of English Language and Literature, Glasgow. 4to. 6*s.* 6*d.*

TABLES OF ANCIENT LITERATURE AND HISTORY, B.C. 1500—A.D. 200. By the same Author. 4to. 4*s.* 6*d.*

NORDENSKIÖLD'S ARCTIC VOYAGES, 1858-79.—With Maps and numerous Illustrations. 8vo. 16*s.*

VOYAGE OF THE *VEGA* ROUND ASIA AND EUROPE. With a Historical Review of Previous Voyages along the North Coast of the Old World. By Baron A. E. VON NORDENSKIÖLD, Commander of the Expedition. Translated by ALEXANDER LESLIE, Author of "Nordenskiöld's Arctic Voyages." With 5 Portraits engraved by G. J. Stodart, and nearly 400 Illustrations, Maps, &c. 2 vols. Medium 8vo. 45*s.*

OLIPHANT (MRS.).—THE MAKERS OF FLORENCE: Dante, Giotto, Savonarola, and their City. By Mrs. OLIPHANT. With numerous Illustrations from drawings by Professor DELAMOTTE, and portrait of Savonarola, engraved by JEENS. New and Cheaper Edition. Crown 8vo. 10*s.* 6*d.*

OLIPHANT.—THE DUKE AND THE SCHOLAR; and other Essays By T. L. KINGTON OLIPHANT. 8vo. 7*s.* 6*d.*

OTTE.—SCANDINAVIAN HISTORY. By E. C. OTTE. With Maps. Extra fcap. 8vo. 6*s.*

OWENS COLLEGE ESSAYS AND ADDRESSES.—By PROFESSORS AND LECTURERS OF OWENS COLLEGE, MANCHESTER. Published in Commemoration of the Opening of the New College Buildings, October 7th, 1873. 8vo. 14*s.*

PALGRAVE (R. F. D.)—THE HOUSE OF COMMONS; Illustrations of its History and Practice. By REGINALD F. D. PALGRAVE, Clerk Assistant of the House of Commons. New and Revised Edition. Crown 8vo. 2*s.* 6*d.*

PALGRAVE (SIR F.)—HISTORY OF NORMANDY AND OF ENGLAND. By Sir FRANCIS PALGRAVE, Deputy Keeper of Her Majesty's Public Records. Completing the History to the Death of William Rufus. 4 Vols. 8vo. 4*l.* 4*s.*

PALGRAVE (W. G.)—A NARRATIVE OF A YEAR'S JOURNEY THROUGH CENTRAL AND EASTERN ARABIA, 1862—3. By WILLIAM GIFFORD PALGRAVE, late of the Eighth Regiment Bombay N.I. Sixth Edition. With Maps, Plans, and Portrait of Author, engraved on steel by JEENS. Crown 8vo. 6*s.*

ESSAYS ON EASTERN QUESTIONS. By W. GIFFORD PALGRAVE. 8vo. 10*s.* 6*d.*

DUTCH GUIANA. With Maps and Plans. 8vo. 9*s.*

PATTESON.—LIFE AND LETTERS OF JOHN COLERIDGE PATTESON, D.D., Missionary Bishop of the Melanesian Islands. By CHARLOTTE M. YONGE, Author of "The Heir of Redclyffe." With Portraits after RICHMOND and from Photograph, engraved by JEENS. With Map. Fifth Edition. Two Vols. Crown 8vo. 12*s.*

PAULI.—PICTURES OF OLD ENGLAND. By Dr. REINHOLD PAULI. Translated with the approval of the Author, by E. C. OTTE, Cheaper Edition. Crown 8vo. 6*s.*

PAYNE.—A HISTORY OF EUROPEAN COLONIES. By E. J. PAYNE, M.A. With Maps. 18mo. 4*s.* 6*d.* [*Historical Course.*

PERSIA.—EASTERN PERSIA. An Account of the Journeys of the Persian Boundary Commission, 1870-1-2.—Vol. I. The Geography, with Narratives by Majors ST. JOHN, LOVETT, and EUAN SMITH, and an Introduction by Major-General Sir FREDERIC GOLDSMID, C.B., K.C.S.I., British Commissioner and Arbitrator. With Maps and Illustrations.—Vol. II. The Zoology and Geology. By W. T. BLANDFORD, A.R.S.M., F.R.S. With Coloured Illustrations. Two Vols. 8vo. 42*s.*

PHEAR.—THE ARYAN VILLAGE IN INDIA AND CEYLON. By Sir JOHN B. PHEAR. Crown 8vo. 7*s.* 6*d.*

POOLE.—A HISTORY OF THE HUGUENOTS OF THE DISPERSION AT THE RECALL OF THE EDICT OF NANTES. By REGINALD LANE POOLE. Crown 8vo. 6*s.*

PRICHARD.—THE ADMINISTRATION OF INDIA. From 1859 to 1868. The First Ten Years of Administration under the Crown. By I. T. PRICHARD, Barrister-at-Law. Two Vols. Demy 8vo. With Map. 21*s.*

RAPHAEL.—RAPHAEL OF URBINO AND HIS FATHER GIOVANNI SANTI. By J. D. PASSAVANT, formerly Director of the Museum at Frankfort. With Twenty Permanent Photographs. Royal 8vo. Handsomely bound. 31*s.* 6*d.*

REMBRANDT.—THE ETCHED WORK OF REMBRANDT. A MONOGRAPH. By FRANCIS SEYMOUR HADEN. With three Plates. 8vo. 7*s.* 6*d*

ROGERS (JAMES E. THOROLD).—HISTORICAL GLEANINGS:—A Series of Sketches. Montague, Walpole, Adam Smith, Cobbett. By Prof. ROGERS, M.P. Crown 8vo. 4*s.* 6*d.* Second Series. Wiklif, Laud, Wilkes, and Horne Tooke. Crown 8vo. 6*s.*

ROUTLEDGE.—CHAPTERS IN THE HISTORY OF POPULAR PROGRESS IN ENGLAND, chiefly in Relation to the Freedom of the Press and Trial by Jury, 1660—1820. With application to later years. By J. ROUTLEDGE. 8vo. *16s.*

RUMFORD.—COUNT RUMFORD'S COMPLETE WORKS, with Memoir, and Notices of his Daughter. By GEORGE ELLIS. Five Vols. 8vo. *4l. 14s. 6d*

RUSSELL.—NEW VIEWS ON IRELAND, OR IRISH LAND GRIEVANCES AND REMEDIES. By CHARLES RUSSELL, Q.C., M.P. Third Edition. Crown 8vo. *2s. 6d.*

SEELEY (PROFESSOR).—LECTURES AND ESSAYS. By J. R. SEELEY, M.A., Professor of Modern History in the University of Cambridge. 8vo. *10s. 6d.*

CONTENTS :—Roman Imperialism : 1. The Great Roman Revolution ; 2. The Proximate Cause of the Fall of the Roman Empire ; The Later Empire.—Milton's Political Opinions—Milton's Poetry—Elementary Principles in Art—Liberal Education in Universities—English in Schools—The Church as a Teacher of Morality—The Teaching of Politics : an Inaugural Lecture delivered at Cambridge.

SHELBURNE.—LIFE OF WILLIAM, EARL OF SHELBURNE, AFTERWARDS FIRST MARQUIS OF LANDSDOWNE. With Extracts from his Papers and Correspondence. By Lord EDMOND FITZMAURICE. In Three Vols. 8vo. Vol. I. 1737—1766, *12s.* ; Vol. II. 1766—1776, *12s.* ; Vol. III. 1776—1805. *16s.*

SIBSON.—COLLECTED WORKS OF FRANCIS SIBSON, M.D., Lond., Fellow of the Royal Society, Honorary M.D. Trinity College, Dublin, and D.C.L. Durham, Fellow of the Royal College of Physicians, &c. Edited by WILLIAM M. ORD, M.D. With Illustrations. Four Volumes. 8vo. *3l. 3s.*

SIME.—HISTORY OF GERMANY. By JAMES SIME, M.A. 18mo. *3s.* Being Vol. V. of the Historical Course for Schools. Edited by EDWARD A. FREEMAN, D.C.L.

SQUIER.—PERU: INCIDENTS OF TRAVEL AND EXPLORATION IN THE LAND OF THE INCAS. By E. G. SQUIER, M.A., F.S.A., late U.S. Commissioner to Peru. With 300 Illustrations. Second Edition. 8vo. *21s.*

ST. ANSELM.—By the Very Rev. R. W. CHURCH, M.A., Dean of St. Paul's. New Edition. Crown 8vo. *6s.* (Biographical Series.)

STATHAM.—BLACKS, BOERS, AND BRITISH : A Three-Cornered Problem. By F. R. STATHAM. Crown 8vo. *6s.*

STEVENSON.—HOUSE ARCHITECTURE. By J. J. STEVENSON, Fellow of the Royal Institution of British Architects. With numerous Illustrations. Royal 8vo. 2 Vols. *18s.* each. Vol. I. Architecture. Vol. II. House Planning.

STRANGFORD.—EGYPTIAN SHRINES AND SYRIAN SEPULCHRES, including a Visit to Palmyra. By EMILY A. BEAUFORT (Viscountess Strangford), Author of "The Eastern Shores of the Adriatic." New Edition. Crown 8vo. *7s. 6d.*

TAIT.—AN ANALYSIS OF ENGLISH HISTORY, based upon Green's "Short History of the English People." By C. W. A. TAIT, M.A., Assistant Master, Clifton College. Crown 8vo. *3s. 6d.*

TAIT.—CATHARINE AND CRAUFURD TAIT, WIFE AND SON OF ARCHIBALD CAMPBELL, ARCHBISHOP OF CANTERBURY: a Memoir, Edited, at the request of the Archbishop, by the Rev. W. BENHAM, B.D., Vicar of Marden, and One of the Six Preachers of Canterbury Cathedral. With Two Portraits engraved by JEENS. New and Cheaper Edition. Crown 8vo. 6*s*. (Biographical Series.)

TERESA.—THE LIFE OF ST. TERESA. By MARIA TRENCH. With Portrait engraved by JEENS. Crown 8vo, cloth extra. 8*s*. 6*d*.

THOMPSON.—A HANDBOOK TO THE PUBLIC PICTURE GALLERIES OF EUROPE. With a Brief Sketch of the History of the various Schools of painting. From the Thirteenth Century to the Eighteenth inclusive. By KATE THOMPSON. Third Edition. With Illustrations. Crown 8vo. 7*s*. 6*d*.

THOMPSON.—HISTORY OF ENGLAND. By EDITH THOMPSON. Being Vol. II. of the Historical Course for Schools, Edited by EDWARD A. FREEMAN, D.C.L. New Edition, revised and enlarged, with Coloured Maps. 18mo. 2*s*. 6*d*.

THROUGH THE RANKS TO A COMMISSION.—New and Popular Edition. Crown 8vo. 2*s*. 6*d*.

TODHUNTER.—THE CONFLICT OF STUDIES; AND OTHER ESSAYS ON SUBJECTS CONECTED WITH EDUCATION. By ISAAC TODHUNTER, M.A., F.R.S., late Fellow and Principal Mathematical Lecturer of St. John's College, Cambridge. 8vo. 10*s*. 6*d*.

TRENCH (ARCHBISHOP).—For other Works by the same Author, *see* THEOLOGICAL and BELLES LETTRES CATALOGUES, and page 27 of this Catalogue.

GUSTAVUS ADOLPHUS IN GERMANY, and other Lectures on the Thirty Years' War. Second Edition, revised and enlarged. Fcap. 8vo. 4*s*.

PLUTARCH, HIS LIFE, HIS LIVES, AND HIS MORALS. Five Lectures. Second Edition, enlarged. Fcap. 8vo. 3*s*. 6*d*.

LECTURES ON MEDIEVAL CHURCH HISTORY. Being the substance of Lectures delivered in Queen's College, London. Second Edition, revised. 8vo. 12*s*.

AN ESSAY ON THE LIFE AND GENIUS OF CALDERON. With Translations from his "Life's a Dream" and "Great Theatre of the World." Second Edition, revised and improved. Fcap. 8vo. 5*s*.

TRENCH (MRS. R.).—REMAINS OF THE LATE MRS. RICHARD TRENCH. Being Selections from her Journals, Letters, and other Papers. Edited by ARCHBISHOP TRENCH. New and Cheaper Issue, with Portrait. 8vo. 6*s*.

TREVELYAN.—THE IRISH CRISIS. Being a Narrative of the Measures for the Relief of the Distress caused by the Great Irish Famine of 1846-7. By Sir CHARLES TREVELYAN, Bart., K.C.B. 8vo. 2*s*. 6*d*.

TROLLOPE.—A HISTORY OF THE COMMONWEALTH OF FLORENCE FROM THE EARLIEST INDEPENDENCE OF THE COMMUNE TO THE FALL OF THE REPUBLIC IN 1831. By T. ADOLPHUS TROLLOPE. 4 Vols. 8vo. Cloth 21*s*.

TYLOR.—ANTHROPOLOGY: an Introduction to the Study of Man and Civilisation. By E. B. TYLOR, D.C.L., F.R.S. With Illustrations. Crown 8vo. *7s. 6d.*

UPPINGHAM BY THE SEA.—A NARRATIVE OF THE YEAR AT BORTH. By J. H. S. Crown 8vo. *3s. 6d.*

VICTOR EMMANUEL II., FIRST KING OF ITALY. By G. S. GODKIN. New Edition. Crown 8vo. *6s.* (Biographical Series.)

WALLACE.—THE MALAY ARCHIPELAGO: the Land of the Orang Utan and the Bird of Paradise. By ALFRED RUSSEL WALLACE. A Narrative of Travel with Studies of Man and Nature. With Maps and numerous Illustrations. Sixth Edition. Crown 8vo. *7s. 6d.*

WARD.—A HISTORY OF ENGLISH DRAMATIC LITERATURE TO THE DEATH OF QUEEN ANNE. By A. W. WARD, M.A., Professor of History and English Literature in Owens College, Manchester. Two Vols. 8vo. *32s.*

WARD (J.)—EXPERIENCES OF A DIPLOMATIST. Being recollections of Germany founded on Diaries kept during the years 1840—1870. By JOHN WARD, C.B., late H.M. Minister-Resident to the Hanse Towns. 8vo. *10s. 6d.*

WARD.—ENGLISH POETS. Selections, with Critical Introductions by various writers, and a General Introduction by MATTHEW ARNOLD. Edited by T. H. WARD, M.A. 4 vols. Crown 8vo. *7s. 6d.* each.

Vol. I. CHAUCER to DONNE.
Vol. II. BEN JONSON to DRYDEN.
Vol. III. ADDISON to BLAKE.
Vol. IV. WORDSWORTH to SYDNEY DOBELL.

WATERTON (C.)—WANDERINGS IN SOUTH AMERICA, THE NORTH-WEST OF THE UNITED STATES, AND THE ANTILLES IN 1812, 1816, 1820, and 1824. With Original Instructions for the perfect Preservation of Birds, etc., for Cabinets of Natural History. By CHARLES WATERTON. New Edition, edited with Biographical Introduction and Explanatory Index by the Rev. J. G. WOOD. M.A. With 100 Illustrations. Cheaper Edition. Crown 8vo. *6s.*

WATSON.—A VISIT TO WAZAN, THE SACRED CITY OF MOROCCO By ROBERT SPENCE WATSON. With Illustrations. 8vo. *10s. 6d.*

WESLEY.—JOHN WESLEY AND THE EVANGELICAL REACTION of the Eighteenth Century. By JULIA WEDGWOOD. Crown 8vo. *8s. 6d.*

WHEELER.—A SHORT HISTORY OF INDIA, AND OF THE FRONTIER STATES OF AFGHANISTAN, NEPAUL, AND BURMA. By J. TALBOYS WHEELER, late Assistant-Secretary to the Government of India, Foreign Department, and late Secretary to the Government of British Burma. With Maps and Tables. Crown 8vo. *12s.*

WHEWELL.—WILLIAM WHEWELL, D.D., late Master of Trinity College, Cambridge. An account of his Writings, with Selections from his Literary and Scientific correspondence. By I. TODHUNTER, M.A., F.R.S. Two Vols. 8vo. 25*s.*

WHITE.—THE NATURAL HISTORY AND ANTIQUITIES OF SELBORNE. By GILBERT WHITE. Edited, with Memoir and Notes, by FRANK BUCKLAND, A Chapter on Antiquities by LORD SELBORNE, and numerous Illustrations by P. H. DELAMOTTE. New and Cheaper Edition. Crown 8vo. 6*s.*

Also a Large Paper Edition, containing, in addition to the above, upwards of Thirty Woodburytype Illustrations from Drawings by Prof. DELAMOTTE. Two Vols. 4to. Half morocco, elegant. 4*l.* 4*s.*

WILSON.—A MEMOIR OF GEORGE WILSON, M.D., F.R.S.E., Regius Professor of Technology in the University of Edinburgh. By his SISTER. New Edition. Crown 8vo. 6*s.*

WILSON (DANIEL, LL.D.)—Works by DANIEL WILSON, LL.D., Professor of History and English Literature in University College, Toronto:—

PREHISTORIC ANNALS OF SCOTLAND. New Edition, with numerous Illustrations. Two Vols. Demy 8vo. 36*s.*

PREHISTORIC MAN: Researches into the Origin of Civilization in the Old and New World. New Edition, revised and enlarged throughout, with numerous Illustrations and Two Coloured Plates. Two Vols. 8vo. 36*s.*

CHATTERTON: A Biographical Study. Crown 8vo. 6*s.* 6*d.*

YONGE (CHARLOTTE M.)—Works by CHARLOTTE M. YONGE, Author of the "Heir of Redclyffe," &c. &c.:—

A PARALLEL HISTORY OF FRANCE AND ENGLAND: Consisting of Outlines and Dates. Oblong 4to. 3*s.* 6*d.*

CAMEOS FROM ENGLISH HISTORY. From Rollo to Edward II. Extra Fcap. 8vo. Third Edition. 5*s.*

SECOND SERIES, THE WARS IN FRANCE. Extra fcap. 8vo. Third Edition. 5*s.*

THIRD SERIES, THE WARS OF THE ROSES. Extra fcap. 8vo. 5*s.*

FOURTH SERIES, REFORMATION TIMES. Extra fcap. 8vo. 5*s.*

HISTORY OF FRANCE. Maps. 18mo. 3*s.* 6*d.*

[*Historical Course for Schools.*

POLITICS, POLITICAL AND SOCIAL ECONOMY, LAW, AND KINDRED SUBJECTS.

ANGLO-SAXON LAW.—ESSAYS IN. Contents: Law Courts—Land and Family Laws and Legal Procedure generally. With Select cases. Medium 8vo. 18*s.*

ARNOLD.—THE ROMAN SYSTEM OF PROVINCIAL ADMINISTRATION TO THE ACCESSION OF CONSTANTINE THE GREAT. Being the Arnold Prize Essay for 1879. By W. T. ARNOLD, B.A. Crown 8vo. 6*s.*

BALL.—THE STUDENT'S GUIDE TO THE BAR. By WALTER W. BALL, M.A., of the Inner Temple, Barrister-at-Law. Crown. 8vo. 2*s.* 6*d.*

BERNARD.—FOUR LECTURES ON SUBJECTS CONNECTED WITH DIPLOMACY. By MONTAGUE BERNARD, M. A., Chichele Professor of International Law and Diplomacy, Oxford. 8vo. 9*s.*

BIGELOW.—HISTORY OF PROCEDURE IN ENGLAND, FROM THE NORMAN CONQUEST. The Norman Period, 1066–1204. By MELVILLE MADISON BIGELOW, Ph.D., Harvard University. 8vo. 16*s.*

BRIGHT (JOHN, M.P.).—Works by the Right Hon. JOHN BRIGHT, M.P.

SPEECHES ON QUESTIONS OF PUBLIC POLICY. Edited by Professor THOROLD ROGERS, M.P. Author's Popular Edition. Globe 8vo. 3*s.* 6*d.*

LIBRARY EDITION. Two Vols. 8vo. With Portrait. 25*s.*

PUBLIC ADDRESSES. Edited by J. THOROLD ROGERS, M.P. 8vo. 14*s.*

BUCKNILL.—Works by J. C. BUCKNILL, M.D., F.R.S., late Lord Chancellor's Visitor of Lunatics:—

HABITUAL DRUNKENNESS AND INSANE DRUNKARDS. Crown 8vo. 2*s.* 6*d.*

THE CARE OF THE INSANE, AND THEIR LEGAL CONTROL. Crown 8vo. 3*s.* 6*d.*

CAIRNES.—Works by J. E. CAIRNES, M.A., Emeritus Professor of Political Economy in University College, London:—

POLITICAL ESSAYS. 8vo. 10*s.* 6*d.*

THE CHARACTER AND LOGICAL METHOD OF POLITICAL ECONOMY. New Edition, enlarged. 8vo. 7*s.* 6*d.*

COBDEN (RICHARD).—SPEECHES ON QUESTIONS OF PUBLIC POLICY. By RICHARD COBDEN. Edited by the Right Hon John Bright, M.P., and J. E. Thorold Rogers, M.P. Popular Edition. 8vo. 3*s.* 6*d.*

COSSA.—GUIDE TO THE STUDY OF POLITICAL ECONOMY. By Dr. LUIGI COSSA, Professor of Political Economy in the University of Pavia. Translated from the Second Italian Edition. With a Preface by W. STANLEY JEVONS, F.R.S. Crown 8vo. 4*s.* 6*d.*

FAWCETT.—Works by Right Hon. HENRY FAWCETT, M.A., M.P., Fellow of Trinity Hall, and Professor of Political Economy in the University of Cambridge:—

THE ECONOMIC POSITION OF THE BRITISH LABOURER. Extra fcap. 8vo. 5*s.*

FAWCETT—*continued.*

MANUAL OF POLITICAL ECONOMY. Fifth Edition, with New Chapters on the Depreciation of Silver, etc. Crown 8vo. 12*s.*

PAUPERISM: ITS CAUSES AND REMEDIES. Crown 8vo. 5*s.* 6*d.*

SPEECHES ON SOME CURRENT POLITICAL QUESTIONS. 8vo. 10*s.* 6*d.*

FREE TRADE AND PROTECTION: and Inquiry into the Causes which have retarded the general adoption of Free Trade since its introduction into England. Fourth and Cheaper Edition. 8vo. 3*s.* 6*d.*

INDIAN FINANCE. Three Essays, with Introduction and Appendix. 8vo. 7*s.* 6*d.*

ESSAYS ON POLITICAL AND SOCIAL SUBJECTS. By Right Hon. HENRY FAWCETT, M.P., and MILLICENT GARRETT FAWCETT. 8vo. 10*s.* 6*d.*

FAWCETT (MRS.)—Works by MILLICENT GARRETT FAWCETT:—

POLITICAL ECONOMY FOR BEGINNERS. WITH QUESTIONS. New Edition. 18mo. 2*s.* 6*d.*

TALES IN POLITICAL ECONOMY. Crown 8vo. 3*s.*

GOSCHEN.—REPORTS AND SPEECHES ON LOCAL TAXATION. By GEORGE J. GOSCHEN, M.P. Royal 8vo. 5*s.*

GUIDE TO THE UNPROTECTED, in Every Day Matters Relating to Property and Income. By a BANKER'S DAUGHTER. Fifth Edition, Revised. Extra fcap. 8vo. 3*s.* 6*d.*

HAMILTON.—MONEY AND VALUE: an Inquiry into the Means and Ends of Economic Production, with an Appendix on the Depreciation of Silver and Indian Currency. By ROWLAND HAMILTON. 8vo. 12*s.*

HARWOOD.—DISESTABLISHMENT: a Defence of the Principle of a National Church. By GEORGE HARWOOD, M.A. 8vo. 12*s.*

HILL.—OUR COMMON LAND; and other Short Essays. By OCTAVIA HILL. Extra fcap. 8vo. 3*s.* 6*d.*

CONTENTS:—Our Common Land. District Visiting. A more Excellent Way of Charity. A Word on Good Citizenship. Open Spaces. Effectual Charity. The Future of our Commons.

HOLLAND.—THE TREATY RELATIONS OF RUSSIA AND TURKEY FROM 1774 TO 1853. A Lecture delivered at Oxford, April 1877. By T. E. HOLLAND, D.C.L., Professor of International Law and Diplomacy, Oxford. Crown 8vo. 2*s.*

HUGHES (THOS.)—THE OLD CHURCH: WHAT SHALL WE DO WITH IT? By THOMAS HUGHES, Q.C. Crown 8vo. 6*s.*

JEVONS.—Works by W. STANLEY JEVONS, LL.D., M.A., F.R.S. (For other Works by the same Author, *see* EDUCATIONAL and PHILOSOPHICAL CATALOGUES.):—

THE THEORY OF POLITICAL ECONOMY. Second Edition, revised, with new Preface and Appendices. 8vo. 10*s.* 6*d.*

PRIMER OF POLITICAL ECONOMY. 18mo. 1*s.*

LAVELEYE.—PRIMITIVE PROPERTY. By EMILE DE LAVELEYE. Translated by G. R. L. MARRIOTT, LL.B., with an Introduction by T. E. CLIFFE LESLIE. LL.B. 8vo. 12*s*.

LEADING CASES DONE INTO ENGLISH.—By an APPRENTICE OF LINCOLN'S INN. Third Edition. Crown 8vo. 2*s*. 6*d*.

LUBBOCK.—ADDRESSES, POLITICAL AND EDUCATIONAL. By Sir JOHN LUBBOCK, Bart., M.P., &c., &c. 8vo. 8*s*. 6*d*.

MACDONELL.—THE LAND QUESTION, WITH SPECIAL REFERENCE TO ENGLAND AND SCOTLAND. By JOHN MACDONEL, Barrister-at-Law. 8vo. 10*s*. 6*d*.

MARSHALL.—THE ECONOMICS OF INDUSTRY. By A. MARSHALL, M.A., late Principal of University College Bristol, and MARY PALEY MARSHALL. late Lecturer at Newnham Hall, Cambridge. Extra fcap. 8vo. 2*s*. 6*d*.

MARTIN.—THE STATESMAN'S YEAR-BOOK: A Statistical and Historical Annual of the States of the Civilized World, for the year 1882. By FREDERICK MARTIN. Nineteenth Annual Publication. Revised after Official Returns. Crown 8vo. 10*s*. 6*d*.

MONAHAN.—THE METHOD OF LAW: an Essay on the Statement and Arrangement of the Legal Standard of Conduct. By J. H. MONAHAN, Q.C. Crown 8vo. 6*s*.

PATERSON.—Works by JAMES PATERSON, M.A., Barrister-at-Law, sometime Commissioner for English and Irish Fisheries, &c.

THE LIBERTY OF THE SUBJECT AND THE LAWS OF ENGLAND RELATING TO THE SECURITY OF THE PERSON. Commentaries on. Cheaper issue. Crown 8vo. 21*s*.

THE LIBERTY OF THE PRESS, OF SPEECH, AND OF PUBLIC WORSHIP. Being Commentaries on the Liberty of the Subject and the Laws of England. Crown 8vo. 12*s*.

PHEAR.—INTERNATIONAL TRADE, AND THE RELATION BETWEEN EXPORTS AND IMPORTS. A Paper read before the Exmouth Liberal Association, on July 22, 1881. By Sir JOHN B. PHEAR. Crown 8vo. 2*s*. 6*d*.

PHILLIMORE.—PRIVATE LAW AMONG THE ROMANS, from the Pandects. By JOHN GEORGE PHILLIMORE, Q.C. 8vo. 16*s*.

PRACTICAL POLITICS.—ISSUED BY THE NATIONAL LIBERAL FEDERATION. Complete in one volume. 8vo. 6*s*. Or:—

I. THE TENANT FARMER: Land Laws and Landlords. By JAMES HOWARD. 8vo. 1*s*.

II. FOREIGN POLICY. By Right Hon. M. E. GRANT DUFF, M.P. 8vo. 1*s*.

III. FREEDOM OF LAND. By G. SHAW LEFEVRE, M.P. 8vo. 2*s*. 6*d*.

IV. BRITISH COLONIAL POLICY. By Sir DAVID WEDDERBURN, Bart., M.P. Demy 8vo. 1*s*.

RICHEY.—THE IRISH LAND LAWS. By ALEXANDER G. RICHEY, Q.C., LL.D., Deputy Regius Professor of Feudal and English Law in the University of Dublin. Crown 8vo. 3*s*. 6*d*.

STEPHEN (C. E.)—THE SERVICE OF THE POOR; Being an Inquiry into the Reasons for and against the Establishment of Religious Sisterhoods for Charitable Purposes. By CAROLINE EMILIA STEPHEN. Crown 8vo. *6s. 6d.*

STEPHEN.—Works by Sir JAMES F. STEPHEN, K.C.S.I., Q.C.:—

A DIGEST OF THE LAW OF EVIDENCE. Fourth Edition, with new Preface. Crown 8vo. *6s.*

A DIGEST OF THE CRIMINAL LAW. (Crimes and Punishments.) 8vo. *16s.*

A GENERAL VIEW OF THE CRIMINAL LAW OF ENGLAND. Two Vols. Crown 8vo. [*New edition in the press.*

STUBBS.—VILLAGE POLITICS. Addresses and Sermons on the Labour Question. By C. W. STUBBS, M.A., Vicar of Granborough, Bucks. Extra fcap. 8vo. *3s. 6d.*

THORNTON.—Works by W. T. THORNTON, C.B., Secretary for Public Works in the India Office:—

A PLEA FOR PEASANT PROPRIETORS: With the Outlines of a Plan for their Establishment in Ireland. New Edition, revised. Crown 8vo. *7s. 6d.*

INDIAN PUBLIC WORKS AND COGNATE INDIAN TOPICS. With Map of Indian Railways. Crown 8vo. *8s. 6d.*

WALKER.—Works by F. A. WALKER, M.A., Ph.D., Professor of Political Economy and History, Yale College:—

THE WAGES QUESTION. A Treatise on Wages and the Wages Class. 8vo. *14s.*

MONEY. 8vo. *16s.*

MONEY IN ITS RELATIONS TO TRADE AND INDUSTRY. Crown 8vo. *7s. 6d.*

WILSON.—RECIPROCITY, BI-METALLISM, AND LAND-TENURE REFORM. By A. J. WILSON. Author of "The Resources of Modern Countries." 8vo. *7s. 6d.*

WORKS CONNECTED WITH THE SCIENCE OR THE HISTORY OF LANGUAGE.

ABBOTT.—A SHAKESPERIAN GRAMMAR: An Attempt to illustrate some of the Differences between Elizabethan and Modern English. By the Rev. E. A. ABBOTT, D.D., Head Master of the City of London School. New and Enlarged Edition. Extra fcap. 8vo. *6s.*

BREYMANN.—A FRENCH GRAMMAR BASED ON PHILOLOGICAL PRINCIPLES. By HERMANN BREYMANN, Ph.D., Professor of Philology in the University of Munich, late Lecturer on French Language and Literature at Owens College, Manchester. Extra fcap. 8vo. *4s. 6d.*

ELLIS.—PRACTICAL HINTS ON THE QUANTITATIVE PRONUNCIATION OF LATIN, FOR THE USE OF CLASSICAL TEACHERS AND LINGUISTS. By A. J. ELLIS, B.A., F.R.S., &c. Extra fcap. 8vo. *4s. 6d.*

FASNACHT.—THE ORGANIC METHOD OF STUDYING LANGUAGES. By G. EUGENE FASNACHT, Author of "Macmillan's Progressive French Course," Editor of "Macmillan's Foreign School Classics," &c. I. French. Crown 8vo. *3s. 6d.*

FLEAY.—A SHAKESPEARE MANUAL. By the Rev. F. G. FLEAY, M.A., Head Master of Skipton Grammar School. Extra fcap. 8vo. *4s. 6d.*

GOODWIN.—Works by W. W. GOODWIN, Professor of Greek Literature in Harvard University:—

SYNTAX OF THE GREEK MOODS AND TENSES. New Edition. Crown 8vo. *6s. 6d.*

GREEK GRAMMAR. Crown 8vo. *6s.*

A SCHOOL GREEK GRAMMAR. Crown 8vo. *3s. 6d.*

HADLEY.—ESSAYS PHILOLOGICAL AND CRITICAL. Selected from the Papers of JAMES HADLEY, LL.D., Professor of Greek in Yale College, &c. 8vo. *16s.*

HALES.—LONGER ENGLISH POEMS. With Notes, Philological and Explanatory, and an Introduction on the Teaching of English. Chiefly for use in Schools. Edited by J. W. HALES, M.A., Professor of English Literature at King's College, London, &c. &c. Fifth Edition. Extra fcap. 8vo. *4s. 6d.*

HELFENSTEIN (JAMES).—A COMPARATIVE GRAMMAR OF THE TEUTONIC LANGUAGES: Being at the same time a Historical Grammar of the English Language, and comprising Gothic, Anglo-Saxon, Early English, Modern English, Icelandic (Old Norse), Danish, Swedish, Old High German, Middle High German, Modern German, Old Saxon, Old Frisian, and Dutch. By JAMES HELFENSTEIN, Ph.D. 8vo. *18s.*

MASSON (GUSTAVE).—A COMPENDIOUS DICTIONARY OF THE FRENCH LANGUAGE (French-English and English-French). Adapted from the Dictionaries of Professor ALFRED ELWALL. Followed by a List of the Principal Diverging Derivations, and preceded by Chronological and Historical Tables. By GUSTAVE MASSON, Assistant-Master and Librarian, Harrow School. Fourth Edition. Crown 8vo. Half-bound. 6*s.*

MAYOR.—A BIBLIOGRAPHICAL CLUE TO LATIN LITERATURE. Edited after Dr. E. HUBNER. With large Additions by JOHN E. B. MAYOR, M.A., Professor of Latin in the University of Cambridge. Crown 8vo. 10*s.* 6*d.*

MORRIS.—Works by the Rev. RICHARD MORRIS, LL.D., President of the Philological Society, Editor of "Specimens of Early English," &c., &c. :—

HISTORICAL OUTLINES OF ENGLISH ACCIDENCE, comprising Chapters on the History and Development of the Language, and on Word-formation. New Edition. Fcap. 8vo. 6*s.*

ELEMENTARY LESSONS IN HISTORICAL ENGLISH GRAMMAR, containing Accidence and Wood-formation. Third Edition. 18mo. 2*s.* 6*d.*

OLIPHANT.—THE OLD AND MIDDLE ENGLISH. By T. L. KINGTON OLIPHANT, M.A., of Balliol College, Oxford. A New Edition, revised and greatly enlarged, of "The Sources of Standard English." Extra fcap. 8vo. 9*s.*

PEILE (JOHN, M.A.)—AN INTRODUCTION TO GREEK AND LATIN ETYMOLOGY. By JOHN PEILE, M.A., Fellow and Tutor of Christ's College, Cambridge. Third and revised Edition. Crown 8vo. 10*s.* 6*d.*

PHILOLOGY.—THE JOURNAL OF SACRED AND CLASSICAL PHILOLOGY. Four Vols. 8vo. 12*s.* 6*d.* each.

THE JOURNAL OF PHILOLOGY. New Series. Edited by JOHN E. B. MAYOR, M.A., and W. ALDIS WRIGHT, M.A. 4*s.* 6*d.* (Half-yearly.)

THE AMERICAN JOURNAL OF PHILOLOGY. Edited by BASIL L. GILDERSLEEVE, Professor of Greek in the John Hopkins University. 8vo. 4*s.* 6*d.* (Quarterly.)

PHRYNICHUS.—THE NEW PHRYNICHUS. Being a Revised Text of *The Ecloga* of the Grammarian *Phrynichus.* With Introductions and Commentary. By W. GUNION RUTHERFORD, M.A., of Balliol College, Oxford, Assistant-Master at St. Paul's. 8vo. 18*s.*

ROBY (H. J.)—Works by HENRY JOHN ROBY, M.A., late Fellow of St. John's College, Cambridge.

A GRAMMAR OF THE LATIN LANGUAGE, FROM PLAUTUS TO SUETONIUS. In Two Parts. Second Edition. Part I. containing:—Book I. Sounds. Book II. Inflexions. Book III. Word Formation. Appendices. Crown 8vo. 8*s.* 6*d.* Part II.—Syntax, Prepositions, &c. Crown 8vo. 10*s.* 6*d.*

A LATIN GRAMMAR FOR SCHOOLS. Crown 8vo. 5*s.*

SCHMIDT.—THE RYTHMIC AND METRIC OF THE CLASSICAL LANGUAGES. To which are added, the Lyric Parts of the "Medea" of Euripides and the "Antigone" of Sophocles; with Rhythmical Scheme and Commentary. By Dr. J. H. SCHMIDT. Translated from the German by J. W. WHITE, D.D. 8vo. 10*s.* 6*d.*

TAYLOR.—Works by the Rev. ISAAC TAYLOR, M.A.:—

ETRUSCAN RESEARCHES. With Woodcuts. 8vo. 14*s.*

WORDS AND PLACES: or, Etymological Illustrations of History, Ethnology. and Geography. By the Rev. ISAAC TAYLOR. Third Edition, revised and compressed. With Maps. Globe 8vo. 6*s.*

GREEKS AND GOTHS: a Study on the Runes. 8vo. 9*s.*

TRENCH.—Works by R. CHENEVIX TRENCH, D.D., Archbishop of Dublin. (For other Works by the same Author, *see* THEOLOGICAL CATALOGUE.)

SYNONYMS OF THE NEW TESTAMENT. Ninth Edition, enlarged. 8vo. cloth. 12*s.*

ON THE STUDY OF WORDS. Lectures Addressed (originally) to the Pupils at the Diocesan Training School, Winchester. Seventeenth Edition, enlarged. Fcap. 8vo. 5*s.*

ENGLISH PAST AND PRESENT. Eleventh Edition, revised and improved. Fcap. 8vo. 5*s.*

A SELECT GLOSSARY OF ENGLISH WORDS USED FORMERLY IN SENSES DIFFERENT FROM THEIR PRESENT. Fifth Edition, enlarged. Fcap. 8vo. 5*s.*

VINCENT AND DICKSON.—A HANDBOOK TO MODERN GREEK. By EDGAR VINCENT, M.A., and T. G. DICKSON. Second Edition, revised and enlarged. With an Appendix on the Relation of Modern Greek to Classical Greek. By Professor R. C. JEBB. Crown 8vo. 6*s.*

WHITNEY.—A COMPENDIOUS GERMAN GRAMMAR. By W. D. WHITNEY, Professor of Sanskrit and Instructor in Modern Languages in Yale College. Crown 8vo. 6*s.*

WHITNEY AND EDGREN.—A COMPENDIOUS GERMAN AND ENGLISH DICTIONARY, with Notation of Correspondences and Brief Etymologies. By Professor W. D. WHITNEY, assisted by A. H. EDGREN. Crown 8vo. 7*s.* 6*d.*

The GERMAN-ENGLISH Part may be had separately. Price 5*s.*

THE GOLDEN TREASURY SERIES.

UNIFORMLY printed in 18mo, with Vignette Titles by J. E. MILLAIS, T. WOOLNER, W. HOLMAN HUNT, SIR NOEL PATON, ARTHUR HUGHES, &c. Engraved on Steel by JEENS. Bound in extra cloth, 4s. 6d. each volume. Also kept in morocco and calf bindings.

"Messrs. Macmillan have, in their Golden Treasury Series, especially provided editions of standard works, volumes of selected poetry, and original compositions, which entitle this series to be called classical. Nothing can be better than the literary execution, nothing more elegant than the material workmanship."—BRITISH QUARTERLY REVIEW.

THE GOLDEN TREASURY OF THE BEST SONGS AND LYRICAL POEMS IN THE ENGLISH LANGUAGE. Selected and arranged, with Notes, by FRANCIS TURNER PALGRAVE.

THE CHILDREN'S GARLAND FROM THE BEST POETS. Selected and arranged by COVENTRY PATMORE.

THE BOOK OF PRAISE. From the best English Hymn Writers. Selected and arranged by LORD SELBORNE. *A New and Enlarged Edition.*

THE FAIRY BOOK; the Best Popular Fairy Stories. Selected and rendered anew by the Author of "JOHN HALIFAX, GENTLEMAN."

"A delightful selection, in a delightful external form; full of the physical splendour and vast opulence of proper fairy tales."—SPECTATOR.

THE BALLAD BOOK. A Selection of the Choicest British Ballads. Edited by WILLIAM ALLINGHAM.

THE JEST BOOK. The Choicest Anecdotes and Sayings. Selected and arranged by MARK LEMON.

"The fullest and best jest book that has yet appeared."—SATURDAY REVIEW.

BACON'S ESSAYS AND COLOURS OF GOOD AND EVIL. With Notes and Glossarial Index. By W. ALDIS WRIGHT, M.A.

"The beautiful little edition of Bacon's Essays, now before us, does credit to the taste and scholarship of Mr. Aldis Wright."—SPECTATOR.

THE PILGRIM'S PROGRESS from this World to that which is to come. By JOHN BUNYAN.

"A beautiful and scholarly reprint."—SPECTATOR.

THE SUNDAY BOOK OF POETRY FOR THE YOUNG. Selected and arranged by C. F. ALEXANDER.

"A well-selected volume of sacred poetry."—SPECTATOR.

A BOOK OF GOLDEN DEEDS of All Times and All Countries. Gathered and Narrated Anew. By the Author of "THE HEIR OF REDCLYFFE."

". . . To the young, for whom it is especially intended, as a most interesting collection of thrilling tales well told; and to their elders as a useful handbook of reference, and a pleasant one to take up when their wish is to while away a weary half-hour. We have seen no prettier gift-book for a long time."—ATHENÆUM.

THE ADVENTURES OF ROBINSON CRUSOE. Edited, from the Original Edition, by J. W. CLARK, M.A., Fellow of Trinity College, Cambridge.

THE REPUBLIC OF PLATO, TRANSLATED INTO ENGLISH, with Notes by J. LL. DAVIES, M.A., and D. J. VAUGHAN, M.A.

"A dainty and cheap little edition."—EXAMINER.

THE SONG BOOK. Words and tunes from the best Poets and Musicians. Selected and arranged by JOHN HULLAH, Professor of Vocal Music in King's College, London.

"A choice collection of the sterling songs of England, Scotland, and Ireland, with the music of each prefixed to the words. How much true wholesome pleasure such a book can diffuse, and will diffuse, we trust, through many thousand families."—EXAMINER.

LA LYRE FRANÇAISE. Selected and arranged, with Notes, by GUSTAVE MASSON, French Master in Harrow School.

"We doubt whether even in France itself so interesting and complete a repertory of the best French Lyrics could be found."—NOTES AND QUERIES.

TOM BROWN'S SCHOOL DAYS. By AN OLD BOY.

"A perfect gem of a book. The best and most healthy book about boys for boys that ever was written."—ILLUSTRATED TIMES.

A BOOK OF WORTHIES. Gathered from the Old Histories and written anew by the Author of "THE HEIR OF REDCLYFFE."

"An admirable addition to an admirable series."—WESTMINSTER REVIEW.

A BOOK OF GOLDEN THOUGHTS. By HENRY ATTWELL, Knight of the Order of the Oak Crown.

"Mr. Attwell has produced a work of rare value. . . . Happily it is small enough to be carried about in the pocket, and of such a companion it would be difficult to weary."—PALL MALL GAZETTE.

GUESSES AT TRUTH. By Two BROTHERS. *New Edition.*

THE CAVALIER AND HIS LADY. Selections from the Works of the First Duke and Duchess of Newcastle. With an Introductory Essay by EDWARD JENKINS, M.P., Author of "Ginx's Baby," &c.

"A charming little volume."—STANDARD.

THEOLOGIA GERMANICA. Edited by Dr. PFEIFFER, from the only complete manuscript yet known. Translated from the German by SUSANNA WINKWORTH. With a Preface by the Rev. CHARLES KINGSLEY, and a Letter to the Translator by the Chevalier BUNSEN, D.D.

SCOTCH SONG. A Selection of the Choicest Lyrics of Scotland Compiled and arranged, with brief Notes, by MARY CARLYLE AITKIN.

"The book is one that should find a place in every library, we had almost said in every pocket."—SPECTATOR.

DEUTSCHE LYRIK: The Golden Treasury of the best German Lyrical Poems. Selected and arranged, with Notes and Literary Introduction, by Dr. BUCHHEIM.

"A book which all lovers of German poetry will welcome."—WESTMINSTER REVIEW.

HERRICK: Selections from the Lyrical Poems. Arranged, with Notes, by F. T. PALGRAVE.

"For the first time the sweetest of English pastoral poets is placed within the range of the great world of readers."—ACADEMY.

POEMS OF PLACES. Edited by H. W. LONGFELLOW. England and Wales. Two Vols.

"A very happy idea, thoroughly worked out by an editor who possesses every qualification for the task."—SPECTATOR.

MATTHEW ARNOLD'S SELECTED POEMS.
(Also a Large Paper Edition. Crown 8vo. 12s. 6d.)

"A volume which is a thing of beauty in itself."—PALL MALL GAZETTE.

THE STORY OF THE CHRISTIANS AND MOORS IN SPAIN. By C. M. YONGE, Author of the "Heir of Redclyffe." With Vignette by HOLMAN HUNT.

LAMB'S TALES FROM SHAKESPEARE. Edited by the Rev. A. AINGER, M.A., Reader at the Temple.

POEMS OF WORDSWORTH. Chosen and Edited, with Preface by MATTHEW ARNOLD. (Also a Large Paper Edition. Crown 8vo. 9s.)

"A volume, every page of which is weighted with the golden fruit of poetry." —PALL MALL GAZETTE.

SHAKESPEARE'S SONNETS. Edited by F. T. PALGRAVE.

POEMS FROM SHELLEY. Selected and arranged by STOPFORD A. BROOKE, M.A. (Also a Large Paper Edition. Crown 8vo. 12*s.* 6*d.*)

"Full of power and true appreciation of Shelley."—SPECTATOR.

ESSAYS OF JOSEPH ADDISON. Chosen and Edited by JOHN RICHARD GREEN, M.A., LL.D.

"This is a most welcome addition to a most excellent series."—EXAMINER.

POETRY OF BYRON. Chosen and arranged by MATTHEW ARNOLD. (Also a Large Paper Edition, Crown 8vo.) 9*s.*

"It is written in Mr. Arnold's neatest vein, and in Mr. Arnold's most pellucid manner."—ATHENÆUM.

SIR THOMAS BROWNE'S RELIGIO MEDICI; Letter to a Friend, &c., and Christian Morals. Edited by W. A. GREENHILL, M.D.

"Dr. Greenhill's annotations display care and research to a degree rare among English editors. The bibliographical details furnished leave nothing to be desired."—ATHENÆUM.

MACMILLAN'S BIOGRAPHICAL SERIES.

Crown 8vo, uniformly bound, price 6s. each.

CATHERINE AND CRAUFURD TAIT, Wife and Son of ARCHIBALD CAMPBELL, Archbishop of Canterbury: a Memoir, Edited, at the request of the Archbishop, by the Rev. W. BENHAM, B.D. Vicar of Marden, and one of the Six Preachers of Canterbury Cathedral. With two Portraits engraved by JEENS. New and Cheaper Edition.

THE LIFE AND WORK OF MARY CARPENTER By J. ESTLIN CARPENTER, M.A., with Steel Portrait.

BERNARD (ST.)—THE LIFE AND TIMES OF ST. BERNARD, Abbot of Clairvaux. By J. C. MORISON, M.A. New Edition.

CHARLOTTE BRONTË: a Monograph. By T. WEMYSS REID. Third Edition.

ST. ANSELM. By the Very Rev. R. W. CHURCH, M A. Dean of St. Paul's. New Edition.

GREAT CHRISTIANS OF FRANCE: ST. LOUIS and CALVIN. By M. GUIZOT, Member of the Institute of France.

ALFRED THE GREAT. By THOMAS HUGHES, Q.C.

BIOGRAPHICAL SKETCHES, 1852—75. By HARRIET MARTINEAU. With Four Additional Sketches, and Autobiographical Sketch. Fifth Edition.

FRANCIS OF ASSISI. By Mrs. OLIPHANT. New Edition.

VICTOR EMMANUEL II., First King of Italy. By G. S. GODKIN. New Edition.

Now Publishing, in Crown 8vo. Price 3s. 6d. each.

The English Citizen.

A SERIES OF SHORT BOOKS ON HIS RIGHTS AND RESPONSIBILITIES.

This series is intended to meet the demand for accessible information on the ordinary conditions, and the current terms, of our political life. Ignorance of these not only takes from the study of history the interest which comes from a contact with practical politics, but, still worse, it unfits men for their place as intelligent citizens. The series will deal with the details of the machinery whereby our Constitution works, and the broad lines upon which it has been constructed.

The following Volumes are ready:—

CENTRAL GOVERNMENT. By H. D. Traill, D.C.L., late Fellow of St. John's College, Oxford.

THE ELECTORATE AND THE LEGISLATURE. By Spencer Walpole, Author of "The History of England from 1815."

THE NATIONAL INCOME, EXPENDITURE, AND DEBT. The Taxpayer and the Ratepayer. By A. J. Wilson.

THE POOR LAW. By Rev. T. W. Fowle.

FOREIGN RELATIONS. By Spencer Walpole, Author of "The History of England from 1815."

THE STATE AND THE CHURCH. By the Hon. A. D. Elliot, M.P.

In Preparation:—

LOCAL GOVERNMENT. By M. D. Chalmers.

JUSTICE AND POLICE. By C. P. Ilbert, late Fellow of Balliol College.

THE STATE AND EDUCATION. By Henry Craik.

THE STATE IN RELATION TO TRADE. By T. H. Farrer.

THE STATE IN RELATION TO LABOUR. By W. Stanley Jevons, LL.D., F.R.S. [*In the press.*

THE STATE AND THE LAND. By F. Pollock, late Fellow of Trinity College, Cambridge.

INDIA. By J. S. Cotton, late Fellow of Queen's College, Oxford.

COLONIES AND DEPENDENCIES. By E. J. Payne, Fellow of University College, Oxford.

LONDON: R. CLAY, SONS, AND TAYLOR, PRINTERS.